D0336489

WITHDRAWN FROM
THE LIBRARY

UNIVERSITY OF
WINCHESTER

KA 0240763 9

SIGNALLING
FROM MARS

THE LETTERS OF
ARTHUR RANSOME

SIGNAL STATION AND OBSERVATORY
from *Winter Holiday*

Alphaeus P. Col
1908

SIGNALLING FROM MARS

THE LETTERS OF
ARTHUR RANSOME

Edited and Introduced
by
HUGH BROGAN

JONATHAN CAPE
LONDON

KING ALFRED'S COLLEGE
WINCHESTER

828 RAN | 02407639

First published 1997

© 1997 by Hugh Brogan and
the Arthur Ransome Estate

Hugh Brogan has asserted his right
under the Copyright, Designs and Patents Act, 1988
to be identified as the author of this work

First published in the United Kingdom in 1997 by Jonathan Cape,
Random House, 20 Vauxhall Bridge Road, London SW1V 2SA

Random House Australia (Pty) Limited
20 Alfred Street, Milsons Point, Sydney,
New South Wales 2061, Australia

Random House New Zealand Limited
18 Poland Road, Glenfield,
Auckland 10, New Zealand

Random House South Africa (Pty) Limited
PO Box 337, Bergvlei, 2012 South Africa

Random House UK Limited Reg. No. 954009

A CIP catalogue record for this book
is available from the British Library

ISBN 0-224-04261-0

Typeset by MATS
Printed and bound in Great Britain by
Butler and Tanner Ltd, Frome, Somerset

Contents

Introduction

by Hugh Brogan

Aᴿᵀᴴᵁᴿ ᴿᴬᴺˢᴼᴹᴱ belonged to that world we have lost in which nothing was more natural, commonplace and necessary than the writing and receiving of letters. Today, when a whole week's post may bring nothing but bills, advertisements, offers from moneylenders and appeals from charities, the fact seems inconceivable, but so it was. Ransome in large part lived through his correspondence. In his ordinary course he wrote letters as easily and often as we make phone calls (he did not possess a telephone until he was in his fifties) and because he was a writer by vocation and training his letters are highly enjoyable. Their language is still vital with his character. Hundreds survive, and together add up to a literary achievement that deserves to be in print as much as his books for children, his fishing essays, *Racundra's First Cruise*, his political tracts, and his *Autobiography*. The only serious editorial difficulty lies in deciding which letters to drop from a selection.

In one respect the letters are sharply unlike the writing by which Ransome is best known. There is little of that art concealing art which explains so much of his stories' popularity. He probably had views on the technique of letter-writing – he had views on all literary questions – but very seldom, in his extant correspondence, do we catch him writing for effect. He conveys his news and views in a relaxed and straightforward fashion, scarcely ever blotting a line or correcting a typescript, and although he is often moving and frequently entertaining, he is hardly ever studied. He does not elaborate: for large word-

I

pictures we mostly have to turn to his fiction and his journalism.
Through these letters we seem to come especially close to the
man writing, closer than in any of his other work, closer even
than in the *Autobiography*, which was composed with at least as
much deliberation as his other books, even though it is
incomplete.

With their delightful spontaneity, the letters compose themselves, within a chronological framework, into a portrait of the
writer, in all his boyishness, his energy, his intelligence, his
geniality (and his fretfulness) and the immense variety of his skills
and interests. Though essential evidence for the biographer (they
were invaluable to me when I was writing *The Life of Arthur
Ransome*), the surviving letters do not of themselves tell the
complete story of Ransome's life. They fall into clumps. For
some years few remain, and on some topics they are completely
silent. For example, they do not tell Ransome's feelings on the
deaths of his father, his brother, his best friend and his mother;
there was perhaps a weeding of the archives before his death. On
other subjects we have too much material: on his homesickness
during the Russian Revolution, on the various ailments which
so regularly afflicted him, and on the hellishness of new typewriters. Nevertheless a balance can be found, giving no more
than proper weight to each theme; and so we can meet Arthur
Ransome as yachtsman, book-lover, fisherman, chess-player,
bird-watcher, journalist and traveller; we can glimpse the erratic
development of his literary career; we can observe the mutations
of his relations with his family, his daughter, his wives, and of his
friendships. We can also enjoy his lively eye for character and
incident, and applaud the steady principles, both literary and
moral, which underlay his response to all events.

A few letters survive from before 1914, several of which have
already been published, in whole or in part. The file becomes
continuous only with the coming of the Great War, and for this
reason, and because it was so important not to scant the main
periods of Ransome's life – the Russian years, the writing years
– the earliest letter printed here is dated 2 August 1914. It was
written at the beginning of a long exile. The war and the
revolution thrust Ransome into a vast detour (as he came to feel)
in which he lost touch with the high road of his career as a man

of letters and became a full-time political journalist, writing first for the *Daily News* and then for the *Manchester Guardian*. The articles and pamphlets of this journalistic period (1915-1929) have great value as primary historical evidence: Ransome had a seat in the front row at what was not so long ago believed to be the greatest event of the twentieth century, the Russian Revolution. His letters have less historical interest: it is not surprising that he did not feel obliged to describe to his family and friends events of which his version could be read in newspapers, and at times when he could not send copy to his editor (for instance, in the summer of 1918) he could not send private letters either. When writing to his mother he concentrated on personal news: private letters were private. Thereby he achieved a richly interesting account of himself in dangerous times, although I have dropped many of these letters to avoid repetitiveness.

Ransome remained trapped (as he thought) by journalism for years after the Revolution; he was also trapped in his disastrous first marriage. This predicament is only imperfectly shown in his surviving letters. We know that he and his wife Ivy wrote regularly to one another while he was in Russia, but few of these letters survive. Such correspondence as we have dates mainly from the period after their divorce, is mostly about money, and is usually angry or plaintive in tone. I have not dwelt on these. The course of events and of his feelings, however, is vividly conveyed in letters to his second wife, Evgenia, during the divorce proceedings, and to his daughter Tabitha between 1918 and 1935. It is painful to follow the gradual deterioration of relations between Ransome and the child he had so much loved. By contrast, the warmth of his love for Evgenia, and hers for him, is delightful: she brought out the best in him, despite her stern criticism of some of his writing. As well as seeing him through his many illnesses, she contributed greatly to the alteration in his circumstances which made it possible for him to resume his career as an author. Unhappy men cannot write books like *Swallows and Amazons*.

Until her death late in 1944 his mother was his best correspondent, and although his natural affection for her does much to explain his fidelity in writing almost every week (when he could) throughout their long lives, it is impossible not to feel that she must have been a particularly rewarding *destinataire*. Posterity owes much to Edith Rachel Ransome: had she not stimulated her son to write to her so often and so brilliantly, or had she not kept his letters so faithfully (over four hundred survive), we would know much less of him than we do, and a full biography could not have been written. It is a pity that so few of her own letters remain.

The most unfortunate loss is of so many of Ransome's letters to the Collingwood sisters, Barbara (his first love) and Dora (his second). The Collingwood family, whom he first got to know during a Lake District holiday in 1903, and the following year when he stayed at their home, was as important to him as his own. Although both Barbara and Dora declined Arthur's proposals of marriage, they were in constant epistolary touch throughout the Russian Revolution and the decades which followed. But not until Ransome's old age do letters survive in any number, and then they are not his best. Fortunately a few important ones from earlier dates have been preserved.

The list of loss might be extended, but so much material is available that to dwell on inadequacies would seem ungrateful to all those relations and friends of Ransome, and indeed to Ransome himself, who saved so many papers. Anyway, by the time of his great success as an author, from 1932 onwards, there is no shortage, rather an over-abundance, as his world opened out and more and more people realised that letters from Arthur Ransome were worth preserving. The majority of these people were women. Sir Rupert Hart-Davis is a notable exception, as was his publisher G. Wren Howard of Jonathan Cape, but otherwise it is plain that Ransome was happiest when writing to such friends as Margaret Renold, Pamela Whitlock (Bell) and Barbara Collingwood (Gnosspelius). All readers of this book are in debt to their sympathy and intelligence.

I have tried to be as light-handed an editor as possible, correcting punctuation and spelling only when necessary for clarity or consistency, silently supplying the occasional accidentally omitted word, and generally correcting slips of the pen and typewriter. Ransome's handwriting is almost always legible, and his typing is that of a professional journalist. Since this is only a selection of letters I have tried rather to produce a reader-friendly volume than a definitive edition of the documents, and with that in mind have, I hope, under- rather than over-annotated. I have not tried to explain every allusion, and the reader is free to assume in any particular instance that my failure is the consequence of ignorance rather than of policy.

The addresses of the letters are given in full when first they occur, and thereafter in abbreviated but unambiguous form. When the address, or any other important detail is hypothetical, square brackets have been used, [thus]. Except in a few letters by other people I have standardised dates, where known, in the forms preferred by Arthur Ransome, e.g., Jan. 13 1925. Sometimes he spelled out the full name of the month (February 15 1915); when he did, I have followed his example. Abbreviations in his text (such as M.G. for *Manchester Guardian*) have been lengthened the first time that they occur in a letter, and after that have been left as Ransome wrote them. The printing of titles and names has been standardised: ships, books, pubs, plays and periodicals are printed in italics; poems, stories and articles in Roman type between quotation marks. All dates not given by Ransome are printed within square brackets; conjectural ones are preceded by a question mark. Arthur Ransome was a great one for afterthoughts, which he often scribbled or typed at the head of his letters or in the margins. I have placed almost every such postscript at the foot of the letter to which it belongs.

Here and there – in the notes and linking passages of narration – I have quoted letters which do not otherwise appear. The editorial principle has been that letters printed in full must self-evidently earn their keep; yet there are many letters which do not meet this case and yet contain valuable passages. For this reason I have occasionally printed extracts rather than complete texts. I have not hesitated to include passages of trivial matter where not to do so would be to destroy the authenticity of letters.

For making available the letters which I have used I warmly thank the following: John Bell, John Berry, Janet Gnosspelius (who was also particularly helpful with advice and information), Sir Rupert Hart-Davis, Francis Lupton, Tania Rose, Richard Tizard and Barbara Ward. I am grateful to the Estate of J. R. R. Tolkien for permission to quote from a letter, and to Arthur

Ransome's grandchildren, Hazel Vale and John Ransome-Lewis, for permission to use letters written by their mother, Tabitha Lewis. I am also very grateful to those kind souls who sent me material that, in the end, I was unable to use.

For help of various kinds I must thank, above all, the Brotherton Collection at Leeds University Library, and Ann Farr in particular; and also, most sincerely, Taqui Altounyan, Captain Sir Thomas Barlow, John Bell, John Berry, Humphrey Carpenter, Fabian Russell-Cobb, John Cowen, Eamon Dyas of *The Times* archive, Donald J. J. Gillies, Sir Rupert Hart-Davis, Francis Lupton, Penelope Renold, Brigit Sanders, John Walter and Roger Wardale (for exemplary proof reading and much else). Finally, I would like to acknowledge how much I, in common with other writers on Arthur Ransome, owe to the unfailing assistance and great encouragement of Tony Colwell of Jonathan Cape.

Hugh Brogan
Wivenhoe
November 1996

Chronology

Principal dates in the life of Arthur Ransome

1884   *January* 18. Arthur Michell Ransome born at 6, Ash Grove, Headingley, Leeds, son of Cyril Ransome and Edith Rachel Ransome (*née* Boulton).

1893   AR goes to Old College, a prep school at Bowness on Windermere.

1897   Death of Cyril Ransome.
       AR goes to Rugby.

1901   AR leaves Rugby, goes to University College, Leeds.

1902   Leaves university to work for a London publisher.

1903   He meets the Collingwood family, and gives up publishing to become a writer full-time.

1904   *The Souls of the Streets*, his first literary book.

1907   *Bohemia in London*.

1909   AR marries Ivy Constance Walker.
       A History of Story-Telling.

1910   *May* 9. Birth of Tabitha Ransome.
       AR takes up fishing.
       Edgar Allan Poe.

1912   *Oscar Wilde*. Alfred Douglas sues for libel.

1913   *April* 17. Verdict for the defendants in *Lord Alfred Douglas v. Ransome and Others*.
       AR's first visit to Russia.

1914   *May*. Second visit to Russia.

1915   Third visit to Russia.
       August 9. Operation for piles.
       AR starts work as correspondent for the *Daily News*.

1916   *Old Peter's Russian Tales.*
1917   AR reports the Russian Revolution for the *News.*
        December 30. Meets Evgenia Petrovna Shelepina.
1918   *The Truth About Russia.*
        August 5. AR reaches Stockholm, and is soon joined by
        Evgenia Shelepina.
1919   *February* 3. They re-enter Russia.
        March 25. AR reaches London and is interviewed by
        Scotland Yard.
        AR is hired by the *Manchester Guardian.*
        Six Weeks in Russia in 1919.
        AR and Evgenia settle in Estonia.
        Aladdin and his Wonderful Lamp.
1921   *The Crisis in Russia.*
1922   *Racundra* is built.
1923   *Racundra's First Cruise.*
1924   AR and Ivy divorce. He marries Evgenia. They move
        to England.
1925   Low Ludderburn bought.
1927   *The Chinese Puzzle.*
1928   The Altounyan family's long visit to Coniston.
        Swallow and *Mavis* bought.
1929   AR begins to write *Swallows and Amazons.*
        Rod and Line.
1930   *Swallows and Amazons.*
        Treatment for ulcers.
1931   *Swallowdale.*
1932   The Ransomes visit the Altounyans at Aleppo.
        Peter Duck.
1933   *Winter Holiday.*
1934   *Coot Club.*
        Appendicitis operation.
1935   Low Ludderburn and *Swallow* sold. The Ransomes
        move to Levington on the River Orwell.
        Purchase of *Nancy Blackett.*
1936   *Pigeon Post.*
1937   AR sponsors *The Far-Distant Oxus* by Katharine Hull
        and Pamela Whitlock.
        He is awarded the Carnegie Medal.

1937   Umbilical hernia operation; embolism.
        We Didn't Mean To Go To Sea.
1938   First fleet on the Broads.
        Selina King launched. *Nancy Blackett* sold.
1939   Second fleet on the Broads.
        The Ransomes move to Harkstead Hall.
        Secret Water.
1940   The Ransomes move to The Heald, Coniston.
        The Big Six.
1941   *Missee Lee.*
1943   *The Picts and the Martyrs.*
        The River Comes First abandoned.
1945   The Heald is sold. The Ransomes move to London.
1946   *Selina King* sold; *Peter Duck* built.
1947   *Great Northern?*
1948   Lowick Hall bought.
1949   *Peter Duck* sold.
1950   Lowick sold. The Ransomes return to London and
        settle at Putney.
1952   Purchase of the first *Lottie Blossom.*
        Prostate operation.
        AR is awarded a doctorate of letters by the University
        of Leeds.
1953   The second *Lottie Blossom* is built.
        AR is awarded the CBE.
1954   Last voyage in *Lottie Blossom.*
1956   First visit to Hill Top, Haverthwaite.
1957   Strangulated hernia operation.
1958   Fall in Bedford Square brings on a long illness and slow
        convalescence.
1959   *Mainly About Fishing.*
1960   Hill Top bought.
1963   Putney flat given up.
1964   AR's eightieth birthday.
1965   AR is moved to Cheadle Royal Hospital, Manchester.
1967   *June* 3. Death of Arthur Ransome at Cheadle.
1975   *March* 19. Death of Evgenia Ransome.
1976   *The Autobiography of Arthur Ransome* published.

PART ONE

War and Revolution

1914–1917

As all visitors to the Kremlin in Moscow will agree, one of the most impressive sights in the fortress is the Great Bell, so tall and heavy that it cracked during its casting and could never be rung. It stands outside the Bell Tower of Ivan the Great. As Arthur Ransome tells us in his *Autobiography*, when as a child he saw a photograph of it he 'inexplicably' promised himself that one day he would see the bell. It was twenty years or so before the promise was fulfilled.

His earlier life never seemed to be leading him towards Russia. True, the refugee anarchist Prince Kropotkin taught him to skate; he did not try to interest the infant Arthur in Russian politics. Ransome's father was professor of history at the Yorkshire College, Leeds (now the University of Leeds), but his early death left his widow to bring up four children on her own. She was not rich. Arthur, her firstborn, was expected to graduate in science from Leeds and then get a secure and decently-paid job. He saw the sense of this (he was an affectionate and conscientious son) but he felt his vocation to be that of a storyteller and essayist (as indeed it was) and after two terms he could bear bunsen-burners no more. He left for London, where he found himself a job as office-boy with a publisher. That too did not last. Once he felt that he knew his way around, he threw up publishing and committed himself to the highly insecure life of a full-time writer. He began to make a name for himself, and to feel that he wanted a wife. We know that he proposed to at least five women, and probably more; at length he was accepted, unluckily for both of them, by Ivy Constance Walker, beautiful but unstable, and in every other way unsuitable as a wife for Arthur Ransome. Their marriage was already foundering when in 1912 Ransome was sued for libel by Alfred Douglas on account of his book about Oscar Wilde. Soon after, in the same year, his publisher defaulted.

Ransome, being by nature buoyant and resourceful, survived all these troubles. He rescued his copyrights from the wreckage of his publisher's affairs, and was acquitted in the libel case. He decided to escape from his marriage by running away. Russia seemed a sufficiently remote refuge: Ivy would not come after him there. Besides, he was getting interested in Russian fairy tales. So to Russia he went, for the summer of 1913. He began to learn the language and translate folk tales, and was very happy. On his return to England in the autumn he unwisely reconciled himself to Ivy (he had hated the separation from his daughter, Tabitha), and was soon wanting to get back to Russia as quickly as possible. In the spring of 1914 he was asked to write a guide-book to St Petersburg. Eagerly accepting the commission, he set off at once.

He arrived in St Petersburg on 14 May, 1914, and was soon enjoying Russia as much as ever. He despised the book he was writing ('not a book at all in my sense of the word . . . a great big higgledy piggledy mass of miscellaneous information') but revelled in the process of putting it together. He charged round the city, from museums to monasteries and back, and had completed the sixty thousand words required after four weeks' hard work. It turned out to be wasted labour: the guidebook was never to be published – the Great War putting a stop to it – and years later Ransome destroyed the manuscript. Meanwhile he was in good spirits, and went off to Finland for a necessary holiday. He was there as the great European crisis began to unfold.

★

WHEN this selection of letters opens, Ransome has just returned from Finland. He is thirty years old, and Russia, having mobilised on 30 July, is plunging into war.

To Edith R. Ransome

August 2 1914   Petersburg

My dear Mother,

This is just to let you know where I am and that I am very much all right. I am taking it for granted that you are still in England. I think even England must have waked up to the fact that things were serious some days before you were to have started.[1]

It is of course quite possible that this letter may not get through. However I write it. Things here are extraordinarily interesting. Thousands and thousands of reservists in their coloured blouses are camped all over the town, waiting for uniforms before being sent off to their various fronts. There is no music, no cheering, or very little and that little rather horrible and unreal. There is a feeling of steady and resigned determination, which looks very well. White papers have gone up, proclaiming martial law. I got in by the last regular train from Finland.[2] It took five hours to do the one hour journey. Every station was crowded with people saying goodbye, and reservists joining their regiments, with their belongings in coloured handkerchiefs and string bags, many of them with little tin kettles with a view to home comforts. They pumped 300,000 soldiers into Finland in 24 hours. The gulf at night is ablaze with searchlights.

My Russian friend Nikolai Georgievitch was among the first to be called. I was with him in Finland and travelled up with him. He goes to Kiev.

My plans are very unsettled. I wrote ten days ago asking for an appointment as war correspondent, but the idiots in England, I suppose said What war? and now it may be too late to get anything through.

I telegraphed to Ivy last Wednesday, telling her to sit still in case of war. England is probably the safest place in Europe for the moment. I hope it will go on being so.

McCullagh[3] the war correspondent got here yesterday, by the last train over the German frontier, and he described the Russian troops lying with guns ready all along the banks of the little river at Wirballen. I do not myself think the attack will be made so far down. If the Germans invade, they will come by way of the Northern Baltic provinces, with a sea attack on the coast towns Reval, Riga and Libau.

Aug 4. They have shelled Libau. We are in a state of frantic anxiety to know what England is doing. If she had declared war on Germany at once I think there would have been no war at all. We had the North Sea and could have smashed the German fleet, and she would have had to make peace or starve. The responsibility for not doing this is pretty heavy, and Asquith's waiting and seeing has probably made Armageddon inevitable.

People here expect an airship attack at any minute, because the Germans have moved their big airship up to Posen. I think they will have a lot to think about before they can bother with Petersburg, which, strategically, is unimportant.

Do not tell Ivy I have a chance of war correspondence. I probably have no chance, but of course if anything offers I shall jump for it. It's just possible McCullagh may take me with him. That would be good because he has more experience than anyone else here.

If you write, put via Sweden on your envelope.

Dear old Maw, Good luck to you all.

Arthur

1   Russia declared war on Germany on the day of this letter, 2 August (Western calendar); Britain on 4 August.
2   Where, after finishing his guide to Petersburg, AR had been holidaying and working on Russian fairy tales.
3   Francis MacCullagh, freelance war correspondent.

To Dorrie Collingwood (Ransome's adopted aunt)

August 12 1914

Poste Restante,
St Petersburg.

My Dear Aunt,

I am sitting here in a state of sickening inactivity waiting for a telegram to say I can go to one or other of the innumerable fronts. The *New York World* had the enterprise to wire and ask how much money I needed for this laudable purpose, and I

wired back, and am now sitting and swearing and waiting and
wondering if I asked too much. By the way of suitable
occupation I am translating fairy stories which in the time of
Armageddon I suppose nobody will even read.

All my hairy Russian friends have shaved their heads and gone
into uniform, and wept, and kissed me on both cheeks and gone
off to fight Germans and Austrians, and I am simply longing to
be with them. If only the N.Y. *World* comes up to the scratch,[1]
I am told I shall have a lovely time with an orderly to look after
my chargers (ahem!) the use of the field telegraph, and all sorts
of other joys. Everything is ready packed in saddle bags,
including a compact collection of fairy stories for translation in
idle moments. But the confirming telegram does not come. It's
simply maddening, so I turn to the strange love story of the
Heron and the Crane[2] which I will tell you some evening in the
new world when the war is over and I sit on my hunkers by a
wood fire in the morning room. O Lanehead.[3] It's the only place
I can trust to preserve its character through this upheaval.

The tennis court where I was playing a month ago here is a
cavalry camp. The streets are full of soldiers. And, well, I always
admired the Russians, but never so much as now. You know
how our soldiers go off in pomp with flags and music. I have not
heard a note of music since the declaration of war. They go off
here quite silently in the middle of the night, carrying their little
tin kettles, and for all the world like puzzled children going to
school for the first time. And the idea in all their heads is fine.
They all say the same thing. 'We hate fighting. But if we can
stop Germany then there will be peace for ever.' There is no talk
among the men about Slav versus Teuton. It is all Peace versus
War. 'I have a little boy,' said one man. 'Perhaps after the war
there won't be any more need of soldiers, so he will be free
when he grows up.' It they don't win they jolly well deserve to.
And think of the courage it must need to go off as they go off,
in the middle of the night with no band, no anything, and, in
most cases no knowledge of where they are going to.

England's warfaring seems very far away, and safe in comparison with this. I mean I don't suppose England will be invaded.
Here people know that the first thing the Germans will do if
they get a chance is a landing in Finland and along the Baltic

Provinces and a march on Petersburg. Every little village along the gulf is in a state of siege. Lights out at eight etc. Warships looking for Germans in the gulf. And people on towers squinting through glasses for the distant airship to find out if it really is a boojum.

I suppose there is the same sort of thing going on all round England, only remembering Mafeking I feel glad to taste public sentiment here instead of in London. What are the boy scouts doing, I think of them fortifying High Cross.

I wish I knew what you are all doing.

Goodbye, with very much love

Arthur

1   The *New York World*, a leading liberal newspaper, did not hire AR, and he left for England, to look for war-work there.
2   See *Old Peter's Russian Tales*, 'The Christening in the Village.'
3   Lanehead, the Collingwoods' family home, lies to the north of Ruskin's house above the eastern shore of Coniston Water. From his youth, Arthur looked upon Lanehead as his second home, and it later became the model for Beckfoot, where Nancy and Peggy Blackett lived in *Swallows and Amazons*.

To W. G. Collingwood (Ransome's adopted uncle[1])

November 27 1914

116 Harrogate Road,
Chapel Allerton, Leeds.

Dear Mr. Collingwood,

I have been a bad, unworthy nephew, deserving to be boiled in oil. I never thanked you for digging my notebook out of the coach-house and sending it. It arrived when I was in the middle of a cheerful period of being ill in bed, and in no condition even to open parcels. But since my recovery, and coming up here, I have had ample opportunity of writing. Hence my shame.

Thank you very much for sending the notebook.

Geoffrey,[2] after many difficulties, has got a commission in the 23rd. West Yorkshire Regiment, and is billeted near Aylesbury, and enjoying himself enormously, and looking forward to spitting Germans early next year. I doubt if he will ever be content to return to his printing. If he gets a chance I expect he will stay in the army. He lived until recently in a tent, with a river running through the middle of it, and a leak over the place where he slept. He had no proper bed, and yet he emerged fitter than ever, without even a cold in the head. Also he gets on very well with his men, and when the regiment as a whole refused to go on parade, his platoon sent him a note to say they intended to turn up, and did so, to Geoffrey's lasting honour. They are mostly Northumberland miners, and he likes them very much.

I am working away at Russian fairy stories, which seems a rubbishy thing to do in these times.

I have heard one good joke about the war, which I tell you, in case it hasn't been in *Punch*. It is a riddle. 'Why do the Germans spell [Cult *erased*] Kultur with a K.? Because Great Britain has command of all the seas.'

Please give my love to my aunt, and everybody else at Lanehead. I hope Ursula is back, and that Miss Powell is better.[3]

Yours sincerely,

Arthur Ransome.

1   The Ransomes and the Collingwoods once shared a picnic on Peel Island but it was not until he had grown up, in 1903, that Ransome met the other family again. In spite of great initial shyness, the encounter was the beginning of the most important friendships of his life, especially with the two elder daughters, Dora and Barbara. 'Mr and Mrs Collingwood were to become touchstones by whom to judge all other people that I met' (*Autobiography*, p. 81).
2   AR's young brother.
3   Ursula was the Collingwoods' youngest daughter. Miss Powell is unidentified. She was not the Miss Powell of Pin Mill.

To Barbara Collingwood

Central Station Hotel,

December 22 1914   Newcastle-on-Tyne.

Dear Barbara,

I feel so wretchedly sorry because I have had not one single minute in which to bring you your drawing, or anything. I've

been racing with all sorts of things and only just got done at 10
last night, when I thought it too late.

I sail by the *Venus* tomorrow morning for Bergen, and then
go up the edge of the Gulf of Bothnia, to where the railway
ends. Then sledge and then, if unfrozen, on by the Russian
railway. The whole thing promises to be interesting but cold. I
have been eating fish hard for the last three days, so as to have
some sort of revenge, before the fact, in case a mine so contrives
that fish shall eat me.

You will be amused to hear that *Aladdin* is sold.[1] I finished
him last Sunday, and I've actually had an advance on account. I
am thinking of letting my hair grow long again, to help out the
bad rhymes. But it's a lark, being a poet, and a *paid* poet at that.

Good luck to you, and as merry a Christmas as possible. The
same in suitably less degree to my enemy! My own Christmas
will be on or in the North Sea.

O! Please! My address will be Poste Restante, Petrograd.[2] I
shall be very cold and very lonely, and I would like letters. Please
prod the family.

If I don't have time to write to them, will you tell them how
very much I wish them everything that could be nice. Nice is
not the word. But you know what I mean.

Good luck,

Arthur.

1   *Aladdin and his Wonderful Lamp.* Not published until 1919.
2   Formerly St Petersburg.

To Dora Collingwood

January 12 1915   Moscow

My dear Dora,

Very many thanks for your letter which was the first to reach
me since I left England. I got it yesterday, just before starting for
Moscow, where I now am. You have no idea what a gorgeous
town this is. The morning after I got here I walked round the
Kremlin, and saw the great broken bell that I learnt about as a
child,[1] and the high brick walls, just looking as if they were built

against the Tartars, and the little river running below them, mostly frozen over, with people skating on it. Snow everywhere, some of it looking as if it had been splashed on the green roofs of the old towers. It's the finest place I've ever seen in my life.

January 14. New Year's Day in Russia. Last night I went to one of the cathedrals in the Kremlin, and lost a hat and a glove in the tightest packed crowd I have ever been in. The Metropolitan was there and spoke till midnight, when a fuse was lit, and a little flame ran round the cathedral lighting all the candles. The background was white, and the priests' robes were silver, the whole in the dimmest possible light until the candles were lit. It was very beautiful, but the scrum was so awful that it was not easy to enjoy it. Afterwards I walked along the edge of the hill, looking down from the Kremlin over the frozen river, and then went to the house of some Russian friends, and drank non-alcoholic drinks and ate smoked salmon till about three in the morning. Then I had a long sledge-drive home to my hotel, and now, at half past twelve I am hanging about waiting for my coffee. While hanging about my least sleepy eye happens to drop on a typewriter with an unfinished letter on it, which accident is the onlie begetter of these preceding and ensuing words.

I would love to write a story about the old Moscow of Ivan the Terrible. Perhaps I shall, when I know something about it. It's the most historical feeling place I know.

Oh, you asked who was the idiot who bought my epic.[2] The name of that unfortunate firm is Nisbet. May they suffer less for it than is to be expected. 200 pages of verse. There are going to be eight coloured pitchers, and fifteen or twenty plain. And six copies are to be mine. One of which will, of course, go to Lanehead to be used as an object lesson for young poets. 'This, you see, is what you may some day attain. Work hard, and learn the rhyming dictionary by heart, and even this will in the end not prove impossible to you, etc.'

I am so awfully glad to hear about the Skald's[3] new book. Tell me as soon as it's done, because then I shall not so much mind leaving Russia. I shall come with the snow still on my boots, claim bed, bunloaf and box of matches, and settle down to read it.

It's very pleasant to think of Lanehead away here. In a sort of way, you know, you have all been in the Kremlin with me, and seen the broken bell.

Love to everybody,

Arthur Ransome

1 'In Moscow I was in a magic world. I saw the Great Bell, the picture of which in that old-fashioned book had inexplicably made me promise myself that I should one day see the bell itself.' (*Autobiography*, pp. 172-3).
2 *Aladdin.*
3 The Skald: W. G. Collingwood, Dora and Barbara's father, and AR's honorary uncle (see List of Correspondents). His new book was probably *The Likeness of King Elfwald*, which was to be published in 1917 (Kendal: Titus Wilson).

To Edith R. Ransome

Moscow.
But I shall be
in Petrograd before you
February 15 1915   can reply to this.

My dear Mother,
    This is merely a bulletin, to say that I have not been very well,[1] but am now again in good condition, and that my articles have got on very slowly, but my notes are increasing in bulk, and that I have written a fairy story about Helen of Troy, and two Russian ones, and the rough draft of a third.
    Two days ago I fished for three hours in an open hole in the ice under the walls of the Kremlin. Lots of peasants were there fishing. I saw one fish caught and one only, and instantly all the peasants rushed to the place and threw in their lines. It was quite like Roundhay Park.[2] I made several of them show me their tackle, which was quite different in plan from ours. I have made diagrams of it, and it will turn into a nice little article for *Country Life*, when I get back to England.
    Last night I killed three unmentionable insects, and spent about five sleepless hours in switching the light on and off, in the

hope of a larger bag. They are large and flat and odorous, and they are imported, I fancy, from the dreadful little hole in the kitchen where the servants sleep. A very handsome and filthy *Zuiranka*,[3] of non-Russian race, makes my bed in the mornings, and I believe she is the vehicle of their introduction, for the room itself is very clean and so am I.

I protested about this, and suggested that there should be a clean up of the pigstye in which she lives, but the proposal was met with a horrified almost religious disgust by the maid and the cook. The room never had been cleaned. It never need be cleaned. And as for the unmentionable insects, God made them, so it was to be supposed that he intended them to live. I was made to feel a murderer.

Today the thermometer has gone up to zero, so everybody is complaining of the heat. We have had up to and over forty degrees of frost. The snow in the garden is very deep, and the house is fringed with a beard of icicles some of them four and five feet long.

I expect by this time you will be back from Edinburgh, with, I sincerely hope, a better report of your eyes.

I have got hold of a splendid book of Russian apocryphal legends of Christ and his disciples, all taken down from oral traditions, which will give me (1) a delightful article (2) either a beautiful little book or at any rate some very pretty stories. They are the simplest, sweetest things.

The illustrator of *Aladdin* has suddenly gone off to Serbia, so I have not got the least idea about what is happening. I expect, however, to hear one of these days, perhaps tomorrow. It will be most awfully disappointing if it is postponed for another year. I have written protesting.

I have a very jolly letter from Barbara, and another from Dora. But I am afraid the Collingwoods are having a bad time financially, because of the war taking all their pupils away.

The new stories in the children's book are:–
'Salt'
'The Kingdoms of Copper, Silver and Gold'
'The Seven Simeons'
'The Magic Bird and Vasilissa the Very Beautiful'
'The Golden Fish'[4]

Much love to you and everybody. I wish Joyce and Kitty would take up their pens and write.

Your affectionate son,

Arthur Ransome

1 Ransome was beginning to suffer dangerously from piles.
2 In Leeds.
3 Gypsy.
4 With the exception of 'The Seven Simeons', all these stories eventually appeared in *Old Peter's Russian Tales*, though not always with the same titles.

To Dora Collingwood

February 27 1915   Petrograd

My dear Dora,

This is merely a note of exclamation. I must boast to some-body, and as there is no one here I have to put my shame on paper and boast through the post. I am having the most exciting adventure of my life. I am . . . you need not believe it unless you want to but it's perfectly true . . . writing a romance.[1] The idea got stuck in my head, and would not get out. I ought, as you know, to be doing serious work, and there is plenty to do, but this wretched tale kept dangling itself in front of my eyes, until at last I made a bargain with it. I said, 'If you will let me write you in three weeks, I'll do it', and the tale, humble beggar, said, 'Fire away', so I chucked all other work and fired away. This is the end of the first week, and behold six chapters, 20,000 words are written, and the rest is still seething. The whole book will be sixty thousand, about as long as *Bohemia in London*, and if I really do get the whole thing into rough draft in the three weeks it will be a record, for me at any rate. You can have no conception of the excitement of the performance. I start out each day at nine sharp, and go it all day, knocking off finally at seven. Then in the evening I smoke pipes and gossip with my heroes and heroine, and discuss next day's business. Then I sleep. Then up, wallop down two glasses of coffee and a whack of bread, and off again.

The tale itself seems to me prodigiously intriguing. I won't tell you the main idea ... but it includes one murder, several attempted murders, the finest uncle ever was, a big Yorkshire cake, an alchemist, a housekeeper, a pedlar with the voice and manner of Jeremiah the prophet, an old man, a weird and ancient house, six family portraits of horrible significance, and, of course, the prettiest heroine in the whole range of English fiction.

The worst of it is that the minor characters insist in coming out of their places and occupying the stage to the annoyance of the stars who are kept fuming in the wings. The uncle for instance, simply won't lig whyst in Bigland Hall[2] whither I sent him in the first chapter.

I'd give my last rouble to have the Skald's knowledge of technique in this business. I know something about the technique of essays and such, but this here is an entirely different matter, and it keeps me on the perpetual jump. I never can be sure whether the narrative is moving too slowly, or else tripping over its own knees and becoming horrid and spasmodic. It's dreadfully difficult. Of course when it's written, if I succeed in keeping up the pace to the end, I'll put it aside and have a thorough go at it when I get back to England. But it is so easy to make hashes in the rough copy that can never be straightened out. I wish I were at Lanehead for an hour or two, and with the Skald a free man and very kind, so that I could fairly flood him with questions. The beastly thing needs a special technique of its own.

As for the love scenes! I think it was a pity love was ever invented to prove a stumbling block to the author of shockers. I do my best to wriggle out of the worst by making the interest of the love scenes wholly subservient to something in the story, but I feel it's a mean dodge and blush as I do it.

But really it's an unholy lark, and I do believe that in the end it will find its way into a list of 'Spring Fiction'. If it does it will be the greatest joke of my somewhat serious life.

There. I feel better. You don't know what it's like to burst to boast, and have no one within reach but a cook, and she a Zeeranka[3] with a very poor knowledge of Russian. The story by the way is set in the year after the publication of Berkeley's 3 Dialogues, about 1716, I think,[4] but some of its events occur two centuries before. As soon as possible after getting back to

England I hope to bring it up to Coniston to give it the benefit of the sane and useful criticism that prevails at Lanehead. On March 13 or 14 I ought to be able to send a postcard with the statement that the rough draft is finished.[5] If it really does come out as quick as all that I shan't feel so naughty at wasting time over it. Indeed I shall glory in my wickedness.

There: I've boasted enough, and my trumpet can go back into its case. Goodbye, and much love to all of you, and please forgive my proud arpeggios.

Arthur Ransome

N.B. Letters with news will be thankfully received. Who is at home? What pictures are being painted? Is the Skald's book done? The thought of 'Dutch Agnes'[6] makes me groan at my ignorance of the tools necessary for the job.
P.S. When I come to Coniston, I'm going to catch a pike.

1   *The Elixir of Life*, published in the autumn of 1915. The Skald (W. G. Collingwood) and Barbara corrected the proofs for the exiled author.
2   A real place, east of Haverthwaite and south of Newby Bridge.
3   See letter to his mother, 15 February 1915.
4   George Berkeley, *Dialogues between Hylas and Philonous*, published in 1713.
5   Ransome was too optimistic, but the final revision of the *Elixir* was finished on 17 April.
6   W. G. Collingwood, *Dutch Agnes Her Valentine: being the journal of the curate of Coniston, 1616–1623* (Kendal: Titus Wilson, 1910; second ed., London: Heinemann, 1931).

To Edith R. Ransome

July 27 1915   Petrograd

My dear Mother,

I have just heard from Ivy that she has left Tabitha with the Thomases in a cottage near Petersfield!!!!! You can imagine how delighted I am. And after all the fuss about nobody being able to touch her except Ivy herself, to leave her with the incompetent Helen Thomas, with three other children and no

maids of any kind, so that Helen's incompetence is shared between four.[1] I simply don't understand it at all. I do wish I could
remove Tabitha altogether, but I can't so it's no use thinking
about it.

My own health has been worse this week than I can remember
it. I can't even walk upstairs without almost collapsing. I don't
think I've ever had such a bad go before. I can't do anything at
all. I go on from day to day hoping for a turn, because these bad
goes do not last for ever. But it's sickening being unable to work,
and also unable to keep still, and waking every day with a most
frantic headache which only clears off for a few hours in the
middle of the day. There is nothing to worry about in all this,
because it will go again, but it is a satisfaction to grumble.

I think it would probably be better if it wasn't for worry about
Ivy and Methuen. I worry about Ivy because I cannot be sure
how things are in any way. I worry about Methuen[2] because
they say nothing at all in answer to my two prepaid telegrams.
Also the postponement of the Russian fairy stories has made me
feel that I am not being the slightest use to anybody.

Yesterday there was a fire in a village near here.[3] I went and
sweated for a couple of hours till it was put out, cursing in
Russian as if I was a native. Then I paid for it, and had to lie
flat on my back by the side of the road three times before I
could get home again, though the total distance is only a mile
and a half. I nearly howled with mixed feebleness and rage. The
fire had its amusing points. The peasants were finely incompetent. I fell upon two who were trying to get a pig out of a
cottage. One had a rope round its hind leg, and another a rope
round its front leg. Both, regardless of the howls of the animal
were pulling like blazes. There was only one well in the village,
and it was emptied in half an hour, and we had rough carts with
barrels racing to the ponds by the river and back, with branches
of trees shoved into the barrels to keep the water from splashing
out. The charioteering was considerable fun, full lick, over
ruts and holes as deep as the dining room chairs, with herds of
old women, children, pigs, hens, cattle, flying in all directions,
and independently negotiating the mattresses, samovars, beds,
chairs, pictures, piled everywhere at large. I saw a screaming
pig take a broken sledge with a mattress and an old woman on

it in a single flying leap in its frenzied escape from under my chariot wheels. If the wind had been a point or two different the whole village would have burnt, but, as it was, they got off with a single hut, though as the average time for the burning of the whole of one of these wooden villages from end to end is forty five minutes, everybody removed their things at once in case. The row was deafening. The inhabitants of three other villages came to help. I am glad I went, in spite of the after effects.[4]

I have got through the rough copy of the second chapter of my new book,[5] but it is uncommonly like its author in general feebleness.

My charming old lady with whom I used to walk and talk here has gone off to the Crimea. It is much too hot to follow her, though it is nice to know that I can go there as soon as I feel inclined. If I manage to have my operation done here, I shall probably go to stay with her after it, for which reason, I would like to have the said op. later if I can hold out, because the Crimea in August is several times worse than an oven, and would be bad instead of good.

Oh blow, I do wish I could be put right internally, so that I could have a little more energy to shove into the work that is opening out in front of me. I see such ripping things to do, and haven't the driving force to do them. All I'm really doing is getting a jolly good knowledge of Russian, and heaven knows if it is ever going to be useful to anybody except myself. I feel it will be useful someday, if and when my inside gets put right. For one thing, Russian speaking Englishmen will be wanted badly as soon as we take Constantinople. And, I do hope that you will take any opportunity of jamming into the Aclands the fact that I want to be used. If a job turns up for me, I would have my operation at once.

Apart from that there are such a lot of things I want to write, if only I can manage to do so without starving by the way. An awful lot depends on the *Elixir* and what happens to it, and still more on how I get on with the thing I'm now on, which, unfortunately needs twice the energy which I can call together even on a good day.

August 2.

My dear Maw,

My health has finally smashed. I can't cross a room without nearly collapsing, and the day before yesterday I fainted in the street. I have seen a first rate doctor, and he said that I must be operated upon at once. I then saw a surgeon, who prodded me about in a cheery way, and, after two examinations, one of them in hospital, also said operation at once. Probably by the time you get this the business will be over, though perhaps not, as they have given me various medicines to get things into a slightly better condition before operating.

That is my bad news. The good is that just when I was feeling most desperate a letter came from Methuen, saying that my book is to be published early this autumn. I have asked Mr. Collingwood to correct the proofs, but a set is to be sent to you so that you can see what sort of a book it is that is dedicated to you.

DO NOT ON ANY ACCOUNT tell Ivy that I am having the operation or that my health has gone wrong. Nothing would be more awful than a sudden appearance of her over here.

The operation will be cheaper than in England. I do not think it will cost altogether more than twenty pounds. After it I shall go down to the Crimea to lie about in the sun and shall return I hope a new man full of beans, and able to do something better than imitate the habits of a maggot crawling miserably about.

I am borrowing the money for the operation, because they say I must have it at once, and I have now got slightly less than my fare home. That I shall spend on going to the Crimea,[6] if indeed when I have paid minor expenses there is enough left for that. I am awfully sorry about all this from the financial point of view . . . but I can't help it. I could not get home in my present condition even if I were such an ass as to try.

There is no need to worry about me. *I will post another letter to you the day I actually am finally taken into the hospital,* and I will have a wire sent as soon as I can after the actual affair is over. It ought to improve my knowledge of the language, being operated on in Russian. The only worry is money. Both doctor and surgeon say waiting is impossible.

If you are able to send any money, the best way is a cheque payable at the Crédit Lyonnais Petrograd. This your bank can arrange. I hate even the possibility of this, but as far as operation goes I have no choice.

Anyway, it is cheering that the *Elixir* is going to be published at once. I feel a thousand times more cheerful since I got that news.

Don't worry about me. Remember you'll get another letter before I'm actually dealt with.

Your affectionate son

Arthur.

But do send a nice lot of letters to read when it is over. Arthur.

1   Helen Thomas was the wife of the poet Edward Thomas, at one time a close friend of AR.
2   The publisher of *The Elixir of Life*.
3   'Here' is the Tyrkov family house at Vergezha on the river Volkova, where Ransome was staying.
4   AR was to put this incident to good use in a short story, 'The Shepherd's Pipe', published in *Coots in the North and Other Stories*, 1988.
5   Presumably the historical romance about Novgorod.
6   In the event, he did not go.

To Edith R. Ransome

August 8 1915   Petrograd

My dear Mother,

The hospital is delightful, and I began to write a story yesterday, which I hope to finish today, in case the operation turns me out very different, in which case I should spoil it. It's rather a jolly story of Russian village life. I want to get several stories done soon, as the publication of the romance may, in case of success, create some sort of mild demand.

My little room looks out on a courtyard where the partly cured hop about on crutches. It's a very nice little room, with a bed, a couch, table and chairs, all as white as white can be, like me. I am white from head to foot, with a special sort of white dressing gown and shirt. I have no objection to make of any kind, except that it is beastly lonely, and that food is practically prohibited. Unlimited Russian tea is provided, and I drink all day long. Smoking, thanks be to God, is also allowed, even encouraged. The nurses are nice, one especially, but I don't get much chance of talking. They just charge in, give me a thermometer or worse, and disappear. A stubbly man also in white gave me a very thorough bath. Everything is clean and efficient. I am quite sure I could not be anywhere better either in England or here . . . The surgeon has just been to see me, and says the operation will be tomorrow at ten. Twenty four hours from now it will be over.

The only worry is money, and that, I admit, is a limit, because I have come to the very end of my resources. The best way of sending any that is possible is via the Crédit Lyonnais Petrograd. Any English bank can arrange that. But, if it were possible to telegraph a small amount in advance to the Post Restante, it would be a good thing, though in that case I fancy I lose instead of gaining by the exchange into Russian money. But the main thing is that if anything is possible it should be done at once.

Do let me know as soon as possible what you think of the romance. If you notice any howling errors in it, will you please announce them at once to Mr. Collingwood, who is correcting the proofs for me. It's an awful thing not seeing the proofs at all of a book that was written as fast as that was, especially when it's dedicated to one's Maw.

With much love,

Your affectionate son,

Arthur

*

The operation was a success, but was no fun for Ransome. Two days or so afterwards, in an undated letter, he wrote to his mother: 'I have had a lively time and know more about the nature of pain than I have ever known in my life before. They tried to deal with me with cocaine but it did not work, and, after the operation had begun!! they tried ether which did not last till it was over. Then, afterwards they tried so many things that they dared try no more in the effort to get me to sleep. I was 56 hours

after the op. without sleep. They said that it must mean that
writers are special beings with most anarchical nerves.' His con-
valescence was drawn-out, but seems to have been fairly steady.
His money-anxieties were relieved when the London *Daily
News* began to employ him as its Petrograd correspondent. But
he suffered acutely from home-sickness, especially in the immediate wake of the operation. In the same letter he lamented: 'I
long for Leeds today with an overpowering desire. I want to
have brandysnacks for tea, and eat them all, and to sit in a tram
and see the smoke cloud in the valley, and to smoke shag in the
garden, and to hear Aunt Mab's voice laughing over the telephone, and to go fishing with Uncle John and no doubt catch
grayling in trout time and vice versa. Oh Lord if only England
did not mean Tisbury and the shadow of Tisbury.' Tisbury was
the village in Wiltshire where his wife and daughter lived.

★

To Edith R. Ransome

Glinka d.3 kv.48.,

March 6 1916   Petrograd

My dear old Mother,
    It is a bright sunshiny day, and my huge room is fairly slopping
over with gold light, which is very jolly after my four months of
living in the shadow of a brick wall.[1] I've sent no telegram today,
but written an article instead, and finished the rough copy of it
about an hour ago. Then they brought in the wing of a goose
which I gnawed and then sucked, and so imbibed nutriment.
Then they brought in the samovar, and I made tea, and while it
was getting cool enough to drink, shaved. Now, you have a
cleanish faced son sitting down to drink his tea, and to talk to
you by medium of the typewriter. N.B.: I have cut off my col-
laborators, and have now only the most modest of moustaches.
    It's very jolly talking to you, but you really are an abominable
long way away, and I feel inclined to press too hard on the
typewriter keys, as if that would raise my voice. It doesn't you
know. Not a bit. I've tried it. So I go on typing in a whisper,
and I hope you'll manage to hear.
    I am extremely busy, and every day now expecting to be very

much more so. So I sit up pretty late, and rise at eight, and lunch in, and do all sorts of other little time-saving tricks in order to push on with the romance[2] while I can. 41,000 words of it are done, that is well over half. And I am very depressed about it, although the Scotch economist[3] who obligingly acts as fool-ometer is very keen on it, and always ready to come half across Petrograd when I have a new chapter ready to read to him. But he is a very kind-hearted man and in matters of writing books kind hearts are not the things to trust to. No. What is wanted is the steely conscientiousness of my respected mother. I wish to goodness I could have your remarks on the first eight chapters as they stand. Yesterday I nearly chucked the whole thing into the stove. But then the economist came along, and asked for more, so I made up my mind to go through with it, if only as an exercise. Ouch, I do envy Joyce having hers at the typists, all done except for printing. And I'm sure hers is jolly good. And if it isn't it doesn't matter, because she is a babe. But I am getting old, and cannot afford dead failures.

By the way, you must get from the library at once and read *The Dark Forest* by Hugh Walpole. It is the first book I have read which gives anything like a true impression of Russians as seen by English. And it gets the spirit of the war here in the most wonderful way. It's an astonishing piece of work, especially considering he's not had a year of Russia and is still very shaky in the language. It's the best book I've seen which is a direct result of the war.

About Russian. It seems that the other northern universities, besides Liverpool, are taking up Russian studies, and the idea is to establish a professorship, or at any rate to begin with a lecture-ship in each of them in language, history and literature. Well now, Professor Pares[4] asked me if I'd like Leeds supposing it was offered me.[5] It would mean coming to Leeds for two terms in the year, from October to March, and being free for the rest of the year for my own work, and for coming to Russia. Of course it would be a perfectly marvellous piece of good fortune if it did come to me. It would mean a small safe income for one thing, without tying me either to England or to Russia all through the year. If I am to try for it something ought to be said at once, and I thought of writing to Dr. Eddison.[6] Also, because of father, I'd love to be connected with the university. And the actual work would be extremely interesting. And it would give me a fine chance of doing some real good with my Russian studies after the war. Say a word to Dr. Eddison and see what he says. If it did come off it would solve the problem of keeping alive after the war, which looks as if it were going to be pretty difficult, unless I am content to turn into a journalist simply, and do no more decent writing at all. However, we'll see.

Did I tell you I've had a letter from Jack, saying that they have decided to let me have coloured illustrations to my Russian fairy tales, and that I am to find an artist out here to do the job?[7] That means the book really will be out this autumn, and, if the pictures I get are really decent, it should be a jolly book, which will console me if I fail to get my romance finished in time. This last possibility is becoming ghastly like a probability. I don't get ahead anything like so fast as I did with the *Elixir*, even apart from the fact that instead of having all day to give to it, I only have an hour here and an hour there, with continual interruptions. As for 'Aladdin: an Epic' I hear nothing of it. It is most disappointing, and I could tear my hair for ever for having sold it to that wretched man. I long to have that book out, for my own joy, and there it is lying waiting for pictures which the blighter will not get. It's a most cruel business. They'll probably be pictures only fit for grown-ups when he does get them. And I had set my heart on letting it be a real children's book. However, there's no help for it. And at least I've had the pleasure of writing it, and the pleasure of being paid for it. All the same I would like to have the thing in my hands to fling at the heads of serious friends.

I say, it's all very well my grumbling about being worked off my head and feet. I am. I work absolutely continuously all day, and through a very long day. But the point is that with my improving health, I both thrive on it, and like it. I enjoy it like fun. It will be like returning to a thoroughly artificial existence when the war ends, or my job ends, and I come back to getting up late, and having nothing to do but a book with almost unlimited time to get it done in, and half the day spent in slacking about. I don't believe I shall find it possible. The whole business of superabundant work is ripping, especially now that I

am beginning not to be so worried by the writing of my telegrams. I fairly charge out of bed, and start getting ahead while I
make my tea and drink it, and after that it's hammer and tongs
hammer and tongs, first one thing and then another, and the
romance messing about in my head when I go out for anything,
and before I know where I am, the electric light (controlled by
a severe landlady) gives a flicker and I know that it is midnight,
and that in another two minutes it will be out altogether. Then
I light my candle, scribble down in my diary the result of the day
in number of pages written or typed etc., and start hurling off my
clothes. Five minutes after that I am asleep and before I know
where I am, it's next morning, and I'm at it again. Altogether,
it's ripping. My only complaint is that I haven't time to do all I
want. E.g. I have no time for reading. I've never read so few folk
stories a week since first I came to Russia. And that's one of the
things I don't want to let slip. As for literature, I practically read
none, except the *Golden Treasury*. Any reading I do, is usually a
frenzied plunge into history or geography, and out again before
I've done more than get rumpled and wet.

As soon as the Spring comes I am going to take one day a
fortnight in the open or bust. Then things will really be ripping,
especially as I think I'm to have a little fishing within reach of
Petrograd. By the way, the *Yorkshire Posts* you sent me have not
got the 'Notes on the Rivers', which is what I wanted. I think
someone might have looked to see. Perhaps it's the Saturday
Yorkshire Post that has them.

I wish Geoff knew Russian and were out here. He could be
jolly useful. I had a letter from him a little time ago, from
Rugeley,[8] where he seemed to be having a loathsome time. I do
wish I could foresee a chance of getting home if only for a week
to see you all again. But it looks more than unlikely. If a chance
does come I shall take it, but there won't be one for months and
months.

My dear Mother, my tea is drunk, and I have no excuse for
not getting back to work. So I get. Goodbye, Your affectionate
son,   [no signature]

1   An allusion to the room in the Hotel Continental where he
     stayed before moving to Glinka Street. Research has not yet

established where he lived before he went to the Continental though we know that in 1914 he had a room in an unnamed hotel near the Nikolai Station. Glinka Street (above) was his first home-like base, and he kept his possessions there even after the Russian government moved to Moscow in 1918.

2   *Piscator and his Phillida.* Never finished, and the manuscript now lost. AR abandoned it soon after writing this letter.

3   Will Peters.

4   Bernard Pares, correspondent of the *Daily Telegraph*. Later (1931) published *My Russian Memoirs* which AR reviewed pettishly in the *Manchester Guardian*.

5   It wasn't.

6   Dr John Eddison of Adel, uncle of E. R. Eddison, the author and boyhood friend of AR.

7   He found Dmitri Mitrokhin.

8   Geoffrey had been wounded and was recuperating at 'the Research Hospital' in Cambridge from which he wrote to AR on 9 March, 'What you say about joining as a Private is absolute rot. Now that I have been wounded twice I am sure that the family has done enough, and you could not possibly join for months and months as you won't be fit enough for a long time yet. I know exactly what your training would entail by personal experience, and your health would never stand it, let alone your eyes. So you had better not go on bothering about it. You are doing a very useful work where you are . . . I am glad you liked my poem. I liked yours very much.'

To Edith R. Ransome

September 7 1916   Glinka Street

My dear Mother,

I am writing this in the train on the way to the Russian Roumanian frontier. In another six hours I shall be a lone and helpless creature in a country whose language, so far as I can judge from my urgent efforts to acquire it is one of the most difficult on earth. I have been at it hard on the journey, and can now read it with some difficulty, but enough, I think, to tell the head from the tail of a newspaper.

I've had a very amusing journey, though my day in Kiev was so full up with business – seeing the staff, arranging with a Kiev Bank to send me money, etc. – that I had no time to do any of the things I had planned to do, which had included a trip on a Dnieper steamer. However I shall do that some time or other, and there's the Danube to look forward to, which I shall probably see quite soon. And Bucharest! I've read *The Prisoner of Zenda* in the train on the way down, and am told the real thing is very like it. But you will begin to see what sort of impression it makes on me because I shall be telegraphing pretty freely to the *News*.[2] And writing a whole series of articles. At least I hope so. The *News* has told me to cable freely.

You have no idea how jolly it is to come back to summer after the cold ceaseless rains of Petrograd. I have again shed all my underclothes. The sun is boiling hot, and soldiers by the side of the line are eating big melon-like fruit called arbusts, and lying asleep in rows under trains in the sidings in order to get the benefit of the shade. I expect in Bucharest it will be hotter still. But it's sickening to think that but for this sudden affair I should now be on my way not to Bucharest but to Leeds and Finsthwaite and Coniston.

Never mind. It will mean that when I do come back they will let me stay longer, a month at least, and if I get a really good set of photographs in Roumania it will mean a second lantern lecture at my disposal for future money-grubbing. Also I wonder if my Roumanian will get on fast enough to open a new source of fairy stories for me. There is a lot of Roumanian folk-lore, but I have no idea how much of it has got into books.

There are crowds of blue cornflowers growing by the side of the line.

Botheration, I wish I were coming home. Then, the next minute I rejoice at the idea of seeing a new country and one quite different from any I already know. Also, from the point of view of eventual stories and romances, nothing could be better. And, when Joyce and I set to work somewhere away in the hills, it will be jolly to have had this experience as well as the Russian.

I send much love to you all.

Write to me as usual, but also write to the Consulate at Bucharest, as if I am kept here a long time it will be beastly to have no letters at all.[1]

Arthur

1   AR left Bucharest for Petrograd on 12 October.
2   Ransome was now the full-time Petrograd correspondent of the Liberal newspaper, the *Daily News*.

To Edith R. Ransome

British Consulate,
September 10 1916   Bucharest.

My dear Mother,

I arrived here at four this morning, after a terrific journey. It was all right as far as Kiev. But the train was seven hours late at the frontier, and I had to sleep in a siding, and wait twenty four hours before I could get on. Ungheni is a jolly little town, filthy beyond description. Inhabitants Jews out of the most lurid parts of the Old Testament. Houses one storey white huts each one with a booth attached. Streets mainly manure, pigs, goats and geese filling main highways. I walked out of the town and slept on the bank of the Prut, after very sleepily watching through binoculars wild Roumanian soldiers in white shirts and pointed fur caps with long guns like Corsican brigands guarding the other bank and the bridge. A Russian sentry came and lay down beside me, and we had a good talk. He knew my part of the Russian front, and we had a good jabber, my last in Russian. Then, at last, over the frontier and into Roumania, with French as main means of communication. Slept at Jassy, till morning, when started on long journey down the eastern perpendicular part of Roumania, round the corner and south to Bucharest, weather getting hotter all the time.

Part of the time I was with some French officers, the rest of the time with Roumanians. I made violent friends with a little girl of twelve, who mothered me throughout the journey, and talked about Robinson Crusoe, and Sir Gulliver, her two great British heroes. Also two small boys, who played with everything I had about me, compass, camera, binoculars, top boots, forage cap, etc., and insisted on feeding me with sweets, which they put forcibly into my mouth by somewhat grubby hand. After a bit I left the aristocratic inside of the carriage, and climbed up and travelled on the roof with Roumanian soldiers, with whom I got on famously in a mixture of my three days old Roumanian and vigorous sign-language. They forcibly fed me with melons. Then I went down again and made friends with two delightful Roumanian girls, who fed me, less forcibly, with cheese, and caramels. Then two Roumanian men introduced themselves with great grandeur, and took me off at a station and forcibly fed me with cold chicken, hard boiled eggs and chocolate, plus soda water and yellow wine. MY STOMACH STOOD IT! Think of that! Then the two Roumanian girls fired away with my first lesson in Roumanian, took my book knowledge, turned it inside out, and gave me a really good start. Taught me the numerals, how to tell the time, and a thousand other things. We passed crowds of troop trains. The Roumanians had not enough wagons, so just before declaring war they told the Germans that if they wanted corn they must send wagons to fetch it. The Germans fell into the trap, and provided a good half of the transport for the Roumanian mobilisation. The train grew later and later, and fuller and fuller. I stood for the last eleven hours, and we arrived thirteen hours late at about four in the morning. No cabs. Streets dark. Pressed a porter into service, and taking my two language mistresses in tow, set off on foot. They got me a room, and I then saw them home, and came back and went to bed for a couple of hours. At seven I had coffee and a bath. At nine I had coffee and another bath, and at ten was at the British legation, where I saw Sir George Berkeley,[1] and Carnegie the secretary with whom I take tea this afternoon. In spite of starting last, I have the satisfaction of knowing that I am the first English correspondent to get through. I went to the French legation, and was on my way to look for Anet, who started a week before I did, when I met him on the street. We dine together tonight, and tomorrow I shift to his hotel, where I have taken a nice room at an exorbitant price, which is however cheaper than anywhere else. So that is all right, and we shall be able to play chess as much as we like. I am calling on the father of one of my language mistresses today. He is a *sénateur, très anglophile*, and his daughter promises that he will help.[2] I have also seen the Russian General in chief command, so that altogether I have wasted no time.

Bucharest is ripping. Hot, white, a regular French town. I am delighted to have been sent here, even though it means postponing my visit home. I hope to come home directly after my return from Bucharest. Sir George Berkeley is putting me in touch with our military attaché, with a view to helping me to get on the Roumanian front, and I am myself going to try and arrange a visit to the Russian front in the south against the Bulgars. I am as happy as a bird, and burnt as red as a brick. Really I do have the luck to have the most extraordinarily interesting time. Now, after my somewhat strenuous morning, I am going to have lunch. I will add to this letter later. It does not leave till Tuesday,[3] when it goes by courier, and will therefore reach you in pretty quick time. Now 'Please God give me a good luncheon!'

Later:– 'Thank God for my good luncheon!'

I had luncheon and it wasn't half bad, and then charged off, and had a charming talk with an old Roumanian gentleman who produced the last version of the Roumanian Code of Civil Law.[4] A spoonful of jam, a glass of cold water, and a tiny cup of Turkish coffee was brought in. You first lick up the jam, then wallop down the cold water, then sip the coffee. Most oriental and extremely good. Then you smoke cigarettes and discourse, using your arms, hands, fingers, eyebrows and nose as a kind of multiple windmill given you by God as a machine of expression. It was very jolly, and the old bird has given me the run of his house, his maps, his books and his capacious knowledge of things Roumanian historical and contemporary. I read through a Russian history of Roumania on the way down, and with wily exhibition of shallow information coupled with addressing him in Roumanian won his heart and we are now firm friends. His wife is also quite charming. From them I went on to have tea with Carnegie of our Legation and he and his wife poured out most useful information of all kinds. No bad, considering I got here at four this morning. I am tomorrow to have a letter for the prefect of police and also to see Colonel Thompson and, I hope, Take Ionescu, the Great Man of Roumania. For resulting interview you must look in the *Daily News*.

Later. Lunched with Colonel Thompson[5] who is as good a man as ever I've met, absolutely first rate, so good at his job that it is a miracle he's got it. He is going to do his best to fix me up with the Roumanian army. With the Russians I got my own way because it turns out that the man in command is a man I knew on the southern front, in fact the same general who re-commended me for a George[6] which I have never got and probably never shall. His Chief of Staff I also know.

I have just come in after a talk with the Minister of Pub. Instruction,[7] a young man, very quick and alive, acting as Chief Censor for the time being. Says if in doubt can always see him. So that is all right. Sent off my first telegram, a very long one, and am now banging at articles for all I'm worth. No time for a word more.

With much love, your affectionate son,
Arthur

Send a postcard to the Collingwoods to say I've arrived in Bucharest, and do the same to Ivy. Please. Tell Ivy my address in Petrograd as usual. But yourself write here, and if I leave I'll have your letters sent after me. I can't do that for many letters as it would be too much to ask of a very busy consulate.

1 British Minister to Roumania.
2 Perhaps 'the famous Ghetsu' (*Autobiography*, p. 199) – see note 5 below. If so, this letter contradicts the *Autobiography*, according to which Ransome met Mme. Ghetsu (one of the 'language mistresses') not on a train, but through the Minister of Education.

3   12 September 1916.
4   Ghetsu. 'He was living in retirement, a very eloquent old man
     with the most uncompromising notions of what Roumania
     would be able to claim after the war. On the wall he had a huge
     map showing Austro-Hungary and the Balkans and on the map
     he pointed to the whole of Transylvania as ethnographically
     Roumanian property.' (*Autobiography*, p. 199).
5   Christopher Birdwood Thompson (1875-1930), later Lord
     Thompson of Cardington. AR devotes two lively pages to him
     in the *Autobiography*, including the story of how he left
     Bucharest by motor-car, giving a lift to Arthur Ransome and a
     great many bottles of champagne. He was an army engineer;
     became Secretary of State for Air in Ramsay Macdonald's first
     and second administrations; and died in the R101 crash.
6   A Russian decoration of some kind.
7   Dukas, according to the *Autobiography* (p. 198).

                          To Edith R. Ransome
February 26 1917   Glinka Street

My dear old Mother,
    I wonder whether you are in London yet. I had a letter from
you the other day saying you thought you would be going there
about half way through February. If so do see something of
Barbara. I feel hopeless about letters. I've written often both to
you and to her, and it seems hardly a letter has reached either of
you.
    I have got a beastly cold, which is not surprising, as we have
run out of wood and my stove has not been lit for a week. I
shiver in my big fur coat (*fur* is polite for sheepskin) and the
balaclava helmet which Kitty[1] made but did not make long
enough in the neck. By my side I have a spirit lamp, and when
my fingers get too cold to twiddle on my typewriter, I warm
them in the flame of the spirit lamp and then proceed. Also, it's
two weeks since I was able to get any bread for breakfast. Most
disgusting. And difficult to work under such conditions. But as
you will have seen from my telegrams a good deal is going on of
very great interest, and I am hard at it from eight in the morning

to midnight every day. I haven't touched my fairy stories for nearly a month.

I believe in the end I shall be driven to writing a book about Russia in the faint hope of getting people to understand just a fraction of the puzzle. The only book that's any good is Williams'.[2] And it's so packed with information that it's difficult to read. The book in my head would be about as big as my books on Wilde and Edgar Poe,[3] and done in something the same way, with a historical section instead of a biographical, and chapters on Politics, Town, Village, Church, Men, Women, the Constitution, Railways, Roads and Waterways, etc. It would be pretty interesting, and it seems a pity to have learnt a good deal about it all without slopping over into a book.[4] But I much prefer Russian fairy stories.

My operation has definitely gone wrong, and I have got those wretched things again, which means that eventually I shall have to be operated on again. Nothing could put it right except a good long spell of thoroughly regular existence, punctual meals and decent ones, and so on, none of which is at all possible. I do not see much hope of getting home this year, although the *Daily News* said I might come back in the autumn.[5] It looks to me as if I shall be here till well into 1918 if not till autumn 1918, living my forlorn and industrious existence. It's very rotten because it's exactly as if real life had meanwhile stopped. If there were two of us here it would be all right. But to exist here alone producing telegrams is about as like humane existence as being a mechanical saw. I haven't even a book of fairy stuff going to make it all right. I asked Maurice Macmillan about a book, but have had no answer.[6] If he wants one he must communicate by telegraph. Please tell him this, and say that if he telegraphs fairly soon to say he wants a book of (1) ordinary fairy stories like those in *Old Peter* or (2) stories more or less bearing on peasant attitude towards morality and religion or (3) Russian stories of the saints, he must telegraph at once if I am to get it done in time.

I spend most of my spare time at present sweating up Russian Constitutional Law. It's interesting, but only like chess, and I'd give anything to have another of my own books instead.

Never mind. Some day or other, regardless of the advantages of a settled income, I shall fling my typewriter over the moon, catch it with a joyful yell on the other side, and spend three years in pouring out novels – at least romances – in collaboration with Joyce, and a mass of fairy stories in collaboration with myself. We will live in a farm. We will live on my boat.[7] Said yacht meanwhile is decaying away, and will be in an awful state when the war is over. Still, I daresay with plenty of candle grease in the worst leaks she'll float in smooth water, and allow me to sit in the cabin and hammer out books worth writing. But when is that time coming? Because, unless the *News* chucks me, and we are not on too good terms at present,[8] I shall feel more or less responsible and unwilling to turn over my job here to some inexperienced ass who will make a mess of it. And I do so want to be at home, and to go to Coniston, and to walk over Wrynose with Barbara and to feel that there are other things in life beside exceedingly complex politics. I expect when it's all over I shall be a dry political old oracular idiot with no power whatever of playing with imps and other merry devilments through the jolly forests of fairy books. I shall be bald, 'orrid serious, and altogether contemptible.

On that melancholy note I think it would be dramatic to close. So I close.

Your very affectionate son,

Arthur Ransome.

1   Mrs Ransome's adopted daughter.
2   Harold Williams (1876–1928), at this time Russian corres-pondent of the *Daily Chronicle*. AR was devoted to him, but the Russian Revolution eventually separated them, since Williams was implacably anti-Bolshevik. For their relationship, see *Life*, and *Autobiography*, especially p. 167: 'He was a very quiet man, unselfish, extraordinarily kind. I do not think it possible that he can ever had had an enemy.'
3   *Edgar Allan Poe, a critical study* (London: Martin Secker, 1910); *Oscar Wilde, a critical study* (London: Martin Secker, 1912).
4   The notion of writing a book about Russia haunted AR for years, but ended up as one among his many false starts.
5   The publisher. 'My father's and mother's oldest friends were the Maurice Macmillans' (*Autobiography*, p. 68).
6   AR had left Petrograd for England on 29 October 1916 and returned on 11 December.

7   When Ransome acquired this boat, what she was called, and what happened to her, are all unknown.
8   The *Daily News* thought he was needlessly excited about Russian developments.

To Edith R. Ransome

May 1 1917   Glinka Street

My dearest old Mother,

A whole bundle of letters from you and Joyce turned up together this morning dated March 11, March 27, simply March, and March 13. I was awfully glad to get them, and to hear that you are having an amusing time in London. Simultaneously I had letters from Barbara, and a parcel which Acland[1] sent for her through the bag containing tobacco (shag) most urgently needed, Robin's book,[2] a lovely drawing, and some bull's eyes to fill up. She told me she'd seen you and that you were very nice. Also I had a jolly letter from Mr. Collingwood with a scrap from Mrs. scribbled on it. Altogether I have a most comfortable warm feeling of not being so alone in the world as I thought I was. It was ripping hearing from Joyce about my beloved zoo. It's five months since I left. Perhaps in another six I shall be on my way back, and we will all go to the zoo together and feed monkeys and watch the sea lions and the adorable penguins.

There's a gorgeous demonstration going on all over the town today, and one of the centres is under my window, so I write with the Marseillaise pouring in from the street, and red flags and happy people as far as I can see.

Last night I was at a meeting of Servian professors who made me a member of a wonderful society. But the best thing I've had so far was the conference of all the councils of workers,[3] who came and asked me to sit with them. No other journalists there at all. It was the first proletarian parliament in the world, and by Jove it was tremendous. They said very nice things when they asked me to come. It was because of the stuff I got through on their behalf before the revolution.[4] Gummy what a row. There is a band of about forty fiddlers playing the Marseillaise, and a brass band playing a Russian revolutionary song. And about fifteen thousand people partly singing one and partly singing the other. Russia is a great place, and I shouldn't be surprised if in the revolution here I wasn't assisting at the birthday of a new and honest Europe.

But I am tired cOMPletely OUT. It's the most terrific difficulty to get up the force for a telegram, and as for my book about the revolution I've so little energy left in me that it will read as if the revolution had had the same operation I had myself. Never mind, if I survive, some day I'll get the original feeling into a myth, a flaming legend which is beginning to light up somewhere away in the cloudy back kitchen of my weary old mind. I'm glad Joyce spots the bits of my telegrams which are meant for family consumption. It's rather amusing knowing that my telegrams are in a sort of way letters home. At least you know more or less what I'm doing.

Your two pictures of Coniston hang on the wall beside a bit of heather from Peel Island and an ikon of Saint Nicholas. They give me great pleasure every day. I do so often wonder whether I shall ever be back with you all again and thinking about better things than correspondence. Joyce and I MUST some day do a book just as full of lake country as ever it can be. Hestbank [sic] and the sands and the whole lovely place.

Peters the economist has come in and is slowly trying to perform with my old cup and ball. Do you remember the thing?

While solemnly playing with it he announces that the war is going to end by the end of September. As he spends his whole time in sweating over information about it, he may be right, but personally, though I like Peters, I have small faith in economists.[5]

I hear the Leeds professorship has been given to Boswell of Liverpool, so I am probably out of the running altogether. Never mind, I have had the best end of the thing in the revolution, and I must be content with that. But I am tired. Williams has broken down altogether and gone away to the Caucasus to recover. I haven't bust as badly as that, but I am tired out, and one of my kidneys has gone wrong, probably after-effect of that damned operation. Still I am all right in bulk so to speak, and unless the summer is jolly tough I think I shall be able to keep it up with some vigour. Though I don't think there's any chance of getting any book done beside my account of the revolution. Macmillan I rejoice to say has agreed to do a book of Russian

Folk Tales, like 'The Soldier and Death' which I think I read to you when I was in England.[6] But I am not letting myself touch it until the revolution is done, copied and sent off to England. There's packs in it that Joyce will like, and it's real live history right enough, but all the same I want to get back to my fairy tales. A lovely character comes into one of the new ones. She is simply known as 'the old woman in the back yard.'[7]

    Well, my dear mother, I send you much love,

Your affectionate weary son,
Arthur

1   Sir Francis Dyke Acland (1874-1939), Liberal M.P. 1906-24, 1932-9; Under-Secretary for Foreign Affairs 1911-15, etc. A member of AR's enormous cousinage, he was extremely helpful to him in the early years of the war. He too had been at Rugby, and his recreation was fishing.

2   Presumably *Religion and Philosophy*, published in 1916 by R. G. Collingwood – 'Robin', (1889-1943), son of the Skald. It seems to have been he who taught Ransome to sail.

3   i.e., Soviets.

4   AR had passed to the British Embassy the manifesto, written in prison, of the arrested War Industry Committee. See *Autobiography*, p. 221.

5   Nevertheless, the influence of Peters on Ransome's interpretation of the Russian Revolution was, and was to remain, huge.

6   'The Soldier and Death' was to be published on its own in 1920.

7   She has not survived in any Ransome manuscript known to me.

To Edith R. Ransome

June 6 1917   Glinka Street

My dear Mother,

    I am so sorry you've had so few letters from me. I've written plenty, at any rate until the revolution, since when I've probably written rather less, because I've been worked off my head and off my feet and into a state near hysterical delirium.

    I simply have no time for anything, though when I get a headache so rotten that work is an absolute impossibility I bolt to the suburbs of Petrograd and get sunburnt and catch, actually catch, roach. The other day in two hours in the evening, I caught enough to feed a family of eight persons for lunch, which is not bad, besides doing me no end of good.

I am in the throes of trouble with Garvin,[1] who sent me a long and most excited telegram about Allied policy because I had had to telegraph that the Russian socialists were by no means satisfied with the same. That is of course unfortunate for us, but I can't alter it by telling lies about it, and pretending that all is for the best in this best of all possible worlds, so I think it quite possible I shall have to stop being correspondent for the *Observer*. I shall be very sorry if so, because though he may easily get a less well-informed correspondent to write him more cheerful telegrams from his point of view, the result will only be that he himself will get a false notion of what to expect. I do my very level to give an accurate idea of things here, but, bless my soul, only God who knows all things could really give an accurate view. I think I give a more accurate view than anybody else, judging from the way in which the Russian papers almost exclusively quote from the *News* as the only paper which gets near understanding the position.

To make up for the difficulty with Garvin, my other employer followed up a whole series of congratulatory telegrams and letters by sending along a cheque for fifty quid, I suppose to emphasise that he really meant it. My first inclination was to send it back and say I wasn't in the habit of taking tips. Then I remembered the amount of fishing tackle I could buy with it after the war is over, and the length of time I could live on it in my little boat while writing books for their own sweet sake, and finally remembering that I belong to the casual labouring proletariat I jolly well decided to stick to it with appropriate joy. 'Enry Straker would have stuck to it, and grinned.[2] Well, you should just see my grin. Fifty wholly unexpected Egyptian quid!

Praised and glorified for ever be the name of Hans Christian Andersen. But for him, I do believe these politics would have sent me mad. They nearly do anyhow, but I read a story of Andersen's every day after sending off my telegram, and so catch hold of a swan's feather and get ashore somehow or other though very out of breath.

I am very sorry to hear that Acland is ill. Please tell him to get better and come out here. It would be a thundering good thing if he did, and came unofficially simply to try to realise the actual state and needs of the country. Incidentally it wouldn't do Acland any harm.

I am getting more and more restive in Petrograd, and wanting to get off either to the front or to the interior, to get a first hand knowledge of how things are there. But I cannot stir for more than twenty-four hours at a time. Things happen too fast. I do my best to get a clear view of them, and to preserve some sort of smooth efficiency in judgement, but it's a queer job for me, though most people have queer jobs at the present time. Still to deal with politics day after day, with a cupboard full of folk-lore, is really rather comic. I never thought when I came to Russia in the beginning, and spent my first summer here hunting fairy tales that it would end in this sort of business, of which I foresee at least another year, and indeed begin to fear that long after the war is done the revolution and its developments will keep me conscience-bound to the treadmill. Never mind, some time or other a fine morning will find Joyce and me producing our masterpieces, either on my boat, or in a cottage in the lakes. And then, if not tired out, I have about fifteen lovely books waiting to be written, two plays and a pantomime, plus a whole series of new Aladdins. What do you think? Will that time come? Or shall I always have a sense of guilt in even thinking about fairy tales? N.B. Guilt or no guilt, just you wait till I tell you the idea of my pantomime. It's an absolute darling, even though I may never be able to write it.[3]

Please prod Kitty, Joyce and Geoffrey into some faint remembrance of their brother.

Your affectionate son,

Arthur Ransome

1 The editor of the *Observer*, then a Conservative newspaper. Ransome had been hired to write for it (as well as for the *Daily News*) a few months previously.

2 Enry Straker is the well-educated chauffeur in Shaw's *Man and Superman*.

3 He never was.

To Edith R. Ransome

July 23 1917   Glinka Street

My dear Mother,

Your July 17th letter came today, much quicker than most, and I was very glad to get it, as I've been in the rottenest condition for ages and had very few letters indeed. I can't understand why you seem to get so few letters from me because I write a tremendous lot.

It was very jolly hearing about Tabitha though I'm sorry you think her 'penny plain'. She ain't beautiful I admit, but that would be much to expect. Still, plain? No. She's better than that. I'm very glad you liked her.

Events of this week have definitely knocked on the head all chance of my getting home this year. I don't think I can even take a holiday of any kind here. You see nearly two months ago when I first crocked I wired for a holiday, and then was unable to take it, and had dysentry instead combined with an extra special dose of work. I sort of scramble on from day to day, in hopes of getting my second wind and feeling full of what Tabitha calls 'good beans' again.

My *Daily News* telegrams must be pretty rotten. I can't judge, because it's simply a case of forcing out something somehow. I WON'T lose faith in Russia. Nor will I lose faith in democracy. It's not democracy that's to blame for Russia's troubles, though plenty of evilly disposed persons will try to make out that it is. For months I've been wiring till my typewriter was blue in the keyboard that these things would happen unless certain other things were done which have not been done. Still that is not satisfaction.

It really was jolly hearing about Tabitha and you playing at retrieving grouse. All that, however, seems so very far away, and every sentence in your letter which touched on Russia showed that people in England, even intelligent birds like yourself, have not the faintest notion of the condition of things here. I think of England as of a sort of dream country, in the world and in the war but not of it. Everybody, I know, is either working or fighting, but for some reason or other the war does not hurt every man, woman and child in England permanently, continuously as it does those of the continental nations, and Russia most of all. Partly it is the laziness of our imagination, partly because the actual sufferings of England are so much less. You do not see the bones sticking through the skin of the horses in the street. You do not have your porter's wife beg for a share in your bread allowance because she cannot get enough to feed her children. You do not go to a tearoom to have tea without cakes, without bread, without butter, without milk, without sugar, because there are none of these things. You do not pay seven shillings and ninepence a pound for very second-rate meat. You do not pay forty-eight shillings a pound for tobacco. That is why those English papers who rail at the Russians are criminally wrong. It is because things are like that here that German agents and extremists[1] who promise an immediate millenium do succeed in carrying away the absolutely simple-minded Russian soldier whose poor head is cudgelled with long words till he does not know where he is, and does exactly what they tell him, even though it may be to his own ruin and to that of his country.

The time may come when England will be the best-hated country in Russia, and that would be a German victory of the most real and valuable kind, whatever may be the nominal terms of peace. It is just that which I fear. And we, here, are a handful of Canutes stopping the deluge. It *will* come right. It *must* come right. But it *won't* come right until England with knowledge learns sympathy. When I hear that Englishmen say, 'well, we must make up our minds not to count on Russia any more', and when I know that they mean by that that their attitude towards Russia is that of a man towards a tool that has worn itself out and is no further use to him, then indeed I see a pretty black future.

But, my dear mother, I won't talk politics to you. It's just occurred to me that perhaps the reason my letters don't get to you is that they are stopped by the censorship. Still, I hardly think so, because there's nothing in them that, alas, isn't printed with emphasis in the German newspapers. I never start my letters meaning to talk politics, but my mind is so crammed with the beastly stuff, and my days are so full of it, that I can't get away from it even in writing to you.

I can't get on even with my book about the revolution which

was wanted in a hurry. I am at it every minute of the day, rushing about, and talking till my throat's sore, and there's no time for books. As for *decent* books, I've forgotten I ever wanted to write them. I doubt if I ever shall again. If ever I do get home, my sole interest will be gluttony.

> Your affectionate son,
>
> Arthur

1　The Bolsheviks.

To Geoffrey Ransome

July 24 1917　　　　　　　　　　　　　　　　　Glinka Street

My dear Geoffrey,

It is just conceivably possible that you may be sent for to do a job here that requires a thorough knowledge of printing.[1] If only you had the rudiments of Russian, it would be pretty certain. Anyway, if you have any spare time at all, peg into Russian like a forty horse power and learn as much as you can.

Things here as you can jolly well imagine keep me fairly on the go. I haven't had one day's holiday out of this beastly town since I came back from the front in January. I am permanently hungry, permanently tired out, and permanently on the job, only getting about five hours' sleep most nights. Last week with the rows[2] on I was up three nights in succession. You may gather from this that I am in a mood to be grumpy with the devil himself.

Momentarily in the town, things are better. On the front as you see from the papers things are rotten. The disease afflicts only the infantry who are, of course, the least educated, and therefore easiest diddled by agitators. The bicycle corps, the artillery, all the sections that are made up of cleverer, better-trained men are unaffected. Don't (like other thoughtless asses) blame the Russians and call them traitors, cowards, etc. They are nothing of the sort. The same men who walk off today are those who have stuck it out through the previous two years under infinitely worse conditions. They are first-rate men, but week in week out agitators have been telling them that their real enemies are the bourgeois, that is, to their simple minds, men who wear collars, women who wear hats, or officers generally, and this is the natural result. If the retreat[3] goes far enough to affect the big towns in the rear, things will be gay in the extreme, and we shall be unlikely to meet again, but I take a more cheery view myself, and believe that things will automatically right themselves before irreparable harm has been done. If this had happened in France, it would mean the end of all things. But Russia is so mighty big that here that is not necessarily the case.

The fact that I can take a view so much more cheerful than that of the surrounding population, after over a month's dysentry, means a lot. But the blighters who are wringing their hands over here have most of them never anything to do with the Russian army except to yell when they saw a bit of it walking through the streets. I've seen the Russian army at work, and I *can't* lose faith in it. Although mind you, I thought when I came back last autumn that Russia could not stick another winter. I still think that. The war has hit Russia a lot harder than it has hit anyone else, and the poor old country has been tired and hungry for a very long time.

I wish I could see any prospect of leave and a week in England with you. But it's impossible. I can hardly come now, and in the autumn things will be even busier. And I cannot get anyone else who could take on the job. The last man who could have done it has been snapped up by the F.O. and leaves for England, lucky devil, on Monday.

Letters are doubly welcome just now, and come with corresponding rarity. From you, never, you infernal swine.

Your affectionate brother,
Arthur

1 Geoffrey Ransome was a printer by trade. Arthur had long wanted him in Petrograd, partly for company, and partly, no doubt, to save him from the trenches.

2 The so-called July Days, when the Bolsheviks tried to seize power and were defeated. Lenin had to go into hiding and Trotsky was briefly arrested. See Brogan's *Life*, pp. 137-8.

3 The Russians, under General Kornilov, had that summer launched their last offensive, which had failed like all the others and turned into a retreat.

The Daily News
& Leader

LONDON AND MANCHESTER.　　　　　SATURDAY, JULY 28, 1917.

RUSSIANS FIGHT HARD AT THREE POINTS.

Still Retreating, But Resistance Strengthening.

LOSS OF KOLOMEA.

Rumanians Pushing Their Way to the Frontier.

More effective resistance is now being offered by the Russians to the German advance in Galicia.

Last night's Russian official reports that the enemy has been repulsed at three points, but the retreat continues. The Germans report bitter but successful fighting on the eastern bank of the Sereth near Tarnopol, in which "thousands and thousands" of Russians were mown down. The enemy further reports the capture of Kolomea, south-east of Stanislau, but they admit the evacuation of the Susitza Valley, owing to the pressure of the Rumanians, who are setting the Russians a fine example.

In another long dispatch from Petrograd Mr. Arthur Ransome states that "if the Germans had been in great force the retreat of Russia's southern armies would long ago have been cut off." This danger now appears less menacing.

Our Special Correspondent discusses at length the military situation, and ascribes the retreat to the influences of the Petrograd Extremists. He predicts that "the same troops who to-day voluntarily retire will to-morrow voluntarily advance."

HARD FIGHTING.

Successful Actions by Russian Rearguard.

RUSSIAN OFFICIAL.　　　　　Friday.
To the north of Tarnopol the enemy occupied Plotytch and Chystyloff (on the ─eth). His attacks to the south-east of

THE 7th AND 8th ARMIES.

Difficulties of Retreat Not to be Underestimated.

From Our Special Correspondent,
ARTHUR RANSOME.

PETROGRAD, Thursday, 1.30 a.m.
(Received yesterday.)

The Russian retreat continues on a front of about a hundred miles. It is due to events in Petrograd and the success of the Extremist agitation. Those troops behaved worst who had received most reinforcements from Petrograd. The troops in certain cases actually retired voluntarily after fighting a successful engagement. This is to be explained by the fact that the officers being wounded or killed, the simple soldiers fell immediately under the influence of the Extremists.

There is no need again to outline the Extremist arguments. The main one is always the absence of an agreement between the Allies so simply and clearly worded as to make it obvious to the soldiers that Germany and not the Allies are responsible for the war's continuance.

Extremists at the Front.

After this the Extremists ingeniously insist that the real enemy of the Russian soldier is the bourgeois—that is to say, that his real enemy is behind him, not before him. Add to that the events in Petrograd, ─h made it possible for the Extremist ─　front to talk of

be establis
mous an a
at a halt
alike by f
give the R
ment and
the capit
the expo
on the ─

The ─
selves a─
in the w
the Extr
them one
by an ad
wards, ─
voluntar
tarily a─
tremist ─
the min─
in the ─

DE

Gre─

Th─
impr─
M. ─
the ─
seems
noff's ─
by th─
effort ─
feat of
Baltic ─
mands,
be re-el
to give ─
Extremi
the effe─
could n─
present─
Govern
by na─
given ─
aded.─
in th─
surre─
has b─
from ─
of Le─
comple
which ─
handed ─
The a─
towards ─
be held
clearly t.
forces ca─
and rear.

*

AMONG Ransome's other difficulties was the depletion of
his financial resources due to escalating prices. On 30 July
he had to explain to his editor in London why he had allowed
The Times to scoop the *Daily News* with reports of the partici-
pation of a British armoured-car squadron, under Commander
Locker-Lampson, in a new Kerensky offensive against the
Germans. 'I am fully conscious that my recent telegrams are
rotten like their author who telegraphed you weeks ago that he
was pretty well dead after the continuous rush,' Ransome wrote
bitterly. 'Three days later I broke down with dysentery which has
lasted till now intermittently. Therefore I am working under
extreme difficulties. I am unable to exist further on my present
income in view of the quadruple prices. Unwant increase salary,
but I think I should have a living allowance.'

*

To F. J. Hillier, *Daily News*, London

Aug. 12 1917

Glinka Street,
Petrograd.

Dear Mr. Hillier,
Here are my accounts up to the end of June. They need
explanation on three points.
(1) Committee of Journalists. This is a Russian association
which runs a room with typewriters etc. in the same building as
the Cabinet, and sends out reports of proceedings to the Russian
newspapers. Immediately after the Revolution it was extremely
useful to me, since then less so, although I think it worth while
to keep up my membership as in times of crisis, which are pretty
frequent, I can get there what I can't get elsewhere. However if
you think the expense is too great for its occasional usefulness, I
can drop it. The other subscription (to the Committee in the
General Staff) is not monthly. There is now and then a demand
made to cover running expenses and that is all.
(2) Enormously increased cab expenses. Cabs have become a
much more serious item since the Revolution, firstly because
there is infinitely more running about to be done, and secondly
because after the Revolution trams became next door to im-

possible and cabdrivers threw over even their quasi-statutory
fares and put up their prices to an extraordinary degree from
which so far from lowering they are still increasing them. I only
count those cabs on newspaper business.

(3) Enormously increased expenditure on newspapers. Before
Revolution there were only about half a dozen papers. Now there
are more like a score, and it's unsafe not to take pretty well all,
because first one section of the press and then another becomes of
capital importance. Also they too are steadily raising their prices.

I think these are the only points so far as the accounts go.

Now then, there is another matter which ought to be thought
of now. It was agreed when I came out last year that I should
come home as usual for three weeks (or a month?) in the autumn
to report on things, and to get up steam to meet the winter. This
is the more necessary since as you know I got jolly ill about two
months ago, and had to keep it up regardless of that fact, telegraphing pretty well every day because of the unfortunate fact that
Petrograd politics took no account of the dysentry and nervous
collapse attendant on the efforts of the *Daily News* correspondent.
I'm better now, although for weeks at a time I could not get a
telegram done without bleeding at the nose and other unpleasant
phenomena. However, the point is not to lament the past. The
point is that if you want decent telegrams this winter your
correspondent has got to be put into better condition. Otherwise
I should myself propose going straight on without a holiday at all.

I simply must be here and not in a state of being tired out at
the time of the Constituent Assembly.[1] Therefore I want to
come to England earlier this year than last. Last year I left Russia
at the end of October. This year I think I should be back here
by then. I think I should leave about the end of August.

I want you to telegraph to me that I may prepare things for an
efficient service in my absence, and use my own judgement
about leaving. You can have absolute confidence that I shall do
my best to choose a time so as to lose as little as possible of what
is happening here.

The beginning of winter is going to be a very critical time
here, and I want to get back before it comes on.

> Yours sincerely,
>
> [no signature]

1   The Constituent Assembly had been postponed until October, and was to be postponed (fatally) yet again.

To Edith R. Ransome
August 12 1917   Glinka Street

My dear Mother,
   My spirits are slightly better, principally because I did actually get out of Petrograd a week ago for three days of which I spent two and a half and two nights in the train, going to and from Headquarters, where I got through the business I was there for without any difficulty, and had half an hour free, which I used in getting a dirty boy in a dirty boat to row me up the river above the town drains, and hold the boat while I bathed. Well that was jolly, and though the water was like pea-soup, the evening light was all the better on it on account of its opacity, and I splashed about in it with great joy and some humiliation at finding how weak a swimmer I have become. Further my spirits are bucked up today, because yesterday after sending off my telegram, and mopping up the consequent nose-bleeding which too often accompanies that job, I resolved to strike, and flung some tackle into a bag, grabbed my rod, telephoned to a friend of mine, Arnatt, and set off for Lachta. The train crosses a long bridge over the river where we fish, and the station is two miles further along a very dusty road, and I filled my self with joy by jumping out of the train at the bridge, and landing BEEootifully, running like a hare and not even falling on hands and knees. So I saved the two miles walk, and lay on the bank of the river until my astonished friend turned up hot and dusty from the station. I know what you are remembering . . . that shameful tramway episode of early youth.[1] Well, this was better, and I felt so bucked about it, it put a glow on the whole day. We got a boat, and found a jolly place by reeds, and we caught fifteen fish, perch, half a dozen of them being really respectable ones. Then coming back I got a cab with a really good horse, which in these days is a rarity, and had a spanking run home. Altogether a ripping half holiday, and I feel better for it.
   Further I've had satisfactory news from the *Daily News* about

an allowance to help in meeting the gigantic expenses incident on living here. So the barometer stands momentarily set fair. Except that it's ages since I had any news from home of any kind from anybody. And of course, I think it's very unlikely I shall get a holiday at all although they promised me three weeks in England this autumn, and even said I might make the round trip by Japan to get an interesting series of articles. That is off anyhow, and I shan't complain, because I see the futility of it myself. But I am very sick about not seeing England and all of you for so long. And three weeks in England would make the winter here infinitely easier.

However, you never know. Something may happen at the last minute to make my coming possible. In which case three cheers for seeing you all, and Coniston, and Tabitha. Tabitha does seem a charming infant. We might even be able to manage Finsthwaite this year. But I won't think about it, because at present it looks as if I were not going to get away at all.

Aug. 13

Your letter of June 29 has just turned up. It held some jolly bad news about your eyes, and did not say what decision you felt like taking about an operation. Operations are beastly things, but I always remember the happiness of old Puff when he had it and was able to go back to his botany and tell a birdseye from a forget-me-not. Of course I don't know whether your operation is the same as his or not. But his was a cataract. And it would be worth while to you if only you got a little sight out of it. At present your typing goes to my heart. Although I fancy the typewriter itself is a little to blame and that it is a case of the blind leading the blind. Anyway do let me know what you decide, and I'll burn a candle to my dear Saint Nicolai and ask him to do what he can for you.

It seemed so queer to hear of Robin[2] 'coming to dinner' tonight, and to get the letter six weeks later, when that dinner has long ago been eaten, and you have watched Robin's steel blue and polished manner with which he always enters upon such functions, turn to softer metal and even to cheerful remnants of Rugby, as humanity makes itself felt. Barbara I suppose is still at Coniston with Dora's baby. Oh hang! Wouldn't I like to see that said brat. Her name is Barbara Harriet,[3] and Barbara says 'She seems to be angry about something or other.' And in another letter. 'She howls like a Turk.'[4]

Today again there is a faint glimmer of hope that I may get home. The Cossacks have asked for a postponement of the Constituent Assembly. Well that gives the Government a good lump of public opinion to back them in putting the thing off, and it's obvious to all observers that the thing will have to be put off somehow or other, if it is to be a real test of the country's feeling. Well if it is put off till December or January my prospects much improve. It was to be October. That meant that either I had to go at once, or else risk being late for it. And I've got to be here for it anyhow. Well, if it is postponed, then I *may* be able to barge home bursting with stupendous joy in about a month's time, stay three weeks in England, and get back in plenty of time to have all the various political threads properly sorted in my mind before the Assembly comes off. You don't believe in St. Nick, or I'd ask you to pray to him.

Don't say anything in the direction of Hatch about my possible coming home.

But, if you get a wire from me saying I am coming, be a good and sainted although agnostical mother, and send a letter to the *Daily News* for me marked vastly 'TO BE CALLED FOR'. (Called for . . . By Jemima Ann!) And in that letter give me such information as you may possess as to people's whereabouts. E.g. Shall I find a bed at Cecily's? Is Barbara in town or at Coniston? Are you at Finsthwaite or Duddon or Leeds? Lord what fun to come walking down from Walna Scar to find you in Duddon valley as once I did years ago, and arrived in disgraceful circumstances after falling among gipsies.

But I WILL NOT allow myself to raise my hopes only to see them dashed. Still, there's no denying it. It is possible, if the Assembly is postponed, that in five weeks from now, I shall be sailing about in England looking just like any other person, but actually not touching the ground, lighter than air, my gross corporeal envelope distended and supported by sheer unconquerable busting braggadocious joy.

Geoffrey is a swine, although he has the doubtful privilege of being your son and my brother. HE NEVER WRITES. I've several times written to him but never know whether he gets my letters.

I go on, lobbing letters into the infinite, not knowing where they fall, in much the same spirit as that of the gentleman in the house next to mine who during the revolution tossed hand-grenades out of a garret window down to the pavement which he could see, merely in the hope that they would meet something. Well, goodbye for now. IF if if I come, I may be in England about as soon as you get this.

[no signature]

1   'My mother used to tell of her shame when she had set out for Leeds leaving me, not ready, at home and, sitting in the tram, looked back and saw me running steadily down the hill from the Horseshoes a very long way behind. She said nothing, hoping that I would give up and turn back . . . at last the conductor saw that he was being pursued. Kindhearted man, he stopped his tram. I panted up, plumped myself down on the seat beside my mother and remarked happily "Just in time" to the unfortunate passengers whom I had thus delayed.' (*Autobiography*, pp. 16-17.)

2   While still a schoolboy at Rugby, Robin Collingwood had brought home to Lanehead on Coniston Water his friend Ernest Altounyan, the son of an Armenian surgeon, whose affection for Dora made Arthur jealous (*Autobiography*, p. 130). Eventually Ernest married Dora and took her away to Aleppo. Four of their five children – Susie, Titty, Roger and Bridget – became models for characters of much the same names in Arthur Ransome's *Swallows and Amazons* and its successors; and Captain Nancy Blackett bears some resemblance to the eldest Altounyan, Taqui.

3   Her name was soon changed to Taqui.

4   A tactless remark about a half-Armenian baby. Possibly an allusion to Belloc's Lord Lundy, who bellowed like a little Turk?

                    To Edith R. Ransome
September 1 1917   Glinka Street

My dearest Mother,
    Hang on at the Duddon for as long as you can. I shall, I hope,

be leaving Petrograd next Thursday or Friday on my way home.[1] I bust. I have broken a mouth-organ already with melodious enthusiasm. The only piano I know has been locked up to protect it from my need for self-expression. Unless something quite unforeseen happens between now and then, this day next week should see me on my way.

Keep this information within the family: e.g. I am not announcing my return at Hatch. So please be equally discreet.

With luck I may be fishing in the Duddon in three weeks' time. I shall only have a very short holiday and of course a lot to do in it. I wish Tabitha were with you at the Duddon. Still. Good Lord, it is too ripping to think of. I shall probably sleep either at Robin's or at Cecily's, if Cecily is in town.[2] If you get a wire saying I have started AND NOT UNTIL write to me care of the *News*, Bouverie Street, marking the envelope TO BE CALLED FOR and saying where Cecily is and if I can sleep at her place. Then I propose to go to Coniston, and repeat with Barbara the walk over Walna Scar into the Duddon valley, where I hope to find you. It is really too gorgeous to think about.

Altogether, I don't quite believe it. And it may not be true.

But it looks true at present. And I've already set about speeding up my passport etc. Tell Kitty to leave one trout in the Duddon for me. A little one, very energetic.

I shall have to be dentisted as soon as I get to London. I shall combine that with other unpleasant operations like reporting on the situation and things like that. And then. Oh shiver my fountain pen. The temptation to hurl my new typewriter through the double windows was terrific but I withstood it. I said to myself 'Be calm'. I said, 'There is nothing to get excited about. You are going to England, where you will have a worrying time and a short one.' It was no good. Myself replied by yelling hurroo and jumping over my camp bed.

Also today is sunny. Also, after yesterday's two telegrams I went out, gathered worms and a boat and anchored or at least tied up to a buoy in the Gulf where it was so rough that I thought I should be able to do nothing. I made a temporary paternoster[3] like we used to make at Coniston, and though the waves nearly swamped the boat I got out fourteen decent perch on which my porter's wife and her vast family are feasting today.

In three weeks' time I will catch a pike at Newby Bridge.

The only blemish is that this is the first year since I was nineteen in which I haven't a book coming out. I feel lost and wretched without one. *Aladdin* is all in print, but postponed. *Revolution* unfinished, and I haven't the power of finishing it yet. I want the Constituent Assembly for its last chapter. Fairy stories next year. So there's nothing this year. It's beastly. However

> Who cares for lack of printed books
> While there are fish in southern brooks?
> And who enforced oblivion recks
> With better fish in northern becks?
> To me indifferent is the frown
> Of publishers in London town.
> Perdition take all printed yarns,
> While there are trout in moorland tarns.
> Be literary if you like!
> Give me the evil-snouted pike,
> The red-finned perch, the spotted trout,
> The quill float, hovering in doubt,
> Then slipping sideways in the stream,
> Tugged by a shy gigantic bream.
> Sunshine and water . . . give me these.
> Give books to anyone you please.
>
> Arthur

1 In fact he did not leave until 9 October.
2 Cecily was the elder of his two sisters.
3 A fishing-line, with hooks attached at intervals, and weights to sink it.

*

RANSOME'S return to England meant that he was not at his post when the Bolsheviks seized power. He had foreseen the swing to the Left, but thought that he would have plenty of time to visit home and get back to Petrograd before the Kerensky government fell. In London he did his best to interpret events for readers of the *Daily News*, but 'lately as I had left Petrograd, I could not trust myself to be sure of the truth in this welter of contradiction'. (*Autobiography*, p. 224). He felt he must get back to Petrograd as soon as possible, and with the assistance of the British Foreign Office reached Stockholm on 11 December. It took him more than a week to persuade the local representative of the Bolsheviks, V. V. Vorovsky, to stamp his passport, but at length Vorovsky did so, and Ransome reached Petrograd at last on Christmas Day.

★

To Edith R. Ransome

December 30 1917[1]   Glinka Street

My dear Mother,

I hear a bag is leaving for England today, so I just scribble a few lines to you.[1] I have no time for more.

Things here are such as to keep me most frantically busy. I wish to goodness I had been able to get back before. It's too late to do very much good now; but there is a lot that must be done unless we are to throw up our hands and leave Russia to the Germans.

I am so busy seeing people that I am afraid my telegraphing is likely to suffer. Yesterday for example I saw in the course of the day something like eighteen or nineteen various folk, ranging from the present dictator of Russia[2] to our ambassador through pretty well every shade of contradictory Russian opinion.[3]

The people taking the most sensible line here are a small group of Americans, including a Col. Robins, and a Mr. Sisson, whom probably Mrs. Macmillan saw when he was in London.[4] The people taking the maddest because the angriest view are the French.

As things are now, I doubt if Geoffrey could have done any good here, although I should have liked him to be here for the sake of his education. And for my own sake. Practically every one of my friends has left, unlikely to return.

The situation is beyond all things extraordinary, and from the point of view of social study most violently interesting and suggestive.

I have no time for another word. So I say goodbye till I get another chance.

I send you my very best wishes for a happy New Year. To you and to Cecily, Joyce, Kitty, Geoffrey, Sidge,[5] the Weasel, the Other One, that exuberant black devil dog of Kitty's, the hens, and even the garden.

Your affectionate son,

Arthur

1   The letter is typed. The exact date is not clear, but 30 seems more probable than 31.
2   Lev Davidovich Trotsky.
3   It later became clear that, to AR, the most important person he met on 29 December was his future wife, Evgenia Petrovna Shelepina, then Trotsky's secretary (see *Autobiography*, pp. 229-31).
4   Raymond Robins, head of the American Red Cross and unofficial diplomatic agent; Edgar Sisson, American journalist – also an unofficial agent, and eventually the author of *One Hundred Red Days* (Yale University Press, 1931). For AR's relations with these men, see *Life*, pp. 156-7, 165-7, 196-7, *et passim*.
5   Miss Sidgemore, Mrs Ransome's companion, and formerly the Ransome children's governess. 'The Weasel' was a maid-servant.

PART TWO

Love and Journalism
1918–1929

THE YEARS OF WAR and revolution had transformed Ransome
from a struggling man of letters into a professional journalist, and one, moreover, with great responsibilities. After his
return to Russia in December 1917, the responsibilities grew
greater, and he had less and less help in carrying them out. By
February 1918 Ransome of the *Daily News* and Philips Price of
the *Manchester Guardian* were the only two British correspondents in Russia who were sympathetic to the Bolsheviks'
foreign policy. Ransome urged that in spite of appearances
the Bolsheviks were the most reliably anti-German force in the
country. This infuriated the British Foreign Office and the
British military authorities who were soon to launch the anti-
Bolshevik 'intervention' at Archangel. Before long Ransome's
only reliable Russian friends were to be found among the supporters and associates of the Bolsheviks. One of these was
Evgenia Petrovna Shelepina, Trotsky's secretary, with whom
Ransome fell in love; another was the leading Bolshevik Karl
Radek. When, with the coming of intervention in the summer
of 1918, Ransome's personal position became impossible,
Radek helped him to escape to Stockholm, where Shelepina,
now a member of a Bolshevik diplomatic mission, joined him.
It was the beginning of a fifty-year union.

For the next fifteen months Ransome struggled to report
events to his paper and his countrymen, and to rescue his own
affairs from the chaos of revolution. He did not stay long in
Stockholm. Under British pressure, the Swedish government

63

expelled the Bolshevik mission (including Shelepina) in January 1919, and for good measure Ransome, 'the Red journalist', was thrown out too. He returned to Russia with Shelepina on 3 February, leaving again for Britain on 14 March. Arriving in London on 25 March, he was met on King's Cross station by a plain-clothes policeman, who summoned him to Scotland Yard, where he was questioned by the head of the Special Branch, Sir Basil Thomson. Ransome's opposition to intervention had made him a deeply suspect figure, but he managed to convince Thomson, though not the Foreign Office, that he was more interested in fishing than in politics. Next he went north to his mother's house in Chapel Allerton. Mrs Ransome was now living in Kent, but Ellen and the Weasel looked after him (they 'stuffed me like a Strasbourg goose' he reported) while he hammered out his book *Six Weeks in Russia in 1919*. All the while he worried about what was going to happen to Evgenia Petrovna, for the White Russian armies were getting nearer and nearer to Moscow. By the end of September his anxiety had become intolerable, but at last he was able to wrest a passport out of the Foreign Office, thanks in part to Basil Thomson, and left for Scandinavia and Russia.

He arrived in Stockholm on 7 October and next day wrote to his mother, 'I have not a regret in my mind . . . I know I must go, I want to go, and whatever happens, it cannot be worse than my own self reproaches if I had avoided going.' Clearly he had by now told Mrs Ransome all about Evgenia. From Stockholm he went to Estonia, and then began the most hair-raising adventures of his life. He had to get across the Estonian-Soviet front line with a whole skin; with the assistance of the Estonian government, for whom he was carrying an important peace message, he managed it, and arrived in Moscow to deliver his message and rescue Evgenia. She did not believe she needed rescuing (and indeed before long the White threat receded) but she agreed to travel back with him to Estonia. The return was, if possible, more dangerous than the journey out; at one point Shelepina bought their lives by presenting a Lettish farmer's wife with a tea-kettle; further on Ransome assuaged suspicions by playing a chess-game with a White officer, an old acquaintance. Ransome lost the match, and the White commander was so pleased that he sent the fugitives down to Reval (Tallinn) by special train. In reaction to all the nervous strain, he went down with what he said in his *Autobiography* was 'something like brain fever'. But thanks to Evgenia Petrovna and a good local doctor, he soon recovered.

First Estonia and then Latvia served as his base for the next five years or so. Evgenia passed as his wife. He earned his living as Russian correspondent for the *Manchester Guardian*. It was convenient to reside just outside Russia, to which frequent visits were possible, since from Reval or Riga telegrams could be sent uncensored. He would have preferred to live in England, but it was impossible to say when or if Ivy would agree to a divorce, and until she did so, it was socially prudent to live with Evgenia abroad.

Superficially the end of the first phase of the Russian Revolution and the return of peace made little difference to Ransome, but his new arrangements left him plenty of spare time. His creative impulse slowly began to reassert itself. He took up sailing, to which he had never been able to devote himself fully. Soon he started to write imaginatively again, in a very different style from that of his earlier years. *Racundra's First Cruise* (1923) was the result.

This phase of Ransome's life came to an end in 1924 a year crowded with incident. He was in Moscow in January, and covered the funeral of Lenin for the *Guardian*. Then it was back to Britain, where Ivy had at last begun divorce proceedings. There were long wranglings over the terms of the settlement before she completed in April. Ransome hastened back to the Baltic and married Evgenia Petrovna on 8 May at the British Consulate in Reval. That summer they visited Moscow and cruised in *Racundra* before laying up the ship in November and travelling to Britain together. The *Guardian* immediately sent its Special Correspondent off to Egypt, where he spent Christmas, while Evgenia stayed with her mother-in-law. After Ransome's return in February 1925, he and Evgenia went house-hunting in the Lake District, where they soon found Low Ludderburn, the hill cottage near the eastern shore of Lake Windermere that was to be their home for the next ten years.

Life settled down into an agreeable routine, now and then tiresomely interrupted by the *Guardian*, which repeatedly sent

Ransome on foreign missions at Christmas time and summoned him to Manchester. Apart from that, his time was his own, and he filled it in his usual manner, with fishing, sailing, writing, and making friends with children. He began 'Rod and Line', a fishing column in the *Guardian* which rapidly attracted an enthusiastic following. Except for internal ailments, of which he was never to be entirely free, and which grew worse whenever he was away from the sea, by the late '20s Ransome had little cause to complain about his fate. He was happily married, agreeably employed, and was at last beginning to put politics behind him. A way seemed to be opening to the achievement of his dearest literary ambitions.

★

To Edith R. Ransome

send letters addressed   Foreign Office,
                                                 for Arthur Ransome,
                                                 c/o Bruce Lockhart,
                                          British Mission in Russia.[1]

May 21 1918   [Moscow]

My dear Mother,
    Letters addressed like that might possibly reach me. I do not know how you have been addressing letters, but anyhow I have not had a single one dated after December. The last four months have been complete silence from all my belongings, so that I begin to feel I haven't got any. Also as we get no newspapers England begins to seem a sort of Atlantis, a fantastic island of last year, that this year has sunk beneath the sea, where perhaps on clear days, when the water is smooth, travellers will be able to see it, and through special glasses inspect you and Joyce in a subaqueous Chapel Allerton, subaqueously feeding subaqueous hens. Writing letters to England is like writing letters to Father Christmas, and putting them in the drawing room fire to see their ashes blow hopefully up the chimney into the mysterious infinite.
    This time, though, I have real hope of my letter getting through. It is going by a Soviet courier, I suppose to Berlin,[2] and thence to Denmark, and so at last to England, if it does not get interned on the way.

Anyway I do hope it gets to you.

Tomorrow, I think, is your birthday, though I am not at all sure. You will be walking about a little bit in the open and making good resolves. I know you. And Joyce will be striding longleggedly by your side and looking over the hedgetops of the immediate future into the pleasant fields where there is nothing to do except write romances, and Michael Boo[3] is much more real than Lord Robert Cecil.[4] Well, he is that anyway.

Do try to get a letter to me. I have not the least idea how or where is any single one of the whole family.

Here in Moscow, I have a room as big as a matchbox in the top of the beastly expensive hotel[5] which houses my American friends,[6] and the British Mission. But I had about a week in a little palace, requisitioned by a bunch of Bolsheviks,[7] where we ran a sort of Lunatic Commune, and gave ourselves indigestion by eating nothing but cheese. Some day I will write an account of that performance which was really extraordinarily comic, although it ended in awful idiosyncratic rumpuses where temperament met resolute temperament and rent souls wailed and howled their woes.

I had a jolly good picnic one day, but mostly it's impossible to get out of town. Every time I plan to get out, some rush of work comes along and keeps me here.

I have had a jolly bit of real work last week, writing a sort of Open Letter to America, about the Soviets, which Colonel Robins has taken there, for the benefit of Wilson and other people.[8] I had only 36 hours in which to do it. So I started at eight in the morning, and went at it steadily without sleep until six o'clock the following evening, wrote something over ten thousand words, and got them done just in time to give them to the Colonel before he was off, via Siberia and Japan. By now he must be somewhere beyond Irkutsk. Of course a statement written out without any preparation, without any revision, at such a rate, straight on the typewriter, could not be as good a thing as I should have liked to have done. But, reading it over afterwards in copy, I think it gives a fair idea of the truth, and perhaps, when I revise it and expand it, will make a good sort of first chapter to my book Portraits of the Revolution.[9] It beats the big drum a bit too much and there are too many trombones in it for my mother's refined taste, but the old Colonel who read parts of it while I was writing the rest, says it will hit Americans where they live, and that is what it was written for. It's got some very rude remarks in it about English brains, but you know my views on that subject.

Not a single one of my English friends is left in Russia. They've all gone home, lucky brutes.

My principal friends here are Radek,[10] his wife, and two huge young women, Bolsheviks, as tall as Grenadiers, who prefer pistols to powder puffs, and swords to parasols, the heroines of exploits that would make Michael Boo seem a mere carpet knight. One of them succeeded in extracting over a million *poods* of corn from the south under the very noses of the Germans, she at the time commanding an expedition of 300 wildly devoted sailormen.[11]

All this is very jolly, but my gloom increases daily when I see that people in England continue to trust the refugees, not realising that the fact that they are refugees puts them out of court in estimating the true balance of things here. We could have easily saved much if we had recognised and supported the Bolsheviks in December. One thing is perfectly clear and that is that from the merest selfish motives we shall find ourselves very seriously regretting their departure if they depart, whatever party succeeds them. Whatever party succeeds them will be bound to look for help from Germany. And these brave, honest folk, whom England mistrusts because they see visions . . . It's a tragic business. And England is unfortunately going to pay most dreadfully.

I would like to be able to tell you what I am going to do next, but I do not know. I am learning Tartar, because I think that by this time next year the interest of the world may be concentrated on the Mahommedans, in which case every man who is on the spot will be useful. I am not sure whether, if things end badly here, and I am able to get away at all, I shall go south or try to get into Scandinavia so as to be able to get Russian news from both sides. Anyway, I MUST somewhere or other have three months in which to write the bulk of the material I have before it fades and becomes useless. I don't think anyone has seen this thing as closely as I have, and I absolutely must write its history.

And things go on happening so fast that it looks as if I shall never get a moment for writing the sort of report of it that would be really worth while from all points of view.

I must stop. I send my very best love to you, and Joyce, and Sidge, and my beloved Geoff,[12] and Cecily, and Samuel who will I hope wag a tail at me from the other world, and everybody else.

Your very affectionate son,

Arthur Ransome.

1　Robert Bruce Lockhart headed one of the several British missions to Moscow which at this time were meddling counter-productively in Russian affairs. He and Ransome were good friends.

2　Since the treaty of Brest-Litovsk, signed on 28 February 1918, Russia and Germany had been nominally at peace. AR had been told about the courier by Evgenia Shelepina, then working as Trotsky's secretary.

3　Presumably the hero of a romance which Joyce was writing. If so, he never appeared in print.

4　Cecil had succeeded Francis Acland as Foreign Undersecretary. In the *Autobiography* (pp. 224–5), Ransome describes a conversation with him just before the return to Russia in December 1917: 'He stood in front of the fireplace, immensely tall, fantastically thin, his hawklike head swinging forward at the end of a long arc formed by his body and legs.'

5　The Elite.

6　Colonel Raymond Robins and company.

7　Among them the Radeks and the Shelepina sisters.

8　See Ransome's book, *The Truth About Russia*, published 1918 by the *New Republic* in New York, and reissued (along with *Six Weeks in Russia in 1919*) in London in 1992, with an introduction by Paul Foot, by RedWords.

9　Another unfulfilled design.

10　Karl Radek, a Polish Jew, was AR's closest friend among the Bolshevik leaders – indeed, in any real sense, his only friend. He figures prominently in the *Autobiography*, for instance on pp. 227–8. His wife's name was Rosa.

11　The 'huge young women' were Evgenia and Iraida Shelepina; Iraida was the heroine of the corn expedition. Evgenia, at least, would in later years have objected strongly to being called a Bolshevik: she said that she worked for Trotsky only as a matter

of common sense patriotism. A *pood* is equivalent to 36 lb. or
16.38 kilograms.

12 AR had not yet heard of Geoffrey's death in January. No surviving document shows his response to the news, though we
can be sure it distressed him greatly.

                    To Tabitha Ransome

May 28 1918[1]   Russia.

MY DEAR BABBA

        AT   LAST DOR·DOR   HAS GOT A LOT OF

GREEN   AND   PURPLE   INK   AND   A LITTLE A VERY

LITTLE   TIME   AND   SO   HE   CAN   WRITE A PROPER

   TO   HIS   WOOLLY BABBA.

ALL   MY   BEASTS   ARE   WELL

THE HEN.

            THE OWL

                                                AND
                                                THE ELEPHANT
                        THE PEACOCK   ALTHOUGH AS YOU CAN SEE
                                               FROM THE PICTURE THE ELE
                                               IS RATHER HUNGRY AND HANGR
                                               FROM HAVING HAD NO DINNER.

DOR-DOR IS BUSY EVERY DAY TRYING TO MAKE
IMPERIALISTS SEE SENSE

OBSERVE THE GRASS
GROWING UNDER THE
IMPERIALIST.

THIS IS MEANT TO BE AS
MUCH LIKE A BARN-DOOR AS
POSSIBLE. BUT THE IMPERIALIST
WON'T SEE IT.

DEAR BABBA YOU MUST ASK MUMMUM TO EXPLAIN.
THIS AND SHE WON'T BE ABLE. NEVER MIND.
THAT IS BECAUSE SHE IS A GOOD MOMMUM WHAT
KNOWS ALL ABOUT WITCHES AND PUDDINGS AND
DONKEYS AND BABBAS AND NOTHING WHATEVER ABOUT
POLITICS. IF YOU WANT TO KNOW WHAT POLITICS
ARE DORDOR CAN TELL YOU. THEY ARE A KIND OF
PORRIDGE WHICH DORDOR HAS TO EAT THREE WHOLE
PLATESFUL EVERY DAY EVEN WHEN HE'D LIKE TO
·BE FISHING OR PLAYING CATCH. POLITICS IS
WHAT KEEPS DOR-DOR IN RUSSIA AND MAKES
HIM SICK

MUMMUM WILL SAY THIS IS A
NAUGHTY DORDOR TO MAKE SUCH
A PICTURE.
BUT IT IS THE TRUTH AND
DORDOR DRAWS IT WITH HIS
WHOLE HEART.

HA! DORDOR HAS NOW BOUGHT A WHOLE
BOTTLE OF  RED INK. HE SPILT
HALF IN OPENING IT BUT THERE
IS A LOT LEFT BESIDES A RED
SEA ON DORDORS PAPERS
ANY WAY THERE IS ENOUGH
TO MAKE MORE MESSES
WITH NEXT TIME.

DORDOR WISHES HE AND HIS BABBA WERE
LYING IN THE LONG GRASS SINGING THEIR

SONGS AND SMOKING

THIS IS US IN THE LONG GRASS. THE RED IS POPPIES

OR IF ONLY WE WAS FISHING

THIS IS A RUSSIAN BOY
IN SUMMER

THIS IS THE
SAME
BOY
IN
WINTER

Лебеть Факсомь = FOR TABITHA RANSOME

Лягушки на прогулкѣ

THESE ARE FROGS WALKING

THE DRAWING OF THE FROGS IS DONE
FOR A BABBA BY A BIG GIRL AS
BIG AS DORDOR WHO CARRIES A
REVOLVER AND A SWORD AND IS
A FIERCE REVOLUTIONARY [2]

DORDOR MUST NOW STOP BECAUSE
THE MESSENGER IS GOING.

MESSENGER   BOAT.   BABBA AND
                                        THE POST.

DOR DOR

1   AR's diary makes it clear that most of this letter was actually
     written on 21 May ('wrote Ivy. Babba. Mother. Gardiner.')
     but he no doubt sent it on the 28th with the letter he wrote to
     Ivy on 27 May.
2   Evgenia Petrovna Shelepina. This enclosure may not have
     pleased Ivy Ransome, who would soon be warning Tabitha
     that there might be a divorce (see *Life*, p. 199).

To A. G. Gardiner [abridged]
(Editor of the *Daily News*)
care of the British Legation,
August 11 1918   Stockholm.

Dear Gardiner,

I have had nothing from you since December, and one telegram from Hillier which told me something was on the way. It never arrived. Hillier told me that my telegrams were from seven to twenty-one days late, and arriving with whole sections missing and so often useless. I began then to make preparations for shifting, but wanted to stay on till the last possible minute.

I left Moscow one or two days before the internment order,[1] and with a Russian diplomatic passport, two bags full of rubbish (in case of accident I sent my best documents out separately) and a Lettish soldier of the Red Army, who in dealing with the Swedes on the boat most solemnly translated for me from my Russian into his American,[2] sailed from Petrograd. I betted (1) on the cholera, knowing that the Finns had closed their land frontier on account of it and therefore that it was more likely that the usual German examination at Helsingfors would not take place, and (2) on the Bolsheviks who fixed my passport and guaranteed that if I should be collared they would stop a German courier and hold him till I should be let go. I had not much faith in this project being put into action, but taking (1) into consideration thought it worthwhile to take the risk.

The journey was pretty nervous, but my guess about Helsingfors[3] came right and though we stopped in harbour there four beastly hours no Germans came aboard, and when we left I felt happy till I heard we were to stop at Mariehamn the German base in the Aland Islands. However I'd let myself get in such a stew at Helsingfors that I had no nerves left with which to be in a stew at Mariehamn. In Helsingfors while waiting I solved one chess problem and failed dismally at two, whereas at Mariehamn I solved three one after the other, a very good barometrical indication. Through the porthole I had a look at a German gunboat, I think No. 74, and an auxiliary cruiser, and lots of German sailors on the quays behaving laughably like English ones.[4] After leaving Mariehamn there was nothing more to be worried about, and though we were stopped for quarantine and medical examination at Foya we were let go at once and I came ashore in Stockholm very cheerful indeed. I don't think anyone else has got through that way, though earlier in the year several tried and were collared. I could make an amusing story out of it, but unfortunately must not write it, nor must it be written, because it is possible that for other than newspaper purposes I may have to get back in the same or some very similar way.

Parts of this letter are for you containing information and suggestions as to what is likely to happen in the new circumstances created by the state of war which already exists, and parts for Hillier, explaining what arrangements I have made for Russian, Ukrainian and occupied province news service from here. The point is, that as far as I can gather from occasional papers you have been taking a strong line against intervention.[5] With that, as you know, I entirely agreed, being convinced that support of the Soviets was our cheapest way of doing more vital damage to Germany, and having on the spot plenty of evidence to show that an understanding between the Soviet and the Allies was the thing Germany most feared. This of course apart from the question as to whether or not the downfall of the Soviets will mean the end of the Revolution and sooner or later the establishment of a government in Russia which, perhaps not at once, but in the future will be bound to work with and not against Germany. But that line of policy having been rejected, and Intervention being now an accomplished fact, it seemed to me that telegrams that could be only protests would be only a nuisance and no sort of good and that the thing to do is to see what can be done in the new conditions regardless as to whether they are not worse than those one had hoped would be created. This, of course, was an additional reason for coming out besides the obvious one that an internal correspondent or one who, uninterned, is unable to telegraph freely is no use to anyone.

You may have guessed or heard that I had got, to an extraordinary degree, the confidence of the Soviet folk who certainly allowed me to see much more of what went on than was seen by any other foreigner, and were willing to talk straight to me when they would not do anything but put official representatives of England off with fair words. My position with them has been useful not only from the point of view of information but also from that of getting things done and of preventing other things being done (for example of preventing the whole of the Allied representatives at Vologda being put in a saloon car under guard and brought to Moscow by force, which Radek whom I accompanied to Vologda had the authority and the inclination to do).[6] Lockhart in Moscow and Lindley[7] our chief of Missions at Vologda are agreed that it would be very unwise to throw this position away. It became clear that there was no longer hope of preventing intervention, and also clear that I should lose the confidence of the Soviet folk if I remained in Russia and refrained from using the Government wireless to issue loud howls about spilt milk. Lindley agreed with me that the best thing that could be done would be at least temporarily to put me into cold storage at Stockholm with a view to the possibilities in the future. If I started corresponding with the other side in Russia it would serve no purpose at all and I doubt if I could do it effectively. Lindley therefore approved of my coming out this way, and gave me letters to Sir Esmé Howard[8] and to the Swede in Petrograd with a view to getting fixed up here.

(Hillier) The Soviet people themselves had complained to me about the need of getting information out of Russia and from the German-occupied provinces to Stockholm, but lamented their shortness of hands, and left me free to do what I liked, merely giving other people leave to help me. I have arranged accordingly to get pretty regular Ukrainian information, all possible Russian information, and with less certainty Baltic province information, sent to Stockholm, where I shall naturally have first call on it myself. All Russian Government publications, newspapers, both official and other, will be coming to Stockholm for me twice weekly. Probably, like everything that depends on Russians, it will take a little time before it works smoothly, but I think that within a week or two I should be able to keep up a better Russian news service from here than any other paper has got.

Russia from the military point of view is going to become two: Russia on our side of the Murman-Archangel-Ural front, and Russia on the other side of that front. The front will shut the lion and the lamb of Germany and the revolution up together. On the position of that front depends how much of the revolution will be in a state of irritation against Germany and how much in a state of irritation against the Allies. I propose to send you a series of articles on various aspects of this business, as, severally, various aspects definitely promise themselves. There are so many cats to jump so many various ways that I don't like prophesying. One thing however is quite certain, and that is that the strongest thing that has come out of the revolution is the Soviet organisation (I have very nearly completed a translation of the Soviet Constitution, with notes explaining odd points, which I shall send to you, not for publication, as soon as it is done). Conditions in Russia are going to be so bad for so long that whatever Government may replace the Soviet under the combined pressure of the Allies and Germany, it will be under the constant threat of fresh revolt under Soviet auspices. The possibilities are so manifold that, from a general, not news point of view, some future turn of events may make it very well worth while to lump any immediate hampering in order not to sacrifice the position which the attitude of the *News* and my own telegrams have got me with the left wing of the revolution. That position is such that supposing we remain at war, and supposing the lion allows the lamb to continue existing, lest it should turn into something worse, I think that as historian, not journalist, I should be able to get back into what will be in a sense enemy country. The question of my doing so must be decided by what happens between lion and lamb.

If, as I think likely, Germany momentarily supports the Soviet, it will only be until she is free to suppress it, until she sees some other force which will take the responsibility of suppressing it for her, or if, being really severely threatened in the Ukraine, she takes the desperate course of trying to appease and stifle one country in revolt by taking on the additional task of stifling another. Anyhow, I think that it will very difficult for Germany to work smoothly with the Soviet for more than a short time. I think she may try to spin that time out, simply because the Ukraine has taught her that interferring with a revolution even when invited by 'The Real Ukraine' uses up a very great many more troops than she supposed when she brought the Rada[9] to Kiev, and threw it away in disgust and found the sticky thing (that's what revolution is) un–get–riddable–of. This experience may make her anxious if possible to let the Soviet die a natural death, or one that shall seem to be caused not by herself but by the Allies. Starvation for example may swamp the Soviet. It will not provide an alternative Government. And already the Germans are making the best use of the fact that Central Russia is cut off from Siberian food supplies, not by Germans but by the Allies (Czechs). However, no one can imagine that the Germans *like* the Soviet. The Soviet, in connection with the Ukraine, and as a centre for Austrian revolutionary organisation, is altogether too dangerous to them. I have watched at very close quarters, for example, the German bargaining after Mirbach's murder,[10] and I know that there was no collusion or anything like it. It was simply two sets of people in a horrid fright. Ritzler of the German Embassy panicking and actually himself appealing urgently for armed defence to be sent at once from Germany . . . not a sham panic . . . the man was nearly ill with fright. And, on the other side, the Soviet people for two days expecting an immediate German advance, against which they knew they could do nothing but bolt (and their old line of retreat to Ekaterinburg and the Urals, long planned, dished for them by the Czechs), madly enquiring several times a day for telegraphic reports from all the stations on the frontier. Then a reassuring wire from Joffe[11] in Berlin. Hearts lightened visibly, though Ritzler hurried round to say 'Don't you believe it, we shall demand a battalion', and it was decided that since the Germans had not advanced it meant they could not and that therefore it would be possible to refuse any such demand if it should come. Then the demand for the battalion refused point blank, and finally the compromise on 200 German prisoners as an Embassy Guard. Then later, when news came of the assassination of Eichorn in Kiev, Radek gleefully pointing out to Ritzler, 'What would have been the good of your battalion, since Eichorn could not defend himself with a number of corps, that you, Herr Doctor [*sic*], probably know better than I?'

In Moscow I lived for some time in a Commune, which had requisitioned a small palace or *osobniak*, where also lived besides the secretary of the Commissariat for War and the secretary of the Eastern Branch of the Commissariat for Foreign Affairs,

Radek. Radek, who controlled the Central Europe Department of the Commissariat for Foreign Affairs, used to conduct all relations with Germany except the actual exchange of official notes. Radek used to come bubbling in with chatter about his last encounter with Ritzler, and when I have time, I hope to do an account of Soviet-German relations of the most entertaining kind.

There is such a lot to talk about that I can't help zigzagging into digressions. The main point is, whàt will happen, now that non-recognition and intervention are forcing the lamb into the rather unwilling jaws of the lion, who is not at all sure how good the lamb is going to be for his digestion.

Germany must realise pretty thoroughly to what an extent the Ukrainian revolutionary activities are dependent on Moscow, not for motive, but for their organisation and directives. The Ukrainian Soviets, for example, continue to exist, and over seventy of them succeeded in smuggling their delegates over the frontier for the Assembly of Ukrainian Soviets which was secretly held in Moscow at the time of Mirbach's murder and the Fifth All-Russian Assembly. As fast as the Germans get machine-guns and rifles away from the Ukrainian peasantry, they are replaced by arms smuggled through by the Ukrainian Bolshevik organisations which have their headquarters in Moscow. The chief Ukrainian leader is Pyatakov, whose brother was tortured to death in the Ukraine. Pyatakov's last words to me last time I saw him were an urgent request to find some means whereby the Allies could get machine-rifles (he wanted small machine-guns that one man could carry) through for use against the Germans by the Ukrainian peasantry. I told him that it would be impossible to send them through the front, because we should have no guarantee that they would not be used at once against us, and he said they would do anything possible by way of guarantee, even to having the things in sealed cases accompanied by someone who should personally see that they reached their destination. Impracticable no doubt, but given here as an illustration of temper. Pyatakov himself makes periodical illegal journeys into the Ukraine, and comes out again . . . so far successfully, though he does not doubt that sooner or later he will share the fate of his brother. His reports from the

Ukraine will reach me here in Stockholm. The Germans must know of this and many other ways in which Moscow and the Ukraine help each other. For example no sort of secret is made of the fact that the Ukrainian railway strike, which when I left had lasted already for over a fortnight, is not only approved of but actively supported by Soviet Russia, Russian railwaymen and factories independently getting up subscriptions to help the Ukrainian strike funds, and members of the Soviet Government openly putting their names down for such sums as they can afford.

All this goes to suggest a motive which may precipitate the Germans into encouraging anti-Soviet movements and even helping them in Russia, in the hope of thereby weakening the steady gnawing resistance of the Ukraine. (This of course was one of the reasons why I held it to be to our interest to strengthen the Soviet instead of weakening it. In weakening it we were helping Germany in the Ukraine.) As things are now, it is no longer a question of saving the Soviet as a weapon against Germany. It is simply a question as to what will happen if (1) Soviet Russia is forced to seek support in Germany, and (2) if Germany as a result is sucked into the same kind of action there as the action which is costing her so dearly in the Ukraine.

If the Soviet goes down, then the whole left wing (probably swiftly followed by the right wing) of the revolutionary parties will once more be *underground*. The rottener elements will cease to enter into our calculations because only the good ones will continue to risk their lives without the hope of material profit. But it takes fewer people to disorganise a country than to run it, and I can best suggest what will happen by quoting what was said to me on that subject by one of the leading Bolsheviks: 'You carp continually at our slowness in organisation, forgetting that we are trying to organise against the resistance of all who stand to lose by our revolution, and against the opposition, armed or otherwise, of both the Imperialistic groups. And I tell you, we may, perhaps, be bad organisers, but no one will deny that we are the best disorganisers that the world has ever seen. And I tell you now, that if ever Germany drives us underground, you will see that she will not be able to run a single train unguarded, that she will find the factories breaking down, munition stores

blowing up, workmen striking, peasants revolting, telegraphs
and telephones going wrong, etc. etc. so that even if she does not
try to steal bread, she will yet be forced to repressive measures
which in their turn will create such resentment as the Ukrainian
resentment. Yes, the putting down of the Soviets in Russia will
in the long run cost whoever does it, Russian or foreigner or
both, more troops even than in the Ukraine, and it may so
happen that little as your folk deserve it, we revolutionaries may
win you the war.'

I can imagine a state of things in which the Allies might find
themselves consciously and effectively making use of the
revolutionaries to bother the Germans, just as, indirectly,
Germany made use of them to bother the Allies. The revolutionary mind itself rather resents being useful to either
Germans or Allies, but the Brest peace and the behaviour of the
Germans generally has made them bitter against Germany to an
extraordinary degree, although that bitterness is now partly
directed against us. It has been most interesting to see the
Germans gradually creating an anti-German national spirit in the
Russian working classes.

There is another possibility, which is now less likely than it
was owing to the weakening of the Soviet Government by the
loss of Siberia and food together with the loss of raw material on
which it was counting for recuperation. That possibility is that
serious revolt in the Ukraine may spread to Austria or be
inspired by Austrian revolution. (Note. The prisoners I have
examined who have escaped or been sent back from Austria vary
considerably in their views on this, but those who seemed to me
most credible do not think revolution in Austria likely before
the autumn of next year, and not then if the food supply is
improved.) Revolt of this kind would be as good as anything we
could hope, because it might save us the hardest, most difficult
stage of the war, the Eastern stage, for which Germany is steadily
preparing. In the days before it became clear that we were
determined to work with the Russian minorities other than the
Russian government, Joffe's reports from Berlin, some of which
I had the opportunity of seeing, urged with great emphasis the
need from the Soviet point of view of co-operation between
Russia and England, because Russia and England were the two

Powers most closely threatened by the German preparations in the east.

It may be objected that Germany will not have the force for any extensive eastern operations.

She will not need such force, if she can create a Mohammedan block that will seek to expand towards Afghanistan and the Indian frontiers, and towards Turkestan and the cotton fields which Germany needs. Such a Mohammedan block (Ottoman I suppose in general character) would be a powerful moral wedge for detaching from us our Mohammedan supporters in India. It would cost Germany little, and even if it failed in its more grandiose intentions would compel us to undesirable activity at a great distance from home and over lines of communication peculiarly difficult to guard. It might even be that a moment might come when Germany could with satisfaction to herself make apparently equitable peace with us, secure in the knowledge that we should be forced to continue something in the nature of war during the period when she may hope to be recuperating. (I don't think much of her chance of recuperating with Russia in the state it is at her doors . . . However that is the subject for an article.)

So far as we are concerned that is more or less the idea of Joffe's confidential communications to his government. From the Russian point of view the German plan involves German retention of the south of Russia as a way of land communication, and of the Black Sea as a German canal, together with a steady diplomatic offensive aiming at the severance of the Caucasus in small flattered national units looking to Constantinople and to Berlin for light leading and support against Soviet activities beneath them. With regard to this, I may say that I learned from the Eastern Department of the Soviet Foreign Office (with which I shall, I hope, even if there is a war, continue to be in touch) that representatives of Georgia, Azerbeijan and two other new states which for the moment I cannot remember (I have not yet got my notes, which I sent out of Russia by another route)[12] have, under German auspices, gone to Constantinople with a view to establishing intimate relations with Turkey.

The motives for Soviet hostility to these schemes are pretty obvious.

No one will have such good opportunities of watching as those I have made for myself from here, at any rate for the present. Nor do I think the paper is likely to do anything but gain. On the other hand I do not like to fix a definite length of time for my staying here, because, in the event of war continuing between the Soviet and ourselves, and of the Soviet seeming to Germany too prickly a hedgehog to be crushed, it might be my job to use the special position which I have got to go back into the country looking for knowledge rather than for news. In which case I am sure the *Daily News* would give me temporary leave for the purpose.

(Hillier) I propose to send articles on the following subjects, or shorter things, which, anyhow will reach you sooner than telegrams from Russia:

Mirbach's Assassination and the Left Social Revolutionary Revolt. (I was present at these negotiations as translator.)

The attempt to persuade the Ambassadors to come to Moscow from Vologda.

Revolutionary activities in the Ukraine.

Kiev and Moscow as the centres of revolution and counter-revolution.

The Soviet's attitude as [*sic*] the centres of revolution and counter-revolution.

The Soviet's attitude towards America (for *New York Times*).

Character of the opposition to the Soviet within the country.

The purpose of the Soviet in stirring anti-German and anti-ally feeling.

With regard to this last, nothing has been more interesting than to watch how the 'bourgeois' parties veered gradually, perceiving their chance of coming to power on, as the American politicians would put it, a pro-ally ticket. A pro-ally counter-revolution in Moscow, which would immediately need Allied help, is now certainly possible. And it might even be considered desirable by Germany, since we should then be in the position of having to suppress the revolution and that task might prove as troublesome to us in Russia as it is to Germans in the Ukraine.

I do not think you should publish anything that is in this letter. In fact I send it to you on the understanding that you will not publish anything from it that is not included in articles and telegrams which I shall send you myself expressly for publication.

Yours sincerely,

[no signature]

1 On receiving news of the Allied landing at Archangel the Bolsheviks arrested and interned, on 5 August 1918, two hundred British and French residents of Moscow, including the consular staffs of both nations.
2 AR was masquerading as a Soviet courier.
3 Modern, Helsinki.
4 He tried to photograph them through the porthole.
5 The Allied intervention was carried out with the vague idea that it might somehow do something against Germany, possibly by overthrowing the Soviet government.
6 See *Autobiography*, pp. 249-258.
7 Sir Francis Lindley, British *chargé d'affaires* in Russia.
8 The British minister in Stockholm.
9 The Ukrainian parliament. At this stage of the Revolution the Ukraine was desperately trying to assert its independence against both Germany and Russia, but German oppression soon drove it back to the Bolsheviks.
10 The German ambassador murdered by the Left Social Revolutionaries in Moscow on 6 July 1918. There is a vivid description of the affair in *Autobiography*, pp. 244-8.
11 A. A. Joffe, Soviet representative in Berlin.
12 Evgenia Petrovna, no doubt, who had not yet reached Stockholm. See *Life*, pp. 204-5.

*

Ransome's residence in Stockholm came to a humiliating end (which he did not like to hear mentioned in later years) when on 30 January 1919 he was expelled from Sweden with Litvinov, Evgenia Petrovna, and the other Bolsheviks. He went with them to Moscow, though even that at one stage seemed unlikely: there were suspicions that he was a capitalist spy. As his letters show, he had long anticipated this move; on January he had ended a letter to his mother with a spirited drawing of what was going to happen.

Moscow

The official boot

To Edith R. Ransome [abridged]
November 12 1918   Stockholm

My dear Mother,

No letter from you for ages, and no excuse for you for not writing. Please bear in your revered head the fact that already there is vastly improved service between England and Scandinavia, so that you could, if you were up to your job as a mother, write at least twice a week. Please do.

I have still some slight hope of being home for Christmas, but it's a very little one. As soon as the Swedes kick the Russians out of Stockholm, which is not impossible, the main point in my being here goes, and I shall probably shift to Viborg, or some other abominable Finnish town, where I can fix up some sort of arrangements for getting Russian newspapers etc. In which case, I think I should feel I owed it to myself to catch a pike in England before going into such a particularly loathsome exile. The other possibility is that I go back into Russia for a month to collect material, after which I should naturally convoy the said material home with a view to reporting on conditions. But things are developing so fast that it's quite impossible to say for certain what comes next.

I do most awfully want to come home. This last year has had such a lot in it, of such a brain-tearing, heart-wearing, and latterly heart-breaking kind, that I feel I have been away from home for a very long time indeed. And, as you know, a year ago when I was in town, it was such a hectic Russian period that I was really mostly in Petrograd. It seems at least five years since I was really solidly with both feet in England.

The *Daily News* sent me some tobacco, including four blocks of black plug, guaranteed to kill at ten yards. I cut up some, stuffed it in a clay pipe, and at the first puff I was back at home drinking beer with Lascelles Abercrombie in the 'Hark to Melody' by Haverthwaite. Then I was talking to the charcoal burners who used to bake clay pipes for me in the wood above Coniston. Then I was in a good old stinking Furness Railway third class railway carriage with a lot of miners going oop Millom way. It's no good; the Russian Revolution has failed utterly in altering me personally. And once I get a little peace and quiet and get my sketch of the development of the revolution written, I shall write FINIS and fetch politics a good boost with a boot in the latter parts, and return with no regrets whatever to pen, ink, tobacco, fishing and the lake country.

I think we have every chance of escaping revolution, if only some wise man comes along, like the Duke of Wellington, who has the sense and the strength of mind not to meddle with other people's revolutions however little he likes them. In 1830 every country in Europe had trouble except us. We were exempt because old Wellington had refused to intervene anywhere.[1] Germany 'restored order' in a good big bit of Russia,[2] and look at the result. There is a sort of fate in these things. You get the attribute of the thing you fight. However this is getting near the province of the Censor. So I slide off to safer things.

I went out for an hour's fishing on Sunday and caught a lot of little fish, but got so cold that I could not take my rod to pieces. Dukes, whom I knew at Petrograd,[3] was here from Archangel, taking photographs and playing chess . . . Bless my soul, my dear. Now you've got your eyes again,[4] you'll be able to play chess again. How simply ripping. My dear, I do so much want to see you again.

Well, Goodbye for now. Love to Joyce, Clum, Kitty, Sidge and Sam and of course the Weasel, Ellen, etc.

Arthur

1 The Duke of Wellington was Prime Minister in 1830, when
   the July Revolution swept away the last Bourbon king of
   France and made Belgium independent of Holland. AR gives
   Wellington too much credit.
2 After the peace of Brest-Litovsk.
3 Paul Dukes, British intelligence agent; later, author of *The Story
   of 'ST23': adventure and romance in Red Russia*. According to AR
   (*Autobiography*, pp. 262-3) he was knighted for getting some
   members of the Imperial Family out of Russia.
4 Mrs Ransome had just had an operation for cataract.

To Tabitha Ransome[1]

[December, 1918]   [Stockholm]

My dear Tabitha

            I hope this letter finds you well and
                                    good.
                                    Especially I
                                    hope you are

having   a   very   jolly   Christmas

I hope the Donkey   is   also   feeling
Christmassy. [2]

Where I am there are no nice donkeys—
only dachshunds which are more like pieces of
tape than dogs. They curl round the leg of the table

Once upon a time, except for bad drawing the
dachshund was short like an
ordinary DOG. He lived in Germany and
belonged to a giant's mother, who gave him to
her two sons

The Mother   of   Fritz
                                   . Hans

But the two giants began to quarrel at once.
Fritz said "he is my dachshund". Hans said
"he is mine". Fritz said "Anyhow I am going to
have him." Hans said nothing but gave Fritz a
black eye. Then Fritz took the dachshund by the
head . Hans took him by the tail — and
they pulled and pulled

TO THE PULLING →

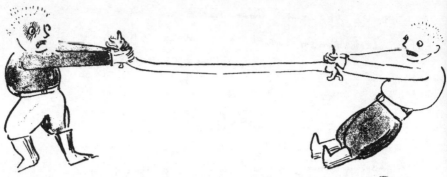

They pulled and pulled, until they were tired. Then they rested ● with the dachshund stretched between them like a telegraph wire. But when the German fraus came with their clothes from the washing, and began to hang them on the dachshund to dry, Fritz ● Hans dropped him in disgust, ● the dachshund crawled like a snake from under the mile, or so of wet clothes which had been hung on him. He has been long ever since. One of him at this minute is twisted like a bangle round my leg.

So much for dachshunds!!

Last summer I had a hedgehog, who was much nicer than dachshunds. He used to run about the room and catch ants and other insects, and he slept in a blue hutch on the balcony outside, where also

there was   a   Snake

He was a
Viper and
full of poison and wickedness.

Next year I hope I shall have
a new fairy story book to send you.
This year I have no new book at
all. But I send a cheque for you
and your mum mum to buy something
you want for yourselves.

Well you lazy young Cockyolly bird,
have you yet read Robinson Crusoe?
If not, why not? Read him at once, and
then you will have a happy New Year

This is a young
Cockyolly bird,
reading Robinson Crusoe.
Observe her contented
expression.

Goodbye for now

1   Date and address are both conjectural; but the style of this letter
     (red, green and black ink, and all the pictures) is so similar to
     the letter of 28 May 1918 that the guess seems reasonable. The
     snake referred to may be the one that AR caught in the summer
     of 1918 and gave to Evgenia.
2   The donkey was Moab, a most important person in Tabitha's
     childhood.

                         To Edith R. Ransome
December 18 1918   Stockholm

My dearly beloved Mother,
    Yesterday I got three letters from you, including one written
with your spectacles on, which was a model of copperplate
calligraphy, and a source of huge pride to me, who showed it to
Captain Grenfell,[1] who is passing through Stockholm to show
him how you had come on. You remember his coming to the
Rembrandt[2] last year, and you being so blind you could not tell
him from his bearded brother. The three letters had been at the
Legation some days, but I had happened not to call there.
    Your letters are the greatest delight to me, especially when
you harangue me about politics, and tell me the truth that I am
not fitted to have anything to do with them.[3] I agree most
heartily. I am no good at them and I hate them, and as you know
it's only accident that I've had to take an interest in them. But
there was no question about the compulsion. I should have been
the worst kind of rotter if, having been sent to Russia to supply
accurate information, I had given false information because it
would have been more welcome. I've been through all my *Daily
News* dispatches, and, modest though I am by nature!!!, I must
say I was astonished at their accuracy, seeing that they were
always written in great haste, and in circumstances which made
it very difficult to get at the truth. Everything I have said about
the actual nature of your loathed Bolsheviks, has been confirmed
over and over again since. So I cannot find it in me to regret
having told what I knew was as near the truth as I could get. As
for me myself mixing in politics, I hope I never never will. (Beg
your pardon . . . Macaulay would have written 'shall').[4] Quite
apart from the fact that it's impossible, I rather gather from what

friends from England tell me, that I have earned an unpopularity as colossal as it is underserved. Malevolent devils seem to be inventing all kinds of lies about me. That, however, can't be helped, and lies however flourishing for a time in the long run defeat their own ends. I should be more worried about them if I were a politician, and not a mere writer who wants nothing more than to be quit of war and politics alike, and free to write fairy stories.

I got a long letter from Barbara adding her 3 stone of weight to your philippics, and asking me 'how I think I'm going to face my creator with all my notebooks stuffed full of unused Russian folk lore? Do you think He won't see your pockets bulge?' She objects most violently to my leaving fairy stories and being busied in 'attending the births and death-beds of revolutions'. She doesn't object more violently than I do. But I can't help it. So long as the turmoil continues, so long is it essential that anybody who has a chance of getting at any truth out of it [sic] must use that chance, remembering always that now, just as a hundred years ago, for every man who tries to go below the surface there will be hundreds who do not, and by loud shouting about individual trees deafen people into forgetting the wood.

As for the *Daily News* I sympathise with your tears. At least I should if I read it regularly. But, as a matter of fact I don't think I have seen two dozen copies since I left England more than a year ago. I got one yesterday, and was amazed to see it has turned into a fair sized paper again, eight sides instead of four, and pictures once more. That means I shall have to produce some more little solemn articles to go in its middle. I've got several in my head, Swedish ones. I don't trust myself to write about Russia, because such appalling lies are being told that I find myself almost forced to be extreme in the other direction, and that is as bad.

My work here looks like ending up about New Year, and then, as far as I know, I shall be coming home, although I have made another suggestion that, if accepted, would postpone my coming for another six weeks.[5] Then, I do not know quite what will happen. The *Daily News* is quite evidently hankering to send me to Berlin. But I am not having any, thank you. I've had the unpopularity of telling the truth about one damned revo-

lution, and nothing will induce me to touch another at the end
of a barge-pole. Let them send some one there blind and deaf
and without imagination, who will find out the popular thing to
say and say it in the ordinary time-honoured fashion. I'd like to
go to Berlin to look at things, and I have no doubt that with my
Russian experience behind me I should be able to form a fairly
accurate estimate of what is going on. But I would not like to go
if I have to publish my results. I mean I'd like to go as an official
observer but not as a miserable journalist.

Ivy writes that Dan[6] and his *mésalliance* came to stay, and were
very nice, the girl not all that an ambitious mother would wish
but gentle and decent, and Dan apparently much in love, though
fretful. She says he isn't on speaking terms with either his people
or with you. I beg to enter a protest if that is so. Hang it all, Dan
is married. You can't undo that, and what you can do is to
prevent a very risky affair from additional embitterment. Of
course Ivy's report as to Dan's international relations may be like
most reports from that quarter. If however it's true, I do beg you
for my sake[7] to take the sensible human line of accepting Dan's
wife, for his sake if not for her own. The next step should be for
Dan's parents to discover that Dan is still Dan and very much
worth having even if his wife were blue with green spots. In fact
I should think, if you put it to them, the parents would be rather
glad to have you keep in touch with him, until they have the
sense to do so themselves. I'm very sorry for them over the
whole thing, but I shall stop being sorry if they make Dan's job
harder than it anyhow will be. Dan, as they know and you
know, is one of the very decentest straightest humourous witty
affectionate creatures that was ever invented.[8]

Hi! I do wish you would make Denny's Bookshop in the
Strand send me AT ONCE Hazlitt's *Winterslow* and *Spirit of the Age*,
any cheap edition. But not a day's unnecessary delay. I've been
panting for those books for four months.

Also, will you please send me a book of English penny and
halfpenny stamps. PLEASE.

I am awfully interested to hear about the new house in Kent.
Do please, in choosing a house, remember for the sake of Kitty
and me that it should be in a place where there is fishing. No
house is worth looking at without. There are lots of good places

in Kent. If you get on the coast, so much the better. I will bring my yacht round from Southampton.[9] What about Maidstone? Anywhere along there. N.B. there is a lovely harbour at Ramsgate. My boat must have some sort of harbour to lie in, she being too big and deep-keeled to be beached. On fine days you shall lie on the deck in the sunshine, and on rough days I'll make Joyce and Kitty seasick. All the same I'm more sorry than I can say that you are leaving dirty old Leeds.

Goodbye for now, my dear. If I do get to England as soon as I hope, I'll spend the night at Leeds on the way down, and go on first thing in the morning. Then perhaps I'll get back for a few days. But I'm sorry you won't be in London, because I shall be working there for at least a fortnight.

Your affectionate son,

Arthur

Dec. 20 1918   Stockholm

Postscript. Violent haste.

This is to regret most woefully that I shall not be in England for Christmas, and to tell you that I shall think about you all on Christmas Day, and further to send you the dullest of all Christmas presents. I can't send parcels, so I send a cheque[10] to be divided thus: Mother, Joyce, Cecily, Kitty, Sidge, one quid apiece (to be spent at once not hoarded . . . this is addressed to the ear of Sidge) and ten bob each for the Weasel and Ellen with my love.

Your affectionate son,

Arthur

1 Harold Grenfell, formerly Naval Attaché in Petrograd.
2 Apparently a residential hotel in Leeds where Mrs Ransome spent the later years of the war.
3 As the widow of an ardent Conservative activist, AR's father, Mrs Ransome no doubt felt well able to judge.
4 Ransome had been reading Macaulay's collected *Encyclopaedia Britannica* articles.
5 The impending expulsion of the Bolshevik representatives from Stockholm had given AR the idea of returning with them (and with Evgenia) and making a book, or a set of articles, out of the experience; a scheme duly realised as *Six Weeks in Russia in 1919*.

6 Daniel Macmillan (1886-1965); his wife, Margaret ('Betty')
Matthews, who died in 1957. Her crime, in the eyes of her
mother-in-law, was that she was 'Welsh and unsuitable'.
(Alistair Horne, *Macmillan*, vol. i, p. 80.)

7 AR is pleading his own case as well as Macmillan's, though his
mother could not know it.

8 Daniel Macmillan had been of enormous comfort to AR
during the Douglas case; see *Autobiography*, p. 154.

9 Presumably the same mysterious boat mentioned in the letter
to Mrs Ransome of 26 February, 1917.

10 This detail perhaps tends to confirm the dating of the preceding
letter to Tabitha, in which AR sends a cheque to her and Ivy.
The current letter is wrongly dated in *Life*, p. 229.

                        To Edith R. Ransome
                                                    82, High Street,
June 13 1919   Hampstead.

My dearest Maw,

Thank you for your letter which arrived today. I got back late
last night, after a very jolly time in the north, which however did
nothing except clear my head. I have not written a word.

The *Manchester Guardian* of yesterday had a two-column
article on my book, in evident effort to outdo the *Daily News*,
and today I have a letter from Scott,[1] repeating his offer that I
shall become their correspondent in Russia. I am writing to him
to say I will come over and see him from Leeds. I think I must
go to Leeds for another go of frenzied work at 'The Pathology
of Revolution' or 'The Muddle in the East End of Europe', title
as yet not fixed, which is my next effort. At the same time I may
have to scoot off to Russia again. 'At the same time' is the wrong
phrase, because it's precisely that fact of possible scooting that
makes it urgent that I should get this second book done,[2] so that
I can leave it behind me to ensure that my name will stink again
in the nostrils of all decent people in the autumn. The first book
as you know has already sold more than four times as many as
my wildest hopes, something well over eight thousand copies.

Mr. Collingwood was sweet.[3] He knew I knew of his violent

anti-bolshevism, and I think he thought I was rather avoiding discussion. Well, one day he just walked round the table after dinner and collared my right hand secretly with his left one, and said it was very nice to see me again or something like that . . . the words didn't matter. But the whole incident nearly made me weep. Also something has happened which has made him see that I was a great deal nearer the truth about our policy than he supposed. A quite independent source has informed him of our annexation plans for Turkestan, which of course corroborates all I have been saying. Mrs. was as sweet as ever. Ditto Dora, Barbara and Ursula and Ernest Altounyan. The wind was awful and I caught nothing till the last day, when, seeing that the drought made trout hopeless, and as pike were having none, I fished otherwise and caught a dozen good perch and two eels which made a breakfast. But at Kentmere, my hat, 36 trout in four days.

In two hours' time I join Hirst[4] to go down to the Mill. Grenfell is back from Helsingfors and is coming. When I come back after a few days in town next week, I return to Coniston, where I shall wait till you go to Leeds, or I shall go straight to Leeds.

With much love, your loving son,
Arthur

1 C. P. Scott, the legendary editor of the *Guardian*. For his recruiting of AR, see *Autobiography*, pp. 270-1, and *Life*, p. 244.
2 He never got it done.
3 Ransome had revisited Lanehead.
4 Francis Wrigley Hirst (1873-1953), editor of the *Economist* 1907-1916, and as dedicated an angler as AR himself.

To Edith R. Ransome
c/o British Consulate,
Reval.[1]
[Estonia]

Dec. 2 1919

My dearest old Mother,

I am now quite recovered from my illness, and am fat in face, cheerful (moderately), and very much better in every way with a peace of mind that I have not had since I came to England in

March. I know I have done what I had to do. So there can be no argument about it. What the future will bring, God knows, but that one step at least was right.

The weather has turned autumn again, and the snow has left the streets, or rather leaves them every day, coming again at intervals. It's going to be a long beastly winter, and I wish I were in England, or should wish it if I were not so interested by what is happening here.

Tomorrow night I go down to Dorpat for the peace conference there which will certainly be highly amusing, though probably unproductive of peace. I think that both sides are expecting too much from each other, and that they will find mutual concessions next door to impossible.

I was over in Finland for two days, but saw nobody except Holsti, the Foreign Minister, who is an old friend of Petrograd days. He was very jolly and his wife too, and laughed at the infernal White Russian stories about my being a Bolshevik. Those idiots are so bitter that they will go on yelling that to the end of the chapter. Holsti knows better. He used to visit me regularly in Petrograd during the revolution, and knows jolly well exactly what my attitude is. Also he knows that all the things I then used to prophesy have actually come to pass. Of course beside Holsti I saw Miss Hopper, an old friend who used to be in Moscow with the Lockhart Mission, and Miss Lunn whose brother is still outside Moscow, and is an old fishing friend of mine. I had quite a nice time, except that when I was dining with two other correspondents we were joined by Princess Bariatinskaya[2] who made an entirely unprovoked and hysterical attack on me, obviously mixing me up in her mind with Goode.[3] That gave a nasty taste to one evening, but the rest was all pleasant excepting five minutes of the first crossing, in which I was sick. Most unusual for me, but quickly over. It was very rough indeed. The trip back was also pretty rough, but had no ill effects.

Here in Reval I work pretty hard with nothing whatever to show for it. I put in a bit every day on my book, and am beginning to translate a rattling good history of nineteenth century Russia. I left all my fairy story material in England, or I would be tinkering at that too.

By way of recreation I play skittles very regularly. This is very like the old English skittles, played in a wooden paved alley, such as you find attached to some old inns in the south of England. The balls are very heavy, and I get as stiff as an ambassador after an hour and a half of it. I can beat all the other correspondents, but that means nothing, because we are all pretty bad.

My other amusement is prancing round the town with Evgenia looking at the historical remains, of which the whole place is built. For sheer compressed history this place beats any place I know, except London, and even London has not got such a collection of different civilisations imposed upon it as this place has, beginning after the Esthonian[4] fortress rock dismantled in 1290, then the Danish, then the Hanseatic German of the Middle Ages, then the Swedish, then the Russian, and finally the German of the last fifty years. There is least of all Russian. It's a regular little mediaeval town built round and on a fortress rock. Incredibly picturesque and interesting. I am going to write something very jolly about it, if I do not have to shift elsewhere before I've got it fairly in my head.

Evgenia is learning English as hard as she can from a translation of Hans Andersen. I want her to learn English from something better as English than any translation can be, and I want her to learn English history at the same time and get a good sound idea of what we stand for in the world as opposed to the choice picture of us and our doings now current in Russia. I want her to begin by reading a *First History of England* by my respected Mother[5] (incidentally I'd like to read it again myself) and would take it very kindly if you would write 'Evgenia. Christmas 1919' in a copy and send it here by the very next post. She'll be through Hans Andersen by the time it arrives (I was only able to get a very small selection of him). I think you owe her at least that for lugging me through my deliriums and other wretchednesses after I came out. I am now very well, and getting visibly fatter . . . far far better than I was during any of those appalling months of worry in England.

I am not sure if parcels are allowed. But I think such a little book as yours sent bookpost would be allowed anyhow. Newspapers get here all right. I am getting hard up for tobacco, but there is no way of sending that out, so I must stick it on what I can get.

Evgenia stands in need of outdoor shoes, but I doubt if they are made big enough in England.[6] Perhaps in Edinburgh. That too, like tobacco, must be managed without, until we come home, or until I send her on to Mrs. Hamilton,[7] who has promised to look after her and do necessary shopping.

Please write. And remember that it is best to register your letters. I have had several unregistered from the *Guardian*, but, so far, nothing from you since I left England over two months ago. There is a censorship of course, because this country is at war.

If you want to send me a Christmas present, do a little copy of any lake country picture of yours on a postcard and put it in an envelope between cards. I would most awfully like a permanent window into the lake country that I could carry about with me.

I shall not be permanently at Dorpat, but shall be there and back about once a week while the conference lasts, Then I intend to go down to Riga and have a look at the Lettish republic, get material for an article or two, and back again.

But, of course, out here it is impossible to prophesy what one will be doing in a month's time. Scott wants me to settle at Helsingfors for the winter. I am not at all keen on it, because the place is chock-a-block with the extremest of the reactionary Russians who love me just about as much as I love Gregory Powder, and will certainly make things as uncomfortable as they can. Reval is altogether more friendly, and if only I can satisfy Scott with a good supply of telegrams from here I shall be well content to stay at any rate until the Spring.

Do let me know if my little fairy story is out, which Jones and Evans were doing for me.[8] Their address is 77, Queen Street, Cheapside, London, E.C. I told them to send you a copy as soon as it was out. Also, let me know if you hear any news of *Aladdin*. *Aladdin* was to be published early in December.[9]

Now I must stop. I send my love to everybody.

Oh yes. Do send me a photograph or two of the new house.[10]

I wish I could be running down there for the week end, to bicycle over to Wateringbury and Teston Halt, to catch a good fat pike or two. The season is just right now, and I survey my fishing reel, which I have with me, with considerable sorrow at heart. I shan't have a chance of fishing till May, unless I come home before then, which is not very likely, although my contract with the *Guardian* ends on April 1. If it is not extended I shall come home gladly and spend the whole summer writing and fishing, going off on a new expedition in the winter. It's the only satisfactory way of earning money, and I must keep on with it at intervals, writing books in between whiles. The book I am messing at now will please you in parts. It will annoy most people, and will enrage the extreme Left, so you will be quite happy.

Well, my dear, Goodnight, and please remember that I am still the same old rapscallion I always was, and, as ever, your loving son,

Arthur

Dec. 12.

I am down at Dorpat watching the conference which at present looks like ending in cannon smoke.[11]

1   Now Tallinn, capital of Estonia. Ransome always used the Russian name.
2   Unidentified; presumably a Russian *émigrée*.
3   AR's predecessor as *Guardian* Russian correspondent. After interviewing Lenin he had disappeared in odd circumstances, and was kidnapped by a British destroyer at Reval. See *Life* p. 244.
4   *Sic.*
5   Edith R. Ransome, *A First History of England* (London: Rivington, 1903). Reissued in 1905 as *A Primary History of England*.
6   For Evgenia's feet, see *Life*, p. 156.
7   Mary Agnes ('Molly') Hamilton (1882-1966), F. W. Hirst's assistant on the *Economist* and *Common Sense*, later, in the 1929 Parliament, an M.P. and Parliamentary Private Secretary to Clement Attlee. Occasionally a novelist, she was one of AR's most valued friends. 'To have the friendship of Molly Hamilton was like having an army at one's back.' (*Autobiography*, p. 223).
8   *The Soldier and Death*, published in 1920 by J. G. Wilson.
9   It was.
10 At Malling, Kent.
11 It ended in peace between Estonia and Soviet Russia.

To Edith R. Ransome
[abridged]

Dec. 17 1919

Reval [Dorpat]
[Estonia]

My dearest old Maw,

I am working very steadily, taking exercise regularly, and getting stronger and fitter every day. And the part of my inside that matters is happier than it has been for the last ten years or more, and is quite confident that you will some day be very happy about it too. I am unhappy only about Ivy, although actually things are no worse for her than they have been, and two unhappinesses do not make one happiness but rather make each other worse. Anyway as things turned out there would be no possible choice, as Ursula [Collingwood] would explain.

There has been a lot of snow, and for days the trees have been furred all over, every tiny twig, with fine snow crystals. I walk in the gardens of the old Domberg, on the hill looking out over the low country (I think I described it to you six years ago when I was here) and really it is better than anything in an artificial fairyland. This is the real thing, with those sparkling snow-crusted trees, and the nuthatches and creepers running up and down wherever a strip of bare trunk shows, pecking out their food with their long beaks. Then sometimes I walk in the gardens by the frozen river covered with children skating, or over the old stone bridge built by Catherine II and back over the wooden bridge, and through the open air markets, where by the light of kerosene lamps, in little wooden stalls in the snow, the countryfolk sell apples and bread, and the town folks sell at enormous prices cigarettes marked 'For H.M. ships only', and bartered by the English sailors.

All that is jolly. And then, besides that I'm immensely interested in this democratic little republic, socialistic only in its land law, and therefore, as it seems to me, possibly a sample in miniature of the sort of thing which Russia itself will develop, if only we have the sense to stop trying at great expense to turn her into a reactionary, and consequently into an ally for a reactionary Germany. Here one sees, as it were, a later stage of the revolution, and it is most extraordinarily interesting. One friend of

mine here, a member of the Constituent Assembly, and of the
Esthonian peace delegation, used to sit side by side with me in
the press box of the old Duma in Petrograd before the revolution. The Commander-in-Chief of the Navy is an old shipping
master. And so on, and all as keen as mustard. I am very glad to
be here . . .

Once more I send you my love,
                Your affectionate son,
                                              Arthur

                    To Edith R. Ransome
April 19 1920   Reval.

My dearest old Mother,
    I am writing in the coupé of a saloon car which is conveying
a couple of Russian couriers to Reval, also two female typists,
and myself. And not a single one of the four can play chess. We
are waiting for the moment just inside Russia, and in a minute
or two shall be passed over the frontier into Esthonia. This
wagon is going the whole way to Reval and I have come in it
from Moscow, so you see there are faint traces of civilisation
beginning to show themselves even here. The bridge at Jamburg
which Judenitch[1] destroyed in order to save himself and the rest
of his crowd is a fine sight. The river is in flood, foaming and
roaring with white foam churning up out of a ruddy brown
torrent which moves at such a rate that as it breaks over the mass
of twisted girders and iron bars lying in the stream between the
broken piers, you can see great lengths of iron bending and
waving like grass in a strong wind. The Russians have already
built up a wooden bridge, over which we crossed at the rate of
about a yard a minute, getting a glorious view of the river and
the wreckage below.
    In Petrograd yesterday between arrival and departure I rushed
round to see what had become of my old rooms. The infernal
idiots had made a search there. They found my collection of
newspapers, every copy of every paper issued in Petrograd from
Feb. 1917 to Feb. 1918, an absolutely priceless and irreplaceable
collection which I had intended for the British Museum. THEY

BURNT THE LOT amid the protests of my old landlady, who, however, succeeded in saving my favourite fishing rod, a few pictures and my Turkish coffee mill. Boots, felt winter boots, the files of my old telegrams,[2] cameras, practically everything of value stolen. I was very angry for a moment when I heard it, and saw my bare and ruined room, and then I grinned a deep and solid grin. It is after all only just that I as a bourgeois should suffer like the rest, and now at least I have the necessary feeling for the chapter on that subject in my history. I had such contempt for the Russian bourgeois that I had difficulty in thinking of him without impatience, and found it hard to take him seriously when he complained of losing his piano and what not. I despise him as much as before, but in describing his mental state after the revolution I have now the best of subjective material. Devil take it. I forgive them for stealing my boots, which were no doubt wanted for the army, but to burn that collection of papers, to destroy such material for the chronicling of their own revolution, and to BURN it (if they had collared it for their own archives I should not have cared a damn) . . . but to burn it . . . Forty thousand million dancing devils with pink tails and purple stomach aches.

I have done a lot of work in Moscow, and collected material for a small book on the economic crisis and the means being taken for dealing with it, which should be pretty useful for everybody if I can get it written in time.[3] I shall probably go into the country with my good Evgenia, and write like blazes for the next six weeks, not bothering about telegrams.

I am very happy, in a solid farmerly rather than intellectual manner, feeling myself very much alive, full of plans and beans, expecting my first day's fishing in the near future. And I have so much material and of such a new kind (almost entirely economic and requiring hours and hours of detailed work) that I think I can go with a good conscience into the country and work and not go back to Russia for a long time. Best of all I'd like to come to England. I want Evgenia to get her English into really good form, and I want badly to fish in Hirst's new bit of river. Walking to the old bit of river last year we used to see the fish rising in it in the most regular manner whether they were rising in our water or no. My fingers fairly itch to feel a rod in my hand

and to chuck a Wickham's Fancy on one particular pool. But if I do come to England, I should like to stay a good long time and write my big book. Well, it's no good writing about it. You know I want to come. Evgenia is bursting to come. I've told her so much about England, and so on, that she is simply mad to see what a really decently organised country is like. And it would be a very good bit of her education. I think it very unlikely that I should come without her, because I must have her as secretary to wade through masses of Russian material which, if I had to do all the wading myself, would mean I could not finish my book in twenty years. I think that with Evgenia to do the dirty work, I could get the first volume done in two years. Then I should have to earn some money, so that there will probably be a year's interval between finishing the first volume, and starting work on the second. Five years should see the whole thing finished, as far as I can take it with the intimate knowledge of persons and events which is necessary, that is up to the Armistice and the breaking out of revolution in Germany.

You see I am already planning to be alive later than 1924,[4] by when I had always supposed that I should finally crock up. But I am now so solidly happy, and so confoundedly interested in things, that I really do want to last a little longer.

And you see the worst of it is that there are always little jobs turning up that want doing at once. This book I'm at now, a little book, about the same size as *Six Weeks*, on the Economic Crisis of Russia, simply must be done at once. It explains the position of the Co-operatives, tells the bitter truth about Russian transport, and the means being taken to improve matters, contains a complete list of the concessions offered, showing exactly where Russia can and cannot get on without foreign help, and works out certain inevitable changes in the industrial geography of Russia. In fact it will, I hope, be the sort of little book which the British Government ought to have issued itself, if it had been really studying the question instead of trying to blot it out. Now that at last, two years late, people have come round to my way of thinking on the main point of war and peace in Russian policy, the information which in spite of folk, I have been able to keep on getting, knowing that eventually we should behave sensibly, ought to be awfully useful. But I am afraid it will also be awfully dull except to people interested in such things. It will be much harder to humanise than anything I've done, and yet, as it is private enterprise and not official, I must make it human, or else people will not read it. So it should be a comic work, partly a series of hard facts about the economic smash and partly such articles as have already been in the *Guardian*, and some small things yet unpublished . . . one very nice one about a Moscow cabby who cabbed in the winter and spent the summer poaching in the country, total effect a sort of mixture of Gregory Powder and small beer. My publisher will tear his hair.

Then besides that I've begun the translation of the *History of the Nineteenth Century in Russia*,[5] which unfortunately requires so much knowledge of Russian history in general that I shall have to write so many notes and of such a character that they almost mean a book in themselves.

April 21.

I was optimistic when I said that in a moment or two I should be in Esthonia. The Esthonians for reasons best known to their own wooden heads refused to let us cross. They kept me waiting 36 hours and more without a chance of getting any food, on the edge of their blessed country. Permission to let me in from Reval has still not arrived, but I finally lost my temper on purpose in the best possible manner, and roared at the Esthonian frontier officer so effectively that he let me through to Narva where I did the same with the Commendant [*sic*] of the town, and am now actually on my way to Reval, though extremely illegally. Tomorrow I shall find out at the local Foreign Office if they did it on purpose. If it was an accident then well and good. If not then I will write an account of the whole performance which will make them pretty sore. Ever since Piip left and Wirgo, the Foreign Office here has gone to pieces.[6] Piip and Wirgo were decent people and behaved decently, and I can count on them to wring the necks of their idiotic successors.

I had an amusing time last night, hunting round Narva in the dark to find a doctor to certify that I was free from LICE. Then to get supper, which I got in a horrid little restaurant where the waitresses were painted like Dutch dolls, and Russian officers of the White Army with nothing to do lolled about looking beastly. Bolsheviks or not Bolsheviks, I prefer the hardworking whitefaced hungry Puritans of the other side. (This does not apply to the real Esthonian army, which is a very decent institution for which I have nothing but liking and respect. But the White Russian officer with a very few exceptions is about the most worthless hound that was ever allowed to grow up with an unclipped tail.) Of course the Red Officers are not all Puritans by any manner of means, but public opinion among them is against debauch generally and with the Whites it is openly the other way. And public opinion is the only thing to judge by in judging a mass.

It is a jolly sunny day, but very cold. We are passing through endless pine forest, and the little pools of water along the edge of the forest and in there under the trees are all frozen and the bare thin stems of the white birches scattered among the pines look as if they could not keep warm even in the sun.

I wish I were coming straight back to England. But perhaps I am. I shall telegraph to find out as soon as I get to Reval. Well. Please give my love to Sam, and tell him I'll take him for a walk if he promises not to run sheep. The same though perhaps of a superior quality to you, Joyce, Cecily, Kitty and Sidge. If you cross the Medway in Kitty's little car, whisper my love to the pike as you go over the bridge. I caught a walloper in a dream only last night.

Your affectionate son,

Arthur

1 The commander of the unsuccessful White offensive against Petrograd in 1919.
2 A puzzling statement, since a thick file of these telegrams is preserved in the Ransome papers at Leeds.
3 *The Crisis in Russia*, London: George Allen & Unwin, 1921; republished, with *Six Weeks in Russia in 1919*, by Redwords, 1992.
4 When he would be forty.
5 Unidentifiable.
6 For A. Piip, Estonian Foreign Minister in 1919, see *Autobiography* pp. 275–86, *passim*. According to Ransome, he was the only person who ever said Thank You 'for any of my amateur meddling in public affairs'.

To Edith R. Ransome

January 19 1921   Reval.

My dear Mother,

Very many thanks for the sailing book which arrived yesterday and has been delighting me ever since and making me forget the abominable cold which has been more or less prostrating me for the last week.

The Baedeker arrived earlier, but I did not write because I was waiting day by day for the other books which I made sure you had sent off at the same time as I asked. If you have not sent them already, please DO send them off the very morning you get this. Although they will probably arrive too late, still it is worth trying. I have wanted the big two-volume history[1] for something I am writing, urgently for the last fortnight. Now I absolutely need them. I may be leaving Reval any day, and particularly want to take them with me. If I start I will telegraph. If you get a telegram to say I have started BEFORE you get this letter, then of course do not send the books. If however this letter arrives first, or even simultaneously with the telegram, then do PLEASE do what I asked weeks ago, and post them at once. Even if they arrive after I have started, I shall probably be more or less accessible for another week or ten days and it will be possible for the books to catch me up. After that it will be hopeless, for I shall be miles from anywhere, and adding new miles every day. I have put in an application[2] for leave to make a gigantic journey, which will take about two months if all goes smoothly.[3] Allowing three weeks for unforeseen delays, I hope to be back in Reval in the very early Spring, to have a jolly summer and do my Esthonian book. Of course I may not get leave, in which case we shall probably have to come to England, as the *Manchester Guardian* job ends almost at once. This trip should give me articles and a book, which should provide enough money to pay for the summer here while I do the Esthonian book.[4] The Esthonian book is sheer luxury, because I cannot hope to make a penny out of it. People won't read a serious book on Esthonia. The only hope of making them read it is to make it a jolly sort of travel book, with lots of camping and fishing and sailing shoved in, together with the essential historical material.

Thus I hope to do jolly chapters about the big islands of Oezel and Dago, and have a good chapter about the sailing trip I am making with Col. Meikljohn after gulls' eggs on some of the little uninhabited islands. Then a regular little voyage of discovery to the island of Runo, in the middle of Riga gulf, a little island inhabited for hundreds of years by Swedes, still talking Swedish, and wearing Swedish national dress on holidays. For this sort of thing I must be here for the good weather, and the Russian trip must provide the money to pay for the fun of doing the Esthonian book.

But the end of the M.G. job means that I shall have to find a cottage in England just as soon as possible, so as not to lose any time in settling down to work there on the big *History*. I shall still write for the *Guardian*, of course, but shall not have a regular salary, and I therefore cannot afford to waste any more time. I MUST settle down to finish the big book, before taking another spell of correspondence. So do PLEASE keep an eye out for a cottage, on the coast or on the Thames estuary, or east Kent, or best of all the Broads. But it does not so frightfully matter where, so long as it is near water.

I have got a publisher for the Esthonian book; at least I think so, but as I have already remarked, I shall make no money out of it, lucky if it pays for the boat.[5]

I am sending you by a safer way a cheque for the Burberry coat (which I ought to be wearing on my new trip), and for the Legg and Millard suit, with a bit over to pay for the postage of books etc., buying books and so on.

Could you buy *The 'Falcon' on the Baltic* by E. F. Knight, 3/6, and send it. You can get it from G. Wilson, 23 Sherwood St., Piccadilly Circus, W.[6]

With much love,
  your affectionate and now thoroughly middle-aged son.[7]
  Arthur

1 Unidentified.
2 To the Bolshevik government.
3 This was Ransome's tour of the famine areas, which resulted in some powerful articles in the *Guardian*.
4 He seems to have been planning a book on the famine in the style of *Six Weeks* and *The Crisis*, but it was never written.

Need it be pointed out that 'the Esthonian book' is what was
to become *Racundra's First Cruise*, although *Racundra* herself had
not yet been conceived?
5   Presumably *Kittiwake* (see *Autobiography*, pp. 301–2).
6   Eventually included in the Mariner's Library, with an introduction by Arthur Ransome.
7   The day before had been his thirty-eighth birthday.

                        To Francis Lupton[1]
Aug. 4 1921   Reval.

My dear Nephew,[2]
    In the first place I must congratulate you on your choice of
parents, grandparents and other relations. You are born into a
family remarkable less for beauty (though your mother is not bad
looking, as, if you have the rudiments of taste, you have already
discovered) than for the sterling virtues. There will be no
flightiness in your upbringing. You will get your meals at proper
times, and that, but you know it already, is one of the prime
essentials of a man's life. Further, you will not be fussed over.
You will be given a chance to show by growing up a sensible
decent person that your fortunate choice of parents was no mere
accident, but a proof of the superior qualities with which I feel
sure you are endowed.
    And then it is not as if you had shown wisdom in the matter
of parents only. You have had the good sense to be born in the
most lovable, energetic, pleasant dirty town in the county which,
as your mother will some day inform you, is the best county in
England, and therefore in the world. You will grow up hardened
from birth to the smell of smoke. Smuts falling on your veil will
bless you from the first as with black kisses. When you climb your
first tree your hands will teach you universal tolerance. And,
when you go into the country, you will enjoy it with a zest quite
foreign to persons born in any other place but Leeds.
    If I know anything of your mother, she will take you at the
earliest possible moment to the Lake Country, so that from early
youth you may know the outline of the Old Man, and the smell
of rain on bracken. By Jove, Sir, what a life you have before you.

Your father specially skilled in all the things you will surely most admire,[3] to build your first engines with you, to balance you upon the swaying bicycle, to explain everything that is to be explained in all the newest complications of human ingenuity, your mother to stuff you full of history and prevent you from thinking that the world began and will end with yourself (*Michael Boo and his Brother* and I hope a succession of others will make a perfect playfield of the past for you while your father's solider inventions will let you into all sorts of adventure places in the future). You seem to me to be in for no end of a good time generally. At Ilkley, close at hand, you have a great-uncle who will teach you as few in England can how to fish for trout with a fly, and I, if your parents will allow me, shall be awfully glad to go fishing for perch with you with red-topped green-breeched floats, and perhaps, when you are a little older, show you how to be the third of your blood to catch a pike in Allan Tarn.

Well, Sir, I will not detain you further. I see your face is growing rather red and crinkly with impatience. No. No. Hi. Put it off half a minute. Help. Nurse Ho. No. Steady on. She's coming. There's a beauty. On your stomach. So. A pat on the back. Another. Ah. Better now. O. Crinkles again. And a quadrilateral mouth. Joyoyoyoyoce. Quick. Take him. There now. I've handed you over and remain your affectionate uncle.

A.

1   Sent with a letter to Joyce and Hugh Lupton. They had married in 1920.
2   The envelope is addressed to 'Master (x) Lupton (minimus)'. AR did not yet know his nephew's name.
3   Hugh Lupton was an engineer by profession.

To Edith R. Ransome
23 Stralsunder Strasse,
Kaiserwald,
Riga. [Latvia]

April 11 1922

My dear Mother,
    I enclose with this a photograph of me, looking as cross and worried as possible, in the agony of watching somebody else

manipulating my camera with imperfect knowledge under my directions. Also Tom and Evgenia.

Will you please order to be sent out here by LETTER POST any small good handbook on photography. I am still working with the rather loose knowledge acquired with a TitBit camera at Rugby, and want to learn a little more about it. About long distance photography, for example, about enlarging, making lantern slides, etc. I think Bumpus[1] is sure to know of a good practical handbook.

Yesterday a big steamer arrived in the port. The river is clear of ice to the mouth. Our lake is of course still frozen. On Sunday, I had a fine sail on a big ice yacht. The snow on the lake had melted and frozen again, so that there was a fine surface of smooth ice, with only the most occasional hummocks, which sent us flying into the air, as we shot over them at terrific speed. There was a very uneven wind, with hard squalls, and with even a moderate wind an ice yacht on smooth ice goes over forty, and often over sixty miles an hour. It felt most odd, to cover in a few minutes distances that I used to regard as a good hour's sailing last autumn. It's very exciting, but I should not care to have an ice yacht. You go so fast that you use up your available space. Our lake is about five miles long, and careering up and down it at that pace is like running backwards and forwards at full speed in a drawing-room. It soon palls. Yesterday, however, there was a tug breaking up the ice in the broad arm of the river across which our new boat is lying in a shed.[2] It was a most wonderful sight, icebergs floating down, the tug charging into the ice, cutting off fresh hunks, big grey hooded crows perched on icebergs, shifting into the air and settling again as their ice rafts turned over in the swirl of waters, and fishermen and their wives throwing out nets in the open spaces between the icebergs, waiting for a clear moment and then hauling them out again into their little boats, and then desperately beating their hands to get warm again. I saw a beautiful big pike lugged out in this way. The reason why they are breaking up the ice is that there are enormous floods a hundred miles or so away up river, and they want to give the water a clear run, to prevent a similar flood here. We shall ourselves be good deal happier when that danger is past, as a flood would sweep the island where the new boat is, and we might lose it before ever we put to sea.

I am thinking with envy of your diplomatic skill in getting away for the spring cleaning. It burst upon my head this morning like a thunderstorm. Every single room in the house is hell, to put it mildly. I encamp desperately first in one place, then in another, but am kept on the move like a vagrant in a London street. I have been made to take down a hanging cupboard, to do appalling gymnastics to open a window from within, to climb on the roof of the verandah and burst it open from without, to clear away my things from a thousand places. You may picture me, clinging to my sextant, camera and compass, defending them wildly, and afraid to leave the house until some island of calm in the tumult has appeared where I may leave them. All the doves I have tentatively sent out have returned dusty and discomfited. I thought the bedroom was done. Not a bit of it. Then I tried the dining-room. Carpets proceeded to come up. I tried the garrets, and behold they were to be used for storing furniture during the washing of the upper floors. I think of you, and sigh. I used to think Sidge was a whirlwind during Spring Cleaning. I now know that in comparison with Evgenia she was a storm in a teacup compared with a tornado.

Tom, our cat, has wisely absconded for the day.

I wish I could.

Interval for shifting a cupboard from the downstairs to the upstairs. The house owners are coming back for the summer, when we shall retain the upper floor, and they will have the lower floor, where we lived during the winter.

Yes, it is pretty sad to know that Lloyd George knows what to do, and yet has not got the force to enable him to do it. And it does seem still more ridiculous that a handful of wild Unionists in England should be able to prevent L.G. from doing with regard to Russia what the countries on Russia's own borders want him to do. I think politics are beastly, and the only thing to do is to forget them for as long periods as possible. This, as soon as we have finished fitting out the *Racundra*, we propose to do.

I have done the bulk of what I had to do, and now have merely to see that a certain amount of material from other people, Russia, Esthonia, Lithuania etc., comes through to Manchester according to programme. So I think that about May 15 I shall be able to set my sails and sail away to the islands of the Blest, or rather to the islands of the Damned Thieves who stole my mainsail two years ago. However, this year I shall be living on board all the time, and shall try not to give them a chance.

It is, thank goodness, thawing this morning, though it froze like anything in the night, and the whole place is still white with snow.

In another two weeks, I should think I should have a chance of rather frigid fishing.

Your affectionate son,

Arthur

1   Thought by many to be the best bookshop of the day in London. It was run by J. A. Wilson, who published *The Soldier and Death*.
2   *Racundra*.

To Edith R. Ransome

June 8 1922   Riga.

My dearest Mother,

We are still wrestling with difficulties here in getting ready for sea. The boat itself is nearly ready, and we are busy with mattresses and things of that kind. But nothing on earth will induce the swine who is alleged to be doing some metal work for the mast to deliver the goods, ordered about three months ago. However, the little tiny motor I am sticking in to push us along in calms is now being installed, though I admit, it looks rather toylike, its propellor looking rather like a little brass flower attached to the big hull of the *Racundra*. You will be pleased to hear that I have persuaded the old man who looks after our dinghy to come with us on the first trip to Reval. He is very ancient (sailed with Lady Brassey in the *Sunbeam*[1] about the time that I was born) but very efficient, and highly entertaining.[2] He wants to sail to England with me next year. He is quite the best sailor in these parts, and I shall be glad to have him if only to pick up hints from him, to polish up what, hitherto, I have been finding out for myself. I think I can now safely say that on Midsummer Day I shall be able to date a letter to you from on board the *Racundra*.

During the Whitsun holidays, when the land was a sort of hell of ginger beer bottles, gramophones and waste paper, spread all over the place by family parties, each, of course, accompanied by a dachsund, we spent the whole time on the water in the little boat, and had some very good sailing. I am learning all the time and can now do things in the little boat that I should never have dared in *Slug* or *Kitty*, though they were twice the size. It remains to be seen how I shall handle *Racundra*, but certainly I am much better fit to handle her than I was a year ago.

Your Bantam Coffee has been religiously kept (not a tin opened) and lies in a place apart, the first stores to go on board *Racundra*. Tomorrow I am buying a lifebelt, which I hope will be less useful than the coffee.

But it is very sickening how much of the summer has gone, although perhaps it is as well, for I am not really free to start on a real cruise until the Russian Number of the *Guardian* has gone to press. Still, we could have been living on board, which is a joy in itself, or would have been. Among the joys which I remember, even one day's sleep in *Slug*, with stone ballast for pillows, after a thirty hour sail, stands out. And *Racundra* will be luxury compared to that. Actually horsehair mattresses.

I wish we could see any chance of making our trip to England this summer. But I think it is impossible. Already too late. Chatterton and other great men tell me that there is such a prevalence of N.W. winds from June on in the North Sea, that it is a miserable job crossing from the east after the end of May. So I suppose I shall have to put that off until next year. However, when at last we get going, I am going to try to keep going as hard as I can, for practice sake, and try to cover in distance the journey to England, even if it will not be in the hoped-for direction. The trip to Reval is about 250 miles It will be 500 if we go straight there and back. I should very much like to do a thousand miles this year. The trip to England is about 1500 allowing for calling at a number of ports. Well, if I do a thousand this year successfully, what with Reval, Helsingfors, Kunda,

Arensburg, Pernau and the other Esthonian ports, I shall be pretty confident of being able to bring *Racundra* home next year, when you shall motor over to Ramsgate or the Medway or somewhere, and have tea in the cabin under the barometer and clock (which said clock keeps time accurately enough to allow me to navigate with her, and duly find out where I am by observing the sun).

My friend Wirgo, the Esthonian Minister in Stockholm, is back in Reval, and wants to come down here to sail up to Reval with me, so we shall probably be four on board and something of a tight squash. However, it will make the work easier. He has become as mad on boats as me, and has brought his yacht back from Stockholm, and also a folding boat with which, under sail if you please, he navigates the rivers of Esthonia.

If you are doing any knitting in these days, may I put in a humble request for dark blue socks? I am very hard up for them. My dark blue ones have shrunk, and five minutes is enough to bring my toes through. BUT IF YOU ARE NOT KNITTING ANYWAY PLEASE DO NOT BOTHER ON MY ACCOUNT.

Our pansies are doing well, and though we pick for all we are worth, they keep pace with us, and fairly blaze in the garden, the sweet peas are coming up, and should be in flower when we get back from Reval.

I may have to visit England during the summer, but can pretty well promise to be home in November for a month. I want to be home then, because there is going to be a big Small Craft Show, at which I am sure to pick up wrinkles, and see a decent little stove and other dodges for *Racundra*. I am fitting her out just as cheap as ever I can, with the idea of probably wanting to get really decent things at the Show. It is to be in the Agricultural Hall, and will probably be the finest collection of all the latest tweaks ever seen.

This is merely a gabble about nothing.

So I stop.

> your affectionate son,
>
> Arthur.

---

1   Anna, Lady Brassey (died 1887), was the first wife of Thomas Brassey, a Liberal politician, Rugbeian, and dedicated yachts-

man, who sailed over 400,000 nautical miles in his yacht, *Sun-beam* (but according to the DNB 'never undertook a long voyage unless it was to fulfil some public purpose'). In 1878 Lady Brassey published a cruise book, *Voyage in the 'Sunbeam'*, which described a tour round the world in 1876-7.

2   Karl Hermann Sehmel, born 1861; the Ancient Mariner of *Racundra's First Cruise*, and the original of Ransome's fictional character Peter Duck.

To Edith R. Ransome

Aug. 17 1922   Riga.

My dear Mother,

After all kinds of tribulations which I will not recount in detail, I have got *Racundra* in the water, taken her away from the swine, and with a couple of workmen have got her almost ready for sea. Ship's papers are ready, and I hope on Saturday to move down to the mouth of the river, starting for Reval (about 250 miles away) with the first S.W. wind. I have slept on board since getting her, the workmen turning up at six and working till dark, and today really all the important things are done. I had to make a new centreboard, the old one being stuck and hopelessly warped, and took her up on the slip, after which I made sail and brought her back to the little harbour all by my wild self, the two workmen hammering away in the cabin did not know we were moving till I had got half way and they put up astonished heads. She is very easy to manage, and so slow on her helm that I have plenty of time to run about and do things while she takes care of herself. But SLOW. My word. Something terrific. Our motion has a stately leisuredness about it that is reminiscent of the Middle Ages. I have just come home for clock and barometer which can now be put up in the cabin. Compass is already there. Lamps polished. Water casks oiled and their hoops painted with silver bronze. Anchors fixed. One on deck. She is riding to the other. Lamp in the cabin fixed. Mattresses now going down. Sweet peas on the cabin table and His Brittanic Majesty's Minister coming to tea on board this afternoon.

Everything except final stores, Customs examination, and Insurance is done. By the time you get this, we shall pretty certainly be rolling about somewhere in the middle of Riga Gulf.[1]

Please address your next letter c/o British Consulate Reval Esthonia, marking the envelope *To be called for*, as we may be a week or ten days on the way, if we stop for weather or in any port. It will be very jolly to find a letter there when we arrive.
                    Your affectionate son.
                                        Arthur Ransome

My dear Maw, the socks will be the very nicest I have ever had. There could not be finer knitting mixture. Don't send them. I'll do as I am till I come home.

1   *Racundra* left port
    on 20 August.

                    To Edith R. Ransome
October 2 1922   *Racundra*, Riga.

My dear Mother,
   You will by this time have heard of how the Equinox flung us home with a flick of his mighty tail after giving us a lively time for a fortnight or so. I wrote at once, but was too tired to tell you much about it, and now the freshness has worn off and you will have to wait for a detailed story till you hear the final chapter of my Log. In the way of writing I did pretty well, and came home with eighty photographs (sixty of which I have still to develop) and over 30,000 words written of my first little sailing book. I want to make it sixty thousand altogether, that's the same length as *Bohemia*,[1] and I think that when I have revised the stuff I wrote while actually sailing and worked in the material I collected last year, I should have a pretty jolly little book. It fails rather badly however from Mr. Christian's[2] point of view by having no feminine interest whatever. All the dialogue in it is between the Ancient and myself and the various odd folk we

met, the most interesting of which were the seal-hunters, armed with eighteenth century flintlocks which might have been used by the Jacobites. Generally it was a pretty successful trip, though with so much bad weather as to make the story seem a little exaggerated to anybody who does not know what a stormy sea the Baltic is, and does not remember that we were cruising during the Equinox which is its worst time. We actually sailed over seven hundred miles.

I am still sleeping on board, for fear of pirates, because of the dark nights and because all my most valued possessions are in the boat, but tomorrow or the next day I hope to get everything ashore, and at the beginning of next week, she will be hauled out and put in a shed for the winter.

I do not know whether I told you that your much belated Bantam Coffee, meant for last year, provided many comforting drinks in the small hours of the morning. Nothing is more wonderful than the effect of a hot drink on a weary steersman who has been at the tiller all night. I remembered you every time, and drank your health in condensed milk and Bantam many times.

I feel quite confident of being able to sail to England next year. The passage from Reval to Helsingfors is twice as long as that from Dover to Calais, and the worst bit of the journey from one end of the Riga Gulf to the other is as long as from Harwich to Rotterdam, and in many ways far worse, from a sailor's point of view. *Racundra* managed all this like a bird in the worst possible weather, so if I get free in June next year she ought to make nothing of the trip to England, which should take her about six weeks, going comfortably. But, of course, I do not know what next year's work will be, or whether I shall be able to be free for so long. I am very anxious to do it, so as to have a second book ready to follow up RACUNDRA IN THE BALTIC or whatever else we call it. Titles thankfully received.

Of course my greatest joy is the navigation, which went through in all four of the out-of-sight-of-land passages without a hitch. It made all my mugging up of books seem really worth while. The sheer excitement of being out of sight of land for twenty-four hours and then seeing the land appear and finding that you have hit it exactly as you had intended is something not to be equalled in any other way. Incidentally my colour is Indian Red and I am said to be very fat. Fat that is for me.

I shall be working on the book until I start for England, in the hope of having the rough copy pretty complete. Then while in England I want to do the revision and get somebody to help in redrawing charts and things necessary for illustration, so as to be able to leave the book in England finished for publication in the Spring. It's a huge joy really doing a non-political book at last. And in fact it is almost violently non-political, so complete a contrast is it to the things I have had to do during the last few years. I feel almost like starting author again, and somehow think that this will be a sort of breaking of the ice. Parts of it at any rate I think you'll like, though parts of it may seem too technical. At the same time I do not want to leave them out for I expect the book will be read quite considerably by people like me, and I rejoice in detailed accounts of other people's navigation of difficult bits. The worst trouble is that there are three several storms in it while at sea, and several which we dodged in harbour, and though the storms were S.E., N.E., S.W. and N.W. and so had each his quite special character, yet even for a sailing book there seems to be a blessed sight too much wind. There are also calms and one beastly fog, besides several days of simply jolly sailing. On the whole it gives a pretty good all round picture of autumn sailing in the Baltic, enough perhaps for the escape from the particular to the general which is essential for a good book.

I have got so accustomed to writing on board that I may not be able to put a sentence together in a room that does not rock just a little. I wonder whether you will be able to let me have a room to write in at Kemsing[3] while I am in England.

In any case I am enormously looking forward to coming home.

Your affectionate son, [no signature].

1   *Bohemia In London*, first published in 1907; a new edition was published by Oxford University Press in 1984.
2   Unidentified.
3   In Kent, where Mrs Ransome was now living. AR was in England in December.

To Edith R. Ransome

15, Stralsunder Strasse,
Kaiserwald,
Feb. 24 1923   Riga.

My dearest Mother,

Please observe number of street. 23 Stralsunder Strasse no
longer exists. Nothing is left but charred logs, and a chimney
with bits of the lower storey.

I have lost almost everything: new evening clothes not yet
worn, all my boots and shoes except the one old pair I took to
Moscow,[1] your lovely clock, my sextant, and every single
thing belonging to the boat, all the sails, all the ropes, all the
wire rigging, all the lamps, every single thing, even the tiller,
which for safety I had taken home. Nothing is left of the boat
but the bare hull in the Yacht Club. About two hundred
pounds worth of stuff gone. I suppose it would cost at least a
hundred pounds to get again all the boat things, and even if I
were to order the sails and ropes at once, I doubt if I could get
them in time for the summer. That means that not only is the
boat useless for a year but that I cannot get a second book to
follow the first.

Generally the disaster is pretty complete.

Walking about among the frozen ruins I have picked up two
shackles, and the twisted bottom of my beloved cabin lamp, and
a small bit of iron rigging. That is all.

What was not burnt was stolen by the fire-brigade, who
even saved camera cases, from which the cameras had
miraculously disappeared, and were actually seen by a neighbour smashing open the sextant box with a hatchet and breaking the sextant in doing so after it had been saved undamaged
from the wreck.

I am too gloomy to write more for the moment.

But Evgenia fortunately is really all right again now, and I was
much afraid when in Moscow that she had been actually burned.
She had an awful shock, and a frightful cold, but is now more or
less recovered.

We are in a neighbour's house, but shall have to move because the rent is too high. That however does not matter. What

does matter is the complete wreck of all plans about sailing and
doing another book this summer.

Your affectionate but rather unlucky son,

Arthur.

1   AR had been in Moscow when the fire took place.

To Evgenia Ransome

Feb. 21 1924   S.S. *Baltriger*

My dear,

   We spent a day pushing at the ice north of Bornholm, then
went back and round the island and had a go from the south and
got a good long way into it, about twenty miles, as far as Adler
Grund, which you will see on the big chart in my room. We got
so far that we were all but wedged, and then turned back to get
out of the ice, but it had hardened astern of us, and closed in,
and we could not move at all. Meanwhile the ice was moving
east and we were stuck in it, just able to see Bornholm, and in a
rather uncomfortable position. We went down on the ice and
played catch and generally got hot enough fooling about. At the
same time it was pretty uncomfortable as it was found we had
only enough food to last till the day after tomorrow. However,
early next morning I looked out of the window of my cabin and
saw just a dim shadow of a big ship in the mist over the ice about
three miles away. This was one of the biggest if not the biggest
of the German battleships, the *Brunswick*. She saw us, and came
through the ice like a knife through butter, with the tremendous
power she had, and stopped in the ice about a hundred yards
away. A lieutenant and three men with a rope between them in
case of accidents came to us over the ice, and after a little talk the
big ship began going backwards and forwards in the ice cutting
us out. Then she signalled to us to go east in the track by which
she had come through the ice and get to anchorage by
Bornholm. We did, but in one place the track was already closed
up and for a long time it looked as if we were stuck again.
However finally we got through to the edge of the ice and
anchored by Due Odde, the S.W. end of Bornholm. Here the

mate and I with a boat's crew and some stewards went ashore, and got to Bornholm over the ice and repeated the Roogo adventures with buying food,[1] only in this case we were not buying a few eggs, but provisions for the whole ship. By the time the provisions were on board the wind had got up from the S.W. and the ice was drifting up round us, and we were warned that the place was not safe, which was obvious enough with the ice twisting round the corner of the island and the wind making it a leeshore. So we cleared out and came round to the eastern side of the island and are at this moment at anchor off Nexo . . . This looks a jolly little place with a first-rate little harbour for *Racundra*, or at least it looks pretty good seen through my glasses, which I am very glad I brought. It is a tragedy that I have no camera here, because I could have got some perfectly wonderful pictures, the *Baltriger* with the ice piled up all round her, and the propellor fixed in the ice, the great battleship churning backwards and forwards cutting us out, the seals and birds on the ice and the other ships also stuck.

The only blemish to the whole adventure has been that you are not with me. Though I think your feet would be sticking out pretty stiff and angry, to find that even big ships can have bad times and not keep to their timetables. Now it is blowing like blazes from the west, so there is every chance that it will shake the ice up and drive a good deal of it out to the east, in which case we shall probably have another push into the ice tomorrow trying to get through.

I sent a wireless to the *Guardian*, but it is most worrying being held up like this unable to get on. It's already a whole week since I said goodbye to old Top,[2] and I'm only as far as I was on last Saturday night.[3] We are lying well enough in a good place with both anchors down. There are only two other first-class passengers, and they are very decent. We play draughts, bezique, cribbage and dominoes. But I do wish you were here. Then it would be really enjoyable, and I should not feel it were such beastly waste of time.

By the way, Whalley is to be promoted to command this ship on her next voyage.

Sunday.[4] Yesterday with a convoy of thirteen ships we were taken through the ice from Bornholm to Copenhagen, where

we are filling up with oil. With luck we shall get away today or
early tomorrow morning and should reach England about
Wednesday or Thursday . . . Pretty awful isn't it? A whole week
stuck like that. However we were very lucky not to have worse
things happen.

Very much love my dear. It would be entirely ripping if only
you were here too.

Arthur

1   In *Racundra's First Cruise* (pp. 116-118), there is a comic
    account of AR's attempts, as skipper of the *Kittiwake*, to buy
    eggs on little Roogo island, which lies off Baltic Port (Palldiski).
2   At this time they called each other Topsy (as in Turvy) and
    Charlie (as in Chaplin).
3   On 15 February.
4   23 February.

To Evgenia Ransome

Feb. 26, 1924   *Baltriger*

My dear old Woman,

We expect to get to London tomorrow. You will have got
my letter posted from Copenhagen, into which port the Danish
icebreaker *Isbjorn* took us on Saturday night.[1] On the Sunday I
went ashore for an hour while the ship was taking in oil, for we
had run short during our battling about with the ice. In the
afternoon we sailed. It was impossible to get through to Kiel, so
we went north right up the Skagerack and Kattegat (look at the
big chart on the wall) between the Danish and Swedish and
Norwegian coasts, and came round the Skaw with a good S.W.
wind behind us. At Helsingor a pilot boat built just like *Racundra*
took off the pilot, and because the usual channel was blocked by
ice, we went through the western channel between the islands
of Anholt and Lase and the Danish mainland. In the morning of
Monday we were round the point. The whole ship is shaking
and vibrating like anything because the propellor was damaged
in the ice, but we are getting along fast, because just when we
got round the point the wind came from the N.E. where it has

stayed ever since, blowing us down to England at about twice the pace of *Racundra* at her best. With luck we should be getting in the Thames tomorrow and to London tomorrow evening, twelve days out from Libau on a voyage supposed to take four days. Very annoying to lose so much time, though it has been extremely interesting, some new exciting thing happening every day. If only you had been here too it would have been perfect, and I think you would have enjoyed it, in spite of the delays, which considering the size of the ship were much worse than any we have ever had with *Racundra*. The last two days have been lovely sailing days, and we should have been doing fine in our own boat, though we should have taken the mainsail down and hoisted the little squaresail, and found it quite enough. But if we get such a wind next summer on the way home we shall do just fine, and make the crossing in a couple of days. Of course we shall not cross from the Skaw but from the mouth of the Elbe.

I have not the least idea what has happened while I have been at sea, and am terribly afraid that the *Guardian* will have gone and made a mess of things without waiting for me. However, fate is fate, and really I am jolly lucky not to be still in the ice or worse. The propellor is in a horrid mess, and there was one moment when the ice screwing looked as if it might make an even worse mess of the ship. However all ended happily, and now we are bowling along over the North Sea terribly pleased with ourselves.

The worst of the whole thing has been the terrific amount of talk . . . Leslie will explain that to you. He knows this ship.

Don't throw away these two letters, as I may need them to do something about [the] winter Baltic in the next *Racundra* book.

I am longing to get to London, and hoping to find there at least six letters from you . . . At least, knowing how lazy you are I suppose there will really only be five . . . At least remembering how long you sleep I suppose there will only be four . . . and remembering what a lot of work you have to do I suppose I shall have to be content with three . . . and since you have Tom to feed I suppose there will only be two . . . and as it is such a job posting letters, I suppose you'll have put the two into one . . . and it's not impossible that you have put off posting that so that

there will be none . . . in which case I shall say that no news is
good news but that no news means a jolly wicked Topsy.

Now I am going up on the bridge to have some practice in
taking observations of the sun with a sextant.

Wednesday.[2] Got in by this morning's tide, and hurry to post
this at once. I need hardly tell you, you lazy heartless creature,
that I have found no letter at all. But I still hope I shall find one
when I get down to Kemsing.

With much love . . . and a lot of hard scolding.

Arthur

1   22 February.
2   26 February. Assuming this is correct, then perhaps the letter
should have been dated 25 February.

To Evgenia Ransome

Monday   [Kemsing? Postmark
[March 2 1924]   West Brompton]

My dear old Top,

I have just got your letter with the sad news about poor Tom.
I am so sorry for you all alone without him but I know you were
right.

I have been in Manchester and got things started. A good deal
of the material[1] had already come while I was stuck in the Baltic,
so I expect the rest will be on its way. I played two games of
billiards and won one and lost one. I went up to Coniston for
Sunday. It was really most beautiful. The high mountains were
covered with snow and there was a dusting of snow over the
lower ones, like a silver veil over the dark rocks, with a very blue
sky, and the trees ruddy and dark purple. The lake was like black
ink. Then I went across the lake to the village in the old dinghy,
and bought some tobacco, and heard owls in the woods on the
way back. It really was perfectly lovely. I drove to Windermere
station this morning to come back to London, about ten miles
over the hills, with perfectly gorgeous views every few yards,
one after another of the mountains towering up, some with
clouds about their heads and others quite clear against the sky.

In the valley there was a little thin cat ice on the lake, but only round the edges, and the little steamer was puffing up the lake as usual. I wish you could see it.

[Editor's exclusion.]

The old Collingwoods are, I fear, getting very old indeed. He went for a little walk in the evening and got tired at once because Barbara and I walked too fast, and only a year or two ago he used to walk everybody off their feet and I well remember having almost to run to keep up with him. And he himself thinks he is finished, which is awful. But in his brain he is as fine as ever, and has done a lovely little history of the Lake District with pictures by himself,[2] which will be out in a few months. Robin also has a book[3] just coming out, and I saw the proofs but they were very much too clever for me, and I could not make anything of them at all except that they made me very sleepy. I also found a rotten book about a very good cruise, called *The Dream Ship*, the ship a big Norwegian boat rather like *Racundra* only more than twice the size. They went to the South Seas in her, and then like damned idiots sold her and came home to buy another which they could not find. The book was very bad, but the boat made me sick with envy. If I had a ship like that I should not bother to look for a house at all.

Poor old Top. I will write often.

A.

The negatives are all being printed and will be done this week.

1 For a special Russian number of the *Guardian*.
2 W. G. Collingwood, *Lake District History* (Kendal: Titus Wilson, 1925).
3 Presumably R. G. Collingwood, *Speculum Mentis; or, the Map of Knowledge* (Oxford, 1924).

To Evgenia Ransome

March 15 1924   Kemsing.

My dearest old Top,

I was so awfully glad to get your nice long letter with the story about the little girl who did not see the good of wasting arms when tigers had shown they wanted them. I got it last night when I had come home from town extremely miserable after getting an awful letter from Wiltshire [Ivy][1] in which she says that all that she is going to let me have of my things is my father's gun and my writing-desk. She is not going to give up any of my books. Today I saw her solicitor and he says that he sees no reason why an agreement should not be reached at once, in which case he thinks the thing would be finally settled four or five days later, not more than a week anyhow.

I am sending a cheque to Hopper by registered post on Monday. I am sending it to her as it will be easier for her to change it than for you.

I shall be leaving England either this Friday or, if the Wiltshire business shows signs of getting done, Friday week.[2] I should think it worthwhile to stay if I were really going to be able to get it finished up and to come out actually free to make discreet love to a certain young woman in Riga and ask her what she thinks of me as a possible husband.

I spent the whole day at the Boat Show with Barbara, having a special press ticket from the *Manchester Guardian*. A huge pile of *Racundra* was on sale and you would have been much amused. The show was interesting but it made me feel that we are jolly lucky to have got such a stout lump of a boat as *Racundra* so cheap. Not one of the boats shown, though some of them were much bigger, had anything like her cabin. I wouldn't care to live in any one of them unless alone, certainly not with anything less than an angel as a sailor and an archangel as a cook. Anybody with stiff white feet would make one of those boats impossible in five minutes, while in *Racundra* one can rub along for weeks with storms inside as well as out. Plenty of room for cyclone and anticyclone.

The *Manchester Guardian* asked me to stay in England for another six weeks or so, till this number is out. *I have refused.* But, if the Wiltshire business ends all right and if that young woman I spoke of in Riga agrees, we might come back together after getting *Racundra* into the water. But all that is hazy. Anyhow I have refused to stay now and we can decide plans only when we know about the conclusion of the wretched Wiltshire business.

I do wish you had been at the Boat Show. There was lots that would have amused you very much. A dinghy that I could lift in one hand. A very good seagoing motor-cruiser. Beautiful side-lights and dodges for cooking and some charming little tents. But there was nothing I would have liked to buy unless perhaps a sailing dinghy.

The jolliest things were models fully rigged of all the types of small vessels used for fishing, etc., round the English coast. But these were lent by a Museum that is permanently open in London, and you shall see them when (and if) you happen to marry an aged and worn-out Englishman well-known for general worthlessness and laziness and altogether pretty useless as a husband. However, that's as may be. The boats will always be here and they are lovely things to look at. There was a big stout Scotch fishing vessel (model), 50 feet over all, decked completely, which I like even better than the Bristol Channel Pilot Cutters. A beauty of a boat, like a huge *Racundra* in design, but without a centreboard and accustomed to cruise in winter in the Atlantic. Fit to go round the world in easily.

It is quite possible I may get away on Friday this coming week, but I shall let it depend entirely on the Wiltshire business. It would be too sickening to have to come back again. So you must just be a dear good old [word missing] and bear it a little bit longer.

As far as business goes I could get away, I think. But I dread leaving the other thing still unsettled and having it drag on all through the summer.

So bear up. Get the seeds in and be as happy as you can. Remind yourself that you'll be much more unhappy when I've been in the house a few days. So just you do a little caulking and painting and keep the leaks till I come.

Dear old woman. Please give my best handshakes to Leslie. I am very much looking forward to getting back.

A.

1 Ivy Ransome was always called 'Wiltshire' between AR and Evgenia.
2 In fact he was detained in England for another month, that is, until he surrendered to Ivy's demands.

March 22 1924   Kemsing.

My dear,

I am today at Kemsing for Mother's birthday, an occasion on which she is very much younger than any of us. Her place was piled up with presents and letters this morning, and with a great effort I jumped out of bed as soon as I was called and went down the garden and picked a huge bunch of violets out of the cold frame. Mother as pleased and happy and excited as a five year old. Very different from our sober attitude towards those dismal dates. I have been racking my brains to think of yours. March the something or other old style. I believe it is somewhere near April 12 new style.[1] Anyway I must try to bring you something back for it.

Yesterday I went to pay a last visit to the show. There were several new things, the best of which was a very good and cheap collapsible dinghy. Our compass was not ready but will be ready on Monday.[2] Tomorrow I have my solemn tea with members of the Royal and most Kaiserlich Cruising Club, at which I do hope I pass muster and get put on the list of possible members.[3] They say so far that the *Racundra* book is a good enough proof of qualification. They little know. However as you are not here to tell them the horrid truth I may be able to keep them thinking so until the door is open and I have slipped through.

Mother's seeds for this year are already showing, though none have been put in the garden. The proper way is to sow them in boxes or pans of earth, thinning out the weaklings, so that they are about an inch apart and putting them into the garden only when they are already fairly sturdy. I think you might sow some of each at once indoors, in the veranda. That way they will not be so terribly late as they were last year.

The last of the snow patches have gone here, and today the barometer is low, the weather warm and a soft warm rain falling at intervals. I felt awfully sorry for you in winter again. Still even in Riga the winter must be pretty nearly over. I feel a mean beast to have left you to bear all the worst of it. But if you only knew what an awful time I am having here with the fight over the greed and vindictiveness of Wiltshire, I do not think you would want to change places. Now there is additional worry because the *Manchester Guardian* is urging me to be off, and I simply can't go leaving everything unsettled as it is. I am going to send the M.G.'s letter (asking why I have not gone) to the solicitors and that may make them realise that by their greed they may end by having no income of mine at all in which to dip their claws.

The thing will of course clear up, MUST clear up, pretty soon. In the mean time I comfort myself in the middle of all this beastliness by thinking of the good old Topsy who however cross and sulky she sometimes may be is really made up of solid comfortable decency and with whom I always feel as if I were in a comfortable harbour able to laugh at whatever beastly wind may be blowing outside. Good old Topsy. Wicked plump Topsy who will presently get back a very thin and worn-out worried Charles. Never mind. The time of red floats is coming, and we will go after trout to the Brasil, and take *Racundra* up to Mittau all by ourselves and anyhow be together again and quite happy.

Has Juchter ordered my trysail?

I do so awfully wish I were back and that we were putting in the three weeks residence in Reval that will be necessary before the ceremony. During those three weeks we will be getting *Racundra* into the water and rigged, and we will finally have a party on board, consisting of Leslie and myself . . . oh yes, and you too. We shall have to have you if only to make the tea. Of course what will really happen is that you and Leslie will play cards, and I shall sit on the deck in oilskins reflecting on life, and be allowed in for tea when you have cleared the cards away.

By the way, has the little book on piquet arrived?

My new teeth are terribly uncomfortable and fairly glitter with gold. They asked me in the office if it was a new way I had thought of for carrying my money about. Also on Monday I have to have a tooth stopped, and possibly more than one. Most unpleasant.

Next week will be the deciding week, I think. And I am buying your stockings and getting everything ready to start the moment the thing is settled.

In general, except for the appalling worry of the Wiltshire

demands, the outlook for the future is not half bad. Ted[4] really does seem to think that I have a good chance for the literary editorship as an armchair for my old age. We could manage well enough with that, supposing I don't succeed by then in getting out some sort of moneymaking books. If only I could write stories, we should be all right. But after all, we shall be all right anyway, or at least I shall, thanks to your admirable powers of getting along in whatever circumstances you may happen to be placed. You will always be able to keep us going somehow or other even if we are very hard up. And you and I can always be happy on very little money, if we can only have a bit of a garden and some water handy and even the most diminutive boat upon it.

Now I must stop gabbling to you, which I am only doing just by way of trying to feel that you are somewhere comfortably near instead of at the other end of Europe. I wish you were stopping me by an angry announcement that the tea is getting cold, and that we were just going to sit down and have it together. I wouldn't care how cross you were, just to have your old mug close by and be able to count the new wounds you have acquired in your daily hand to hand fight with kettles pots pans stoves knives forks wood and primuses.

Well, I kiss your old cheek, give you a hug and say goodbye for now.

Arthur

1 It was 10 April.
2 On 17 March AR had written: '. . . I am bringing back with me a new compass with sights for taking bearings of the sun, so that on any sunny day we can work out and correct our own errors without having to submit the ship to the tender mercies of the official swingers, and actually while in open water.' For swinging the ship see RFC, pp. 92-96.
3 Ransome's account of what happened at his 'solemn tea' is quoted in *Life*, pp. 279-80.
4 E. T. Scott (1883-1932), son of C. P. Scott, editor of the *Manchester Guardian* 1929-1932, and already, in 1924, one of its leading figures. He has been at Rugby at the same time, and in the same house, as Ransome. See Notes on Correspondents.

To Evgenia Ransome

March 30 1924   Kemsing.

My dear Topsy,

I have got a vile stomach-ache, the usual chill, I think, and also, being unable to sleep at night, I kept worrying over all this beastliness. I am so awfully afraid that Wiltshire means to drag the thing right on to the very last minute so that we shall not be free till July. Of course the next few days should show that, and if it is so, I shall stop fighting over it here and come out at once and we shall have to go on as before. I have given up believing in good intentions now, and am come to think that the woman is an incarnate devil and nothing else.

I am simply longing for tomorrow to get up to town and find a letter from you to keep me going. Nothing else does anything to make me mind a little less this long drawn out worry of wretchedness and uncertainty.

Just outside the window a thrush is hunting for worms on the grass. He sticks his head to one side listening. Then he hops a yard, listens again, plunges his beak into the ground and starts a tug of war with a worm. He drags it out, pecks it a few times, and then is off to extract another. At this moment he has three worms out, hopping from one to another to take a peck, keeping all three from escaping.

I have just been out to look. The thrush flew away and I found he had pecked the worms into pieces, so that they could not escape.

It's awfully cold, north-east wind blowing straight from Riga, so I suppose you are still having a freezing time there. Still, it can't last long now.

The thrush has already come back to his mangled worms.

Yesterday I posted Arnold Bennett's *Great Man*[1] to you, and I am sure you will enjoy it and laugh like anything. I laughed at it more than at anything since Inisheeny and Spanish Gold.

I have again got a sort of wish to write another story, and wish I could get the sort of framework I want for it. I have a vaguish kind of idea, which may get clearer, but I don't know. Anyway I am letting it slop about in my head to give it a chance. It's very unlike anything else I know, and would mix up boats, excitement and a good deal of fun. However it may very likely just fade away into nothingness in the way fine ideas often do in lazy stagnant minds like mine.

On the other hand if it continues to harden and take shape I might knock up something out of it and put another book beside the old *Elixir*, though of course it would not be a serious story or any sort of attempt to compete with Hopsha,[2] who is and always shall be the one real novelist of the family.

Now I must go in for lunch.

Returned after lunch. Kitty is unwell and can't go out with the little car, so I am not going over to see the Swing household.[3] I have been talking about houses with mother, and she says the best will be for you to come over here and then we can go and look and find just what we want. She suggests somewhere up the river at Ipswich. I don't much care. I want my good old Topsy, and I am quite sure that she can make any pigsty comfortable anywhere. Much love

A.

1 Arnold Bennett, *A Great Man* (London: Chatto and Windus, 1904).
2 Unidentified.
3 Raymond Swing (1887-1968), American journalist settled in England.

To Evgenia Ransome
Wednesday April 9 1924   London.

My dearly Beloved old Madam,

All clear at last.

I signed documents yesterday. Today at one, we exchange documents with the other side, and on Monday, mechanically the thing becomes absolute.[1]

My solicitor seems to think that I shall have to wait till Monday in order to bring away in my pocket a certificate of the absolute thing, which he says Grove may demand.[2] Leslie certainly would. But I may perhaps not wait for that and have it sent afterwards.

I have got my visas, so that I can come either direct [to] Reval by boat or overland. If by train I shall not bring so many things.

I am very much rejoiced that it has all gone through although Wiltshire has been just about as beastly as she possibly could be, beastlier than I thought it possible for anyone to be.

We lost all my books, but shall have some of the furniture.

Mother says that as soon as we have a house of our own she will give us a lot of the books from home to start a new library.

I am tired completely out but feel a sort of undercurrent of hope and the feeling that now at last we can make a fresh start.

The *Westminster Gazette* has sent me a translation of Aksakov[3] for review. I am bringing it out to have the benefit of your expert criticism. When we are in England we shall probably have books for review regularly.

I shall telegraph as soon as I know which way I am coming.

With very much love darling,

A.

Tell Sehmel to varnish the fishing boat and put it in the water! Make him get it ready at once so that it has time to dry.

1   Only three days before, Ransome had written to Evgenia: '. . . once the decree is absolute, there need be no more bother with Wiltshire except paying her her blood money which will be done through a solicitor.'
2   Grove was the British Consul at Reval. Leslie, a friend of AR and Evgenia, was his predecessor.
3   Sergei Aksakov (1791–1859), Russian writer on fishing. AR wrote a charming essay on him, with plentiful quotations, to be found in *Rod and Line*.

Edith R. Ransome to Evgenia Ransome

42 Harlow Moor Drive

May 4 1924   Harrogate

My dear Evgenia,

I send you these few lines, which I hope you will receive on your wedding day, to welcome you into the family.

You and I hold different views on certain subjects I know, but I want you to feel sure that this will not stand between us, now that you are my son's wife. I send you my love, and I hope and pray that you and Arthur have many years of peace and happiness in store. I know that you have gone through much together – that you have nursed him in sickness, stood by him in some of life's dark hours, and played with him in the bright ones – and that your influence over him has been wholly good. For all this I feel I cannot be too grateful and it fills me with the happiest hopes for the future. I do hope that when we meet we shall understand each other, and be very good friends.

With my love and very best wishes to you both,

Your affectionate Mother-in-law

Edith R. Ransome.

Evgenia

To Edith R. Ransome
c/o The British Consulate,
Reval,
May 10 1924   Esthonia.

My dearest Mother,

It is done. As a matter of fact it was done on May 8 at the British Consulate, by His Britannic Majesty's Consul Grove, who was extremely nice and welcomed Evgenia into the community of British subjects with a really sweet little speech. After the ceremony we went upstairs to Leslie's room, where Leslie had left a bottle of champagne for this special purpose. Evgenia recoiled from it in terror after half a small glass, but Grove enjoyed it very much and would, I think, have felt that there was something definitely missing if it had not been there. So we have something to thank Leslie for even in absence, for we should neither of us have ever thought of it for ourselves.

From the Consulate we rushed off to the shipyard carrying an enormous tin barrel of paint, and found things going on very well, from there we rushed to the train and just caught it, back into the country. I came up this morning alone, getting up at four to walk through the forest to the station, because today *Racundra* goes into the water. E. follows on Monday to help in putting her to rights inside, hanging up clock, barometer, etc. Then provisioning, and then as hard as we can go for Riga, where I want to leave her (the boat) while we go into Russia for the *Manchester Guardian*. I shall collect all the material for articles I can, and then if the weather is suitable we may start for England, shedding articles into the post-boxes at all the harbours on the way.

I found on arrival this morning your letters to E. and to me. Both extremely nice ones. E. will write, though no doubt she will feel shy about it. And when you meet, I am quite sure that you will realise, (1) that you have got a new and extremely loveable and simple-minded daughter, and (2) that I have got one of the staunchest and most capable wives that any man could wish for. Remember that I say that not in the midst of any hectic idiocy of 'falling in love' but after six years of close partnership and friendship. The dear creature is just solidly good and incapable of a single mean or unworthy thought.

I am not writing separately to Joyce, but please give her my very best love and rumple what is left of that mop of hair of which Francis offered me all that I might need.[1] I hope the minor brat[2] progresses. Please also give my best love to Cecily. There is no point in writing to her to repeat what we have already talked over. She knows how things are and will, I know, rejoice with me that (D.V.) the worst days are over.

Always, my dearest Mother,
                Your affectionate and grateful son,
                              Arthur.

1   On 17 March AR had written: 'Francis, Joyce's eldest brat,

tried to pull out some of his hair today to give me, and as in
spite of tugging it would not come out, crawled to me across
the floor and bravely offered his woolly head for me to take
what I wanted. He saw that my need was greater than his.'
2   Arthur Lupton.

To Edith R. Ransome

Grosvenor Hotel,
Kasr-el-Nil,
Jan. 13 1925   Cairo.

My dearest Mother,
    Thank you for your nice letter of Jan. 2 which arrived two
minutes ago and made me howl with laughter. Your second
sentence, 'Evgenia was getting savage', called up a very vivid
picture and I know that it takes the hand of a practised tamer to
deal with it. I laughed and am still laughing, with much affection
both for her and you. I am glad my letter arrived in time.
    She evidently enjoyed Christmas with you very much and
wrote a most jolly account of it, since when nothing, though I
expect something is on the way.
    I have been working sixteen hours a day ever since I got here
and have now amassed a good deal to say. I had a long telegram
in the *Guardian* a few days ago, which got me into hot water
with all parties here, not one of whom can conceive of anyone
being other than a hot partisan of themselves or else an unscrupulous villain. I have now done the rough drafts of five
articles, and shall be copying them out during the next three
days, after which I go to the Soudan.
    I think the Soudan trip will take a fortnight. After that I shall
spend three days here and then come home.
    I suppose by now, poor Evgenia has gone north. I hope you
rammed it into her that she was going to a very cold place and
must take her sweater to wear about the house, and her fur coat.
Poor dear, she is getting a full dose of England's damnedest in
the way of weather. We get nothing like that at Riga you know,
but bright snow and sunshine and a dry cold all through the
winter.

Sir Arthur Downes and his dame to whom I am very much attached[1] together with Sir George Manners[2], who has invited the *Racundra* to come to Woodbridge and even offered us a piece of land on which to build a cottage, have all gone this morning on a long steamer trip up the Nile. They will not be back till I have gone, so that henceforth I shall not even have the momentary escape into non-political sanity that they used to give me every night after dinner. However, that scarcely matters as I am leaving for Khartoum so soon.

By Jove I shall be glad to be out of it and on my way home.

The total impression I have got is that of a most poisonous political cobweb that tangles up even the honestest of people. If you had read my *Guardian* telegram you would still have only a faint idea of the general unscrupulous rottenness of politics here.

Thank you very much for looking after my much beloved old Madam. I am so glad that she got on well with Cecily. And I think you realise too her solid goodness that is really only emphasised by her streaks of intolerance. I admire her tactful protest in preparing the grog by way of escaping the sermon.

Your affectionate son,

Arthur

1   Sir Arthur Harry Downes (1851-1938), medical administrator; AR's friend, Florence Chapman, was Downes's second wife: they married in 1902 and had one child, a daughter. (See *Autobiography*, p. 320.)

2   Sir George Manners (1860-1939), Suffolk country gentleman; President, National Association of Pigbreeders; yachtsman.

To Edith R. Ransome

c/o Mrs. Watson

Where is Hubbersty Head?   Hartbarrow,

Cartmel Fell,

March 5 1925   Windermere.

My dearest Mother,

We have found the cottage, on very high ground but sheltered from the north, overlooking the whole valley of the

Winster. From the terrace in front of the house you can see
Arnside and a strip of sea under the Knott. Away to the left you
can see Ingleborough, and from the fell just behind the house
you can see Ambleside, and all the Lake hills.

The house is called Low Ludderburn and is marked on the
Ordnance maps. It contains two rooms on the ground floor, plus
scullery hole. Two rooms upstairs. A lean-to in bad repair,
capable of being turned into a first-rate kitchen. A huge two-
storey barn in first-rate condition, stone-built, at present with
stables below, and the top part which has a double door opening
on the road is used to put up a Morris Cowley. Water from a
Roman well just behind the house, our title deeds giving us the
right to lay a pipe from it to the house. A lot of apples, damsons,
gooseberries, raspberries, currants, and the whole orchard white
with snowdrops and daffodils just coming.

Blemishes. Very low beams in the rooms. A good deal to be
done to make it really nice. But it is a stout place (walls two feet
six thick) and livable in at once, uncomfortably, while capable of
being pulled about and turned into an almost perfect place, bit
by bit.

They asked £650 but the owner in the absence of the agent
came down to £550. Freehold, with 1¾ acres, including a tiny
scrap of wood, and a jolly rough garden, a terrace jutting out of
the hillside and the orchard sloping beneath it. It is the best *site*
from the point of view of having a good view in the whole
district, and will consequently most certainly go up in value, as
building spreads beyond Storrs.

It is over the top of the hill behind Gillhead, 5 miles from
Bowness.

We can have it on May 12.

There is not room in it for much furniture.

I hope you had a good and satisfactory visit to Joyce. I am sure
you did. And I hope you got back not too tired.

Zhenia sends her love.

I send mine.

Your affectionate son,

Arthur

Please if Aunt Kit is still there, give her our love, and tell her that
Zh. finds she can run up Lake Country hills without the despair

that overcame us at the sight of a slight slope that we decided not to climb near Kemsing.

[*In Evgenia's hand*]

My dear Mother,

We are so overcome by finding ourselves in possession of the loveliest spot in the whole of the Lake District with a very small house that wants a lot of doing to it to make it really nice and comfortable that we can't write coherently about it and we hope you will forgive this very short letter. With much love to you all. Evgenia.

To Edith R. Ransome

May 27 1925   Low Ludderburn

My dear Mother,

We did the final move today in two journeys of our perambulating biscuit tin from Hartbarrow, after which I made a forced dash in the said biscuit tin to Windermere because we found we had no looking-glass even big enough for shaving. We cooked our first meal here, a haddock, in the fish-kettle on the Perfection Stove, a great success.[1] There is a lovely log fire roaring up the chimney, using up the rotten beams from the barn which is now being altered. The lamp is burning on the table, under a sort of inverted soup dish fixed above to prevent it from setting the low ceiling on fire. In a jam-pot are narcissi and bluebells from the garden. Our potatoes are in, and two rows of kidney beans which Ikey, the man we have had to clear up the mess and rediscover what years ago used to be a kitchen garden, 'happened to have in his pocket'.

The little car rattles about beautifully. We drove to Ulverston the other day and did a lot of shopping. I saw Stephen H.J.[2] who was very nice and gave me permanent leave to fish all their part of the Crake above Lowick Bridge.

Major Birkett has given me leave to fish all the upper part of the Winster, which is, I am happy to say, sufficiently open for fly-fishing. I have tried about half of it, and just fishing along, casting in likely places, I got a nice bag of eight the afternoon before last, besides putting back about a score of little ones. I can get down to this fishing by going through a gate in the bottom of our orchard and then just dropping down a footpath through the woods. Half or three-quarters of a mile to the best stretch.

I was down for an hour yesterday evening after a strenuous day's housepreparing and got four, including a sea-trout, the first I have seen this season. Generally, we seem to have done much better in the fishing line than I thought when we first got the place.

The *Manchester Guardian* is still veiled in clouds, but I think now that they will eventually clear.

Aunt Mab has written saying that if fine they propose coming over on Sunday evening.

I have been through the *Storytelling*,[3] and decided what to omit in the new edition. I have also made sure of having the right to republish, and have today written to the American publisher saying that if he really wants the book, and will pay me a satisfactory royalty on it, I will write a preface for the new edition.

Generally Ludderburn has made a satisfactory start and I think that the whole thing, including furnishing, the motor car and the altering of the barn will not come very much over the thousand pounds that I was prepared to invest in settling.

It is a long time since you have given me news of Cecily. I hope she is going on properly. Please give her my love, OUR love.

Your affect. s & d.

A. & E.

1   In the *Autobiography*, pp. 102-3, he writes: 'A solid meal could be made from a haddock and the cooking of it wasted no time . . . I used to buy my haddock and take it home, then boil a kettle of water on the fire, and pour the boiling water over the haddock in a saucepan, put the lid on, read for another ten minutes, when a meal would be ready that would last for twenty-four hours.'
2   Hart-Jackson, who became Ransome's solicitor.
3   *A History of Story-Telling*, published in 1909. No more is heard of the proposed re-issue.

Low Ludderburn, sketched by Roger Wardale from a
watercolour by Edith Ransome

★

ONCE THE RANSOMES had settled in the Lake District, it became impractical to keep *Racundra*. The cost was simply
too high, and with regret Ransome advertised her for sale at
£300 in the *Yachting Monthly*. In his sailing life of Ransome,
Nancy Blackett, Roger Wardale takes up the story: 'The yachting
writer Adlard Coles then twenty-four and recently married, saw
the notice and thought of the book he could write about a cruise
returning the boat to England. Having one cruise book already,
he looked forward to another. He wrote on 21 May 1925, asking
Ransome for details. The letter was sent to Ransome in Riga
and it pursued him to England but was sent back again to Riga
before finally it caught up with him. Ransome replied on June
21st, describing the construction and detailing the equipment.
Coles was very interested, offering £150 in cash and £100
guaranteed – scarcely a high price for such a boat. Ransome
accepted, and letters and telegrams went to and fro almost daily

for the next ten days. Eventually Coles made a new offer: he would pay £220 in cash. This Ransome also accepted, though it led to a misunderstanding. He assumed that Coles meant £220 in cash and a further £30 guaranteed. To avoid a bitter row, Ransome proposed to waive the £30 if Coles would agree to rename *Racundra* and not use the names anywhere in print.'

★

To Adlard Coles, Southampton

July 7 1925   [No address]

Dear Sir,

The price I asked for *Racundra* was £300. You asked if I would sell for £250. I agreed to do this. You then suggested paying a part in cash and the rest by guarantee, the last offer you made being £150 in cash and £100 guaranteed. Finally you telegraphed raising, as I thought, the cash part of your proposal to £220, leaving £30 for subsequent payment. I now gather that you meant £220 in cash to be the total payment.

You have sent me a cheque for that amount which I have paid into my bank.

Now for your various points.

I have told you several times that the yacht is at the Riga Yacht Club, in their private shed, and not at any yard. You cannot and I cannot tell them to caulk and antifoul the yacht. You must personally superintend this. However, I am writing to my friend, Mr. H. Juchter, the best seaman in that club, asking him to do what he can in getting *Racundra* ready for sea. You will find him extremely helpful, and he promised me when I was there to do anything he could.

The Ancient will rig and get *Racundra* ready for sea in a very few days AFTER your arrival. It is quite useless to tell him to do anything before you arrive as he simply won't do it.

He will ship with you for the passage to England if he likes you, not otherwise. He is called Captain Sehmel by me. Other people address him less respectfully and get less out of him. He is an extremely charming old man, and makes himself very useful. You would have to come to some agreement with him about payment, privately, so as to avoid having articles made

out, etc. And, of course, you would have to send him home at
the end of the trip. It is no use having the gear handed over to
the Ancient before you are there and the ship is in the water.
You will see the ship properly antifouled, and on the day you are
ready to put her into the water, you will collect the stuff from
the Express Company on a cart and bring it straight to the Yacht
Club and there put it on board.

I will send you the Express Company's receipt for the stores
and a letter authorising them to hand over the things to you.

There should be no trouble about the Ancient's passport.

German is the most useful language in Riga. But if you go
straight to the Ancient, whose English is copious though ornamented with swear words of whose meaning he is quite unaware
he will see you through with the Yacht Club hands etc.

I had nothing to do with the Consulate, but you will find them
very helpful in every way. The secretary of the Club talks English.

The *Petrograd* is the best hotel, that is the cleanest and
cheapest. You can get beer there but no spirits.

Riga is a perfectly peaceful harmless place and not in the least
like Russia, in fact rather self-consciously the other way. Its
inhabitants are stupid and greedy, and you must deal firmly with
them in the matter of money.

Take with you a tin of Algecide Antifouling, obtainable from
Imray, Laurie, Nory and Wilson.

The dinghy is, I think, seven feet. It is a very strong and
beautifully designed dinghy. I can kneel on the gunwale in the
bows without putting her nose under. A first-rate dinghy for
work.

The charts do not include *Baltic Pilots*. I brought them back as
I am using them in writing another book.[1]

Certainly use my name in filling up your visa[2] forms. You will
have absolutely no difficulty with them. You will do well to
explain that you want a vise[2] that will let you both enter and
leave the country.

I most strongly advise you to take the southern route through
the Baltic. Supposing you got hung up by extraordinarily bad
weather, you could winter the ship at Danzig, Stettin, or half a
dozen other places. If on the other hand you get an easterly
slant, you might run the whole length to Kiel in a few days. By

taking the southerly route, you would be all right either way.

You will want a proper deed of transfer or sale or whatever it is called. I suggest that you should meet me in Manchester on July 10 or 11, preferably 11, when we will get the whole thing done properly.

I am leaving here tomorrow, and shall be in Manchester probably two days later. You will find me either at the office of the *Manchester Guardian*, or care of E. T. Scott, 15, Brook Road, Fallowfield, Manchester. You might telephone to E. T. Scott's on arrival. I think the telephone number is under Mrs. E. T. Scott in the book. We could then have a talk and I daresay that there will be half a dozen things worth talking over.

I will bring the ship's papers and everything else necessary with me to Manchester.

I have left all the cooking things in the stores, two big thermos flasks, oilskins, a vast variable spanner, in fact everything I thought I should need if I were sailing home myself. I have even left my mechanical log. You will need a clock and a barometer.

Yours faithfully,

Arthur Ransome

1   See next letter.
2   Ransome sometimes spelt 'visa' with an 'e'.

To Adlard Coles

at 15, Brook Road,

July 19, 1925   Fallowfield, Manchester.

Dear Sir,

I have had your letter dated July the 9th.

I am seeing a solicitor tomorrow here and will try to get him to draw up a proper document to prove in Riga your ownership of the boat. There is a slight difficulty about this as your letter still does not make it plain what you propose to pay for the boat.

It would naturally be very unpleasant to me if anyone else were to write books about *Racundra* using the name that I had carefully devised[1] with the object of having a name in which no one else could have any sort of copyright. I have another book about her on the stocks.[2] Further you have begun writing books yourself and would no doubt do a book about your cruise home and similarly would dislike being saddled with a name which has already been used in one book and will be in another.

I therefore propose to cry quits over the thirty pounds difference between your first offer to me and the amount sent after your suggestions of a smaller amount in cash and subsequent payment of the rest if you will agree to give your own name to a boat which will, I hope, in your hands, have cruises really worthy of her.

With regard to the Ancient, you need have no qualms on account of the name I give him but by which he is not generally known in Riga. You will get no navigational assistance from him. He is incapable of reading a chart and though a first-rate rigger and admirable seaman, is a very old man. I have never let him stand a night watch alone. You would have to pay him a pound or two a week, and naturally would not discharge an old man in a foreign port without sending him home to the dinghies and little boats by looking after which he keeps alive.

The engine is extremely simple. You heat with a blowlamp or a cartridge, and push the flywheel down twice hard the wrong way, whereupon it takes charge and starts the right way with the utmost enthusiasm. Keep it oiled and you have no trouble whatever.

Will you please telegraph your views concerning the name, whereupon I will send you all the documents and letters to the Ancient Mariner and to Juchter and the Secretary of the Riga Yacht Club.

In this way you will avoid having to come to Manchester. I leave Manchester again the day after tomorrow, and shall be away for some ten days fishing without any certain address, though letters sent here would eventually reach me. If you telegraph tomorrow night or first thing on the morning of the 11th, you will be in time to catch me.

Yours faithfully,

Arthur Ransome

Postscript. Of course if you were to resell the boat I should have no sort of objection to your mentioning in advertisement or otherwise that she was the original *Racundra*. Copies of her are I am told being built in Canada and South Africa.[3]

1   The invention of the name *Racundra* is a process still hidden in
    mystery, though as the Ancient Mariner's daughter suggested,
    it may have been a play on the initials AR.
2   Never finished.
3   Years later Ransome saw *Racundra* again, while he was cruising
    on Chichester Harbour: '. . . a very nice man called Cook . . .
    took me to see *Racundra* lying in the mud, hull looking much
    the same, a very good intelligent hull, but she now has some
    sort of silly doghouse, and, of course, years ago an earlier owner
    had cut the great beam that carried the bridge deck. [Genia]
    would not look at her, but I would have liked to know just
    what has been done to her.' (26 August 1952; see Roger
    Wardale's *Nancy Blackett: Under Sail With Arthur Ransome*,
    p. 218.)

                        To Tabitha Ransome
                                                        P&O.S.N.Co.
[postmark Southampton Dec. 17 1926]   S.S. *Kashgar*

My dearest T,
   I simply cannot find the Scriabin I wanted to send you. But I
have found a collection of Little Russian folk songs some of
which are very jolly. It will reach you about tomorrow or the
next day.
   Christmas. I would have liked to give you books, because
nothing else is a pleasure for so long, but I think you were not
pleased to have books last time I sent some[1] so this time I send a
cheque for two pounds for you to buy whatever you happen to
want. Please buy it with my love.
   Once again I shall be out of England for Christmas. I am
writing this on the S.S. *Kashgar* on the way down the Thames. I
am going to a place called Hang Kow, about 600 miles up the
Yangtze Kiang in China, because there is a beastly war on there.
I don't want to go at all, but it is the only way I can make
enough money. It will be interesting anyhow and I shall send
you picture postcards from China. This time I suppose there will
not be monkeys or camels like there were when I went into
Africa. But there will be Chinese junks and the sort of things that
happen on willow pattern plates. If I come back all right

(according to plan) I shall see if I can find something Chinese for your birthday. But birthdays are a long way off yet.

Now I wish you (and Mum Mum) a very happy Christmas and then a Happy New Year. And when I get back you must see to it that Mum Mum is in good condition and able to bring you to London.

> With very much love
> > from Dor Dor Li Po
> observe pigtail.

1　The previous Christmas he had sent Tabitha four of the Dr Dolittle books by Hugh Lofting, a chief pillar of the Jonathan Cape children's list, as he was to be himself before long. Perhaps the present was not a success because Tabitha, at fourteen, felt herself too old for the stories.

> To E. T. Scott, *Manchester Guardian*

Jan. 8 1926　　　　　　　　　　　　　　　　　S.S. *Kashgar*

My dear Ted,

We are just reaching Colombo.

Your correspondent is still alive though only just. He was inoculated against typhoid and paratyphoid and the doctors gave him the second dose first or most of it with the result that he was knocked flat, with a temperature of prodigious height, unable to eat or smoke or move for two days. He is now taking notice again having eaten an enormous breakfast, the first meal for 48 hours. The second inoculation is yet to come. If he survives that, there is smallpox and plague to follow.

I hope the *Manchester Guardian* has seen the wisdom of insuring its correspondent for this trip.

On the boat is the regular who is being sent out to run the Shanghai volunteers. He turns out to be the man who on orders from the War Office was busy trying to prevent me from getting into Russia in the autumn of 1919 when your father had got permission for me to go in. I beat him at chess three times a day now and he failed then. He is quite a nice man though a convinced believer in poison gas and bombs on villages, etc. We fight continuous and hearty.

To judge from the wireless news, the situation by the time I get there will be one of war, in which it may be very difficult if not impossible to carry out the original programme. It seems probable that there will be no means of getting up the river unless on a destroyer. It also seems possible that I may arrive to find myself automatically mobilized for the said war and set to shoot Chinamen instead of discussing with them Confucian views on revolution. If this happens I shall be immobilised and extremely unhappy. But it's small use looking at messes of that kind before you are properly in them. At the same time, I am increasingly astonished to find a person with my well-established preference for a quiet life moving at fifteen miles an hour relentlessly across the world towards the most uncomfortable spot in it.

In the mean time, physically spotty and morally extremely worried, I send my best wishes for the New Year to you and Mabel, Margaret and the rest,[1] and those, at this moment, almost enviable rabbits.[2]

Yours ever,

I have played five games of chess a day since Dec, 16 and lost four, drawing two.

Arthur Ransome

1   Scott's wife Mabel and daughter Margaret (sometimes Peggy).
2   'Rabbits': AR's scornful term for the editorial staff of the *Guardian*, whom he alleged that Ted Scott kept in hutches on the editorial corridor. Ransome was determined never to become one of them.

To Edith R. Ransome

March 19 1927   Peking.

My dearest Mother,

I had a pretty fair doing getting here, travelling in a tiny little cargo boat and meeting a big storm which made us take a week in getting from Shanghai to Tientsin. I enjoyed the sea part of it very much, as indeed I enjoy all boats. As soon as I got to

Peking, I went off in a rickshaw to find Aunt Edie and after a long wallow through little muddy lanes and appalling stinks found her in a most beautiful old place.[1] She is very old, and blind in one eye, and unable to do any walking without help, but full of clear spirit and amazingly like the impression she left on me as a little boy. We had tea together in her very Chinese room, waited on by an ecstatically grinning old Chinese woman who evidently adores Aunt Edie and is prepared to extend that adoration to even her humblest belongings. She chattered away about all kinds of things in the very liveliest manner. Her bishop (Norris) has just sent round to ask me to fix a lunch, which I shall, though it's going to be a tough squeeze. I shall also see Aunt Edie again. She sent her love to you and particularly wanted to know if you still looked young. I described your kittenish manners and appearance and she said that she had the impression that your physiognomy was so built that you would not age. She really is a delightful old lady. She said Evgenia had a very nice name. She urged me to go and see the horrid Oswald.[2] I said I would.

I have got my appointments with the Foreign Minister and other people here for the early part of the week, and have booked my ticket home, leaving Peking on March the 27th. The journey, if no delays due to snow or anything else, is so amazingly quick that I decided it is worth trying. I come via Manchuria and Siberia, and ought to be in London fifteen days after leaving Peking, about the 11th or 12th of March. It's almost too good to believe.

Six of my articles are already on the way, and I have another seven with the notes for half a dozen more. There will be about twenty altogether. Telegraphing from China has been a complete failure. Also I have had to spend so much of the time simply in getting from one place to another.

I am very tired and most heartily sick of the whole muddling business. It's easily the worst and most hopelessly puzzling problem I have ever struck and I fear the *Guardian* will be very much disappointed with the results.

Well, by the time you get this I shall be well on my way home.
With much love,
        Your affectionate son,
                Arthur

1   Edith Ransome (1852–19??) and her sister Jessie, Cyril
     Ransome's eldest sisters, had gone to China as missionaries in
     1894. 'I had said enviously how lucky she was to be going to
     China. She replied, rather severely, that she was not going there
     for pleasure . . . These aunts were in Peking during the Boxer
     Rising and had been decorated for heroism. One of them had
     a Boxer arrow through her bonnet during the siege.' (*Auto-
     biography*, p. 326.) On 25 March Aunt Edie wrote to Edith R.
     Ransome to say how much she had enjoyed the meeting: 'It
     was funny to be hailed as "Aunt Edith", [and] affectionately
     kissed, by such a tall fine looking man . . . I hope his hair will
     grow before he sees you. He had it cut by a Japanese barber,
     who shaved his head till he looked like a Buddhist priest!!'
2   Oswald Ransome, b. 1881, Cyril Ransome's half-brother, and
     therefore Arthur's half-uncle.

                         To Tabitha Ransome
May 8 1927   Low Ludderburn

My dear Tabitha,
    This is, I think, the day before your birthday and it is, un-
fortunately, a Sunday, so that I can't get it posted till tomorrow
morning, and even then, unless I go to Windermere, it won't
actually leave until the evening, because up here there is only
one post a day. Postie brings letters and takes them away and
sleeps in a little hut in a wood until late in the afternoon when
he starts back in time to catch the evening post for the south.
    Anyhow, you won't mind. Here is a cheque for two pounds
which please spend on whatever you want.
    I brought next to nothing interesting back from China. All
the time I was there I was working very hard and most of the
time I was extremely ill. China is the most horrible place I have
ever been in. In the south it was beastly hot, with cockroaches
as big as mice and butterflies as big as soup-plates and centipedes
bigger than most eels. In the north it was horribly cold. In the
middle it was disgustingly damp and foggy. I don't wonder that
such a climate should produce such unpleasant characters, both
foreign and Chinese.
    I hope I never have to go there again.

Also there is no fishing there, though on the way there I caught catfish in Aden and rose a shark, which came up so close to where I was standing on a raft that I could have kicked his back fin and at Singapore I caught a sea-serpent, a poisonous-looking snake about three feet long. But of decent fishing like the little Nadder, there was none at all. Most wretched.

Have you been doing any fishing?

Up here the weather is most beautiful and in another week or two I shall begin to feel like a human being again. The daffodils are just over, but the narcissi are out under the big yew trees and the wild cherry is blazing out on a background of firs and all the apple trees are just coming into full blossom. We have two pairs of redstarts nesting in the buildings, and the day I got back I found a weasel's nest hole in the garden. A pair of rooks are building in one of the chimneys and we also have long-tailed tits and goldcrests and more than enough blackbirds to make a pie for any king with a good enough digestion. Fishing on the lake last night a big black cormorant came past me in the dusk only a few yards away. He may have caught something. I didn't, last night, but I have had thirty-eight trout since I got back.

With much love and wishes for many happy returns of your birthday.

Your affectionate Dordor.

Dordor

To Edith R. Ransome

Low Ludderburn
Dec. 27 1927

My dearest Mother,

Seated before the fire in your chair and reading by the light of your lamp, with a stomach well packed with your vegetables and a heart made almost too content by Kitty's rum, the book being Sidgie's book, and the hot water for the rum being boiled in Cecily's kettle, I had not got the force of character to get up and sit on a hard chair to write and say thank you yesterday. It would have taken a steam crane to get me up.

Today I am recovering tone, thanks largely to plentiful

supplies of your ginger, which really was a present showing a great deal of forethought and understanding.

That chair is the very ideal of all chairs. It does not repel by over-great importance. It is plain, sober as a Quaker, which gives confidence. And when you are in it, what luxury. It fits me perfectly. I can lounge in it with my feet aloft like a University student. I can sit in it with straight back, in the most comfortable of all positions for reading. It rests one instantaneously, like sleep, when tired. It simply is the chair that in all my life I have neither had nor deserved. I can only hope that, within it, I shall produce something worthy of such an origin.

In more temporal, fleeting pleasures you could have chosen nothing better than your hamper of vegetables. I LOVE Brussels Sprouts and yours were the best I've ever had, little cabbage cherubim. And the leeks, most luxurious things, soft as butter. But the Brussels Sprouts stick in my mind, hanging in memory like those little garlands of angels' heads.

The next thing to thank you for is the pair of bedside tables, which gives just that touch of perfect symmetry that Evgenia enjoys. Nothing could be neater and more practical, and one of the old tables is now freed for service in the barn where it is very useful.

The fender is a great relief to both our minds whenever we go out in the afternoon. It has a delightfully domestic appearance, reminds us of early childhood and in these days of elderly dotage, serves beautifully to dry out frozen fishing socks. It fits the fireplace (which Barbara described as 'a visiting card with a hole in it') and generally gives a finishing touch to our new room.

Lastly, though I think it may give us more pleasure than anything else, is your sketch of the cottage. It is one of the sweetest you have ever done, and its technique is perfect. Not a line too much. Your painting gets better and better. We have hung it at the side of the fireplace under the hawk, so that there are no window reflections on the glass of it and it is the first thing that catches the eye as we come into the room. We are both most awfully pleased with it. It lets us enjoy our cottage both inside and out at the same time.

Now I am going to sit in your chair.

Thank you very much indeed for all your avalanche of Christmas presents.

We both send our love and best wishes for the New Year.

Your affectionate son,

Arthur

To Tabitha Ransome

May 8 1928   Low Ludderburn

My dear Tabitha,

Many happy returns of your birthday.

I send you with this what I imagine will turn under your skilful hands into a frock of some kind. It is Chinese silk brought from Shanghai. If you don't like it white, I believe it will take a dye.

You must be practically grown up and a monstrous great creature. How tall actually are you?

And, more important than size, what are you interested in? When I was your age I had been earning my living for a year and was buying books one by one, sometimes going without meals in order to get them. I thought myself already full grown, though not quite so elderly as another young man who wrote to me on his eighteenth birthday, an almost despairing letter ending 'Eighteen today and NOTHING done!' You, I hope, will not be in such a hurry as all that.

Eighteen is a thumping good age. You have the whole per-formance before you. It's like that gorgeous moment when you have waited a long time in the queue, paid your hard-earned shilling at the little hole in the passage, climbed up the stairs to the gallery, got your front seat and looked down to the gold and brocade of the drop curtain, with a row of hidden lights in front of it and the violins in the orchestra are making all sorts of exciting noises just ready to begin. The whole play is before you and the very sight of the curtain that is still to lift on the first act is intoxicating.

Also time has not yet begun to go too fast. Spring seems to go on and on and summer lasts three times as long as it does in later years. Later on someone seems to unhook the pendulum and the clock unwinds itself at a terrible pace, the hands spinning round, springs and summers flashing by like instantaneous exposures, only winters dragging a little.

The moral of all this is to make the most of being eighteen while you can. But there is no need for forty-four to read that moral to eighteen. Besides, eighteen is far too busy being eighteen to listen to old, bald, doddery forty-four. So the best I can do is to wish eighteen, 'Many happy returns and NOT TOO FAST'.

O.B.D.44.

To Tabitha Ransome

Dec. 21 1928   Low Ludderburn

My dear Tabitha,

I enclose with this a cheque for a pound with which, no doubt, you will be able to buy something that you want.

I suppose you will be having a merry Christmas. I hope so, anyhow, though if this miserable rainy weather goes on it will be difficult to be very merry. We have a Christmas party that begins towards the end of October and lasts until April. The guests are cheerful all the time and the worse the weather the more they enjoy it. The table is spread or rather hung about the branches of an apple tree outside the window of our kitchen-dining-room. It consists of three coconuts, one of which is still full of coconut and the other two are filled with fat. Then there is a big tassel made of strips of bacon rind. Then there is a long thread or necklace made of monkey nuts on a string. This is about two yards long and hangs from the end of a high branch. Then there is a table on the top of an upturned chimney pot, on which there is a bird seed, fat and breadcrumbs. The chief guests are great tits. Then there are blue tits and a few marsh tits (our favourites) chaffinches and robins who come in at the window. Lastly there is one cole tit. He is the smallest of all and there is only one of him and the others in spite of no end of lectures from us are exceedingly beastly to him, chasing him away. Even when one of the others is in a coconut, he keeps one eye on the table, in case the poor cole tit should dare to take a bite. The moment the cole tit comes near the table all the others leave the feast and rush at him. Sometimes he is hanging about for an hour never able to get near the table. The chaffinches are birds of selfish character and we think they have corrupted the others. There is also a bath, on the top of another chimney pot, and unless it is frozen, the robin has a tremendous splash in it every day. Luckily, we have not got a single sparrow, but of the other birds there are sometimes as many as half a dozen all together twirling round the monkey nuts and dodging in and out of the coconuts, and as fast as one goes another comes all day long and at night going round with a lantern, we have found some of them actually roosting in the nuts.

Best wishes for a really happy Christmas and New Year.

Dordor

From Tabitha Ransome

Dec. 26 1928   Hatch

Dear Dor-Dor,

Thank you for sending me a cheque for a £1 and for your letter. But you do not write at all as you used to. The thing that was alive in it seems gone, and you sound decidedly dull!

I have never been able to take an interest in the lives and habits of birds. I like hearing them, especially the owls, blackbirds, and cuckoos – but as to who they make friends with, and how they feed, I cannot be interested in it, sorry.

I don't think I will say anything more to you – except, are you going to stay in England now?

from your daughter

Tabitha.[1]

1   In mitigation of the offence (as his reply of 8 January shows, AR found it very hurtful) it must be said that, according to Tabitha's memoirs, her mother read all her letters from Ransome and frequently dictated the replies. She was determined to stop any friendship developing between father and daughter. Yet there is little reason to doubt the spontaneity of this letter. In January, 1929, AR made a great effort to persuade Ivy to return his books, which was unsuccessful and created bad

blood all round (see *Life*, pp. 283-4). Tabitha bitterly resented the attempt to take the books away – 'all I have got out of ever having had a father' (letter to AR, 14 January 1929).

To Tabitha Ransome

Low Ludderburn,
Cartmel Fell,
Windermere.

Jan. 8 1929

My dear Tabitha,

It's difficult to write to you, when you tell me that my writing is so dead. I cannot help it. Growing old. That is what it is.

But I must thank you for sending me your photograph. You seem to be a good deal better looking than, for example, I was at your age.

Also, when in your letter you said I was so dead in my writing that you did not want to say anything else to me, you asked a question: Was I going to stay in England? Answer: I am not my own master, and must go when I am sent. If I am not sent to some unpleasant place it means less money for your mother and you. So far as I know at the moment the world seems fairly quiet – no wars or revolutions or other kick-ups – so I shall probably be in England. A few weeks ago, when it looked like war between Paraguay and Bolivia, I was practically packed and expecting to be sent to South America. That squabble is patched up and so I have some hope of staying at home.

PART THREE

Storytelling

1929–1935

I N SPITE of the years of separation and dispersion, during which Ransome had taken up residence in the Baltic, while Dora Collingwood had married Ernest Altounyan and gone to live in Syria, the friendship between Arthur Ransome and the Collingwood family had held firm. It was reinforced by Ransome's return to the lake country, and then, in 1928, by a long visit to Coniston by the Altounyans; probably Dora wanted to be with her mother as she entered her last decline (she died in May). The five Altounyan children – Taqui, Susie, Titty, Roger and Brigit – were all, except for Brigit, old enough to sail, so Ransome and Altounyan put their heads together. The result was the joint purchase of two dinghies, *Swallow* and *Mavis* (so-named by their new owners) and a happy summer and autumn afloat on Coniston Water.

Winter came; the return to Syria loomed. On 19 January 1929, the day following Ransome's forty-fifth birthday, there occurred one of the most famous incidents in the history of English children's literature. Altounyan and two of his children visited Low Ludderburn and gave Ransome a handsome pair of red Turkish slippers, as a birthday present. Immensely pleased, he decided to make a return by writing a story about *Swallow* and *Mavis* for the exiles to read in Syria. He finished it, after a long struggle with ill-health and the demands of the *Manchester Guardian*, in April 1930. Its publication was to change Arthur Ransome's life for good.

With *Swallows and Amazons* he had at last found the way to do what he had always wanted to do, which was to write stories for children while satisfying his own exacting literary standards. It was never to be an easy process, as his letters reveal, but in spite of all the pains of composition it was a deeply satisfying vocation. The agonies of self-doubt that increasingly hung about the toil of writing were always replaced in the end by a proper pride in achievement. As the writer he wanted to be, he also attained permanent financial security.

It did not happen all at once. *Swallows and Amazons* earned its advance only slowly, but did well enough to justify a sequel, *Swallowdale*, which did rather better, rather faster. Then the third book in what was beginning to be a planned series, *Peter Duck*, was an instant best-seller, and the sales of the earlier books leaped up too. In 1934 *Swallows and Amazons* went into its eighth impression. More than that, Ransome had emerged, with what in retrospect seems astonishing speed, as England's leading writer for children, with an ever-growing and passionately devoted young public.

This good fortune did not, at first, make much change to his way of life, although it at least enabled him to refuse finally Ted Scott's attempts to make him a regular member of the *Guardian* staff. In fact Ransome's doctor told him to give up journalism entirely, and apart from some book-reviewing, he did. His duodenal ulcers were not improved by a visit to the Altounyans at Aleppo, though Ernest had hoped to cure him. Nevertheless Ransome wrote most of *Peter Duck* there, and in other ways gained immensely from the journey.

On his return to England he was greeted by the news of Ted Scott's death, which greatly saddened him. Another sorrow was the continuing deterioration of his relations with his daughter, but he was not unhappy. He and Evgenia seemed to be content to go on living at Low Ludderburn, with occasional sailing holidays on the Broads. Then literary success began to revive other ambitions. Evgenia could never quite get used to the all-too-frequent rains of the Lake District, and a visit to Cornwall renewed their taste for sea-going yachts. In 1935 they decided to sell Low Ludderburn and the little *Swallow* (which had been all their own since the Altounyans went back to Syria) and move to the Suffolk coast, where they could play with the sea again.

To E. T. Scott

Jan. 22 1929[1]   Low Ludderburn

Dear Ted,

I did not intend to suggest Machiavelli as a model for editors. They're bad enough without.

Do you think Machiavelli was pro-prince or was engaged in exposing princes, or was naturally amusing himself with a chess problem: Prince to play and win? That is the question that has been debated ever since he wrote, at least the first brace of alternatives. The Prince to play and win theory is my own. (Though I dare say it has occurred to other people too).

As for the modern novels of fornication-analysis, I entirely agree with you and it astounds me that no English swashbuckler has laid about him with an oaken club on these lines. Someone will, some day, and put paid to the lot of them. But there are such a lot of them and they hang together so well that they have succeeded in imposing on everybody their entirely false valuation of their game of sexual spillikins.

On Sunday I went over to Coniston to say goodbye to the Altounyans who are off back to Aleppo. We sailed in a dead calm across the lake to buy tobacco. The boat you and I sailed in[2] is now drying out at Windermere, and ready to be painted for the new season, when I hope you will come up and sail her. For a boat that size, Windermere is an inland sea, and we would have some really good sailing. We sailed on Sunday in the other boat,[3] centre-board, out of the same boathouse. There was no wind and she got across the lake and back under will-power alone, but she is not a patch on the little *Swallow*, who will be launched about the first of March. If you are told not to overstrain yourself by overmuch golf, you will be compelled to fall back on something worth doing.

Have you read *Humphry Clinker*? If I did not know of your wide areas of neglected literature, I would not ask. But, knowing of them, I feel there is just a chance that *Humphry Clinker* is one one of them. If so, now is your opportunity. Send me a postcard if you haven't read him. He'll take the taste of Aldous Huxley[4] out of your mouth. I go back to him in most illnesses.

Would you like to read Muhlhauser's account of sailing round the world in the *Amaryllis*? Or Joshua Slocum?[5] (who sailed round the world and had a row with President Kruger because Kruger said that what he was doing was impossible, because the world was flat).

If I don't stop I shall miss the post.

Talking of Elizabethans, why bother with Strachey?[6] Have a go at Hakluyt. You can get him in the Everyman's Library and will never regret it.

Love or more suitable enclosure to Mabel,

A.

1   Ransome wrote '1928', but the reference to the Altounyans shows that this is a slip of the typewriter.
2   *Swallow*.
3   *Mavis*.
4   Huxley's *Point Counter Point* was published in 1928.
5   G. H. P. Muhlhauser, *The Cruise of the Amaryllis*, Joshua Slocum, *Sailing Alone Around The World*; both were eventually republished in the Mariner's Library.
6   Lytton Strachey's *Elizabeth and Essex* was published in 1928.

To Edith R. Ransome

March 29 1929   Low Ludderburn

My dearest Mother,

We are trying to send you some daffodils to grace your Easter table, but are rather doubtful if we shall be able to persuade the post office to send them off today.[1] If not, they will be late, and you must forgive us.

The whole of our estate is gold with them. Also we have a satisfactory little patch of purple and white from the crocuses which we introduced this winter.

I am steadily (when hunger does not make me forget) taking the beastly medicine before each meal and hope soon to report that the swelling under my arm has gone down.

I got a few fish on Monday but only kept the three best, and they were not really good, far too long for the weight. They don't look as if they would be really plump for at least another three weeks. But it was pleasant to be at Horton[2] again and to have a talk with the old keeper.

Swallow, the little sailing dinghy, is launched on the lake and Genia and I have made several short voyages in her, but we have not yet had a chance of one of our old days on the lake but have just slipped down for an hour or two after taking letters and articles etc. to Windermere. I had to do a long leader on the new Chinese kick-up. Then there was *Rod and Line.*[3] Then reviews. More still to do. And when possible I am hammering at a story.[4]

The weather looks like lasting fine over the week-end. I dare say you will be able to keep your rowdy visitors in the garden.

No. I shan't go fishing this Monday, but leave the rivers to the holiday-makers. If there is any wind we are going to amuse ourselves by watching the pandemonium on the lake. 'Taking part in it', I seem to hear your comment. I dare say there will be nobody on the lake but people who have come to see the pandemonium. Several thousand of them, none the less.

Have you read Crabb Robinson's *Diary and Correspondence?*[5] It's full of good stuff. And if you are writing of letters for the Owlet you ought to mention the correspondence of Sir Thomas More and his daughter. You could probably pick up a good many hints and illustrations out of *English Letters, 15th to 19th Centuries,* in the Worlds Classics Series, price 2/-.[6] It's a very good two bobs' worth. It would save you a lot of trouble, and give plenty of plums for your pudding.

Much love from both of us (and to Aunt Kitty if she is still with you).

A. and E.

1   Good Friday.
2   Horton-in-Ribblesdale. 'The old keeper' is perhaps Tom Stainton, the inspiration for Ransome's unfinished story, *The River Comes First;* though Horton is some way from the River Bela, where Stainton was employed (see *Autobiography,* p. 18).
3   *Rod and Line,* a selection of Ransome's fishing articles for the *Guardian,* was to be published in 1929.
4   *Swallows and Amazons.*
5   A modern edition had been published in 1927.
6   Two shillings, written in conventional short form, in today's coin 10p.

To Edith R. Ransome

Dec. 13 1929   Turf Club, Cairo

My dearest Mother,

This is to wish you a very happy Christmas. I am told it should reach you about Dec. 21, but possibly it won't. Anyhow, please take it as meant to arrive on Christmas Day.

I got here last night,[1] still with an awful cold, made much worse by my low-necked dress as a dowager at the fancy dress ball on board ship. I was a good dowager (took you as a model, but improved on your outfit by adding a lace cap and black mittens). I was sad to leave the ship and my table full of friends (six, all nice). I suppose I shall see none of them again, but in a fortnight feeding together and playing games, you get to know people very well. And all the lot were very jolly, especially the two young married couples who upholstered me in the [shocking?] *decolleté* that made my cold so bad.

I have found a lot of my friends of five years ago. Lady Downes will be here in a few days. I missed her daughter (now married) at Port Said. She came to meet the ship, but, unluckily I had just gone ashore to see about tickets and things.

My first telegram should appear about the 18th (before you get this, so it is really waste of ink to tell you). I hope to send about a dozen altogether, with perhaps a fortnight's interval between batches, when I may go up to Luxor and play at being a writer instead of a hack.

Cairo is not what it was. Already it is covered with white skyscrapers put up since I was here. In this part of Cairo almost all the charming old two-storey Turkish houses have gone. Luckily I am on a *seventh* storey, and can see across the town to the old citadel and the great mosque with its 2 minarets, and the Mokattam hills. There are not so many kites as there were, and I have seen no hoopoes. But coming up the Delta from Port Said, I saw a flock of egrets, and lots of camels, donkeys and buffaloes on the roads, and now and then, comic and frantic picture, an Arab in flowing robes, riding a motor-bicycle. My maid is a fellow as black as ink: but he makes my bed quite well.

Now I really must stop, as there are people waiting.

I am being put up for the Mohammed Ali Club, which should

be most interesting: nearly all Egyptian grandees of different kinds. I wish I had more clothes!!!

I do really hope this will arrive in time to wish you *all* a much happier Christmas than can possibly be the lot of your exiled but affectionate son.

Please drink my health on Christmas and New Year's Day in hot rum and plenty of it. For my part, I shall be drinking your health in the same.

With much love,

Arthur.

1   AR left England in November, on the last of his forays abroad for the *Guardian*. In the *Autobiography* (p. 334) he voices his suspicion that the trip had been devised by Ted Scott, in full charge at last, to restore his deteriorating health. If so, it failed in its purpose; Ransome continued to be ill, which 'meant that once more *Swallows and Amazons* was forging briskly ahead'.

To E. T. Scott
c/o Thomas Cook and Sons,

Dec. 15 1929   Cairo.

My dear Ted,

By the time you get this you will have had some telegrams. I hope to get some off for the elections, though it is altogether against my principles to start saying things before I have had time to look around. However . . .

I got flu or something pretty violent in the way of chills on the way round and have been having a horrible time. There was a fancy dress dance on the ship, the day before reaching Port Said, and I rashly put myself in the hands of two young married couples at my table, who rigged me up as a dowager with a lace cap, white hair, black mittens, bust and bustle, and a horribly low neck with pearls and topazes of dazzling effect. The low neck was I think the final touch and I was very bad the next day and indeed still am, though there are signs that I am through the damnablest.

Now then. Crozier[1] said, Go and see our Cairo young man[2] and report. I did go and see him, and though, after my Berlin experience,[3] I feel a little chary of recommending anything, I think it rather more than possible that in this lad you have got the very best possible material for the corridor, though not for Cairo . . . Not for Cairo, because he leaves *definitely* for *good* in May and is *not coming back* (triple emphasis . . . due to headache). He is 26. Married to a niece of Lord Courtney. Son of a Labour member. Calls himself Labour but considers Labour better served by the *Manchester Guardian* than by its own representatives. Wants to write. Has a congenital interest in politics. Has spent some time teaching in an Indian School or University. Then went back to England, married, and came out here to earn a living. Education: Cambridge. Nothing much in the way of fancy degrees, because he read science, then history and finally education. I asked him how long it took him to write the sort of articles he has been sending us. He said he never has time to give more than a morning to doing an article. Concealing my respect behind a pompous manner, I did not let him know that I considered him one of the heavenborn. Languages: French, German and a pretty good elementary foundation for Russian (learnt here), plus a certain amount of Arabic. His ambition is to be a special correspondent. I led the conversation to the subject of journalism in general and asked him if he had ever thought of going into a newspaper office. He did not express the revolted horror that I should have felt at his age at such a suggestion. He wondered if by doing that sort of thing he would be able to earn £400 or £500 a year. He is extreeeeeemly young, but decidedly nice in feel, altogether unlike some other rabbits whose diseased livers and swollen spleens affect the corridor atmosphere. I think he is the sort of lad you would find it refreshing to have about, and one who, as his articles show, has a natural instinct for the M.G. attitude.

His present plan is to get hold of a lectureship in Moscow university (hence the sweating up of Russian), but I imagine that if you were to suggest to him that he might come for a month to the office for a trial trip, he would jump at it.[4] That would do no harm to anybody, and, unless during the ensuing three weeks my opinion changes altogether, I think you would enjoy having the creature about. N.B. He washes, for one thing. And, for another, he is altogether free from conceit.

If you think well of this proposition, write or wire and let me know (so that *in case* my present judgement is upset by further experience of him I can hold up the suggestion) when I would find out when he could come. He reaches England in May. I would suggest having him up there fairly early, to prevent his fixing up with something else before you have made up your mind about him. I mean it would be annoying if you liked him, only to find that out when it was too late to stop him from going off to some other University. He is not keen on University work.

I still shiver when I remember my last recommendation, but I do feel that it is possible that in this lad you have got both better material and more willingly mouldable material than anything of the younger sort in the corridor. The feel of the fellow is thoroughly simple, eager and pleasant, and free from any kind of intellectual cockiness, while at the same time he is extremely clever and has crammed a lot of experience into his 26 years.

Well, that's that. You know what I think about it anyhow. I should invite him to spend a month in the corridor, without committing either it or him.

The weather here is vile, cold and raining. Furness[5] is ill at his cottage outside Cairo. I am ill in my room in a pension inside Cairo. The telephone is at the other end of about three corridors, and all sorts of Ahmins and Mohammads are ringing up to tell me how wrong each other's views are. What a life.

In case this comes in time for Christmas, I wish you a merry one, if not, then a Happy New Year. Love to Mabel and brats.

Yours ever,

Arthur

1   W. P. Crozier, news editor of the *Manchester Guardian*; Ted Scott's successor as editor.

2   Malcolm Muggeridge, destined to be one of the best-known journalists of his generation. His enormous personal charm explains the thoroughly misleading impression he made on Ransome. It was still potent in his old age.

3   AR seems to have made a dud nomination for the post of the

Guardian's Berlin correspondent, which in the spring of the
year he had been threatened with himself (see *Autobiography*,
pp. 331-1).
4   He did.
5   Robin Furness, who had been at Rugby with AR, entered the
Egyptian civil service in 1906 and worked in various posts in
Egypt until 1950. He was knighted in 1951. He was a skilled
translator of Classical Greek poetry.

From E. T. Scott

13, Mauldeth Road,
Withington,
Feb. 22 [1930]   Manchester.

Dear Arthur,
    I am tempted to write you a letter. I daresay it is foolish and I
shall say something which will jar on the mood of the moment.
Doubtless we have both been thinking and may have got quite
a long way apart by this time. Anyway here are some of my
thoughts.
    I don't know what is the reason for your clearly great
hesitation.[1] Is it that you feel even an experiment will in some
way commit you? I do not see why it should. Is it that you
shrink so from the idea of regular journalism that you cannot
bear the idea of even six months of it? Or is it that ominous
word 'defeat' which you keep on repeating to yourself? If
it is this last reason, I can understand that it may be a serious
difficulty. And if you were permanently to feel 'defeated' I don't
think a permanent arrangement would be satisfactory to either
of us. But isn't that one of the things we have got to find out
in the six months? However the sense of defeat may rankle
now, it may pass and you may find yourself thinking (as I think)
that it is not a defeat but a rescue which is being proposed.
And I don't mean rescue in just a material sense. I suppose
people of your kind (perhaps I should be polite and say the
artistic kind) of temperament have an impulse to make an
impression on the world, an impression which will somehow
carry the initials of the artist in the corner, for all the world to

see. So far as that is a purely creative impulse it seems to me to be wholly to be admired, but so far as it is personally ambitious to be despised. Normally, it is mixed, as I think it is in your case. (I may be talking through my hat, as I am nearly devoid of both motives.) But if you have a sense of defeat in anonymity that is a defeat only of the base part of the creative impulse. The admirable part will have freer scope as a regular journalist than ever before. So Montague found for many years and continued to say until the end.[2] The trouble with him was that he and my father disagreed as to his fitness and capacity for writing on politics. As I esteem your political judgment more highly than you do yourself that particular difficulty would not arise.

Journalism, anonymous though it mostly is, seems to me as fine and interesting a job as there can be. It is true that journalists are not mostly artists, but there are some on the *Manchester Guardian* still – Cardus, Bone, Brown[3] – and the more we can get the merrier we shall be. Though of course one wants the hacks, and sloggers too. Don't think that because you are an artist (forgive this rough terminology) you will necessarily find yourself out of place. If you are the right sort and I know anything of my job you should not. But, as I said before, why not give it a trial?

Yours ever,

Ted.

1 The recent retirement of C. P. Scott had left Ted Scott in full charge of the *Guardian* at last, and he was anxious to bring Arthur Ransome into the heart of the paper's work, although Ransome, who only wanted to be writing *Swallows and Amazons*, had actually resigned.

2 C. E. Montague (1867–1928), Ted Scott's brother-in-law and for many years the *Guardian*'s most brilliant and versatile writer. His retirement in 1925 had left a gap on the paper which Scott thought Arthur Ransome might fill.

3 Neville Cardus (1880–1975), pre-eminent writer on cricket and music; James Bone (1872–1962), the London editor of the *Manchester Guardian*, 1912–1946; Ivor Brown (1891–1974), essayist, dramatic critic, leader-writer, and a good friend of Ransome's.

To E. T. Scott
For your most private eye.
                                    Explanation of the word 'Defeat'.
Feb. 24 1930   Low Ludderburn

Dear Ted

I was very much touched by your letter with its obviously real effort to put yourself in my place. I had meant at all costs to stop thinking about anything except my book during this week at least, but I sent off a careless scribble to you this morning and I should not like you to think that it was a reply to this letter of yours, which arrived with the same postman who took my scrawl.

I am not going to answer your letter in full. But I want to make one point clear. You are quite wrong in thinking that I regret the anonymity of journalism or regard it with anything but relief. I have always HATED being mixed up personally in politics. I came to write about them only because I could not stand what other people wrote about certain subjects on which I happened to have special knowledge. That position still holds and to this day whenever I have a choice between anonymity and signature on political subjects I choose anonymity every time.

Why I use the word 'defeat' is that I set out to be a writer of quite another sort. For a great number of years, right up to the war, I stuck firmly to this resolve and had gone a long way towards getting enough reputation to be able to go on living chiefly out of writing books. It was for that I valued the reputation, not for the sake of seeing my name in print or being a personage in the drawing rooms I always avoided from the very first. Then came two things, the war and the Russian revolution on the one side, and the escape from my first wife, which involved what at first I thought was the temporary but afterwards proved to be the permanent loss of the library which was actually to a larger extent perhaps than for writers of other kinds an important part of my own brain.

Now then, the revolution, and subsequently intervention, made it impossible for me to return as everybody else did after the war immediately to the job left behind. But I never lost hope of getting back to it. Then came the final blow of the loss of the books which had an awful effect on me, so that continually even now, when in the middle of something else, I find myself engaged in imaginary dialogues on the subject. Then, in letters from my first wife, came statements that I would never write books again, showing that her object in taking the books, and possibly also in crippling me financially, was to prevent my doing the thing I had set out to do.

There is enough pugnacity in me to keep on wanting to do it, even though journalism kept up for so many years has probably made it more difficult. I find it perfectly impossible to do two things at once, or rather to be two things at once. My actual output has always been rather small and I cannot, like Montague, write one thing in the morning and quite another thing at night. I therefore know very well that coming into the office is going to mean writing nothing but leaders, and possibly writing more of them than I can write well. It means that I shall have definitely turned my back on my original object, an object I still think the one which, but for the obstacles produced by my own folly in my first marriage, I am more or less capable of attaining. That is why I hanker after literary editorships,[1] really because literary editing does not mean this kind of defeat, does not mean writing except on subjects on which I really would in any case want to write. The having to come to an office once a day does not frighten me in the least. It's what I have to do there that worries.

With all this there comes also a sort of feeling that I may be too late, that I may have been defeated already, and that the publishers who are still ready, it seems, to give me any chance I want are mistaken in thinking that I could take a chance if I had one. Not a pleasant idea at all, but the fact sticks out large and prominent, that I simply cannot produce more than a certain amount in a week and that I find it almost impossible to get on with a book when I am busy with something else as well.

I have never even tried to drag out all these things before, and doubt very much whether I ought to be telling them to you, but you know so much about me that you may as well know a bit more. Anyway they will help you to understand why my hesitation is so painful.

Against all hesitation there is a good deal that is quite different. For one thing there is no paper in the world for which I would sooner write than the *Manchester Guardian*, none with which I am prouder to be mixed up. Besides that there is my feeling for yourself.

This does not touch on other things than my insides. The economic side of the business is also snaggish, but that I think we had better leave until we can discuss the whole position with J.R.S.[2]

I daresay I shall get through my measles in the end, but I can't pretend that they are not extremely uncomfortable.

Yours ever,

Arthur

1   AR was interested in the literary editorship of the *Guardian*, which had long been dangled before him, but in no other full-time job there.
2   John Scott, Ted's brother, and the business manager of the *Guardian*.

To Edith R. Ransome

July 4 1930   Low Ludderburn

My dearest Mother,

Carver's satellite duly delivered the books and the desk, at which I am now writing, but did not deliver the picture that you destined for Blawith.

Thank you very much. The desk is placed in the corner of the barn opposite diagonally from the door, so that it gets the light from the window that looks down the road. It is very pleasant to work at it so, in summer, and in winter, I dare say, we shall shift it to where my huge table now stands. I have already cleared lots of fishing tackle into its drawers, to make room for the Scotts on the bookshelves. The top three drawers I am reserving for the more serious affairs of typewriting paper, notes, etc. It is very pleasant indeed to have it, though somehow it seems wrong that my frivolities should be written on the same desk that has been used by two historians.[1]

Genia is very worried about your frock. She worked at it half the night after we got back, and posted it off to you early enough for it to be in Leeds[2] the day before you were to leave, but perhaps you left Leeds earlier than you had planned.

I am extremely sleepy. In emulation of Kelsall,[3] I got up today at 1.30 *a.m.* and set off about an hour and a half later and went to Sedbergh, to fish until breakfast time, getting there a little before sunrise. It was extraordinarily jolly, and I got six brace of nice trout and one mort. Thirteen altogether, and, in spite of the unlucky number, have so far not got my usual after-fishing headache. Of course it may come yet, but so far all is well, although you may think that this letter might have been the better if its writer had had a little more sleep.

I have had a letter from Cape's, to say that all goes well with binding etc., and that they now feel they can count on publishing *Swallows and Amazons* on July 21. I feel quite childish about it, bursting to see the brute and feel it. I haven't been so eager to see a new book since *Racundra* was done. Well I remember the excitement of the parcel arriving in Riga. The only other book of which I can remember the actual arrival of the first copies is *The Souls of the Streets,*[4] at Gunter Grove. Funny, isn't it, to be as much of a baby about it at 46 as I was at 20. Perhaps it is because nowadays I get so very little chance of doing books at all. Anyway I am just starting another book of Russian fairy tales, for next year.[5] Though if *Swallows* fails, I suppose Cape won't be so keen to have it. But Genia has picked out some very good stories, enough to make a very jolly book, if only I can get at it.

I am going to London next week, with a lot of accumulated things to be done, and shall go to see an oculist while I am there. At the same time I shall see a doctor, because something must be done about my getting these beastly glands swelling out under my arms and being so horribly tired for no reason at all. But blow all glooms away and think of better things . . . The garden is fairly surpassing itself. Genia's long bed of mixed Canterbury Bells and foxgloves, against the wall, looks just as if it were lit up from within. Also the roses are better this year than they have ever been. The rock garden is developing fast. All the bits stolen from you seem to have made themselves at home, and the house leeks that we started only last year have now got grandchildren.

Genia has put in a long row of chrysanthemums, which also promise well, though they were the raggedest scraps to start with, and had to be nursed through the drought.

We want rain very badly. Nothing so far but short violent thundershowers that do no good at all. The river was terribly low and there is not a drop of water in our pond.

I wonder how the antiquarium is at Leeds and whether Hugh[6] has succeeded in banishing the sticklebacks for the sake of the microscopic creatures. I think they ought to try to get a baby eel. A workman I know in Manchester had one and kept it twelve years. It got so tame it would come and take food from his hand. It was about a foot long when he lost it for the last time. It had disappeared more than once before that, but was so well known that someone always brought it back. It was a very clever eel, extraordinarily so. It liked music, and he always hoped to teach it to wrap itself round a penny whistle and play tunes by lifting its folds over one hole or the other while he blew. But, as he said, it lacked concentration.

Now I must stop and do some work.

Please give my love to the various aunts, etc. whom you meet in your Jaunts and Jollities.

Very much love for yourself

From your affectionate son,

Arthur

1   AR's parents. The desk is now on display at the Museum of Lakeland Life, Abbot Hall, Kendal, in Cumbria.
2   Mrs Ransome had recently moved back to Leeds from Kent.
3   Colonel Kelsall of Barkbooth in the Winster valley. Like Ransome, he was a keen fisherman; as neither of them had a telephone, they devised the signalling system described in *Winter Holiday* to inform each other of fishing plans (see *Autobiography*, p. 327). Kelsall's sons, Desmond and Dick, became two of AR's favourite playfellows.
4   AR's first book (not counting *The ABC of Physical Culture*, which he never mentioned). It was published in 1904.
5   Never completed. A selection of Ransome's uncollected Russian tales was published posthumously as *The War of the Birds and the Beasts* in 1984, to mark his centenary.
6   Hugh Lupton, Ransome's brother-in-law.

From Dora Altounyan

July 18 1930   Aleppo

My dear Arthur,

Swallows and Amazons[1] arrived yesterday at 1 p.m. and it is
now 6 a.m. and there have been very few hours of those 18
when it was not being read by somebody. I didn't ask Ernest
what time it was when he came to bed – I myself read it till 11,
and got to within 7 chapters of the end. Well, all I want to say
is that we all like it *enormously*. When we've all read it we'll send
you a telegram, which you'll get long before this; and later on
we'll let you know in detail what we all think about the book.
Now I see why you think I could have illustrated it! How I wish
I could! I mustn't write much now because it's nearly breakfast
time. Goodbye and thank you very very much! Love to you
both from us all.

Dora

1   Ransome had sent the earliest available copy of *Swallows and
    Amazons* to the Altounyans. He was a little anxious about how
    it would be received, in view of the liberties he had taken
    with the family names, etc. On hearing from Aleppo he wrote
    back saying how relieved he was, 'because some people, when
    put in books, might feel like butterflies stuck on pins' (Taqui
    Altounyan, *In Aleppo Once*, p. 163).

To Edith R. Ransome

Kenilworth Hotel
[crossed out]
July 22 1930   Back at Windermere tomorrow

My dear Mother,

I am sorry to say that the doctors, after various analyses etc.,
take the view that I have an ulcer in the upper part of the
stomach. They do not want to operate. But I have to go through
a long course of lying in bed and being fed on bismuth and milk
every two hours. They do *not* think that there are any signs of
cancer, which at first they thought possible. So that is all right.

Things might be much worse. At the end of five to twelve weeks in bed they think it will be all right.

The gland business is separate from this, and they say the ulcer affair is urgent and they will not complicate it by dealing with the glands at the same time.

A very nice doctor, with a profound distrust of surgeons.

It's annoying, but so much better than seemed likely yesterday that I feel most cheerful.

To E. T. Scott

12 York Buildings,
Adelphi,
Sept. 13 1930   [London] w.c.2.[1]

Dear Ted,

The doctor came yesterday and prodded me like fun with good (that is to say with no bad) results. He thinks the damned thing has healed. If this is confirmed by tests, I shall probably be out of bed some time near the end of this month. After six weeks of bed I shall be pretty weak, and he wants me to pick up a bit before going on to further repairs. We shall stay somewhere within reach of London, so as to be able to come up for blood tests etc.

I'm going to take a pretty complete holiday for three weeks or a month after I get out of bed, if Ivor Brown or some other hero can keep up the Saturdays for so long.[2]

I am allowed to sit up for a couple of hours a day, if propped, so that I really feel as cockahoop as ever I did in my life.

I was glad to see today that the *Manchester Guardian* have actually realised that my great-grandfather did attend Huskisson.[3] As a matter of fact they sent an engine to bring my great-grandfather from Manchester, and it went all out and returned at what was for many years the record speed, my said g.g.f. protesting that if they went as fast as that their journey would be wasted for there would be no doctor left by the time they got to the patient. I have a bust of the old gentleman.

I forget now how long you are going to be at Polzeath, though I know you are going to be still on holiday on the Hazlitt Day, which is the 18th.[4] I suppose you will be driving straight home from Cornwall, and not coming by way of London.

Well; I have nothing more to say, and I must not waste any time which ought to be going into Hazlitt. The said Hazlitt is coming out very slow. I'm experimenting with an article that tells the story of W.H. by way of explaining his dying words, 'I've had a happy life'. If it doesn't work, I shall have to do it again in the time-honoured weighty manner of centenary articles.

As soon as I hear definite news from the doctor, which will not be for another *five* days (until they have made their tests) I will duly report. But I tell you here and now that I am feeling most cheerful.

The only sad thing is that the summer is so very nearly over. By the time I get fishing again, the trout fishing will be over. However, there are bream to try for near Oxford, which is where we shall probably go.

Now I do indeed stop.

Love to Mabel from Genia.

Yours ever,

Arthur

1   Molly Hamilton had lent them her flat while AR received treatment for his ulcer.

2   At this time, Ransome was employed to write essays for the Saturday *Guardian* every week. Ivor Brown was a good friend and accomplished journalist whose fluency AR greatly envied. He had encouraged Ransome to turn back to imaginative writing.

3   William Huskisson (1770–1830), statesman, was run over by a locomotive at the opening of the Manchester and Liverpool railway. The DNB remarks that he 'had a peculiar aptitude for accidents'. Arthur's great-grandfather was John Atkinson Ransome (1779–1837).

4   AR had long hoped to write a book on Hazlitt, who died on 18 September 1830 of an 'old digestive weakness' (DNB) which can only have increased Ransome's fellow-feeling.

From W. G. Collingwood

Oct. 7 1930   [Lanehead]

Dear Arthur,

Thanks for your kind remembrance and message. As you see,
I can't write, to say write; and I am doing nothing, like you: and
therefore I am feeling better qualified to say I'm sorry.[1] But *you'll*
get well soon and *I* don't seem to mend. That I am still alive is
the wonder, after all.

However, I have today re-read *Swallows and Amazons* and
enjoyed it ever so much. Somehow you have made your Titty
so very like my Titty;[2] and in a degree your Ruth–Nancy is
more like my Ruth[3] than could be expected unless you had seen
her here last month being a savage with a woodland lair, which
was quite realistic. Unfortunately we lost my Titty to join her
parents, and they fizzle out for want of support; but she is a true
pirate at heart!

I'm most sorry for your continued illness, but I live in hopes
of seeing you recovered. And perhaps the Blacketts and Walkers
will do some more lively things: they are too good a crew to be
dismissed in a hurry.

Love to you both from your   WGC

1   For Ransome's troubles with his ulcer. The Skald had had a
    stroke in July and was paralysed on his right side.
2   Mavis ('Titty') Altounyan, Collingwood's grand-daughter,
    born in 1920.
3   Ursula Ruth Collingwood, second child and elder daughter of
    Robin Collingwood; born 9 May 1921, married Donald Parry
    1942, died 18 July 1943. The elder Amazon was christened
    Ruth, but changed her name when her Uncle Jim remarked
    that Amazons were ruthless (*Swallows and Amazons*, ch. X).

To E. T. Scott

Nov. 2 1930   Low Ludderburn

Dear Ted,

I cannot resist the inclination to write off at once to tell you
and Mabel (on account of her American blood) of my very

good news . . . boasting as it is. You know my views on Book Societies in England. Well, in America they have one called the Junior Literary Guild for children's books, and the beauties (I am sure they are) have chosen *Swallows and Amazons*, and are taking a whole edition (whatever that means) from the publisher. It doesn't come out there till after Christmas, but I've had a rejoicing letter from Philadelphia promising what seem to me colossal results, and of course laying down scarlet cloth and putting up an awning for the arrival of the next book (if ever I manage to write one). Well, who would ever have thought it?

I'll never say another word against Book Clubs, or at least, if I do, I'll take a tip from Galileo.

And as for America. Three cheers for the Stars and Stripes!

Oh yes. I was much amused to see young Mug in the Saturday fouling the parental nest. Too easy to do. We've all done it in our time. I remember my first or second essay, somewhere about 1903, was on that identical subject.[1] And not mine alone. Everybody's. Mug is properly in tradition. He'll be a Conservative yet. But I must say I gaped at his theory that all essayists earn fat livings. I'm afraid you're spoiling him by giving him the high rates of an Author chosen by the Junior Literary Guild of Fifth Avenue, New York City. Ahem!

Yours ever,   Arthur

1 AR's father had been an active and ambitious Conservative. Scholarship has not yet turned up AR's 'first or second essay'. For his swerving from his father's principles into Gladstonism, see *Autobiography*, pp. 22-3.

To Edith R. Ransome
Kenilworth Hotel,

Nov. 25 1930   Great Russell Street, W.C.1.

My dearest Mother,

I am afraid the old trouble is still at it. The result of the analysis shows it very clearly and the doctor wants a new and more extensive X-ray business.

Damnable. I look well, and except for this one place feel fine.

The Queen, God Bless Her, pranced into Bumpus' shop and *bought* a copy of *Swallows and Amazons*. She paid cash for it   I asked.

If only all loyal persons follow her Majesty's example, I shall be able to get cured without any worry.

Well, I have only just time to catch the country post. I've been out all day and unable to write.

Much love. Your affectionate son,

Arthur

To Ernestine Evans
(of the American publisher, Lippincott)

Jan. 12 1931   Low Ludderburn

Dear Ernestine Evans,

I think your Helene Carter must be a most charming person. I couldn't have believed that anyone not brought up in this hill country could have done pictures to *Swallows* that I should like at all. And I am absolutely delighted with hers. There's a lovely feeling of careful, unhurried, almost affectionate work in them that I find entirely irresistible. And wherever she had any material to go on, they are extraordinarily right. Where they are wrong, it's altogether my fault, for not having had the imagination to realise that no-one who had not been here could know what our farms are like. And even then there is so much good will about her Holly Howe Farm, that although I laughed like fun when I first saw it (it being a Kentish, or possibly a Shropshire, farm) I realised at once that whatever it was, it was a very nice farm. Our farms have no timbering. They are usually roughcast and whitewashed about two hundred years ago and have lasted like that ever since. They don't know what a wooden fence is, but have instead walls built of loose flat stones put together with great art and without any mortar. Miss Carter couldn't know that, and I, donkey that I am, have lived in such places so long that I always assume that everybody also knows them too. Anyhow that doesn't matter. Her Rio Bay is first rate. So are all the little pictures and the maps have the English one beaten all to blazes, in picturesqueness and general interest. Her island is delicious, and I clean fell in love with her little *Swallow* sailing round the foot of it. Will you please tell her that I thank her very much. I wish to goodness she were over in England to see all the things that are coming into the next book.

Now then. THE NEXT BOOK.

My life won't be worth living over here unless the next book does what all the children I know assume it's going to do, namely, tell what else happened to the Swallows and the Amazons when they met again next year. That is taken for granted and I am told, in every tone of authority, what NOT TO LEAVE OUT. So that is the answer to your question. Between ourselves and very very private. It begins right off with a shipwreck, thus letting me get rid of the boat temporarily, and the subsequent book describes what happens to the ship-wrecked Swallows in their camp in the hills above the western shore of the lake. Enough of seafaring. Here are land adventures, how they live and what they do during the time when, while *Swallow* is being repaired, they are really and truly forced to do the best they can on land. It seems to be generally assumed that there jolly well ought to be a shipwreck. So I've provided a really good shipwreck and the rest of the book follows on naturally. After all, folk have to live, even when wrecked on the mainland.

My notion is to go on and on and build up a regular row of these books, if only I can make enough to live on out of them, which I think I shall. Anyhow I really like writing them and they don't knock me endways like most other sorts of work. I fancy such books all help each other. They do here anyhow. After the direct sequel to *Swallows and Amazons*, on which I am now working, I have an indirect one (not so realistic) the tremendous tale invented by the Swallows and Amazons when they all spent Christmas in a houseboat that got frozen in so that they couldn't go sailing properly.[1] They couldn't actually sail, so they fairly let themselves go in building up the story of what might have happened. This is also begun. But there's no doubt the direct sequel to *Swallows and Amazons* ought to come first.

After that I've a lovely book about an old schoolmaster and a fisherman and a boy and a river.[2] This is going to be my very best book!!! But I want to keep it fermenting for a bit yet. I hope to start it as soon as I've done the present book, which is called provisionally 'The Shipwrecked Swallows' (or 'The Camp in Swallowdale' . . . Swallowdale is the name they give to the valley they discover in the hills).

Stenka Razin not yet.[3] These things are all waiting their turn and I must get them out of the bran-tub before dipping for something else.

There now. I've told you all my secrets.

Do Lippincott's want to carry on with my particular line of children's books? If so I should be pleased, because I think the books ought to be all in the same publisher's list, for one thing, and for another thing because I am extremely sure that no other firm in America has got an Ernestine Evans as miracle-worker.

Well there you are. I hope I've made my programme and views properly clear.

A History of Storytelling was a very early book of mine. It is out of print and I don't know where to get a copy for you. I don't think much of it and you would think less if your judgment is as good as I think it is.

HELP FOR ERNESTINE EVANS IN ANSWERING THIS LETTER.
(1) The first page and a bit needs no answer. It just says how much I like Helene Carter's pictures.
(2) Pages 2 and 3 answer her question as to what the next book is like. Further they set forth an enticing programme of future works.
(3) The last paragraph of page 3 really does need an answer.[4]
(4) Page 4 doesn't.

But I don't suppose it's much good offering E.E. this help, because it assumes she WANTS to answer the letter. And, of course, she doesn't want to answer it. She never does. As I pointed out to her, all her letters break fresh ground and ignore utterly all that has gone before.

> Yours sincerely,
>
> [no signature]

Good luck to you. And don't forget I'm bursting to see copies of the book. On my walks about these hills I often observe that the mountain sheep look up in astonishment at seeing a solitary pedestrian take his hat off when there is no-one in sight. They do not know that he is thinking of Miss Ernestine Evans, Miss Helen Ferris and The Junior Literary Guild.

1   The tale which became *Peter Duck*. In the writing of *Swallowdale* the houseboat became a Norfolk wherry. The houseboat in the ice was used in *Winter Holiday*.
2   *The River Comes First*. Ransome played seriously with this idea until 1943 (see *Life*, pp. 391-8). Two fragments were published posthumously in *Coots In The North* and a third in *Arthur Ransome on Fishing* (edited by Jeremy Swift, 1994).
3   Stenka Razin was a famous leader of rebel Cossacks in the eighteenth century. AR may have had a passing idea of writing a tale about him in the manner of his once-projected Novgorod romance.
4   He refers to the enquiry about Lippincott's.

To Edith R. Ransome

Mar. 1 1931   [Kenilworth Hotel]

My dear Mother,

What is the name of the people who have the Swainsons' farm at Nibthwaite, and what is their proper address?

I need this address and name in a very great hurry to give to somebody.

I'm sure Sidgie knows it, even if you don't, and I expect you do.

I see my doctor on Wednesday, and shall be spending Tuesday trying to find some work. The *Manchester Guardian* hopeless, reducing all round except on essential news services, and, of course, I can't go to Russia or anything like that.

Tabitha, to whom I foolishly sent a copy of the American edition of *Swallows*, writes to say that it lacks spontaneity, and reads as if it had been churned out and 'tried after'. She could not get beyond the first twelve chapters, but she liked the artist.[1]

Nice isn't it from her? I think she might have said nothing about it, when if I have had to over-write myself, which I probably have, the chief reason is that I have to be earning money for her and her mother. She says her mother is in a nursing home and gives disgusting details of an operation for rupture, ending by suggesting that I might send some more money. I have gone all these last years paying at £150 a year although my earnings came practically to an end last July.

Well, well, this doesn't bear thinking about. I dare say they'll write to you next, in which case I hope you'll rub it in that they have been getting much more and not less than they ought to have been getting. I simply can't give them more without being grossly unfair to Genia, who, unlike them, is not safe from starvation supposing I were to die.

Well, I did not mean to write about all that. But Tabitha's letter somehow made me feel that even my children's books were not worth while and that I might as well give up.

I do hope poor old Sidge has shaken off that appalling bogie of a cold. I have at last got rid of mine, I do think, touching wood, but it lasted quite long enough.

Joyce very kindly sent two parrot feathers.[2] I have put them aside in hopes that when the parrot moults any more I shall have them. You need two opposite feathers you know to make wings. The colours are excellent, so I hope the parrot will do a good moult and not forget which feathers he has already dropped so that it will be possible to collect the fellows to them. NO HURRY. Do not PLUCK him.

Much love. Your affectionate son,
Arthur

1   Helene Carter. Tabitha's letter is missing.
2   To make fishing flies.

To Edith R. Ransome

May 5 1931   Low Ludderburn

My dear Mother,

We are back with copper noses that would do credit to South Sea Buccaneers. Ever so much better for our week afloat. We were to have come back on Saturday, but when we began to look for trains we found it was already too late to get back to Windermere in the day, and the people there said we could have

the boat till Monday for no extra charge, so we saved hotel bills
and stayed and had two more days' grand sailing, roaring back to
Potter Heigham against a south-easterly buster with terrific
rainsqualls, getting everything in the cabin soaked and ourselves
as well, and giving the little ship all she could do to stand up to
it . . . the most exciting and best sail of the whole cruise. We
then dried out and stewed ourselves with two Primuses going,
and stuffed all our wet clothes into a sailbag, and had a good
journey home yesterday, though we missed our connection at
Carnforth. You can tell how much good the holiday had done
us from the fact that whereas on the downward journey we were
both dead beat long before getting to King's Lynn where we
broke the journey by stopping the night, on the homeward
journey we did the whole thing in one day and arrived still full
of beans and thoroughly cheerful.

The whole cruise was a huge success. I got a bad whack on
the head, from the boom, which depressed me for a day and a
half, Genia came a terrible cropper on a cinder path and cut her
knees and hand most horribly, which depressed her for about
half an hour, Ted Scott fell overboard but scrambled aboard
again after a struggle which depressed him for about an hour,
and Dick Scott fell overboard and couldn't get back but
wallowed ashore and out on a muddy bank, caked from head to
foot, which depressed him quite a lot but cheered his father very
much indeed, as Dick had been jeering at his father's misfortune.
But we kept sailing the whole time and went everywhere we
could go north of Yarmouth (there would not have been time
to go south of Yarmouth and back in the week unless we had
made up our minds to see nothing but the rivers). We visited
Hickling Broad, Barton Broad, Wroxham Broad, Salhouse
Broad, Whiteslea, Heigham Sound, Acle, Wroxham, Horning,
Stalham, Ludham, Womack Broad, Irstead, and lots more
places, mooring in a different place every night. Ted picked up
the sailing in no time, and went back to Manchester looking
better than I've ever seen him look.

And now here we are and going hard to work again.

There is a letter from Ivy, announcing that she is giving a ball,
if you please, for Tabitha's coming of age. She doesn't invite
me, but she suggests that I should send you her letter so that you

may have the privilege of contributing. I will send you her letter
and my reply to it tomorrow.

With much love, your affec. son,

Arthur

To Tabitha Ransome

May 7 1931   Low Ludderburn

My dear Tabitha,

I am sending you with this a pair of Chinese silver bracelets I
brought back from Manchuria.

Your mother tells me that you will be disappointed if you do
not get a letter from me, and indeed for a long time I had been
wanting to write to you, and would have done so if I had not
been so silly as to send you my book. I tell myself now that you
are still very young and probably do not know how much you
can hurt people, but, at the same time, your letter in reply to my
sending you that book[1] seemed to me deliberately cruel, besides
being just the letter that you of all people ought not to have
written. You told me that my book was 'churned out' and tired,
and yet you must have known that the only time I have had for
writing it was time snatched after doing masses of uncongenial
work in order to earn enough money for your mother and for
you. I dare say you were quite right about the book, but you at
least were not the person to throw my tiredness in my face.

Your other letter[2] that I keep on being unable to forget was
the one in which you said that you thought it right that you
should have your father's library while he was still alive, and that
you could make a better use of the books I had been collecting
ever since I was a child than I could make myself.

With these two letters forcing themselves into my mind
whenever I think of you, it is hard for me to write and harder
still to believe that you want a letter from me. But there is
something that I do want to say to you.

It is very different from anything that you will hear from all the
people about you. Unless I say it to you nobody will, and unless
you hear it and understand what it means, your life, whatever
happens to you, can never be as happy as it otherwise may be.

It is this: THERE IS NO SUCH THING AS UNEARNED MONEY.

This does not mean that you earn all the money you have. What it does mean is that all money that comes to you no matter in what way has been earned by someone. When your mother talks of having a small income 'of her own' it does not mean that some miracle puts so much a year into her hands, but that somewhere or other people are working and giving her a share of their earnings instead of keeping it all for themselves. (I am not here talking of the money I send but to the money left, for example, by her father.) The accident of possessing what is called capital allows her to take a little bit off the earnings of quite a number of people whom she has never seen. That may seem to you to be a little unfair to them, but as things are arranged it cannot be helped, and I don't think you need worry much at present about it, though I hope you will not forget it altogether.

What is far, far worse, what you really have need to worry about, is the use of money to which you have not got any claim at all. In this case you are taking bits of other people's earnings without even the excuse of lending them your 'capital'. Your share of the affair in such a case is no better than that of a bug or flea who sucks blood but gives nothing. It is a shameful part, not worthy of a decent human being.

This is what people do when they live above their income.

Even in the simplest form of borrowing, such as not paying your tradesman's bills the moment they are presented, you are actually stealing because, to all intents and purposes, you are keeping in your hands (so pretending it is yours and getting the benefit of it) money that ought to be his and benefitting him.

What on earth has all this got to do with being 21?

A great deal.

You are no longer a minor. You are no longer in your mother's 'custody'. You are yourself responsible for any debts that you may incur. That being so, it would be only cowardice to allow her to incur debts that in any possible way you can see she would be incurring on your account. It would amount to saying, 'I will not steal, but I will wear the dress that Mother steals for me'. You can't possibly let yourself do that.

You are old enough now to look about you and to understand, for example, what are the things that most easily push people into stealing or putting off paying bills, which is nearly always the same thing. You will find that nearly always the cause of this sort of unworthiness is the telling of big flat walloping lies about your own position and then trying to live up to them.

THUS: Suppose you have a friend who has plenty of money and you have not the courage to make it plain that you cannot (except dishonestly) afford to do the things she does. You pretend, that is, that you are richer than you are. Once you start that pretence you are done for. You find yourself wanting for example dresses quite unsuitable for the work you have to do, and indeed suitable only for the occasions when you share in the sort of life that you cannot really afford. There's no lasting pleasure to be got out of that. Much, much better, buy a good overall, than clothes of the sort that are for you no more than a sort of dressing up or masquerade.

See your own position plainly. Know exactly how much you earn, and how much other people earn for you, and contentedly plan your life to fit your income instead of trying to stretch your income to fit the sort of life that can never be honestly yours. Do this, and you have taken the first step to putting an end to that kind of falsity. Find out exactly what you can afford to spend in a month. Divide it by three. Allot two-thirds of it to food and lodging and clothes. Count yourself lucky if you don't have to make an inroad on the remaining third, but live on bread and water rather than leave a bill unpaid at the month's end or than draw in advance on next month's money.

Regard any breaking of this rule as equivalent to either stealing or lying. Probably it will be both at once.

You will find as a result that the whole feeling of your life is one of richness instead of poverty. You will never know the horrible feeling of skating on and on over thin ice that may let you through at any minute. You will have no creditors. NO ONE WILL RESPECT YOU THE LESS FOR REFUSING TO STEAL OR TO SPEND WHAT YOU HAVE NOT GOT. And, when you get married, the knowledge that he can count on you never to spend a halfpenny more than he can afford, never that is to put him in the loathsome position of HAVING TO STEAL ON YOUR ACCOUNT will go a very long way to making your husband a happy man instead of a wretched one.

On this subject I know a good deal. Thanks entirely to my wife (whom I did not meet until after I had separated from your mother, so you need have nothing against her) we do the whole of our actual housekeeping on £156 a year. At a pinch we know we could do it on a little less. But, with £3 a week to spend on food, lighting, the garden, etc., etc., we do extremely well. And we have the happiness of knowing that not a single tradesman is wondering when he is going to be paid. If we pretended to be other than we are, a working man and his wife, heaven only knows what sort of a mess we should be in now that (thanks to my illness) for months on end I have been earning practically nothing at all, while going on paying out money to your mother just as if I were still making money. The difference between recognising that you are poor and living accordingly, and assuming that you have a right to be rich and living as if you had more than you really have, is precisely the difference between stone and sand foundations for a house, which you will find set out in the Bible.

Your Mother writes as if she thought that a 21st birthday was 'a great event' in some way other than the legal one. Of course the day on which you are 21 is not really different from the day on which you were 20 and 364 days or from the day on which you will be 21 and a day, unless you do something to make it so. It is a purely artificial division of time. But, it has this legal meaning, and it is a very good occasion of making a firm resolve never on your own account or anyone else's to spend or to pretend that you can spend money that you have not got. Make that one resolve and keep it and you will have gone a long way towards ensuring the happiness of any household in which you may have a share.

.   .   .

Indirectly, not from you, I hear that you have several times promised to marry people and then decided not to. On that, too, I have one thing to say.

Remember that for some inscrutable reason, you are more likely to come to care more for a man after you are married to him than he is to come to care more for you after he has married you. So whatever other mistakes you may make, DO NOT MAKE THE COLOSSAL AND IRREVOCABLE MISTAKE of marrying a man if he has shown even the slightest sign of suspecting that he is not quite sure whether he wants you. To do that is to ask for trouble for yourself, besides being wickedly unfair to him. Of course, you can marry him if you like. Any woman can. It's nothing to be proud of. But, if you do, that first little doubt will come up again and grow and grow, and things will end either in a long bicker over who (of two unhappy people) is to have the affection of your children, or (and this is better for any child than to be witness of a long civil war in the house) in his running desperately away. If he does run away, let him. I can imagine nothing worse for a child than to watch a father and mother fight for its affection. Much better that it should have one or the other. But I hope there will never be any need for you to consider such things. Only, be sure at the start not only that you love him but that he loves you. And be sure that you love HIM and not the imaginary person that you think you will be able to make out of him. If you go and try any of the remodelling business he will either submit, when you will know that he was not worth having, or not submit, when you will quarrel or he will bolt and anyway you will lose him.

All this sounds pessimistic. But there's no pessimism in it, because no-one knows better than I how happy and suitable marriage can be, when, after years and years of it, both husband and wife are more fond of each other than when first their friendship started, and they wonder how it was they loved each other so long ago when they knew each other so little that they had not half the reasons for it that they have today. Friendship is the word. Build first of all on that. And don't mistake for friendship any silly mooncalf business of admiring, or seeming to admire anything and everything connected with yourself. A good square honest friendship is the most dependable thing on this earth. The thing they call love may improve it, but, without the friendship, it is nothing at all and not worth two taps of a typewriter. Make sure of the friendship first and you will not go far wrong. And, do be quite sure that you don't mind being laughed at by him.

All this letter seems to be made up of do's and don'ts, but I hope you won't throw it in the fire at once, but will have another look at it, because the do's and don'ts in it deal with just

the things that may easily turn a happy life into a worried one
not only for you but for your husband and indeed for anyone
who happens to be mixed up with you in any way.

But enough of all that.

I wish you many happy returns of the day and I hope that
your life will be one that makes a lot of other people happy as
well as yourself, and that from one end of it to the other you will
never have to ask people to pretend an affection for you which
they do not feel.

Finally, you are now grown up!! and your own mistress, and
I should like you to come up here and see me and Ludderburn
while I still have it. I should like you to see the sort of life that
is lived here, and the country that has been the background of
people of your race for a very long time indeed. Put a nightgown
and a toothbrush into a knapsack, with something to change into
in case you get wet. Choose your own time, the sooner the
better, but give me a couple of days' warning, so that I can try
to be free of work, and also in case someone should be using
the spare room.

Writing this I somehow forget your letters and remember
only a round woolly Babba of long ago, and it's odd to think that
today you would have to stoop to get in through my cottage
door, and that you won't be able to cross the parlour without
ducking your head so as not to crack it on the beams.

May Happy Returns once more, and love and best wishes.[3]

[Unsigned]

1   See letter to Edith R. Ransome of 1 March 1931 (p. 183).
2   The letter of 14 January 1929, when the row about the books
     was at its height. 'My own idea is, that the books are more to
     me than they would be to you. You'd dote on them perhaps. I
     hope to do more than that.'
3   Tabitha replied on 17 May, describing her birthday-party and
     saying *inter alia*, 'look here, *Never* think I try to hurt on purpose
     . . . Thank you for thinking of me as a "Wooly Babba". I am
     still I believe.' She neither accepted nor refused his invitation.
     Her mother forbade her to visit her father on the grounds that
     he would drown her.

★

Rⁿᵉ ANSOME'S illustrations to his children's book are so integral to
their effect, so much part of their charm and character, that
it is perhaps curious that they took so long to emerge. Author
and publisher recognised from the first that the books needed
pictures, and although Stephen Spurrier was commissioned to
illustrate the first edition of *Swallows and Amazons*, Ransome
rejected his efforts with scorn as not being nearly accurate
enough. The first edition appeared without illustration except
for Spurrier's end-papers, title-page, and map of Wild Cat
Island. Ransome had already thought of doing the pictures
himself, but in the event Clifford Webb was hired to illustrate
both *Swallows and Amazons* and *Swallowdale*. Ransome seems to
have been in two minds about Webb and his drawings from the
start, but he exerted himself to be helpful, polite and encouraging, as the following letter shows. But *Peter Duck*, being
allegedly the Swallows and Amazons' own invention, seemed to
demand their own illustrations, which Ransome undertook to
supply; and after that he illustrated all the books (including new
editions of *Swallows* and *Swallowdale*), complaining all the time
about what hard work it was.

★

To Clifford Webb

July 8 1931   Low Ludderburn

Dear Webb,
    With this is another lump of the book.[1] The omissions are to
prevent you from illustrating things that MAY be omitted.
Cape's want the book kept short if possible, and I am seeing
what can be done.
    They sent me the proofs of your pictures. I think they look
very well indeed and that the book[2] as a whole will do you
credit. The only one I really don't like is the picture of Titty
sitting on a rock with a telescope facing the audience.[3] I can't
help hating that one, because, well, you know what authors are
with their favourite characters. And my Titty is a little eager
imaginative child of about nine. Not more.
    But some of the new ones I had not seen are really first rate.

The night scene in the Amazon River. Magnificent. And the fishing scene with Roger attached to the pike. And I very much liked the one with the lot of them pushing off the boat laden with wood. And the delightful thing of the Amazons carrying

LOADING FIREWOOD, Clifford Webb's drawing for
Swallows and Amazons

the puncheon. I'm more than ever convinced that that is the right way with such things, keeping the figures such that any child can identify itself with any character, and throwing the whole energy of the artist into setting the adventure in its romantic landscape that no child can invent but that every child needs as food to its own fancy. In some of these pictures I think you are really pioneering. Do carry on like that through *Swallowdale*.

Good luck to you. I hope all your models are doing well.

I would say more about the pictures,[4] but I must hurry or I shall have you writing to say you are sitting and waiting.

Yours sincerely,

[Arthur Ransome]

1 *Swallowdale*.
2 *Swallows and Amazons*.
3 This drawing was not used.
4 He did, but not to Webb. Ransome complained bitterly of them to Dora Altounyan, whom he would have much preferred as his illustrator. Dora wrote to him: 'I don't think the illustrations are so awfully bad as you seem to think . . . the things in which [they] fall short are the things nobody knows about except us, the secret japes and details that your general public doesn't know anything about. Of course the kind of illustrations you imagine I could have made (though I myself am perfectly sure I never could have done them) would have made a "perfect book" more perfect still, and I do most awfully wish I could have done them.'

From Taqui Altounyan
[The spelling in this letter strictly follows the original.]

Nov. 15 1931   [Aleppo]

My dear Uncle Arthur,

Swallowdal is EVEN BETTER than 'S's and A's' and you needn't have been so pessimistic about it. We do such a lot in the book and so many things happen, and the G.A. though actually a great bore to the Amazons is very amusing to read about. I'm sure no Walker aunt would be such a beast as the G.A. I love that part where Titty does the wax image stunt, and when the Amazons usually much more efficient than the Swallows forgot to take off their red caps. The wreck was terrible but all's well that ends well and I am *so* glad no shriek came from the Swallows. I've been trying to dive like Capt: John ever since I read the book but like Nancy I can't possibly keep under. I don't care what you say we all think Capt. Flint is exactly like you – is you, in fact. Have you got a red and green hanky?[1] If not buy one *at once* and don't forget it when you pack up and start for the golden sands, waving palm trees, and camels.

The Ships Baby[2] says she can make a *much* better B than the one on the ships papers, and we can all write our names without those artifficial looking blots. Those head peices upside-down don't matter much, anyway they are so bad that they couldn't look much better the right way up. The only good picture is the one of the Amazons not in Pirate rig driving with the black G.A. I do wish the best of all natives would do the illustrations.

The race was very exciting and at one time I really thought you were going to be so impartial as to let Amazon win. The next time I'm in a sailing boat alone I'm going to try Capt. Johns trick, but I think I'll wait until we haven't only one boat.

Last Sunday we went to the farm hoping to sail but to our great disgust Beetle (or Swallow)[3] was high out of water wearing a coat of fresh wet paint. And of course there was a lovely breeze!

The ships baby is busy painting 'Xmas cards'. She has just shown me a robin with a red body and blue tail whose yellow legs look like bulging Xmas stockings, balancing imselfe in a sky of blue blots and a brown thing supposed to be the sun. She'd painted over the robins eye but asured me he'd be able to see alright when the paint was dry!!

I'm not going to write to you again until 'Swallows in Syria' is in print, and you can't write that until you've been here so do pack up and come. There is no excuse now for staying where you are.

      With love from

                    Capt. John
                    of S.D. Swallow.

1   See *Swallowdale*, ch. VI.
2   Brigit Altounyan.
3   *Beetle* was a sailing dinghy named after Dora Altounyan,
    'Beetle' being her nickname, deriving from the bespectacled
    character in Kipling's *Stalky & Co. Beetle* was the inspiration for
    the name of the dinghy *Scarab* in *The Picts and the Martyrs*.

                    To Tabitha Ransome
Dec. 23 1931   Low Ludderburn

Dear Tabitha,
    A happy Christmas to you. And here is a pound to help make
it so. There probably won't be one next year.
    Why talk rubbish[1] about wanting photographs, when you
were asked to come here last May and have never come, and
when you passed through London last year while I was ill (on
your way to Scotland) and did not look in?
    No: I don't remember a Captain George Scott in Moscow,
but if he is as unpleasant as you suggest that does not mean he
was not there as, luckily for me, I have a very bad memory
except for friends. As for my being under sentence of death then,
this is the first I have heard of it.
    Well. A Happy Christmas to you and a really satisfactory New
Year. If I could drink your health I would, but it's bad luck,
they say, to drink healths in milk which is the most inspiriting
liquor I'm allowed, and somehow I don't fancy drinking healths
in bismuth.
                                                    D.D.
1   In a missing letter.

                    To Edith R. Ransome
Saturday   Prince Line
January 8 1932   *Scottish Prince*[1]

My dearest Mother,
    We had a goodish journey to Manchester after a most tiring
packing. Got rid of the car at Kendal, slept at the Renolds' on
Thursday and came aboard last night, only to find that we could

have had one more good night ashore. Today, the loading is still going on and I doubt if we shall be off for a long time yet. The cabin is six foot six square and heated like an incubator.

Fellow passengers rather sawdusty.

Money going like water. Still, I do hope and believe that we have come to the end of the essential outgoings for some time. Otherwise we shall get out there and have only just enough to get home again if we start at once.

However, the sun is shining. There is a lovely iridescence on the Manchester sewage in which our ship at present floats. We have *Huck Finn*, *Treasure Island* and Shakespeare and all that Crush, plus the Savoy Operas to read on the voyage.

Our next port of call will be Tunis, from which I hope we shall manage to send a postcard, if the French will allow us to land.

We shall be in Alexandria on Jan. 24. You ought to post not later than the 14th. But DO NOT FORWARD ANY LETTERS to that address. Forward things only to the Consulate, Aleppo.

I have arranged with the *Guardian* to send direct to Grove Road[2] such review books as are to be allowed to accumulate until my return. There will be a few volumes of the big complete Hazlitt, which please put in a drawer and keep most like spun glass. Then there will be all the Spring fishing books on which I am to write a comprehensive article on my return. I don't think there is likely to be much else.

But your discretion is very good. Let me know if there is anything that seems to you urgentish in the way of books. I could wire back if it needed sending on.

Send all letters but not bills, receipts, etc.

ADDRESS.   VIA STAMBOUL,
             Arthur Ransome,
                c/o The British Consulate,
                ALEPPO.
                SYRIA.

It seems quite a decent boat, though very lightly laden, so that we shall probably roll like fun, worse than this

Much love,   Arthur and Genia.

1   Encouraged by Taqui's letter and by her father's confidence
    that he could treat AR's stomach ailments effectively at his
    hospital in Aleppo, the Ransomes were off on a voyage to
    Syria. (See *Autobiography*, pp. 339-40.)

To Edith R. Ransome

Jan. 20 1932   *Scottish Prince.*

My dearest Mother,
    We are getting all too quickly near the end of the voyage.
Yesterday we called at Tunis, but stayed only a few hours. Genia
and I drove out to Sidi Bou Said to see Lady Downes, and found
Sir Arthur a good deal older and deafer but still very cheerful.
She was much the same. We had only just time to gorge a
colossal lunch there and dash back to the steamer. Their house
is right on the edge of a cliff above the Mediterranean. A very
jolly old Moorish house. Genia found Tunis pretty sordid,
which it is, and was disgusted by the hordes of Arabs with
revolting sores whom you met all over the place. We were
shown the way to the Downes' by a stone-blind beggar every
inch of whom seemed covered by some leprosy or other, a
revolting creature. But the blind led the blind to some purpose,
and we found the place in the end.
    We had a pretty good tossing in the Bay but, though Genia
felt a bit bad one day she only missed one meal, and I had the
luck to miss none, though I felt very squeamish and expected to
miss one.
    We sit at a table with the captain, a most amusing old man,
crammed with amusing stories, and as our opposites an Italian
archaeologist and his very pretty (Genia agrees) Canadian wife,
who knows something of the Parkins. Then there is at the next
table a most charming old schoolmarm, who plays all the deck
games with tremendous energy and enthusiasm, and says she will
be much taller at the end of the voyage because of the way in
which everybody has been pulling her leg. Then there is a queer
and nice little person rather hampered by a voice. Then a retired
aviator, who is full of spirits, though he nearly died of the same
trouble that I have . . . Then a sourish Australian schoolmaster.

A young man on some business or other. Two engineers going out to bring a ship home. Generally a very nice decent mixed bunch, with, luckily, none of the usual hard drinkers. Genia has taught them her racing patience, and also dominoes, and time goes by very fast and easily, broken only by colossal meals.

We shall be getting into Malta some time this afternoon, when I hope to have a chance of going ashore and posting this.

Life on shipboard is extremely soporific and leaves one with absolutely nothing to say.

I have done no work, though I have had great fun taking a lot of notes from a copy of the *Channel Pilot*, that will, I think, come in useful.[1]

At the next table there is sitting the archaeologist who is also writing to his mother, but with a fluency that is altogether beyond the reach of such as I. I have told you everything there is to say in these two pages, but he has already covered eight and is still going strong.

The aviator told me a terrific story of how his trouble started, through crashing in the desert, and being four days without water, and then drinking from a putrid puddle. The rescue machines flew over him on the second day without seeing him, which must have been pretty horrible.

Now the steward is coming along to clear me off the table to lay luncheon. I must stop. But this, though brief, is enough to show that so far the expedition is going well.

With much love from both of us.

Your affectionate son

Arthur

1   For *Peter Duck*, his current project.

To Edith R. Ransome

VIA STAMBOUL
c/o The British Consulate,

Feb 3 1932   Aleppo, Syria.

My dear Mother,

Here we are, after a good and lively journey. After the some-what stirring time through the Irish Sea and the Bay we found pleasant weather beyond Finisterre, and in the Mediterranean we were sitting on deck enjoying the sunshine until we left Malta, when we ran into a real buster, that did indeed bust half the crockery in the ship and shifted the piano in the saloon, and flung the captain out of his bed and generally stirred things up. But taking it all round it was a good enough winter voyage, and we both enjoyed it thoroughly. At Tunis we drove out to Sidi bou Said and lunched at the Downes' delightful little house high on a cliff over the Mediterranean. At Alexandria we spent the day with the Fosters. Then we had a dreadful time shifting the luggage etc. from one boat to another, and forcing our way through the red tape of the Egyptians which is the most binding in the world. But it was all done at last. We had a lovely sail in a little boat with a big lateen sail and an Arab skipper across the great harbour to another harbour to join the *Belkas*. I was allowed to take the tiller the whole way across. The *Belkas* was a nice little ship too, very comfortable, only all the stewards etc. were Greek, and the cooking a bit upsetting. But by good luck she was not going straight to Syria, so we had a most interesting roundabout voyage. We went first to Port Said, where we spent some hours and a lot of money ashore. The we sailed across to Cyprus with cargo for Limasol, Larnaca and Famagusta, going to all three ports, in the first two just anchoring in the bay while the local people came off in sailing boats in spite of a biggish sea and wind and took the cargo off out of the bay. At Famagusta there is a proper harbour, and we went ashore there for the best part of a day, and Genia picked and ate her first orange off the tree, and I caught a large green speckled chameleon, and we walked round the old fortifications of the crusaders, and went into their cathedral, now a mosque, and I read the inscription on the grave of an abbot or bishop who was buried in 1315. A marvellous place, all ancient ruin and orange groves. Then we sailed over to Beyrouth and spent a day there. Then up the coast to Tripoli. Here we had some excitement. About half way up from Beyrouth the engines went wrong, and we were drifting at large. Luckily the wind had gone down and was off the shore. For about two hours we were drifting about helpless, while they did some sort of repairs. After Tripoli, where there is a mosque with sacred fish which come up to be fed and smack their lips at

the faithful, we sailed up to Turkey, to Mersin, where I spent the
day fishing, and then the next day came in to Alexandretta, a fine
bay, with huge mountains all round with snow on the tops. Here
after a bit we saw a boat coming off entirely full of Ernest and
his family. We then had a tremendous long drive up into the
mountains and through the pass called the Syrian Gates, a terrifying affair, twisting round hairpin bends above precipitous
drops, and through wild villages in the hills, and then down on
to the plain of Antioch, a lovely place, with the great Sea of
Antioch and mountains all round it, and in the flat plain three
great rivers, like the rivers of Norfolk, running through reedy
banks. This is where we shall be sailing in little boats.[1] Here we
met Turcomans and Kurds and Armenians, all in their primitive
dress, absolutely untouched by any civilisation whatever, except
the fine road across the plain, which the French are making
really very good indeed.[2] Then leaving the plain we climbed up
again, this time through desert stony hills without one particle of
vegetation, though all over the place there were colossal ruins
built with huge stones, so that at some time in the very distant
past there must have been whole towns living there. We saw the
tents of the nomads. Towards evening we saw Aleppo, a magnificent citadel like the castle of Edinburgh, rising up among low
hills covered with ploughed land. Well, that's that. And here we
are. I got through the journey pretty well, only ending up with
rather a bad go of pains and headache, which, however, seems
to have lifted again this morning.

I have been to the Consulate, but no letters from you have yet
arrived. Plenty from other people, and the newspapers from the
Manchester Guardian. I have told the M.G. to send no papers to
Ludderburn while we are away. The only papers that will come
are some Chinese and some New Zealand fishing and shooting
journals, which I want kept. Please throw away the M.G.s, but
keep anything else. I dare say your first envelope is on its way by
now.

Aleppo is a far finer city than I had expected, though the thing
that so far has impressed me most has been the Syrian Gates and
the great plain in which lies the Sea of Antioch.

Ernest and Dora are in good form, and the children as good
as usual, but I must say it seems a little queer now after two years

of living with them all in *Swallows and Amazons* and *Swallowdale*, to meet them once more as actual human beings running about. My lot somehow seem to me the solider, but Ernest's are very nice, and eager to know 'what is going to happen to us next?' They have, of course, adopted Genia completely.

With much love from both of us.

Your loving son,

Arthur

Tell the brats that yesterday we met a long camel caravan, thirty or forty, each with his head tied by a long rope to the tail of the one in front of him.

1　AR brought with him to Syria, as a present, a dinghy, which the Altounyans named *Peter Duck*. She served as sister-ship to *Beetle*.
2　Syria had become a French protectorate after the break-up of the Ottoman Empire in the First World War.

To Edith R. Ransome

Feb. 21 1932　　　　　　　　　　　　　　　　　　　　　Aleppo.

My dearest Mother,

I am today feeling pretty sick and sorry for myself after my first inoculation for typhoid. Much worse than vaccination, though Genia was done at the same time, and does not feel it at all, which makes me feel all the worse. I feel sick, headachy and bone-achy, with a swelled up arm . . . The doctor, blast him, is delighted.

Up to last night, Feb. 20, I have done 101 pages of rather putrid rough copy for the new book[1] I started on Feb. 4. But it is dreadful rough stuff, merely shaping out the sort of way things are to go. Very little of it will be in the final draft. I want very much to have the bulk of the rough copy done by the middle of April at latest. I want about 400 pages of it, so that I can afford to throw away as much as will rightly cut out.

Bits of it are pretty exciting . . . though you won't like it because nearly all of it takes place in a sailing vessel, actually at sea, and in harbour, making ready to leave.

I have been playing tennis with the children every day, and am beginning to hold my own with them!

The day before yesterday Dora, Booshy,[2] Titty and I drove out to a queer little hill about seven miles away, passing over a non-existent road, through a queer stone-built village, and past mud ones, with all the houses with eggshell tops made of mud. Under the little hill is a natural spring coming out of a cave. The spring fades away into the ground quite soon after it rises, but actually in the spring itself are quantities of tiny fish, like minnows, which must have been put there three thousand years ago, by the Hittites, who went in for sacred fish. There are remains of very ancient building by the spring, and the whole hill is one mass of ancient pottery, mostly pre-Roman.

Looking down from my workroom window, I see a long narrow street in which Arabs play with bicycles (half a dozen of them hire a bicycle together, and while one rides, all the others run alongside, sharing the fun by just hanging on). Regardless absolutely of this modernity, long caravans of camels pass bringing in stone from the desert. Also there are donkeys carrying everything possible, from a chest of drawers to a gramophone, from a sack of flour to a gorgeously dressed sheik. It is really great fun. The weather is lovely, though a good deal hotter already than ever we have had it at Ludderburn in midsummer. Sometimes a dull day and hard frost. But as sure as fate the next day will be a perfect specimen of the best kind of midsummer. I work with my window open and no heating, never wear a coat, and mostly go about in shirtsleeves when on the tennis courts. Too hot even for a sweater. Genia is really enjoying the sunshine.

> Much love from your affectionate son
>> Arthur

1   *Peter Duck.*
2   Brigit Altounyan.

To E. T. Scott

March 2 1932   Aleppo.

Dear Ted,

I was delighted to get your letter with the glad news that you are now a ship-owner, same's myself (though I had the news before from less official sources). I am very glad about it.[1] And it was jolly to think of you at the Wateredge.

Storrs is the best place to live at from the point of view of the little boat. They have a good boathouse, and plenty of sheltered water. There is none at the Wateredge. But the Wateredge is our favourite port of call. It's lovely to sail up there from Bowness, tie up to the little private Wateredge Pier, and feed on the lawn with the little boat bobbing at the pier end just below one.

Another thing to do at that end of the lake is to sail and subsequently row up the river. You can get a good long way. Then there is Wray Bay, and White Cross Bay (both good perch fishing places). Have you got your Cruising Association burgee yet? You want the smallest or next to smallest size, and you also want Borwick's to make you a little revolving vane flagstaff for it to hoist it at your masthead. Borwick makes pretty bad ones. I dare say Hanson[2] will tell you where to get something really light and efficient. Do take the very first chance you can of going up to town and looking in at Chiltern Court to see the C.A. rooms, library, etc., and chiefly Hanson himself.

I wish we were going to be at Ludderburn at Easter.

N.B. Don't take the boat out of the water more than you can help. E.g. Don't take her out of the water except for the actual journey to some other water, unless you have real reasons for so doing. Bad for her.

Don't go and get drowned, till I am there to fish you out!![3]

I am getting on with my book and have banged out about 130 pp. but I haven't reached the moment yet when it suddenly begins to hop about on its own legs. The bulk of what I have done will be scrapped before the finish. It has so far only occasional glimpses of the right metal.

But as a health resort this place is decidedly poor. It appears that everybody counts on getting malaria here. Every member of this household has had it. They have also had typhoid in the house and smallpox. I have been having a frightful time with typhoid inoculations, which stirred up my old blood poisoning trouble. I am now through two doses, but there is another to come. Ophthalmia is also endemic, and I am, of course, being bothered by that, too. Great nuisance. Still, the output, mucky as it is, gets kept up, and if I can keep on producing muck at this pace, I shall have caught up arrears by the end of March and be no worse off than I was last year. The mosquitoes are beginning, so malaria may descend on me before then. The locals look on that as inevitable, and are mildly hurt that I curse them for not having warned us.

However, humanly speaking, we are enjoying ourselves. I get in a couple of sets of mild lawn tennis nearly every day between lunch and tea. Work from an early breakfast until lunch. And then again from four until a latish dinner.

I can't pretend to think much of the idea of Ayerst's coming in again through the reporter's room.[4] UNLESS he is as good at concrete description as he is bad at abstract exposition. But I'm glad you've got a second string among the trebles in the corridor. Your Mug news was all new. Mug had told me that they had decided to have no more at least for the present. Gorblimey I'm glad I'm a hundred and fifty.

Oh yes. I meant to tell you about Blakeholme. This is one of the best islands, but the damned parodies of seascouts have been trying to build a causeway to it from the shore, thereby creating a real danger to navigation. It is no longer safe as it used to be to sail between Blakeholme and the shore. The way to the landing-place is now to sail past the island on the outer side, and then, giving a good clearance to the submerged rocks at the south end, to come round it and up the inside FROM THE SOUTH, when you will find a delightful little landing-place of fine shingle, and a very good place for a camp. This was the island mostly used as Wild Cat Island, and you will see Cormorant Island from it (proper name, Silver Holme) with the bare tree and nearly always the cormorants, six of them, perched on the boughs or fishing.

WHY *Pimpernel*?

I am (secretly) horribly homesick, though prepared to stick it a bit longer, so long as I have hopes of coming back with the book more or less done. But the thought that it's already March, with daffodils, and (thank you very much for the snowdrops) fishing beginning, and the time come round to have *Swallow* launched again is very upsetting.

Genia is very well. She has been inoculated too, but the germs simply curled up and ran away or shrivelled. They had no effect on her at all. She enjoys her lawn tennis very much, and is getting to be as good as the children.

Titty A.B. is working hard helping to produce pictures for the new book. She is most comically like her imaginary self. Ditto Roger. The others have rather shot up with the years.

DID YOU FIND A MESSAGE ON THE OUTSIDE OF AN ENVELOPE BEGGING FOR ONE OF THE TYPEWRITTEN COPES of the old *Aladdin* play I wrote for Peggy and her friends at the Withington School?[5] If one can be found I should be most grateful, and would send it back if necessary. This is urgent.

Go on considering your health. Let everything slide but that. Take all the holidays you can get. It's for the paper's good as well as for your own!!!

I don't see why you shouldn't go to the Broads for the last week of Dick's holidays, taking the *Pimp* with you and towing her astern of whatever craft you live in. Think of the fun of going shopping in her. No week ashore will set you up as much as that sailing week did last year.

Yours ever,

Arthur Ransome

1   Ransome had found an unsinkable boat for Scott (see *Autobiography*, p. 340). Scott named her *Pimpernel*.
2   Herbert Hanson (1875–1958), long-serving Secretary of The Cruising Association, to whom AR dedicated *Missee Lee*.
3   Scott died in a boating accident on Windermere on 22 April. (*Autobiography*, pp. 343–4.)
4   David Ayerst, the future historian of the *Guardian*.
5   For the *Aladdin* play, which was performed in 1928. The script is preserved in the Ransome archive at Abbot Hall.

To Edith R. Ransome

April 13 1932   Aleppo.

My dear Mother,
    Please do not forward any more letters, as we are starting back almost at once, though still uncertain by what boat. We are

trying to catch the good old *Scottish Prince*, so as to come back with our nice stewards and skipper, and only a handful of passengers. But she is somewhere in Cyprus, and we do not know yet for certain if we shall be able to join her. If not, we shall be coming much less comfortably by P. and O.

MORNING SPLASHES – Ransome's drawing for *Peter Duck*

I have done 310 pages of the book, and am stuck pretty badly, and much bothered by duodenals. Hence this flight home . . . I dare not risk things going on getting worse, and making it impossible to get the book done in time for this year. 310 pages is a jolly good lot, but the remaining 100 pages or so need a lot of spirit and jump, and, at the moment, I haven't got any.

So, one way or another we shall be on our way home before you get this.

Your letter after your return to Leeds came here today. We were glad to get such good news of everybody.

The fishing seems to have been pretty awful so far. I had a letter from my favourite pupil, Charles Renold,[1] today, and he says he fished the whole of the Easter week-end without getting a single rise, or bite as he puts it. Very sad, as he has spent the whole winter tying flies for himself. He has tied about 500 wet flies and is now starting on dry ones. Undeterred, it seems, by his misfortunes at Easter, because luckily no-one else was getting any either.

Genia is looking forward to getting home.

I want to go to Lowestoft for a few days, to get the background right for some important scenes in the first part of the book, which is now sketched in with blanks, so as to leave room for what I want. I shall probably do that as soon as I get back.

Then I think all will be pretty plain sailing with the revision, though, of course, I shan't be able to do anything else until it's done. Ernest has looked at some of the bits of it, and likes them better than anything in the other two books, but I know very well indeed how thoroughgoing and wholesale a pulling about the whole thing needs.

Well, well. In a way it's sad to be coming back. But it is getting most fiercely hot, and something or other here makes my inside perfectly beastly. Very disappointing. But it has been a most interesting visit, and I have got 310 pp. of rough copy out of it. I've never done quite so much in the time before.

> Very much love,
>> [no signature]

Later. Cyprus.

We caught the *Scottish Prince* and as soon as we have finished loading shall be sailing for Rotterdam, arriving about May 1.

Address: Passenger in S/S *Scottish Prince*,
                   care of Furness Shipping and Agency Co.,
                   Rotterdam,
                   Holland.

We shall probably cross to Harwich, and so *via* Lowestoft home, but the boat is collecting mixed cargo, and we may have a longer voyage than we expect.

1   See Appendix, Arthur Ransome's Correspondents.

To Edith R. Ransome

Nov. 30. 1932.

My dearest Mother,

I cannot resist giving you the good news at once. I have just had a TELEGRAM from the publishers saying that P.D. is already being REPRINTED!!!.......

And it's only been out a month!

We shall pull through after all.

I stand on my cranium   Love. A.

★

PETER DUCK was generally well received by the critics, and Hugh Walpole, in an act which repaired a broken friendship, reviewed the book enthusiastically in the *Observer*, provoking Ransome to comment in a letter to his mother of 29 November 1932: 'this will be enough to make absolutely sure of P.D.'s success'. One reviewer, however, was not judged by the customers to be sufficiently enthusiastic, and in mid-November *Time and Tide* published the following letter from Colin Bradley-Williams *et. al*:

Sir,
    In the Children's Book Supplement of *Time and Tide* [5 November 1932] we read: 'I shall be surprised if the reception given to *Peter Duck* is as cordial as heretofore . . . presumably most young Ransome fans are . . . well up in *Treasure Island*. The few who are not will, no doubt, enjoy this story; but the others – ? to one reader, at least, this book is a sad disappointment.' We wish to protest very strongly against this review of *Peter Duck*. We have all read *Treasure Island* and like it but we do not feel it can be compared with this book. The adventures in *Peter Duck* might happen to any boy or girl nowadays, whereas *Treasure Island* is not so real to us. We feel we are with the children in Mr. Ransome's books, and that we know them as friends. We suggest that the reviewer should have read the other two books carefully before she was sarcastic about one of the best books we have ever read.
                    Yours sincerely,
                            Colin Bradley-Williams (*age 11*)
                            John Craster (*age 10*)
                            Anthony Hancock (*age 9*).

It happened that the Hancock family, inspired by *Swallows and Amazons*, had taken to keeping a Log-Book, in which all important and interesting events were recorded, and important documents were saved; and so we know what happened next. 'Miss Lorna Lewis, the reviewer, wrote to the paper protesting that she had every right to her own opinion – and someone else suggested that children should be seen and not heard – another that 'out of the mouths of babes . . .' However there was no ill feeling [Lorna Lewis sent a Christmas card to Anthony, and wrote to his mother, 'I have been getting into great trouble with my own godson over *Peter Duck* . . .'] And on Christmas morning

THIS CAME!

WITH·BEST·WISHES
FOR · A · HAPPY
CHRISTMAS
&
TO·ANTHONY·HANCOCK
FROM ARTHUR RANSOME

ANTHONY HANCOCK, JOHN CRASTER AND COLIN BRADLEY-WILLIAMS, SAILING TO THE RESCUE OF PETER DUCK WHEN HE WAS IN DANGER FROM TIME AND TIDE.

To Edith R. Ransome

Feb 27 1933   Low Ludderburn

My dearest Mother,

The latest of my mishaps is as follows. Last Wednesday, as work went well in the morning and it was a fine day and I wanted to do something towards the reduction of my fair round belly I went for a walk, and, with a view to having the wind at my back during the long straight walk down the Winster Road, I went the usual way round, to the cross roads, and then down the steep hill to the ford. The hills looked fine and I was prancing along in great good cheer when .... I came to myself to find that I was lying on my back with my head down the hill and a lot too much blood in it, squeaking aloud with a most violent pain in my right ankle. I suppose I had turned it on a stone or something, but the hill there is very steep, and I must have come down a pretty fair wallop. Things out of my trouser pockets were a couple of yards farther down the hill. Well I stopped squeaking and pulled myself to the side of the road, where it was beastly wet but still somehow less inhospitable, and after a bit set out to crawl home. The pain in my ankle was so frantic that I did not know I also cut open the knee of the other leg until I felt it wet in my breeches just as I was getting home. The ankle is not broken.* I got to bed at once, and the next day it was swolled up something wonderful, but the roads were impassable with snow, and anyhow I couldn't put my foot on a pedal to drive the car or anything. So here I have been ever since. Kelsall turned up very nobly to see if he could do anything, but all seems to be going on all right. Swelling gone down a lot, and I think definitely now no actual break, though I must say at first it looked like it. So here I lie, not in idleness, but banging out my regular five to eight pages a day . . . pretty bad pages I fear and all to be thrown away later, but still something in the way of raw material. I've never done such a thing in my life before. I mean I've sprained my ankle dozens of times, but such a violent affair as that never, and I hope I never do again. We both foresaw weeks of beastliness like those poor Genia had to endure when she broke hers. But I think now that it is all in one piece and not broken. Pretty silly wasn't it? Johnny Head in Air, of course, but I'd rather have fallen as he did into nice water full of goldfish.

I've been reading *Catriona*. It really is awfully good. So completely realised in its chosen details.

Just the very day I came my cropper I had put the first coat of ground paint on the back of the car which had peeled to bare biscuit tin and looked most disreputable. As soon as I can hobble again effectively I hope to have the car looking almost

respectable. I've already put a coat of black on the mudguards!
No more news. Much love.

[no signature]

*   It was – E.R.R. (note in his mother's hand).

To Edith R. Ransome

March 2 1933   Low Ludderburn

My dearest Mother,
  Thank you very much for the two guineas though I hate to
think it must go into the pocket of the villain who so stirred up
my leg that I was awake most of last night with the blasted thing.
Everything was quite quiet and happy till he came. But I suppose
he had to examine, and it's no use cursing.
  I did a review yesterday, short, but hope to get at the book[1]
again this evening. It goes very slowly but is beginning to feel
more like a story. But the rough copy which, as always, comes
out mighty slowly, is very very rough. However I've had a nice
letter from Cape's saying don't worry, because my beastly books
always do seem to go through these troubles, or words to that
effect, and to say that they 'very much like the title'. It is a nice
title, though I say it.
  Oh yes, I don't think I told you. Nelsons have climbed down
very handsomely. There is to be no cheap edition[2] until I agree
that it is desirable, and when there is, the original 15% will be
paid on it. I don't want a cheap edition just yet, because the sales
at the full price are steadily going up, owing to the other books.
They are nothing much, but last year they were more than three
times what they were three years before.
  I do not like writing in bed, because it deprives me of the best
part of the business, which is prancing up and down the room.
It's beastly having to stay still when things get stuck.
  All our snow has gone, though of course there is lots in the
district. And Genia was driven into town yesterday, by the
Kelsalls and came back with a commode slung on to the back of
the Kelsalls' car. There was a great time signalling in the
morning,[3] between her and the Ks. The Colonel has added a

new signal to our previous two, raising the number of possible messages to 74. He has devised an elaborate code, hoisting one, two and three of the signals in different orders. Genia was able to arrange from the terrace of our house yesterday that the Colonel could drive her in to Windermere, and that he would call for her for that purpose at three o'clock in the afternoon. General triumph all round!

Well, fishing begins the day after tomorrow, but with all the snow water about, it will be later than usual, and I usually find that March is too early, except for the lake fish which are quick into condition. So from that point of view I don't mind lying [down].

The main point of the new book is two other children turn up and get acquainted with the Swallows and Amazons in a rather amusing way, and then get involved in one of Captain Nancy's colossal plans for adventure. The details I will not tell you. All the others are in it too, but the main character interest of the book is in the new couple, and in Peggy, who in the previous books has never really had a fair chance, being so much dominated by Nancy. One at least of the two new characters you won't be able to help liking. I find her a most entertaining companion, and in fact I more than half owe my broken ankle to listening to her conversation, instead of watching my feet.

The season is darting on in spite of the snow, and we shall be having daffodils in no time. They are well up all over the place. Also the narcissi. And our first primroses were out some time ago. Actually sunshine again today, which will hurry them on still more.

Well, now you have all the news.

So I stop,

                    With much love and thanks,
                    Your affectionate son,

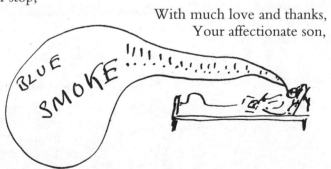

1   *Winter Holiday.*
2   Of *Old Peter's Russian Tales.*
3   For Colonel Kelsall's signals, see *Autobiography*, p. 327, and
    Winter Holiday.

To Edith R. Ransome

March 3 1933   Low Ludderburn
Sunday

My dear Mother,
    Ankle going on a bit better today so I was not kept awake so
much. So I expect all will be well in the end.
    I grimly keep up my five pages a day, but they are dull pages
without the peripatetic stimulus. I need a floor to prance on and
legs to prance with before I can get things going. The swelling
has gone down a good deal, except for the place below the ankle
bone where I am supposed to have torn a muscle a bit.
    But I feel more cheerful than I did last night, when, I fear, I
wrote rather gloomily. No need.
    The new book is *much* more difficult than any of the other
time; it is going to be a tough job all the way through. And *then*
everybody will curse me for not letting the Swallows and
Amazons be the principal characters. They are there all the time,
but the main interest is in my new couple. This makes light and
shade jolly difficult after being accustomed to foreground
treatment in the other books. However, if I can get the thing
roughed out by the end of April and then forget it on the Broads,
I think I ought to be able to pull it into shape in time for the
autumn as usual.
    With much love,
            Your affectionate son,
                                            A.

I am going to
wear nautical
trousers in future
to disguise my
thickened ankle!!

To Norah Templeton Macan
(secretary to Jonathan Cape and
his partner G. Wren Howard)

June 1 1933   Low Ludderburn

Dear Miss Macan,

Thank you for the German books.

The translation is extremely bad.[1] The translator has not been content to leave out parts of my manuscript. He has inserted original remarks of his own, toned up my writing in places where for very good reasons I have been soft pedalling, and gone so far as to put into the mouth of Captain Flint a sentimental comment on the children of the very kind I most detest.

There is nothing to be done about this sort of thing. One simply has to grin and bear it. The translator evidently has thought it his job to bring my book into line with other German children's books (not good ones) and has altered, cut out, and worst of all inserted rubbish, exactly as he liked.

I do not think there is the least likelihood of their wanting *Swallowdale* after this, and, anyhow, *Swallowdale* even more than *Swallows and Amazons* does depend for its effects on the author keeping quiet. It would be worse ruined than S. and A. if treated in the same way. *Peter Duck* would lose less.

Anyhow some of the results of S. and A. Germanised are very funny, and I have laughed as well as being pretty cross. They must not have another without a hard and fast agreement to keep to the text.

Descriptive paragraph about *Winter Holiday*. I can do it in one word. The word is BILGE.

But I suppose for commercial reasons I ought to amplify that and disguise it. I will do my best to send a false, lying and optimistic blurb before the end of the week.

Yours sincerely,

Arthur Ransome

Postscript. I hope you are fully recovered and no longer needing an electric stove to help out the warmth of the year's hottest day.

1   *Swallows and Amazons.*

To G. Wren Howard

July 11 1933   Low Ludderburn

Dear Howard,

Will this do?

['This' was a draft of the 'descriptive paragraph' about *Winter
Holiday* required for the publisher's catalogue.]

I wrote a draft of it some time ago but to tell you the truth did
not like to send it because I was so afraid I was not going to get
done in time.

I have now got the whole thing on paper, and am frantically
working at the revision, having the usual awful struggle with it.

I do wish to goodness you were a little nearer, to tell me how
to work the damned beginning which, as ever, bothers me
simply out of my life.

The pictures are still in the state of the very roughest pencil
sketches or rather suggestions. I go for them when the text is
done.

I am hammering right through to the end and must then
somehow reorganise the beginning.

WHEN DO YOU GO OFF ON CARE-FREE HOLIDAY?
(comparatively care-free?).

Yours sincerely,

Arthur Ransome

*

He was even more despondent when he wrote to Howard again
two weeks later on 24 July: 'I am having the most frightful
struggle to pull it into shape . . . The pictures are started, but I
am letting them slide until I can get the manuscript out of the
house.' His publishers, anxious for Christmas sales of *Winter
Holiday*, could not afford to allow their printing schedule to slip
if the proposed November publication was to be kept. At the
same time, they knew full well that harassing their author might
only result in complete blockage. So it was agreed that Ransome
should send his manuscript as soon as it was finished direct to
J. and J. Gray, the Edinburgh printers, without anyone at Cape
seeing it first. At the end of July Ransome tries, not altogether
successfully, to reassure Howard.

To G. Wren Howard

July 31 1933   Low Ludderburn

Dear Howard,

There's a terrible lot still to be done to the beast.

Pictures. You can count on 20 full-pagers, as in *Peter Duck*, plus a few small insets, not more than four, I think, illustrating particular points in the text, and a bundle of tailpieces to shove in where chapters end high on the page.

I will, in sending the book to Grays, send them at the same time an accurate account of the picture space. The insets, I think, will amount to three thirds of a page and one half page. Not more than two pages in all.

But 'Giminy!' as Nancy would say, it is the very dickens of a job to get some starch into this dish cloth.

Well, I do hope you have a really good holiday, with some sailing in it. If you happen on a nice harbour or estuary, let me enjoy a picture postcard view of it. I promise not to bother you unless in case of the most urgent necessity. Good luck to you.

Yours sincerely,

Arthur Ransome.

★

After three weeks had passed Ransome was still pouring out his troubles. By this time there were scarcely ten weeks left before the books were due on sale in the shops.

★

To G. Wren Howard

Aug 22 1933   Low Ludderburn

Dear Howard,

I have been most horribly bothered by this book, or rather by the end of it. I am absolutely blessed if I know what is wrong with it, but I know jolly well that something is wrong, and I do hope that you will cast an eye upon it, a keen bright eye fresh from the holidays, and spot at once what it is that has gone wrong, and how it can be put right.

I think this time I have got the beginning more or less right, but there is a sort of horrid breathlessness at the end, which is not the sort of breathlessness that is desirable, but something quite different. I may have done it by trying to cut down too much. Or trying to run too many characters at once. Or over-insistence on something or other. Anyway I can't see what's wrong, and yet I know that something is.

So do, for goodness sake, have a look at the proofs when they come along.

I hope you had a really good holiday and got some decent sailing.

Yours sincerely,
Arthur Ransome

My next year's book is going to be done in May.

★

Three days later Ransome reported that the script had finally gone to Edinburgh. 'I am only pleased about the beginning because I am able to compare it with the awful bog it was,' he wrote to Howard. 'Bad as the book is as a whole, I am pretty glad to have got it out of the house. For a long time I thought it simply couldn't be done.' Now it was the pictures that vexed him. 'John is my trouble. In two of my best drawings he has

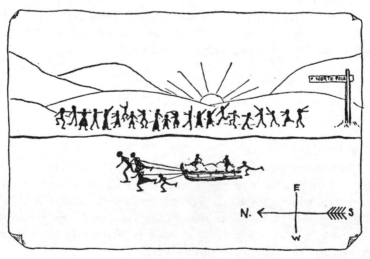

NANCY'S QUESTION

turned into a clumsy lout of seventeen or eighteen. I can't keep him young.' At last, on 11 September, his drawings still unfinished, Ransome accepted graciously a word of praise. 'I am most awfully pleased that you like *Winter Holiday*,' he wrote to Howard. 'I felt so hopeless about it for so long that I was sure everybody else would feel the same, and that you would be dreadfully disappointed. And, of course, I know well enough that there is a good deal of kindness in your verdict. But I am most awfully pleased all the same.'

★

To Edith R. Ransome [extracts]
Sept 24 1933[*]   Low Ludderburn

My dear Mother,

Today, at 12.15 p.m., I finished the endpaper map, very chaste in black and white, with tracks to the Pole in red and the shores of the lake and the islands in blue. That ends the whole job, except for the reading of the page proofs.

I have had a very nice letter from Mr. Wilson of Bumpus', who seems to think the beastly book will go all right. But my hat the pictures are just awful.

I swiped one of your sheep sketches and did one from it for one of the tailpieces, and for another I collared a rock or two, and a curving road from one of your sketches which I liked very much. It does not look so nice in my version as it did in yours, which is, alas, not surprising. Then I got Barbara to do a kettle and a few other details, which I similarly swiped. But these few things stolen from artists do not make up for the great mass of bad drawing contributed by myself.

Genia says I must never try to illustrate a book again, unless exclusively with boats and sea.

On Tuesday I go to Manchester, and then on with Charles Renold for a week's fishing on the Broads (in a motor cruiser!!!)
    Very much love,
          Your affectionate son,   Arthur

[*] Operated on for appendicitis at Norwich – on the 29th. E.R.R.
    (Note written in the recipient's hand.)

To Edith R. Ransome

The Watch House,
St. Mawes,
Cornwall.[1]

Dec 1 1933

My dearest Maw,

Rain today for the first time since we have been here. Really rather welcome. A good big southerly wind, driving the rain up the bay and in at our windows.

It's been blowing hard for some time. Yesterday we had a lively passage on the little steamboat across to Falmouth for shopping. Three or four days ago we saw the two-masted schooner *Mynonie R. Kirby* that sailed from Falmouth to the South Seas, and lost both her masts 100 miles west of Brest and is now adrift somewhere beyond the Scillies, her crew having been rescued by lifeboat and breeches buoy. A rather dismal end to such a venture. She was got up like an old-time man-of-war, with a white band, high bulwarks, and a row of black gun ports, really very much like the *Hispaniola* of *Treasure Island*. She looked lovely, but there must have been something rotten somewhere, for her to lose her masts in the way she did.

Hanson has gone up to town today for a meeting of the Cruising Association. We shall miss him very much, as it will be a fortnight before he comes back.

You haven't answered my question about Joyce's book. Has it got the Methuen prize?

I wish I had a good plot for my next book. It is to be placed on the Broads, with all those rivers, and hiding places in the dykes, and the little stretches of open water. Really a lovely setting, with herons and bitterns, and fish, very wild except just in the holiday months. But, as usual, though I have five youthful characters and one old lady, I haven't a glimmering of a plot. (Keep this secret: about the Broads, I mean.)

We are both enjoying this place very much indeed. And we are very cross with Sidgie that she did not long ago tell us that Sidgland was just about one of the very best countries in England, or rather near England, for the local people talk of going to England when they go farther East than the Saltash Bridge above Plymouth. We shall probably stay here for ever!

On the other hand there is no fishing at all except at sea, and not much there. None of the locals we have met think it worth bothering about. But simply as a harbour and a place for boats, I've never seen a better. I wish I had *Swallow* here . . . though I couldn't really sail her yet, because of not being able to pull or lift. But it's a pleasure just to see other people sailing.

No more news about *Winter Holiday*. I hope there are stacks of it in the Leeds shops.

Much love,

your affectionate son

Arthur

1   Ransome had gone to Cornwall to recuperate from his operation for appendicitis (see *Autobiography*, p. 349).

To G. Wren Howard

St. Mawes,

Dec 3 1933   Cornwall.

Dear Howard,

I say, you really are going it. Today's advertisement in the *Observer* is something tremendous. I couldn't believe it referred to me . . . turned pinker than ever when I saw it. And now Humbert Wolfe. And the Junior Book Club, too, looks well. If it wasn't my book I should buy it at once. Well, I do hope that this time there won't be horrid figures in red ink showing how much you have lost on it, when we meet to argue over next year's illustrations.

We have been over looking at *Industry*. A huge vessel, and with really lovely lines fore and aft. Her twin was sailed home in a gale by her late owner, an old man of seventy odd, who had taken her over to France and was returning single-handed. But, *Industry* herself has had her looks ruined by the silly business of having no side decks, and letting the cabin trunk grow straight up out of the topsides. The result is the most colossal room inside, and a great upper deck fit for forty men to dance a hornpipe on. You must really see if you can't slip down after Christmas to have a look at her, when she is a bit nearer completion.

The size of her is terrifying. A huge galleon . . . God help anything she bumps. 46 feet sounds nothing, but when you stand up inside it, among those ribs, it's like being in a cathedral. And when you look at her from outside, up on the hard, it's like looking at a prehistoric ten times magnified kind of hippopotamus.

Well, I won't babble, even of boats.

But I must say again that I do hope that the sales of *Winter Holiday* will justify the tremendous splash of those advertisements. I should really hate to see those red ink figures once again.

Yours ever,

Arthur Ransome

To Charles and Margaret Renold

Dec 28 1933

St. Mawes,
Cornwall.

Dear Charles and Margaret,

Your card was a real beauty. Who took that photograph? It is a charming thing, Charles to the life, all hope, though fishing the all but hopeless pool, and the old bridge, and the whole a really admirable piece of composition. We both like it enormously.

Was Margaret's uncle's boat called *Norada*? Did she cruise in company with another big yacht? They seem to have impressed the natives. We had luncheon with some people (the Worths)[1] who have built a lovely house on the Helford River, just opposite Manaccan Creek and below Port Navas. We are invited to use their moorings, so really we almost HAVE to get hold of a ship, just in order to sail into the Helford River and tie up to one of their beautiful buoys, guaranteed to hold an eighty tonner. Funny to think that Margaret after escaping from the sea in youth should be fated to come back to it in her wiser years.

I suppose Charles has done no grayling fishing, or I should have heard of it. By now the fish will be thinking of going off. They always seem to be getting flabby in January, though I had a good basket once at Ormside above Appleby about the first week.

I am still putting myself daily in a cider press and trying to squeeze out a plot. I have masses of things to happen . . . stranding on Breydon . . . voyage in a wherry . . . meeting with a Thames barge . . . shopping at Roys[2] . . . night with an eel man . . . But main thread still to find. I think one character ought to be concentrated local knowledge, so to speak, and I think he must be my Principal Boy . . . *aet* 12 or 13 . . . living say at Horning. Then I have a pair of twins, girls, who sail with their father in a racing dinghy. They, of course, have somehow to be seduced from their allegiance to Papa in order to take part in the story. Next property is a most spirited old lady, widow, water-colour painter, living in ?boat or ?houseboat? She, I think, impressed by P.B. and perhaps the Twins also, yearns to tune up her great? nieces? nephews? and therefore gets them down to stay with her for the summer holidays with the object of using the P.B. and the twins to stimulate a livelier spirit than these two well-brought-ups (her nieces nephews?) at present possess . . . There now. What happens? How can I arrange for, say, the Twins to be left behind when the Old Lady and the others sail for Norwich, so that they have the excitement of pursuing without a boat of their own, getting lifts on wherries, tugs, barges, etc.

Do I or do I not bring Dick and Dorothea on from *Winter Holiday*, or is this lot to be an entirely independent world?

Independent, I think.

What can be devised by way of Triumph, to be achieved by effort and so to provide the happy ending that must almost to the end look as if it can't come off?

You will observe that if all the excitement of the chase right round down to Yarmouth and up the other rivers of the south, to Beccles or Norwich, is given to the Twins . . . it inevitably makes them the chief characters of the book, and tends to cut the ground from under the P.B. and the Well-brought-ups, UNLESS some major Triumph, Goal, Aim, Achievement can be devised which will be shared by the whole party, and allow the P.B. a chance of coming out strong, so that the chase etc. while giving the Twins a fine chance of spreading themselves and capturing the reader, will be as it were subservient to the whole . . . or even work as a fuse, delaying, and therefore piling up the interest of the main theme which must for this purpose be already on its way and in the reader's mind.

I am not at all sure that it is not very bad for you, as general readers!, to be let so far into the secrets of the cider press. But you can't really count Margaret a general reader. She knows too much. And Charles, too, as an engineer, knows all about the calculations of comparative weights, stresses, tensions, etc. that lie behind every job worth doing. So there you are. You see what the problem really is, and you are much more likely to spot a solution than I am, who have been in the cider press all this time, submitting to daily, even hourly extra turns of the infernal screw.

The data given above all stand as it were inside the framework of the job. There are a few outside ones which, of course, have to be so dealt with from inside that it is as if they had never existed.

Thus: concentrating the whole interest on ONE character, in the manner honoured by time and by almost all tellers of stories for boys, is easy, but doesn't meet my views. I must have a combination of collective interest and a fair share of the game for all the individuals, girls and boys. Sordid grasp at as wide an audience as possible.

Essential or all but essential to have one or more characters definitely younger than the rest. Otherwise the whole lot are themselves too conscious of infancy in comparison with the other group of characters who are grown up. Shove in a brat, and the rest gain independence at once.

Golly, what a lot of secrets I am giving away.

But, there it is. Now you know just what is wanted.

We are both, I think, wanting to get home.

We are both, I know, hugely looking forward to seeing you.

We both send you, William,[2] and other inhabitants of Turnfield,

Yours ever   A.

Coch-y-bonddhu? What about her sail? Have you been to Arnside? Or, are you letting them go on as they are? The sail is the *last* job and it would not be too late if you put it off till we are back and can all go over to Arnside together. I'd like a word with Crossfield about the angle of the yard in relation to the possible halyard and forestay combined. I think he can improve on *Swallow's*.

1   Claude Worth was an eminent yachtsman.
2   'The World's Largest Village Store' at Wroxham. Not named in *Coot Club*.
3   The Renolds' pug-dog, to be appropriated for *Coot Club*.

To Charles and Margaret Renold
March 6 1934   Low Ludderburn

Dear ?Margaret or ?Charles (whoever is the chief owner of the *Coch-y-bonddhu*)

We very wrongly took the day off today and drove over to Arnside to see the *Coch-y-bonddhu*.

She is all but finished planking, and we have to report that you are in very great luck. How the devil they do it, I don't know, but they have got hold of the most beautiful spruce for the planking, and a really lovely bit of wood for keel and stem and covering board. I think you have got a real bargain in her, and we were both full of envy.

She is too good to paint. You can paint her any time, but for the first few years let her have all the advantage of varnish. Terribly smart she's going to be. All four men were busy batting down first-rate large *copper* fastenings when we arrived. And there she was in the middle of the shop, looking almost ready to be put in the water.

They are producing a sketch for sail plan, and sending it to me, and I will at once get it ordered. I have already written to Andrews and Jeckells at Lowestoft for samples of stuff.

I have also seen Walker about a mooring. And charges for looking after her. He says £5 to cover taking care of her when afloat during the summer, bailing etc., and generally keeping an eye, hauling her up for the winter at the proper time, drying, and keeping her under cover throughout the winter.

Anything *done* to her in the way of painting, rigging etc. would be extra. But for actual looking after and wintering, the £5 would cover everything. It seems to me a lot, but I pay it myself, and I must say the Walkers do make it very pleasant to have a boat there, and I have never once gone down un-expectedly and not found *Swallow* in the pink, so to speak.

In addition to that, you will have to pay Lord Lonsdale half a crown a year.

And you will want some sort of actual mooring. I use an old motor car engine, which is sunk at the right place, and has a chain and hook attached to it with a little wooden floating buoy with *Swallow*'s name on it.

I dare say that could be picked up here as easily as anywhere.

While there at Arnside, I saw a very neat trailer, made from the back axle of a Ford. I should think Peter could produce something even better, with spring chocks to bear the little boat with proper tenderness.

My book is too elaborate, and too thrutched up. It won't go at all.

Love to both of you from us and kitten (Winkle),

A.

They propose to put her on the train to be delivered at Lakeside. You or we could meet her there and sail her to her mooring. Ready in plenty of time for Easter.

From G. Wren Howard

Thirty Bedford Square

September 4 1934   London W.C.1.

Dear Ransome,

You are all wrong of course – both of you. But if your mind is finally made up we can only accept your decision. It is a dangerous decision as you probably know, but I feel I ought to tell you why I consider it dangerous.

The book has already been announced, by means of our lists, and advertised in the trade papers and in letters to our agents all over the world. Orders have begun to come in as a result of this and of the efforts of our travellers. If we now have to say that the book cannot appear until Easter all these orders will be cancelled or reduced in size, and we shall have to start all over again. We cannot, I am sure, expect such large orders or such a big total sale in the Spring as in the Winter.

Think also of the increasing band of Ransome fans who have been carefully and laboriously coached to expect a book from you each Christmas. They are going to be, in the first place, disappointed and possibly annoyed, and then are going to buy or to have bought for them another book instead. Some fortunate ones will be able to afford *Coot Club* also in the Spring, but others will either not afford it or will not hear of it.

And do you hope to write another book for publication next

Autumn, or to appear always like a Swallow in the Spring, or to miss a year, or what?

When I last saw you I think I said that in my view you were over particular and ˙Mrs. Ransome hypercritical. I did not believe then and I don't now that the book is unpublishable even as it stands. What you read me was damn good stuff. And I still maintain that it would be far less dangerous to let the book go to the printer now, even if it were not so highly polished as you both might wish.

My advice, therefore, is, once more, to send off immediately as much of the book as you can to Gray, and to tinker with the balance for another week when it too should go to Scotland.

IT WILL ALL LOOK MUCH BETTER IN TYPE.

But I don't for a moment suppose that you will take this advice, so I have written gloomily to the unfortunate Gray, from whom I had a long letter this morning dealing with suggestions for your projected visit to Edinburgh, to say that it is all off until 1935.

The black edged envelope was indeed appropriate, though until I opened it, for one horrible moment I thought that something terrible had happened to the Chimp.

Yours sincerely,
G. Wren Howard.[1]

1   In response to this masterly letter (which sufficiently illustrates why, according to Sir Rupert Hart-Davis, his publishers regarded Ransome as a 'difficult' author) AR wrote to Howard on 6 September, pleading that 'it is just possible that I have been so close at it all the summer that I don't see clear enough to mend it'. He promised to read through the book again. In the end *Coot Club* was published on schedule. The Helene Carter drawing of Potter Heigham appeared in the American edition.

To Tabitha Lewis
Sept. 7 1934   Low Ludderburn

My dear Tabitha,

I had your letter in which you remarked 'I have married a Dock Labourer', and gave no further information except that he had blue eyes and sunburn. I have now had a postcard from you on which you say 'My name is Lewis'.

I had supposed and perhaps hoped that your first statement was a joke, but, if your name is Lewis, I suppose there is no joke about it.

But, when you tell me as little as that, you cannot expect me to say anything except that I am very sorry for your mother.

I dare say your husband's profession is more interesting than you make it sound. Dock Labourers do not usually take their wives to Paris, or have addresses 'care of' a Bank.

In any case I can have nothing against your husband's profession, even if you have accurately described it, so long as he is good at it and you think it is your mission in life to help him to be good at it. If you really care enough for him to take his friends for your friends, his family for your family (as they will be the family to which your children will belong), if you are ready to give up your dogs and your motor car, and to fill his thermos for him and cook his meals and to scrub his doorstep and keep him a clean house to come home to . . . if all this is so, you may be doing well. If on the other hand you are merely giving him an unreal background, and keeping up yourself friendships in which he cannot share, you will ruin both yourself and him. That way, I can see no hope or self-respect for either of you.

I must also say that I cannot pretend to think highly of a man, no matter what his job, who marries you without having the ordinary decency to tell your parents (or one of them at least) what he proposes to do. But that may be your fault, not his.

You do not tell me where you are living, or where his work is, or even what his name is, or where he was educated, or what are his interests, or how old he is, or what he has done so far with his life, or at whose house you met him, or what his parents are like, or, indeed, anything about him.

Your affectionate   [no signature]

PART FOUR

Before the Storm

1935–1939

Moving south in the autumn of 1935, Arthur Ransome settled on the Suffolk coast, taking with him the unfinished script of *Pigeon Post* which was causing him just as much anguish as some of the earlier books. The story of the Swallows and Amazons prospecting for gold had its roots (recorded in Ransome's diary of 1929) in the discovery by Oscar Gnosspelius, an engineer who had married Barbara Collingwood, of a new deposit of copper on Coniston Old Man. Copper had been mined in the Coniston fells for more than three hundred years but since the beginning of the century it had been increasingly uneconomic to work the mines. Abandoning his own attempts to extract the copper in 1933, Gnosspelius set up John Shaw in a one-man mine known as Horse Crag Level at Tilberthwaite, which resembles in precise detail the old mine in which Slater Bob tells the Swallows and Amazons that gold is to be found on the other side of the mountain.

So, for Ransome, the idea of *Pigeon Post* was real enough, but the writing came hard. 'AWFUL. No grip anywhere,' he confided in his diary after reading his draft script all through. 'Masses of corroborating detail needed and no tension . . . all but lifeless. I can't *think* of it.' After its publication in 1936, the book won the Carnegie Medal – the first to be awarded – though the earlier Ransome stories probably played a part in gaining him this recognition.

Meanwhile, the Ransomes had taken a house at Levington on the north shore of the River Orwell, almost opposite the yacht

anchorage at Pin Mill. Even before moving in, Arthur acquired
a seagoing yacht, a cutter, which he named *Nancy Blackett*,
'feeling that but for Nancy I should never have been able to buy
her'. With young Peter Tisbury as crew, he set sail around the
southern coast from Poole, in Dorset, in a fierce autumn gale to
bring *Nancy* to his new East Anglian home, where she was
almost at once laid up for the winter.

During the next few years his chief happiness was found in
cruising to Hamford Water (which became the setting for *Secret
Water*), down the coast to the Channel, in and out of the Suffolk
and Essex estuaries, and once even across the North Sea to
Holland. Genia refused to go with him, as *Nancy*'s galley was so
small, but he easily found young men to serve as crew, among
them Jim Clay (possibly the original of Jim Brading) and
Richard Tizard. *Nancy* gave Ransome the idea for *We Didn't
Mean to Go to Sea*, and because of her, and the yachting community which she opened to him, he lived cheerfully in Suffolk
until the outbreak of the Second World War, his life disrupted
only by the usual bouts of ill-health.

In the spring of 1939 he and Genia moved across the river to
Harkstead Hall. Of all their many residences this was perhaps
the one which suited them best, but they were only tenants and,
as it turned out, were not to live there long. An even more
important new departure was the commissioning and building
of a yacht, *Selina King*, which was launched as Britain came to
the brink of war in the Munich crisis of 1938. *Nancy Blackett*
was sold, but Ransome was not to enjoy his new ship for long
either. He offered *Selina* when the Admiralty issued an appeal for
small boats to evacuate remnants of the British Army from the
German encirclement of Dunkirk, but the yacht was rejected on
account of her tiny engine.

Pin Mill

RANSOME began 1935 with a lucky escape when he crashed his car on the way home from looking at boats in Brixham, 'It was a whole-hearted skid at pretty good speed', he wrote to Helen Ferris on 26 January, 'and the beast eventually turned over and came right side up again, hurling me out in the process. This ought to have put a stop to the Swallows and Amazons series, but I got off miraculously with a cut leg and a thundering whack on the top of the head.'

★

To the Gnosspelius Family
c/o The Butt and Oyster

Oct. 1 1935   Pin Mill, Ipswich

Dear Barbara, Oscar and Janet,

You have probably heard of the voyage of the *Nancy Blackett* already, but in case you haven't, here are the essentials.

Her name is (officially) *Electron* (until the Board of Trade get her papers through as *Nancy Blackett*, which should be any day now). She is a registered British vessel, with a small Handy Billy, auxiliary to a fine spread of sail as a Bermuda cutter.

I got a fine strong lad as crew to do all the hard work of pulley hauly etc.

We started out from Poole on Sept. 14, just as the famous gale began. We got to Yarmouth, Isle of Wight, where we learnt that the lifeboat had been warned to be ready by the coastguards at the Needles who had observed our approach. We got a few seas aboard, and the dinghy charged our transom and broke its own, but luckily I had foreseen something of the kind, and had coiled thirty fathom of warp in the dinghy, which we hooked out with a boathook and let tow astern, which kept the dinghy quiet, made the seas break a little before they reached us, and so generally made things much better. Sunday we lay quiet in Yarmouth. Monday we bussed to Cowes to get a storm jib made, as we had none. That night when we got back came the climax of the gale, of which you no doubt read in the newspapers. In Yarmouth, two boats were flung on the breakwater, seven or eight sunk, one man was drowned, and the lifeboat was out three times during the night INSIDE THE HARBOUR. On the first occasion it was an hour late in answering the S.O.S. because the boarding boat swamped and sank in the twenty yards between the lifeboat and the quay. We spent the whole night fighting off a huge motor cruiser which had moored alongside us. The rain, wind etc. was quite indescribable, so I shan't try. Poor *Nancy* survived, bruised a great deal but not seriously damaged. The dinghy, of course, swamped and sank, and was further broken up, and we were lucky to get the remnants aboard about four in the morning, in the general turmoil. We could not hear each other speak even when shouting into each other's ears. The only noise to be heard above that of wind and water was the S.O.S., now here now there, from the klaxon horns of terrified motor cruisers.

Next day things quieted down quickly, and late in the day a steamer came across from the mainland, and I went back with it, and so to London, to see what could be done with the insurance.

I got back, loaded with all the things we had found wanting on the first hop, on Friday the 20th, after signing the lease of the Ipswich house,[1] and getting the car from Poole to London (60 yachts were wrecked in Poole harbour, so it was lucky we got her away when we did).

Saturday September 21. Head wind, but sunshine, and we sailed with motor going as well, from Yarmouth to Portsmouth where we tied up in Haslar Creek. Another buster. Saw 'my cousin' Lt. Cdr. Godfrey Ransome, who strongly advised delay. But Monday was a good day with a moderate wind, the first we had seen, and off we went. We sailed from Haslar at 1 p.m. and got into Newhaven at 11 p.m. after a queer long push along the coast watching the blaze of Brighton, etc. In Newhaven we tied up for a few hours, but at 3.30 I woke my young man and gave him some hot soup, and at 4.30 we were off again, just scraping into Dover with another buster, which gave poor old *Nancy* about as much as she could chew.

The night in Dover harbour in the wick, it was so wild that we had to let out every inch of chain we had, and just when the dock gates opened about eleven at night, the wind and rain etc. were such that I could hardly see the lights. It took us three quarters of an hour to get our chain, though we used Billy to steam up to it, getting an inch or two at a time. However it was over at last, and we did not bump anything, and tied up in the

Granville dock alongside a barge at about midnight. Wednesday we shopped and gave this buster a chance to tire. On Thursday we sailed at 11 a.m., passed Ramsgate etc. and were in the middle of the sands, somewhere near the *Edinburgh* lightship as dark came down on us. We got across into Barrow deep, and then in a new buster, struggled up to the *Sunk* lightship, after which, with a foul tide and wind, we were hours and hours making the *Cork*, having to wear ship every time instead of going about, because the spare mainsail we were using did not properly balance her headsails. At dawn we began to get ahead again, roared into Harwich, and up the Orwell river, picking up a mooring at Pin Mill at 9.10.

So here she is, and after ten years with none, I've had a little 'yachting'. It made me feel horribly old, but in a way very young and inexperienced. It's much more difficult than Baltic cruising. But everybody says I picked the worst fortnight for several years, so maybe the next lot will seem easier.

Now the poor dear is stripped temporarily, as I am having all her sails tanned. During all the fortnight we had only one chance of getting them dry, and I took it, for the mainsail, but could not afford to let the jibs rest. So just in case of accidents, the whole lot will be a ruddy ochre. Billy did his stuff beautifully until the soaking at Dover, after which he became hard to start, and he had another soaking on this last Sunday, so tomorrow I have an expert coming to feel his pulse.

I should have mentioned that on the last wild night crossing the Thames estuary, the electric light failed, and we had to rig a pocket torch to give occasional light to the compass. Throughout, the wireless, in spite of all our efforts, failed to give a single squeak. And the miserable navigation lights given with the ship blew out always the moment we showed them. I used a red Woolworth bakelite plate with a strong torch behind it, to frighten off the Flushing Harwich steamer!!!

Good luck to you.

A.

I think you might have sent me word about your Norwegian adventures. Do.

1   Broke Farm, Levington, on the River Orwell.

To G. Wren Howard

Jan. 16 1936   [Broke Farm, Levington]

Dear Howard,

Miss Chafee is a fine young woman and knows her own mind and if she had been writing a letter specially designed to show Lippincotts what hopeless publishers they are she could not have done better.

When you have done with her letter, may I have it again so that when the right time comes I can show it to our mutual friend J. Jefferson Jones.[1]

Miss Chafee is an old-established fan, and wrote to me a couple of years ago . . . 'are they real?' etc. I sent her a postcard. I have nothing to add to whatever reply you make, unless you like to say that you have shown me her letter and that I am pleased she likes my pictures . . . and that I'm doing my best to get another book done before she's forgotten the early ones.

Spirits here are rising again at last. During the last four days I have seen, grabbed, clutched and pinioned a really gorgeous idea for another book . . . Swallows only . . . No Nancy or Peggy or Captain Flint . . . but a GORGEOUS idea with first class climax inevitable and handed out on a plate . . . lovely new angle of technical approach and everything else I could wish . . . So I breathe again . . . I really was afraid I'd done for myself or rather for these stories by uprooting, but I haven't. This new idea is the best since *Swallows and Amazons* . . . And, here's something to sadden niggards in gold leaf (I name no names), there are EIGHT words in its entirely admirable, memorable and inevitable title . . . EIGHT! Cheer up. Monosyllables only. But eight of the very best.[2]

The result of all this is that I don't feel so hopeless about *Pigeon Post*, which I shall be attacking full strength again as soon as the *Swallowdale* pictures are finished.[3] I have been getting ahead with them pretty fast, and yesterday had a lot of them approved by some visiting fans, who really chuckled over some of them, which they certainly wouldn't have done over the old ones.

I hope you will manage to run down about the end of the month, by which time I hope to have the whole lot ready for exhibition . . . when your expert criticism will be much valued.

Love to Michael,[4]   Yours ever,   [no signature]

1   Lippincott was Ransome's American publisher; Miss Chafee, an
     American admirer. J. Jefferson Jones was a Lippincotts executive.
2   Presumably the original title was to be *We Did Not Mean to Go
     to Sea*.
3   It had been agreed that AR would replace Clifford Webb's
     drawings with his own in a new edition of *Swallowdale*.
4   Wren Howard's son, at this time a schoolboy, but eventually –
     before Ransome's death – Managing Director of Cape.

                    To Edith R. Ransome
Aug. 4 1936   [Levington]

My dearest Maw,
     Rouse[1] and I had a couple of really gorgeous sails. We started
on Saturday at 3 from Harwich harbour, and had a grand breeze
just not too much for full sail, all the way past Walton-on-the-
Naze, and Frinton and Clacton to the Blackwater and Colne,
where we had a beat up the Colne River and spent the night
anchored in a creek called the Pyefleet behind Mersea Island, at
just after 9 p.m. That night was pretty wild and blowy and next
day it blew as you know very hard, and we were in two minds
about what to do. In the end we took in three reefs in the
mainsail, and put on my little storm jib, and tried what it was
like. It was pretty well submarinish down to the bar buoy, and
we got very wet indeed, but then, when we came round the bar
buoy and were able to bring the seas on our quarter things were
easier, and we had the best run I've had since coming home to
Riga in the gale back in 1922. With the storm sails she was quite
happy, and fairly flew, big waves picking her up, and she riding
the top of them in a flurry of white foam until they passed her
and she slipped down to be picked up by the next. It really was
gorgeous. We did not see any other yachts on the whole passage,
just one steamship and two barges, which looked very fine
indeed. The three of us, the two big Thames barges and my little
Nancy, all came storming round the Naze together, and we got
good shelter down at Shotley at the mouth of the river, where
we lay all night, coming back to Pin Mill yesterday. The new
anchor is a huge success. I can carry it about the decks in one
hand, and yet it held us perfectly each night, in the strongest

tides of the month, and very hard winds which shifted a good deal, so that it would not have been surprising if she had dragged even with an ordinary anchor. Total distance sailed just about 80 miles. Finally this morning, we set the alarm for six, so as to get all packed and Rouse off to town by the morning quick train, and I tidied up, brushed my carpet, made all neat while waiting for the tide, and then sailed down the river in the little *Coch-y-bonddhu*, which Renold gave me, a rollicking run to Levington creek. Rouse is a charming companion, and a very handy, quick sailor, by many long chalks the best crew I have ever had aboard her. Alas, all the good seamen have got their own boats, and Rouse has his, so it will only be very occasionally that I can get him. This week, luckily, he was without his wife and son, his usual crew, and so he offered himself. And I had far the pleasantest three days I have had aboard her.

While I was away, Genia read the beastly book.[2] That was the idea. I got a version of it finished so that it could be read through, and then cleared out, because I could not have borne being in the house during that grim process. Her verdict is, that it is not very much worse than the worst of the others. Three chapters need complete re-writing, but otherwise she thinks a few minor alterations will be enough to justify me in getting the damned thing out of the house. I hope therefore to be sending it to the printers by the end of this month. But the pictures remain to be done, so I don't suppose I shall get another cruise this year, unless there is good weather in September, when I may manage a week-end or so. But those two sails of Saturday and Sunday, one a fine sail with just the wind she would choose and an easy sea, and the other a snorter with storm sails all she could carry, will be memories for a very long time. Even if I get nothing more but these two and the voyage to the Low Countries,[3] I shan't feel I've done so badly. And, with each time I try her under new conditions, I became more and more pleased with her as a sea-boat. I do wish I could get a picture of her, but of course I can't. On the Saturday, when she was racing along under full sail, about 4 miles off Clacton, she was seen from a motor cruiser, and the paid hand told me today that she had looked a perfect picture,

'and the govner wanted to photo her, but he couldn't what

with his wife being seasick in the cabin, and the little Dutch hound, one of them little hounds like long sausages with claws on their toes, sliding about the decks on his claws, so that we had to put a parcel of cushions round him and rope them, and lash him down on deck so that he would be sick in one place and not every blooming wheres.'
Lovely picture of marine happiness, isn't it?
Well. Much love,
    Your affectionate son,
        A.

Love to Aunt Kit. Sorry to hear she has abandoned her Lime Juice, which though dull will go a long way in keeping her fit.

1 Philip Rouse, who had been at Rugby with AR. He was a cousin of W. H. D. Rouse, the Rugby master (and later head-master of the Perse School, Cambridge) who was the first person to discover that Ransome was myopic.
2 *Pigeon Post.*
3 Ransome sailed *Nancy Blackett* to Holland and back between 30 May and 11 June, researching conditions for *We Didn't Mean to Go to Sea.* The log of the voyage has been published in *Ransome At Sea, Notes from the Chart Table,* edited by Roger Wardale, Amazon Publications, 1995.

To Edith R. Ransome

Aug. 22 1936   [Levington]

My dearest Mother,
    Thank you very much for sending the sketches. The water-colours are charming. I wish I could use watercolour. Ink is a hard, unyielding stuff in comparison.

I hasten to inform you that today, at 4.45 p.m., with a wry grin I posted the complete *Pigeon Post* to Howard. *High Topps*[1] is a much nicer name for it, but they are dead set on using the other. But I am very glad to have got it even temporarily out of the house. I expect it back at the end of the week, when I shall have another go at it. I have asked Howard to suggest any possible shortenings he can see. It is as long as *Peter Duck* and much duller.[2]

But, thank goodness, it is done . . . for the present. I should like to take a day's sailing, and will if I can.

Pictures are urgent now, and I must barge ahead with them as fast as I can, for fear the proofs are ready before the blocks.

Genia is busy ruthlessly dealing with the garden. I expect it will be very nice in the end.

I am most horribly tired after the steady all day every day plug of the last three weeks, and trying to carry the whole book in my head all the time in altering details. I expect a lot of contradictions have crawled in.

Please tell the unlucky Kitty I am very sorry for her. And for Neville.[3]

Museum.[4] I should like to see the things just as they are if you don't mind, before in all probability, handing them on. So please put them away again till I can have a look at them. They will remind me of a lot of things that have nothing to do with museums.

Much love,
Your affectionate son,
Arthur

1   High Topps is the moor where most of the action of *Pigeon Post* takes place.
2   *Pigeon Post* is actually somewhat shorter than *Peter Duck*.
3   Unidentified.
4   A relic of AR's childhood. 'It was a very good museum for a washing-stand drawer. There was a bronze token struck by Wilkinson the iron-master who built the first iron vessel . . . There were sharks' teeth in it, and cowries from the South Seas. There were ammonites, belemnites and other fossils collected by myself, and there was an acorn from Tasso's garden at Ferrara' (*Autobiography*, p. 19).

To M. K. Whitlock

March 30 1937   [Levington]

Dear Sir,

Some little time ago a parcel reached me from two young women,[1] one of whom was your daughter.

The parcel held a full-length book. I read it with a great deal of amusement and profound respect for the sustained energy that had carried the thing through.

I then took it to my own publisher, Mr. Jonathan Cape, and suggested that he should publish it. He read it, agreed with my verdict upon it, and said he would publish it if I would write an introduction. I said I would.[2]

The question of terms for the book was then discussed. Cape offers 10% of the published price in the form of royalties. He will pay a sum yet to be agreed on account of these royalties on the day of publication.

Both authors are under age, and he suggests that his agreement on the subject should be drawn up as between himself and me acting as their agent. The resulting cheques would, of course, be drawn out in their names. If you approve and will write me a letter authorising me to act as agent for your daughter, I will ask Cape to prepare a contract on the same lines as my own.

I propose to ask him to pay them £50 on account of royalties on the day the book is published.[3]

Yours faithfully,

Arthur Ransome

1   Katherine Hull and Pamela Whitlock.
2   He did: *The Far-Distant Oxus* was published in the autumn of 1937. It tells the story of a party of children who spend the summer holidays at a farmhouse on Exmoor where they have all sorts of adventures on horseback, afloat on a raft and lighting beacons at night. It was written in secret by two schoolgirls, admirers of Swallows and Amazons, while they were studying for what would now be called their A-levels and sent by parcel post to Arthur Ransome. The *Daily Telegraph* called the book 'an extraordinary achievement'. The full story of how 'this astonishing book' came to be written and published is told by Ransome himself in his Introduction to it. *The Far-Distant*

    Oxus was republished by Cape in 1978, exactly as it had first appeared forty years earlier.

3   Ransome quickly changed his mind, and Mr Whitlock acted as Pamela's agent; but AR did all the work. No doubt a similar arrangement was made with Katharine Hull's father, but no correspondence survives.

To Richard Tizard

April 11 1937   [Levington]

Dear Dick Tizard,[1]

    I am doing all I can to have *Nancy* ready for a sail this week end, if you would like to come. But, every conceivable thing has gone wrong. They tried to rig her while I was up in the north of England, and, in spite of clearly written labels, managed to get every single halyard and block and shroud and stay in the wrong place. I think it possible I shall have to have the mast taken out of her and start again. Thornycroft's man has promised to come down on Thursday or Friday to deal with the engine. To-morrow a renewed effort is to be made to get her out of her mud berth, where the last lot of high tides did not float her. If we fail, it means getting a gang to dig her out.

    I will report progress, and give you warning as soon as I can if, as the week goes on, it looks as if we shall fail to get her fit to sail.

    Among their other crimes, the riggers actually broke one of the heavy galvanised rigging screws by using it, I suspect, as a sledge hammer.

    Paint and varnish I am not bothering about till later, so she will look like a wreck.

    But it's a maddening business.

    Just let me have a card to say whether IF I do succeed in having her afloat and sailable by Friday you feel like joining. But don't expect anything very much. It will only be local pottering and tuning up.

Yours sincerely,

Arthur Ransome

1   Tizard was an Oxford undergraduate who had volunteered to crew *Nancy Blackett*. See List of Correspondents.

To Richard Tizard

April 14 1937   [Levington]

Dear Tizard,
    Good.
    I'll expect you at Pin Mill when you turn up.
    Don't hurry and bust yourself (and bicycle) on the way. *It doesn't matter when we start*, and I dare say there'll be still a million things to do aboard on the Saturday.
    Mainsail bent last night.
    Engine not yet got its magneto in place. The man from Thornycroft's promises to be here on Friday.
    Dinghy leaking like a sieve.
                    Yours,

                        A.R.[1]

1   Dr Tizard says: 'I arrived at Pin Mill just at the start of a severe frost. We got on board to find that all the ropes were frozen into bars of iron. It was impossible to sail, an impossibility which was reinforced by snowfall . . . We stayed on board that day and in the evening . . . I had the wonderful experience of hearing AR's stories of some of his many adventures. He must have been unequalled as a raconteur.'

To Pamela Whitlock

April 29 1937   [Levington]

Dear Pamela,
    PICTURES[1] I do hope you have done a really good lot, because I want to be able to show them to Cape.
    If they are good enough, as I hope they will be, he proposes to pay for them separately.
    But they must be cram full of larkiness. Keep the idea firm in your mind that you are telling the story in the pictures to Katharine, she being deaf and dumb.
    Thickish nib. J or Relief. Indian ink. White paper. No scratchiness.
    I have written to your father asking you both to come over

on May 8. I shall meet you at Ipswich in the morning. Then you come here. In the afternoon we may have to go across to the *Nancy Blackett*, who is being got ready for sea. We might have tea on board. Then come back here for some sort of supper. Then I'd put you on the 7.56 train which reaches Liverpool Street at 9.24. I hope this will not be too late, as we shall have a very great deal to talk over.

Bring sandshoes in your pocket in case we go aboard for tea.

[Signature cut out]

1   Pamela Whitlock's own drawings for *The Far-Distant Oxus*. For more details, see *Life*, pp. 351-55.

To Pamela Whitlock

July 29 1937   [Levington]

Dear Pamela,

I am so sorry I never answered your very important question about the jacket.[1]

Yes. Go ahead and have a shot. Black counts as one colour. You can have any *two* others.

Do something that looks really *gaudy* when seen from the other end of a LONG ROOM.

This is important; because only that way does a book show up among all the others in a shop.

The Cape people are very pleased with your pictures. I haven't talked to Cape himself yet about how much he is to pay for them, but he will pay all right.

I've gone and been ill, and my book isn't nearly done . . . and I've only done about 4 pictures for it. So I don't know whether I'm on my head or my heels.

TRY to do the jacket design right away.

Your respectful colleague,

A.R.

1   For *The Far-Distant Oxus.*

To G. Wren Howard

Sept. 4 1937   [Levington]

Dear Howard,

Here it is.[1] But I am very dissatisfied with parts of it.

Still, I am prepared to accept your verdict. If you think it doesn't need such wholesale alteration as would take a very long time, I will do what I can with it at once. If on the other hand you think it's in such a hopeless mess that it would take months to put it right, why then I'll sit on it for a bit, go off for a holiday, and rewrite it during the winter.

In no case, of course, is it to go to the printers till I've gone through it again.

Well, I shall turn on to pictures for a day or two until you can hurl it back, with any suggestions you feel like making, for which I shall be very grateful . . . no matter how painful you have to make them.

Yours ever,

Arthur Ransome

I do feel a pig, loading you up with this to read when you must have a pile of extra stuff of all sorts after being away.

1   The draft manuscript of *We Didn't Mean to Go to Sea*. Ransome had been wrestling with revision since June, when Genia had told him that the book was flat, not interesting, not amusing. Fortunately Molly Hamilton had come to stay and proved herself to be a much more helpful and encouraging critic (see *Life*, pp. 355-6).

To G. Wren Howard

Sept. 7 1937   [Levington]

Dear Howard,

Thank you for your letter. Right, I'll get a lot of pictures done.

N.B. I propose to omit the few paragraphs about Jim at the very beginning, and to start with the children in the dinghy.

Also, I think better omit the chapter about the nurse etc. in hospital in the middle of the book. Better leave Jim in suspended animation until he actually wakes up and escapes in chapter XXVI.[1]

The book, when I have cut out a few adjectives and made these excisions, will be about 15 to 20 pages shorter than at present.

Yours ever,

Arthur Ransome

1   This was in accordance with a suggestion made by Molly
    Hamilton in July. AR seems to have taken his time in deciding
    that it was a good one.

★

Wren Howard responded to the new script with enthusiasm. On 10 September he wrote: 'I do honestly think very well of the book indeed. It gathers pace in a most satisfactory manner, and works up through crisis to an admirable conclusion. Dawn and the arrival in Holland are magnificent . . . I am shooting the MS off to you by registered post to-day in the hopes that you may be able to redirect it up to Scotland [to the printers] about Tuesday next. Send me immediate news of its despatch and we will 'dress ship' in Bedford Square! P.S. I have an idea that the next book might perhaps revolve round Roger, presumably Titty, and some new characters from Pin Mill. Temporary exclusion of John and Susan would give a new focal point and age-level.' Was this the germ of *Secret Water*, which introduces the Eels, and in a sense revolves round Bridget, who is even younger than Roger?

★

Sept.13.1937.

Dear Howard,

I am going at it full tilt, and will let you know when it goes off.

I am right, I suppose, in assuming that there will be galley proofs,.?.....I hope to get the pictures done by the time they are ready, and shall bring them to town in the hope of a little first aid for broken bones in the figures.

Your letter was very cheering.....as you meant it to be!

No sailing this week end.

Yours ever,

To G. Wren Howard

Sept. 16 1937   [Levington]

Dear Howard,

I didn't tell Grays [the printers] I would come to Edinburgh to save time in the final proof reading, but I will if necessary. I forgot to tell them in the rush of getting the parcel made up and sent off, catching the post by a minute.

I am still pretty doubtful about the sea chapters, if not a bit too terrific, but I couldn't see how to moderate them without an entire rewriting. Chapter I is now much shorter, and I've got rid of a lot of explanation.

'Hard.' I keep this word, but do not explain it except by a picture of the thing. The word is in the dictionary.[1] With the picture I think it explains itself.

The hospital nurse chapter is OUT, and I've let Jim, wandering round the room, find the card with 'Talks English' on it – to his indignation – in the chapter about his waking up at the end of the book. Account of accident simply left to the bus conductor in the same chapter.

I fear a lot of people will say the thing's too tough for babes. However.

I told Grays 20 full pagers,[2] and about the same number of half pagers.

> Yours ever,
>
> Arthur Ransome

1   'A sloping stone roadway or jetty at the water's edge for landing, etc.' (*Shorter Oxford English Dictionary*, 1936.)
2   Illustrations.

To Barbara Gnosspelius

[October 1937]   M.V. *Royal Star*[1]

My dear Barbara,

Look here: you can't waste real rum from Jamaica on rum butter. Any ordinary pub. Jamaica is good enough for that. To use the real thing that coppered Captain Morgan's mate's nose, that warmed the stone heart of Flint, that turned Teach's beard blue, in any other way than letting it down your throats to send its fiery roots groping through your interiors, is simply blasphemy. What is Oscar doing to allow it? Blasphemy, sacrilege, barbarous vandalism. The thought of it brings me to the boil even in the stoveless cabin of this boat.

Actually the boat is quite snug and till these beastly gales started we were catching lots of fish, a pound perch, a roach well over 1½ lb., pound rudd, and lots of bream. Genia refuses to consider going home, so here we stick, and at the moment listen to a raging hurricane overhead and the groan and sigh of a windmill, or rather windpump, which is whirling like a dervish at the head of the reach.

The Broads are absolutely deserted except for strong fishermen. We haven't seen one moving boat today, except a wherry and a reed boat.

Love to the lot of you but DON'T go and waste the Elixir.

A.

18 lbs of fish today.

1   AR and Genia were on a fishing cruise on the Broads. The Gnosspelius family had visited Jamaica for a holiday in August. Reference to AR's log of the *Royal Star* (*Ransome At Sea*, p. 47) shows that this letter must date from after 22 October.

To J. R. R. Tolkien, Oxford

Nursing Home,
32 Surrey Street,

Dec. 13 1937 Norwich[1]

Sir,

As a humble hobbit-fancier (and one certain that your book will be many times reprinted) may I complain that on page 27,[2] when Gandalf calls Bilbo an excitable little hobbit, the scribe (human no doubt) has written 'man' by mistake? On page 112 Gandalf calls the goblins 'little boys', but he means it as an insult so that is no doubt right.[3] But on page 294 Thorin surely is misinterpreted. Why his concern for *men*?[4] Didn't he say 'More of *us*', thinking of dwarves, elves, goblins and dragons and not of a species which to him must have been very unimportant. The error, if it is an error, is a natural one, due again to the humanity of the scribe to whom we must all be grateful for the chronicle.

I am, sir,

Yours respectfully

Arthur Ransome

1   Ransome was recuperating from an operation for umbilical hernia, incurred on the Broads.

2   Of Tolkien's *The Hobbit*, published in September, 1937. The passage in question originally ran: '"Excitable little man," said Gandalf, as they sat down again. "Gets funny queer fits, but he is one of the best, one of the best – as fierce as a dragon in a pinch."' It was changed for the second edition to 'Excitable little fellow'.

3   When Bilbo Baggins and the dwarves are besieged in the tree-tops by goblins. '"Go away! little boys!" shouted Gandalf in answer. "It isn't bird-nesting time."' This passage was never altered.

4   '"If more men valued food and cheer and song above hoarded gold, it would be a merrier world."' Altered to 'If more of us valued food . . .'

★

Designedly or not, Ransome's letter (perhaps written to pass the time in his hospital bed) touched just the right note for its recipient. Tolkien answered at once – perhaps by return of post:

From J. R. R. Tolkien [extract]

15 December 1937   [Oxford]

I am sure Mr Baggins would agree in words such as he used to Thorin: to have been fancied by you, that is more than any hobbit could have expected. The scribe, too, is delighted to be honoured by a note in your own hand, and by criticisms showing so close a scrutiny of the text. My reputation will go up with my children – the eldest are now rather to be classed as 'men', but on their shelves, winnowed of the chaff left behind in the nursery, I notice that their 'Ransomes' remain . . . I will replace 'man' on p. 27 by the 'fellow' of an earlier recension. On p. 112 I agree in feeling that Gandalf's 'insult' was rather silly and not quite up to form – though of course he would regard the undeveloped males of all two-legged species as 'boys'. I am afraid the blemish can hardly be got over by vocabulary, unless 'oaves' would be an improvement? On p. 294 I accept 'of us' as a great improvement: *men* is there just a loose rendering of Thorin's word for 'people' – the language of those days, unlike modern English, had a word that included the Two Kindreds (Elves and Men) and their likenesses and mockeries. 'Of us' exactly represents this: for Thorin certainly included 'humans' in his comment, for Elves and Dwarves were mightily concerned with them, and well aware that it was their fate to usurp the world; but he was not at that moment thinking chiefly of *Men* (with a capital). The ancient English, of course, would have felt no hesitation in using 'man' of elf, dwarf, goblin, troll, wizard or what not, since they were inclined to make Adam the father of them all . . .

I must apologise for writing at such length. I hope you are well enough to endure it or forgive it, trusting that your address does not indicate a serious illness. I hope the enclosed list of other minor errors will serve to correct your copy – but, *if* there is a reprint (sales are not very great) I hope you will allow me to send you a corrected copy.

Yours very respectfully . . .

To J. R. R. Tolkien

Dec. 17 1937   Norwich.

Dear Professor Tolkien,

Thank you for your most interesting letter.

BUT: I did not intend any criticism whatever of the 'boys' of p. 112. I mentioned it only to illustrate (by contrast) my slight discomfort due to 'man' on p. 27. And that discomfort had no relation to mythology. I had very much admired the delicate skill with which you had made Mr. Baggins so Hobbitty (forgive the word) and the word 'man' on p. 27 seemed a leak or a tear in the veil, undoing just a little of what you had done. That was all. I thought the word had slipped from the scribe's pen by accident. The Hobbitness of Mr. Baggins seems to me one of the most difficult and triumphant achievements of the book . . . And so valuable that, regardless of mythology, it seemed worth while to complain about the one word which in one place, just for a moment, raised a faint doubt.

I have copied your corrections into the book. Thank you for letting me have them.

I had an operation nearly a month ago and hope to get out quite soon now. *The Hobbit* has done a great deal to turn these weeks into a pleasure. And as for new editions . . . there will be dozens of them: of that I have no doubt whatever.

Yours sincerely,   Arthur Ransome

To Margaret Renold

Jan. 24 1938   [Levington]

Dear Margaret,

I made a good lot of notes a couple of years ago for a story bringing in my respected ancestor,[1] fishing, poaching etc., and your letter made me turn them over once more. That book has got to be written some day, but there is one very serious snag about it, and that is its retrospective character.

Genia is strong against it, on the ground that the reason my brats like my books is that they are all something that happens today and MIGHT happen to themselves given only some quite small modification in their circumstances, such as a different mother, or a reformed father, or living a bit nearer a lake, or something like that. She thinks there'd be awful disappointment if I go and tell a story that happened long ago, and in circumstances that can never be the same again. No matter, I have got the notes out, and am having a thorough go into them, to see how far the time element can be dodged.

Detective.[2] Why not? Now then. George Owdon of *Coot Club* is obviously the right criminal. Tom and the Death and Glories are the right detectives, with the help of Dorothea's imagination and Dick's scientific mind. NOW, I see it this way. It would be all wrong for the detectives to snoop out of public spirit with the hope of handing George over to justice. The detective work must be forced upon them TO CLEAR THEMSELVES of some villainy of which, thanks to George Owdon, they are bearing the blame. What the devil can it be? What can George have done and done in such a way that everybody thinks the Death and Glories are responsible? Come on, Margaret . . . Something that can be placed on the Broads, and timed for October or November, or even for the week before Christmas. This because I have a very gorgeous episode with a pike, and a fisherman and an innkeeper and the Death and Glories, which it would be a waste not to work in. And because I want a cold weather story if possible, because of being able to get some fun out of the cabin those three have built in their old boat, with an old coal stove, and a genuine chimney pot on the cabin roof (there is a ghastly episode when they try to smoke eels in the cabin and a fine one where they have a Christmas pudding, and use methylated to get the flames, and subsequently a lot of sugar in the faint hope of taking the taste away). I've got a good lot of stuff simmering about the Death and Glories, and would just love to do you a really good detective story about them if you can get a bit further in devising the crime to make it possible (after *Coot Club* it must have nothing to do with visitors' boats). What the dickens did that beastly fellow father on them, and how the dickens do they contrive to find out the truth, with the help of their various allies? It looks as if it must be a recurrent crime . . . I mean the villain must find it necessary to repeat it, to give them a chance, AFTER their detective work, to lay for him and expose him in the very act. Now then Charles! Speak up, Margaret!

Nancy Blackett, alas, will be for sale. But we shall be fitting her out at Easter, and sailing her till she is sold and till the new boat is ready which won't be before July, I expect.

The new boat has its internal accommodation planned by Genia, who guaranteed that if I built it, she would take up her old job as in *Racundra*. She wants to call her *Selina*.[3]

Gosh, Margaret, if you can provide the right crime, I'll write you the loveliest detective story that ever was.

Yours ever and many thanks

Arthur

1 *The River Comes First*. I cannot identify the 'respected ancestor' (the original of Canon John William in the book) with any certainty. Possibly AR's grandfather, Thomas Ransome (see *Autobiography*, pp. 17–18).

2 Ransome has turned to the subject of a sequel to *Coot Club* – which ultimately became his classic detective story, *The Big Six*.

3 Notice how the pronouns change as soon as the new boat's name is mentioned. Ransome thought seriously of writing a book about her building and prepared drafts for several chapters.

To Helen Ferris
(U.S. Junior Literary Guild)
March 20 1938   [Levington]

Dear Miss Ferris,

Thank you for sending me Miss Burt's hint to His Majesty, which amused me a good deal.

And now then, about this writing for children. I know absolutely nothing about it, for the very simple reason that I NEVER NEVER do it. Unless I am writing something that is good fun FOR ME, not for somebody else, I cannot write at all. The children who read my books are never addressed. I don't even know they are there. They merely overhear me larking about for my own fun, not for theirs. It is just good luck for me that some of them seem to enjoy the same things that I enjoy. I can't claim any credit for it. There is no intention in it. It is simply an accident. It always astonishes me. After all, I am 54 and it is a bit surprising that their tastes and mine should coincide even sometimes.

Writing FOR children is to me something almost incredible. I cannot imagine how it is done. And I don't see why it ever should be done. A book written consciously FOR some audience other than its writer is almost sure to be pulled out of focus by its purpose, so that it cannot be a good book ... whether for children or for grown-ups. That is why I hate the word 'juvenile' applied to my books. 54 is not juvenile, not by long chalks. And they are written for me.

Another result of this way of thinking is that since to encourage the production of 'juveniles' is likely to make people who might otherwise be doing useful jobs turn to writing FOR children, it is perhaps all wrong. Perhaps writing children's books should (instead of being rewarded) be made a punishable offence. This would stop people from TRYING to do it, and would save publishers a lot of money, while people who write books which children happen to like would go on doing it because they couldn't help themselves anyway. And when prosecuted they could honestly claim that they had not done it on purpose, and the judge might let them off.

Further, as there would not be so many books, we should see a lessening of what I think is the worst danger to children's reading at the present day ... namely the dreadful idea that newness is a virtue in itself, and that books are meant to be read only once. (Books written FOR children of course don't deserve to be read even once, and with hundreds of them about it is quite natural that 'Oh I've read that one' should come to seem a sufficient reason for not reading a book again.)

Libraries – and Guilds! – ought to be very careful lest they encourage the idea that books are like newspapers and muffins and herrings, to be served fresh and fresh. Any good book improves on rereading, and I believe that the reason why books meant so much to me when I was a small boy is that I didn't have too many, and that those I did have I knew pretty well by heart. Incidentally a book that really is a book (not a form of grocery manufactured with an eye to the consumer) is usually capable of making people read it more than once, though in the long run, if this business of wholesale writing FOR children and letting children think that a book must be straight from the press if it is to be worth reading goes on to its logical conclusion which is to shorten the lives of all books while encouraging the production of books that don't deserve to live at all ... even the best book will have no chance of being properly read.

Geewhillikins what a sentence! And anyway all this gabble, which is the result of just letting my typewriter have its head, isn't likely to be of the slightest use to you. It hardly touches the real question ... which, on looking at your letter again, I see is 'What is the difference between writing for adults and writing for boys and girls?'

Well, I don't believe there is a difference ... as far as real books are concerned. People write them and some people in pleasing themselves please one sort of person and some another sort of person. The actual age of the reader doesn't seem to matter much. Of one thing I am quite sure, that to set out consciously to write a book FOR an audience of some particular age is a very good way of writing a bad book for persons of any age whatsoever.

Well, well. You had better throw this scribble in the fire quick. And anyhow remember that though I think that artificial encouragement of people to waste their time by writing FOR children is not likely to produce good books, I jolly well don't include in that all the encouragement you and the Junior Literary Guild have lavished on me throughout the last nine years. It has been a continual source of pleasure and cheerfulness and very valuable in all kinds of glooms and difficulties.

Forgive this horrid paper. I have run out of the usual stuff.

The new ship is getting along. Her keel is laid down and her ribs are being shaped, and soon it will be possible to see her whole skeleton.

But as for a new book, I haven't got one. I had one notion but after chewing it over for a bit came to the conclusion that I didn't really like it, so it has gone. Another, a much better notion, is still only a glimmer. There never was in the whole history of the world anybody who had such trouble in inventing stories. Once I have got a story I have a gorgeous time with it, playing with it, but I can't play in a hurry, and if my story doesn't come along pretty quick, I shall have to give up all hope of getting a new book this year. Thank goodness for the boat.

I read a lovely thing somewhere, that in America there are public benefactors who invent plots and do nothing else and call at the door like the milkman, and sell plots for a dollar a time to needy authors. I nearly took the next boat for New York.

At Easter we are going sailing on the Broads, with a fleet of FIVE vessels, mostly sailed by skippers of 16 down to 11, all flying the skull and crossbones. And soon after Easter, *Nancy* will be fitted out and I shall be going to sea again . . . unless these mad beasts loose in Europe ring down the curtain on us all.

Allow me to subscribe myself, as ever,

The J.L.G.'s affectionate and grateful godchild,

Arthur Ransome

To Edith R. Ransome

Oct. 2 1938[1]   [Levington]

My dear Mother,

Useless to comment on the political situation; except that in spite of all that will be said against him, I think Chamberlain has done extremely well.

What has happened is the putting right of one of the worst

errors of the Versailles peacemaking, the giving the Czechs the power to dominate considerable lumps of other nations.. Teschen, for example, they grabbed by force just as the Poles grabbed Vilna.[2] They have had twenty years in which they have shown their inability to think of Germans and Poles other than in terms of conquest. Even now, at the very last minute, they hardly admit the Slovaks as equal partners. To an enormous extent they have themselves to blame. Czechs as Czechs are first rate. As dominant partners they are not good.

Next. Their frontier was a 'military' one. It is a question whether it is best to have a good military frontier that includes a large area populated by the 'enemy', or to have a less easily defensible frontier that is occupied solely by one's own people.

Chamberlain seems to me to have done right WHATEVER the outcome. Because, if we do after all have to fight we shall have the moral support of the whole world, whereas over the Czech question it was impossible not to admit that there was pretty good reason for the German attitude . . . E.g. Benes' calm suggestion of 'ten years' during which progressively to give the Sudetens equal rights.[3] That suggestion was enough to infuriate anyone. Further, the whole thing must have shown the leaders of both Germany and Italy that their own people want peace not war.

I regard Harold Nicholson, Duff Cooper, and the Labour critics of the peace, as persons whose efforts whether they mean it or not, will tend to make less likely the general appeasement which does at the moment seem possible.

London was a queer place last week . . . sandbags, etc., but the queerest of all happenings was the decision of the uneducated idiots in charge of evacuation, to send hundreds of children to Pin Mill, Levington and Shotley, evidently thinking 'a good long way from London', but not realising that these places are in the very heart of an area which will be a military objective, Shotley naval training base, Harwich harbour, with the seaplane base, Bawdsey, Martlesham and Ipswich aerodromes, to say nothing of the river and the Ipswich docks and factories. In other words their motto might have been 'Children to the front lines'. It's a good thing really that there was this dress rehearsal for war, because when war really comes, that particular idiocy will not be committed again. Though perhaps that is hoping too much. Still, I think a pretty good fuss has been kicked up about it, and the evacuators will have been asked to look at a map.

Selina is launched . . . It looked as if she would be just in time for the war. Mrs. King bust the champagne and under protest agreed just to sip a little . . . 'Like Holy Communion,' she said. We had a dinner at the *Butt and Oyster* for the builders, and sat down twelve, in silence but for champing jaws. But it was pretty cheerful because of the turn in the news.[4]

Her mast is not in yet, and they have made some damnable messes only some of which we shall be able to put right. Gale blowing at the moment, so I don't know when we'll get the mast in. Sails have arrived. *Selina* seems most awfully big. Comfortable to live in, but a bit of a handful to sail. However, if war does come there won't be any sailing.

Much love, Your affectionate son,

Arthur

Postscript. I see Joyce asks why we have taken 20 years to find out that the Czechs were not treating the other nationalities fairly. The answer is that Czechoslovakia was artificially created to be an ally of France, and that it is human to turn a blind eye to the defects of an ally.

1   The Munich agreement was signed on 29 September 1938, and is now generally remembered as the most ignominious defeat in the history of British diplomacy.
2   Teschen (now Tesin) was partitioned between Czechoslovakia and Poland in 1920; in the same year Poland annexed Vilna (Vilnius) from Lithuania.
3   Eduard Benes, president of Czechoslovakia twice; his first term of office ended by German aggression, his second by Russian.
4   *Selina King* was launched on 27 September; AR wrote 'War' in his diary. The *Butt and Oyster* dinner was given two days later; the diary entry was 'peace'.

Butt and Oyster and
Alma Cottage, Pin Mill

To Barbara Smith
[Undated; winter 1939/40]¹   [Harkstead Hall]

Now, I am not going to give away secrets, but here is the answer to one of your questions. The lake is Windermere, but in the book I stole a few bits from Coniston and mixed them in for the sake of disguise, because we didn't want everybody to know our best places. Thus the Windermere island has not got such a good harbour. The harbour is really at the S. end of Peel Island on Coniston, where I used to camp when I was a boy.

No further questions will be answered, or I shall get into trouble all round.

Otley is a very good place to have as a base, with moors and rivers close by. You'll get plenty of sailing some day. I was born in Leeds myself, so I know that country very well.

Good luck to you

Arthur Ransome

1   This letter is the earliest extant of those written on postcards ornamented with printed drawings from Ransome's works in the margins, which thereafter AR was to use for much of his correspondence.

To Edith R. Ransome
Sept. 18 1939   [Harkstead Hall]

My dear Mother,

No news from the Admiralty . . . I expect they are snowed under with applications.¹

The book,² I think I told you, has gone to the printers, and I am now full blast with pictures and maps, trying to get them done before the proofs arrive. I've done some big maps and a little one. Four full page pictures inked, six in pencil. Ten small pictures linked.

But it is the devil of a job.

It is the rummest situation. Until the rise of Hitler, the Poles were the worst aggressors in Europe since the Peace Conference.³ They invaded Russia and took Kiev, and were chased back to Warsaw. They stole by force, *and still hold* the capital of Lithuania (because neither the League of Nations nor anyone else could turn them out at the time). They collared a mass of White Russian and Ukrainian land, where they behaved extremely badly. For all this, they will now of course pay.

We are simply backing a small aggressor against a big one, and it is ridiculous to talk otherwise.

The real interest is in the aim of the war, which appears to be the replacement of Hitler by Communism (the only real anti-Hitler force in Germany). This the Russians perfectly well realise, and the next Communist revolution in Germany will have Russian backing (Poland being kindly eliminated for them by Mr. Hitler).

The Russians have always said that the next war of this kind would result in world revolution, and they are following out a perfectly consistent policy to that end, notably helped by both Hitler and ourselves. It will be most interesting to see what happens when for the first time since 1918 Russians and Germans find themselves face to face.

If we win (in replacing Hitler by the Communists . . . We shan't be able to pick and choose) we shall be faced by a Communist block extending from the North Sea to the Pacific. Cheerful look out. However, we seem to have made up our minds to it.

Much love,
Your affectionate son,
Arthur

P.S. I suppose you are on the telephone. I may be able to ring up on Wednesday if I get to town.

1   'When the war came Ransome offered his services to the Admiralty, but they had no use for a "middle-aged crock", and in any case, as he neatly put it, he had "no stomach for the fight",' Rupert Hart-Davis, 'Epilogue', *Autobiography*, p. 352.
2   *Secret Water* was published in November, the last of the Swallows and Amazons series before wartime paper rationing put a restriction on sales and obliged Wren Howard to ask Ransome to accept a lower scale of royalties.
3   The Paris Conference of 1919.

To Joyce Lupton

Harkstead Hall,
near Ipswich,
Sept. 23 1939   Suffolk.

My dear Joyce,
  Sorry my bread-and-butter letter has been so late.
  I saw the blockmaker[1] and got everything fixed up in plenty
of time to catch the 4 o'clock, thus depriving myself of the
pleasure of watching the smooth collaboration of the Lupton
family at chess.
  I much enjoyed seeing you all, and hope there will be another
opportunity at a later stage of getting the beastly book into print.
  And I do very much admire your house. And Mother's.
  No news yet from the Admiralty. I saw one of my chief.
nautical allies, and he says they are cluttered up and fed to the
teeth with elderly birds who offer their services, and it is now
laid down that nobody need expect an answer. We have just to
sit and wait.
  Francis and Arthur much amused the ticket collector by the
way in which they shepherded me on to the platform, and saw
to it that I did actually leave. I liked them both very much.
  The wind is still bang in the North and East, and the days
getting shorter. If the wind don't change soon I shall have to
give up and let *Selina* stay here. But I can't believe it won't
change tomorrow or the next day. It is an extraordinary thing to
get easterlies and northerlies at this time of year. It's usually gales
from the South-West.
  Well, good luck to you all, and love to Mother.
                    Your affectionate brother,
                              Arthur

1 Of *Secret Water*'s illustrations. No letters from AR dealing
   with the genesis of this book survive, although Wren Howard,
   writing on 20 January 1938, says '. . . it is a bit serious about the
   new book. Won't the Walton creek idea work out at all? I liked
   the sound of the skeleton of it. In any case, there ought, if
   possible, I think, to be more land than water this time, though
   a certain proportion of water is always useful and exciting.'

To Katharine Hull and Pamela Whitlock
Dec. 31 1939   [Harkstead Hall]

Dear Katharine and Pamela,

It was nice of you to send me your *Oxus in Summer*.[1] I am very glad to have it and have it with interest . . . and amusement. I particularly like the picture on page 57.

'ARE SHEEP THE SILLIEST ANIMALS IN THE WORLD?'

Are you both going to go to Universities and turn into B.A.s in due course? Or what?

Has Pamela tried her hand at poetry? Katharine, I imagine, will stick to prose.

But I expect this lunatic Europe will upset things a bit for both of you as for everybody else. But ponies, I suppose, will go on much as usual. Boats won't. Poor *Selina* is laid up in a shed at Lowestoft, after her last voyage, which was interesting. She carried a special permit for a war-time voyage by a British merchant vessel, cargo ballast, a beautiful green paper with about a ton of sealing-was on it. I did not sight a submarine, but sailed close by the tops of the masts of one of the sunken ships . . . very beastly to look at.

If the war lasts as long as I fear it will, I don't suppose I shall have much chance of sailing her again. But properly under cover, in a shed by Oulton Broad, she ought not to take much harm.

The cats are well and send their best respects, and best wishes for good mousing in the New Year.

> Yours sincerely,
>
>   Arthur Ransome

1   Their third book, the second, *Escape to Persia*, having been published by Cape in 1938.

To Edith R. Ransome

Dec. 31 1939   [Harkstead Hall]

My dearest Mother,

This is just to wish you a better New Year than it seems likely to be.

People are, I believe, just beginning to realise what is going to happen, but there is always a dreadful time lag in these matters, and, apart from the fact that it is so much easier just to think in terms of fighting Hitler as if we were in a vacuum, final realisation is almost sure to come too late.

Did you read Ryti's broadcast from Finland? It echoes exactly what is being said and thought in many other countries, every one of which is desperately interested that we shall stop collaborating with Hitler in producing economic collapse and clearing the field for Communism, or Reaction, in any case for violence INSIDE every country. Actually, if the war were to stop this minute, the damage ALREADY done in England alone is so serious that it will take years to recover from it . . . if indeed complete recovery is possible.

I find it quite ghastly to listen to people planning what they will do with Europe AFTER the war in the bland confidence that if the war goes on the values they regard as eternal will still exist. They will not. Europe will be fluid, and seething fluid. And not Europe only. Just you remember that income tax at the beginning of the last war was not more than about 1/6.[1] Think of what it is today with the war hardly begun. Consider the complete destruction of almost all our industries. What about the lads now growing up who will NEVER be employed? Foreign markets there will be none. And England is a great deal better off than some others. There will be unemployment on a scale we have never dreamed of. Money will have gone to hell, with the result of continuous violent struggle between employers and employed to let wages keep up with prices and, as well, to keep up with the support of an enormous army who can never be employed.

No wonder the Russians rub their hands as they see their prophecies coming true, and the world shaking itself to pieces. If the thing goes on, it will gradually turn into a vast struggle between economic systems, in which every country will be at war within itself. Already the French newspapers are appearing with huge white spaces where the censor has been at work, and the mutilated papers are not merely the Communist ones. Already the French have begun arresting elected members of Parliament. Those are the symptoms of real trouble ahead. Exactly the symptoms that I saw in Russia in 1916.

Our Ministry of Economic Warfare works in plain fact on behalf of the Communist International. All the damage they do to Germany takes from Germany such reason as she still has for thinking she has something left to defend from Revolution. Drive Germany economically to desperation and naturally you drive her Communist whether she will or not.

The whole affair is turning into a horrible merry-go-round in which all the nations of Europe will collaborate in the preparation of their general collapse.

Well, it's a lovely look out.

                    Your affectionate Cassandra.

1   One shilling and sixpence income tax in today's currency would
     be 7½ pence in the pound. At the start of the First World War
     the standard rate of tax was in fact one shilling and twopence.

PART FIVE

The Home Front

1940–1945

W AR IN EARNEST began to close in on Arthur Ransome, as
on the rest of the country, in the spring of 1940. Living
as they did in a key position in Britain's defences, the
Ransomes were soon subjected to daily and nightly Luftwaffe
bombing raids. 'The row here from the battle is terrific,' he
wrote to his mother. 'Our windows rattle till they roar, and we
can feel the tremors when standing on the drive. Due to some
trick of the earth's strata, I fancy. At a house nearby a farmer
has a watercloset directly connected by a drain to the river, and
the locals appear to take turns in going there to experience the
odd effect of feeling the violent vibration transmitted to their
behinds. Poor Genia is getting very little sleep at night . . .'
Their tenancy of Harkstead Hall was precarious, and it was
always possible that the Admiralty would order them away at a
moment's notice. It seemed best to seek refuge elsewhere, and,
almost inevitably, Ransome found it on the shores of Coniston
Water. There he cheerfully spent the rest of the war, writing
his last works of fiction. In spite of his semi-invalid state, he
took up shooting, char-fishing and riding a motor-bike.
Evgenia was much less contented. Her new house, the Heald,
was too small. Gardening was impossible there, she was remote
from all shops, and the Lake District was as rainy as ever. She
vowed to sell up as soon as the war was over. Perhaps her
sombre mood at the Heald helps to explain why she
condemned *The Picts and the Martyrs* so wholeheartedly when
she read it in 1942.

To G, Wren Howard [extract]

May 18 1940   [Harkstead Hall]

Dear Howard,

I beg to report that I have started full tilt on the revision of
Hot Water, Not Us, Coots In Trouble, Who The Mischief? or God
knows what . . . Not satisfied with any title.[1]

Genia's verdict was in fact much better than it sounded over
the telephone. She even said that the framework was the best
yet, that two of the chapters were good, and that she laughed
several times. So I am full of hope, though very much afraid that
Mr. Hitler, that illiterate bloke, will butt in before I get the
revision typed out. I shan't be worrying you with it till this
second draft is duly done . . . scheduled date June 30 . . .

Two wood pigeons are affectionately seated on the garden
gate taking turns in picking lice from each other's neck feathers,
and a respectable married couple of partridges (those good
bourgeois birds) are taking their morning constitutional across
the lawn. Your delphiniums are shooting up well. The irises full
of bud. The roses survived the rabbits. I do wish you would
come down and have a look at it all. I could take you down river
in the 13 footer [*Coch-y-bonddhu*] to have a look at the war.

Yours ever,

Arthur Ransome

1   It was eventually published as *The Big Six.*

To Edith R. Ransome

June 1 1940   Harkstead Hall.

My dearest Mother,

I do not know if I shall be coming up to town on Thursday
or not. I don't like leaving Genia alone here, unless it seems
pretty sure that nothing serious is likely to happen, and it is quite
obvious that if Hitler turns his attention to England next, the
first thing he will do will be to bomb the ports, and of these
Harwich is one of his likeliest objectives, being the only East
Coast port of real importance between Hull and London. Genia

is quite prepared to be left alone, in fact, as usual, looks forward to it, but destroyers, submarines etc. being in the Stour I think that bombing will be much too near to be other than very unpleasant, especially as the house seems so damned ricketty. So unless a lull becomes obvious, or unless it seems clear that the next item on the programme is France, I shall probably stay at home. Nuisance, as I am invited to meet the Russian Ambassador at lunch on the Thursday, and the whole Russian position is extremely interesting ... and might turn much to our advantage if only that ass Halifax had not made so consistent a series of mistakes. I also rather hanker after seeing Lloyd George, who, I feel sure, will in the end be called in to try to put some of them right.

However, there it is. I may be coming or I may not. If I do, I will do my best to rush down to Kew and back after lunch (I have to be back by about six).

Page by page the revision of my book[1] goes on in spite of everything. Tonight I got to the end of Chapter VII. There are 31 chapters in all. Some are really not bad. Chapter VII, the last one revised, describes the capture of an enormous pike by the united efforts of my three small boys ... a quiet interlude while the clouds of the main story darken all round them. Then there is one about spending the night at an eel sett, and one about smoking eels in the chimney of the stove they have rigged up in their ancient boat. And already villainies multiply, and they are accused, and the police come knocking them up at odd hours of the night to make sure they are at home and not engaged in crime. Dick and Dorothea, complete with camera, have not yet arrived. They come in the chapter after next, after which detective work begins, and the Coot Club shed becomes New Scotland Yard, and the Coots are trying to find the real villains, while everybody else is accumulating proof that it is the said Coots who are to blame. If I can only bring it off right, it will be

great fun, and quite different from any of the others. All this, my dear Maw, is strictly secret, not to be told to anybody.

The irises are really lovely and the roses are beginning to come out.

We still think of getting a small house in London, if we could hear of a really quiet one and could get a lease or something. If you happen to hear of one, or to see just the thing with the notice board up, let me know. Our tenure here is very insecure, as you know, though it is such a nice garden that we'd like to stay if only we could.

Dick Stokes, the Ipswich M.P.,[2] was here to supper last night, full of beans and jokes as usual . . . and as furious as I am with the fools who (a) arranged a war without making sure that Hitler would have to fight on two fronts, and (b) did so when they knew we were in no condition to fight and (c) failed to give our splendid chaps the weapons to match those of their enemies. And to think that Halifax is still in the government!!

much love, your affectionate

Arthur

1   *The Big Six.*
2   Richard Stokes (1897–1957), Labour M.P. for Ipswich 1938–57; Chairman of Ransome and Rapier Ltd. (his mother was a Rapier). AR enjoyed visiting him at Hintlesham Hall.

To Edith R. Ransome

June 24 1940   Harkstead Hall

My dearest Mother,

I am very glad to hear that you are happily at Seend and I hope that you and Aunt Helen will not have too beastly a time. May I give you both one piece of very good advice? Forget to have the battery of your wireless recharged. If that is too much for you, at least have the strength of mind to listen to it only once a day. But better, much better, if you smash the horrid thing and are content to get your news from the newspapers. I think things were much better in the old days when news took a long time to come and if it was bad one had at least the comfort of knowing that it was old. And on the other hand, the battle of

Waterloo was none the less a victory because in the north of England it was a week before anyone knew anything about it. The new illusion that it is essential for the prosecution of the war that the whole civilian population should hear about it minute by minute is a thundering dangerous one for everybody.

Since the Tuesday night before I came to town things have been quite decently quiet here. The funniest episode was Friday night. Stokes the Ipswich M.P. had mentioned to me that if you have no cellar the best thing to do in an air raid is to make a bed up under the table. Well, on Friday he rang up to say he was coming round in the evening, and Genia mischievously put a mattress under my work table with a roll of blankets and a large placard 'RESERVED for R. R. Stokes, M.P.' He came in and roared with laughter. He hadn't been in the house twenty minutes before the warning went, and, as you may not move a car during the raid, there he had to stay, and under my table he had to sleep, and did, until about half past three next morning when the all-clear went.

The garden is looking lovely. Tell Aunt Helen I have a pair of wagtails nesting in the creeper outside my window, full three feet above the ground. We also have some turtle-doves as well as our bourgeois married couple of partridges.

On Saturday I got out for a few hours after tea, and went eeling on the river with Frank the old boatman. We got a dozen.

How lucky for Cecily to be going to Canada, and for Joyce to be able to export the brats. I expect she'll be a good deal happier to have them well out of the way.

We decided to send a couple of trunks to London as a form of insurance, so as to have a few essentials just in case we are ordered to clear out.

My wretched book hardly moves. But I simply must get it done or we shall be in the soup next year.

Two of the cactuses are flowering; the stomatum (not a true cactus) with a yellow flower all very fine spokes radiating from a centre, and the cereus silvestris, a gaudy red trumpet of great size.

Such small things cheer the human soul!

Well, good luck and much love to both mother and aunt,

from an affectionate son and nephew,

Arthur.

To Edith R. Ransome

July 9 1940   Harkstead Hall

My dear Mother,

A grave problem has arisen involving battle royal between me and Cape's. The subject is the title of the new book.

The book is really about the three small boys of the *Death and Glory* and is really a detective story, with those three, plus Tom, Dick and Dorothea using the Coot Club Shed as Scotland Yard and succeeding in exposing a wicked plot against the Coot Club as a whole.

I want to call it *The Big Six*.

They want to call it *The Death and Glories*.

I don't much like the latter title because it has a sort of warlike suggestion . . . though otherwise it is not bad.

Please will you and Aunt Helen give your votes (which I don't promise to abide by).

People here are, as I told them they would, getting entirely accustomed to air raids, and trouble about them little more than they do about thunderstorms, which in these parts they always call 'tempests'. Our beloved Charlie Burgess, the farm bailiff, invited me to see his dug-out. He has dug a deep pit and sunk a chicken hut in it, putting logs over the top and a lot of earth. It has a bench in it and a chair, and he and his wife and his brother-in-law (Genia's gardener) and his wife all crowd in and play cards by the light of a candle. He is laying down a little cellar in one corner for the beer he brews himself. I suggested planting nasturtiums overhead, but Charlie very gravely said that he thought them Germs might see 'em, so he is sowing speargrass instead. Very soon, I think, there will be resentment on those nights if any when 'them Germs' don't show up. During yesterday's go the managing director of one local firm was in the middle of a business conference which was cheerfully continued under the table. And everybody gets a sporting pleasure out of the searchlights, which really are a wonderful sight and extraordinarily quick in picking out the planes.

It begins to look as if we may be driven out of here and have to go to London if they do indeed prohibit the use of cars. We use ours only to go shopping once a week, but if we aren't allowed to do that things will be so awkward, living as we do miles from any shops, that we may have to close down temporarily. Though we don't want to if we can possibly help it. I am sure things are much more cheerful here than they could be elsewhere.

I am perfectly certain there can be no sort of serious invasion until the Germans eliminate (a) the fleet and (b) the air force. Until they do this, which they don't look like doing, there is absolutely no need to worry. So don't you go bothering your head about it. I hereby promise that Cassandra shall duly start prophesying the moment anything like that begins to be at all possible. There is no sign of it now, and you ought to put it right out of your head.

I've got to page 264 and at the moment it's going pretty well. But please advise about the title.

> Much love to both of you,
> Arthur.

> To Edith R. Ransome [abridged]

Sept. 15 1940   Harkstead Hall

My dear Mother,

The weekly bulletin is pretty empty, in comparison with news elsewhere. Our postman had a narrow escape, chucking himself into the gutter with great presence of mind as he saw three bombs coming down at him, and he was very cheerful about it afterwards, except that he said he'd had to come out on the country collecting round without his tea because of their getting a gas main (we think they probably didn't, but that the gas was turned off as a precaution). Anyhow the postman was very lucky. Ditto the schoolmarm's husband who had some down about a hundred yards from his garage. The parson continues to spout hatred and to tell the villagers he would like the chance of killing as many Germans as possible. The village is, I think, much less bellicose. All it wants to know is how soon is the business going to be over, and is it worthwhile digging potatoes? They are pretty sick of never having a quiet night, but are inclined to be more contented with their lot after hearing of the bombing of London. It was in Ipswich that our postman had his escape yesterday, and the village is I think congratulating itself on being a village.[1]

In Ipswich they have asked but not ordered people who can to clear out, but not here, and Genia doesn't want to shift unless she has to.

Caterpillars are a great consolation. I have got a couple of Pale Tussocks, which I never knew as a boy, beautiful pale green creatures with white hair and tufts and bits of velvet black with a plume of red hair for a tail. The first one I got went off its food, but as soon as I got a second it set to again and they are both in great form. Lime leaves, luckily, are not rationed. I have also a couple of Woolly Bears, brown ones.

Yesterday I sent off a complete set of the proofs corrected to Macmillans in London for sending to America. I hope to goodness they get there all right, as if things go on in the way they seem to be, I don't see how there can be much bookselling and publishing here. Howard from Cape's writes that he is up all night putting out incendiary bombs on Hampstead Heath and down all day in the cellars at Bedford Square. His assistant writes grimly, 'The end of the world is not yet', and they are going ahead as well as they can, but are much bothered by the vagaries of the post.

The book is now done except for the endpaper map[2] and the arrangement of pictures and tailpieces, which cannot be done until we have proofs of the blocks.

Are you well supplied with sketching materials? If there is anything you lack, let me know ... Paints ... blocks ... brushes? I can get Rowneys or Reeves to send anything you want, even if I can't find it in Ipswich. So don't hesitate to ask. I think drawing is a very good way of dealing with the situation ... at least it concentrates your mind on things that are not affected by any idiocy of human beings. Anyhow making careful drawings of caterpillars has that effect on me.

I hope that if all goes well till the end of October, there is likely to be some sort of a lull through the winter. Let's look forward to that.

Much love to both of you,

Arthur.

1   Harkstead Hall is very close to Harkstead Church, but the place
    is so tiny that it is perhaps likely that by 'the village' AR meant
    Chelmondiston, of which Pin Mill is a part.
2   As published, the endpaper map in *The Big Six* is a *Coot Club*
    map reused. If there was ever a special *Big Six* map, it may have
    been destroyed in the Blitz (see letter of 27 September 1940).

                    To Edith R. Ransome [abridged]
Sept. 20 1940   Harkstead Hall

My dear Mother,
    Cape's write that they are still hoping to go on publishing.
About half the blocks are made, though the unfortunate blockmaker, deprived of the normal gas supply, is having to hire
cylinders of hydrogen to heat his acids and baths. However, as
Cape's write, 'Up to the time of writing (3.30 p.m. on the 17th)
he has not yet been blowed up.' His works, I think I told you,
are most uncomfortably close to Blackfriars Bridge.
    I have also heard this morning from the English agent of the
American Macmillans, who says he has sent the proofs on their
way to America. So the spiritual barometer at Harkstead Hall has
gone up, though it won't be at 'set fair' till we hear they have
reached the other side. I was beginning to think it quite likely
that the whole year's work would be in vain.
    We have heard from Barbara that Bettyfold, Hawkshead, is to
let (at least it was a few days ago). And to my great and delighted
astonishment Genia says that, given a decent house, water
supply, indoor sanitation, etc., she is prepared to go back to the
Lakes . . . It is very lonely here now that there is no sailing, no
visiting yachts, and our local friends departed. So I have actually
written to enquire about Bettyfold's rent. If we get it (which *I
don't for a minute allow myself to believe*) we both think that you
had better come too, if and when we go there.
    But probably nothing will come of it. Still, if it does come off,
I shall, for one thing at least, be quite grateful to Mr. Hitler. It
really would be rather lovely to be back in the hills.
    The gallant Capes are howling at me to get going on another
book as soon as I can. By 'gallant' I mean 'gallant' in the full

sense of the word. They have had bombs in the British Museum yard, just the other side of the square, and also bombs on Dean Street, and they seem to spend most of their time underground, but are determined to keep on publishing regardless. Of course it means they have to concentrate on what they call 'safe' books, among which, luckily for me, they count mine. Hence their horror at the suggestion that there may be no more.

The cats are well. We now call Podge the Air Raid Warden. She comes dashing in the moment the sirens go. Polly has to be called, and Podge, in shelter, watches anxiously for her arrival. Podge, from the start, has taken aeroplanes seriously, and while anything is on overhead, lies with her eyes anxiously looking up at the ceiling.

Well. Good luck to you both, and much love.

Arthur

I don't think of Bettyfold as at all likely, but the real news is that, given a decent house, Genia thinks of trying the lakes again. I'll let you know if anything more is heard of it.

To Edith R. Ransome

Sept. 27 1940   Harkstead Hall

My dear Mother,

I had a melancholy letter from Cape's, or rather a still confident letter but with melancholy news, to say that by Tuesday all the blocks for my book had been made and that by Wednesday morning they had all been blown up, the unfortunate blockmaker having lost his works, his machinery and everything else.

The original drawings must have been sent back to Cape's the moment the blocks were done, as he says that they are safe. But now the whole business of making the blocks has to be started afresh somewhere else.

Cape cheerfully says he is going to start again but my own private feeling is that publication is pretty doubtful.

Sad about not getting Bettyfold, but Genia has definitely made up her mind she'll go back to the lakes, IF I can get hold of a decent house. The trouble is that the place is chock-a-block and there are none. I have however heard of one place at an awful price, a very small but modern house, 17 acres of grand fell, down to the water's edge, good water supply, and two good sites on it that I could sell off if I found I had to. But, of course, nothing may come of it and I should be terrified by the price if I did not think that land was safer to hold than money.

I haven't got your paints yet, but will at the first opportunity. I think there is a shop in Ipswich that keeps Reeves' colours (which I fancy yours are) or Windsor and Newton. The cards are more difficult. I wanted some myself a year or two ago and could not find anything decent. But I will try. There is nothing in the catalogues of either Reeves or Rowney. What I think the best of all ways is to make the sketch on ordinary Whatman and then put it in one of the folders you can buy for making Christmas cards out of photographs. You know the things . . . some are 'slip in', others have a slit at each corner and you just put the corners of the picture into the slits. That way anybody can frame the picture if they want to or put them into any other mount they happen to prefer.

I do not think in the whole history of the world there has ever been anything so absolutely senseless as this bombing match between Berlin and London and I simply cannot understand why, knowing the conditions, Sinclair was such an ASS as to start it.[1] There may be military objectives in both cities but since Hitler had shown he was prepared to refrain from trying for the London ones we ought to have accepted that 'convention' and not gone for the ones in Berlin . . . especially as London is the more vulnerable of the two. The whole thing is desperate lunacy from which both sides stand to lose and in which civilians on both sides will be the chief sufferers.

However, in a lunatic asylum the sane man and his sane mother hold their tongues, and merely pray that the moment may come when the idiocy of the thing becomes so apparent that even the lunatics bring it to an end.

Love to both of you.

Stick to your painting regardless of the hullabaloo,

Arthur.

1 Sir Archibald Sinclair, Secretary of State for Air; a staunch supporter of the bombing offensive throughout the war.

To Edith R. Ransome

Oct 3 1940   Harkstead Hall

My dear Mother,

Your warning came too late!

Your son is once more a lake country landowner.

I have bought seventeen acres, with *half a mile of lake frontage*, at the bottom of what used to be the Weald Wood on Coniston lake. Fir Island (not mine) is about half way along my half mile. The house is tiny, but civilised in the extreme . . . electric light, central heating, proper water supply and what not. And there is also a cottage which is very tempting as a work room. Both are one storey buildings, very well done indeed. It was built by the Maynards and the whole place has been improved by their successors. The whole of the land on both sides of it and above it belongs to the Forestry Commission, so that it can never be spoilt. And the shoulder of the hill on the other side of the lake just hides Coniston village, so that you see the Old Man and all that as if there were no village there at all. It has its own boat harbour, and a small wooden pier.

The buildings are of gey Coniston stone and they are roofed with green slate from the Old Man.

You will probably remember where there is a sharp bend in the road along the lake a bit above Peel Island and a particularly lovely little wood between the road and the lake. That little wood is inside the southern boundary, and I have the whole strip between lake and road for about half a mile, the bulk of the land of course being above the road where the old Heald wood used to be.

I have plunged with both feet, but, after all, lake frontage is something tremendously worth having. There are also two sites for possible houses without spoiling ours, supposing at some time or other I felt I had to sell some of it. 17 blooming acres.

I have just got back, after a journey too awful to describe . . . The last lap, across from Rugby, I did with an old general last night. He said, 'We'll go in the guard's van'. We did, and shared it with 46 others, no air, and no light, getting to Bury St. Edmunds late last night. I came on today.

No time for another word if I am to catch the post.

Bad news from Capes. Some of the originals were blowed up after all, so I have to set to work to do some more. But they still hope to publish.

Barbara and Gnossy send their love to you. The whole clan, Kelsalls and everybody clustered at Riggs round the returned prodigal, and made me feel very happy.

Genia has always liked the place, ever since we used to go over to see the Maynards in it, and it has been made even more efficient and civilised since.

I wish I had a photograph. But you know the place. The house looks across towards Torver, getting all the sun there is.

But how we are going to cram in, I don't know.

Still it is so small and so well-arranged that I really do believe Genia won't be ABLE to overwork herself no matter how she tries.

Much love

Your affectionate son

Arthur

I will let you know our plans as soon as we know them.

To Edith R. Ransome

The Heald,
Coniston,
Lancashire.

Oct. 21 1940

My dear Mother,

Your welcome letter arrived this morning when I was pounding through the bracken on top of the Heald. I found it here when I came rolling back, a dripping mass of fat. I think I must be losing about a pound a day. Besides our own seventeen acres I have bought the shooting in Machell's Coppice, a very lovely bit of woodland between us and Brantwood. Got it very cheap because it is not worth anything . . . too much poached, I think. But it is a lovely wood for birds etc., and I daresay I shall get a rabbit now and again.

It wasn't tummy that cracked up before we moved. It was my blessed lung, that suffered pretty badly when I had that embolism and bust the blood vessels into it after my last operation.[1] It is a

bit on the wonky side, and I get a touch of congestion or something. All right now. Tummy behaving moderately so I have
nothing to complain of, and being back in the lakes makes
everything look pretty good. You know I had quite made up my
mind that nothing would get Genia to come back. I don't think
anything would have except the war, which of course got lively
in our parts very early on. She had had only three or four good
nights since the beginning of June, and plenty of bad ones before
that. Now she is back, she seems really very pleased . . . though
the rooms are so tiny that we can't move without hitting our
funnybones. There is none of the shut-in feeling she didn't like
at Lanehead, and the house itself though tiny has none of the
primitive savagery of Ludderburn. First-rate water supply for
one thing. Also you are quite wrong about the sun. It always
looks from the lake as if the Heald Brow goes up perpen-
dicularly. It doesn't, and we get all the sun there is except the
very early morning.

Our main trouble is lack of petrol, and there is going to be
great difficulty in keeping up a supply to run the electric light,
let alone getting into Ulverston for shopping.

It is a lovely bit of land, half a mile of the lake front, and it is a
pleasure to think that when we are dead we can let it go to the
National Trust . . . if only I can scrape enough to keep it going
till then. But I have emptied my purse, stocking, pockets and
mattresses! Lake frontage in these parts is valued at diamonds
an inch.

Genia is hard at it from morning to night, fitting blackouts
and trying to squeeze our stuff in. But as soon as that is done and
the place is in working order she does not think the actual house
will be hard work . . . though with seventeen acres to play with
she'll find plenty to do outside. Still, we shall plant trees rather
than try to garden.

One of our boats has arrived, pretty leaky, and I caught four
perch and a minnow just to show that it could be done, in our
own bay. There is good trout ground all along our half mile.

Ulverston is our nearest shopping centre. If we go to
Coniston village it means nearly ten miles (more I think) to go
there and back, and that means not going to Ulverston. More or
less standing a siege until the war is over, but the Ulverston

butcher delivers, and will bring parcels from the grocer etc. So
I think that even if we can't get to Ulverston we shall manage.

To get here by train, which I hope you will, you have to go
to Windermere and get the motor man at Riggs' to drive you
across at enormous expense. Otherwise, you go to Ulverston
and Greenodd, and then have slightly less to drive. Out of the
way it most certainly is.

A big batch of proofs have somehow got lost in the post,
unfortunately the beginning of the book, which is mucking up
the spacing of blocks elsewhere. But I have done the new pictures
to replace the exploded, and the proofs of them came today.

I must say I rather miss the bangs and bumps and the rest of it
as well as the spectacular side, which was very fine. But after all,
not only was it not our house, but we knew that our tenure of
it was extremely uncertain, and that the moment the war ended
we should be kicked out. So I have no real regrets to counter-
balance the joy of getting back to the lakes, and Genia in spite
of the struggle in getting in, is visibly better. I think she would
have had a breakdown if she had not come away, especially as
there was absolutely no excuse for being just where we were and
all our friends had already gone. Further we had been told that
we might be told to go at 24 hours notice and not allowed to
take anything with us but hand luggage. Which left us in the
horrid condition of having no solid ground anywhere. Anyway,
the total effect was that she made up her mind to lump the rain-
fall, and here we are, with 17 acres of our very own.

Love to Aunt Helen. I think you and she must come here
together. Genia will write the moment she sits down!!
Much love,
Arthur

1   In 1937. See *Life*, p. 356.

To John Berry [postcard]
[n.d.; 1940]   [The Heald]

Thank you for a very jolly letter. I think you and Juliet were
a bit young to start on the books at eight.[1] You see they were
really written for moderately grown-up people, like your father

and me. By the way, he must have a grand hard skull. I was knocked out for nearly three days when I got a whack on the head from the boom. Now then, secrets are secrets, and I mustn't let out more than is in the books, but I will tell you this much, that most of your guesses are about right. Walton-on-the-Naze, for example, and Bowness.[2]

Your father was quite right to have strong views about Windermere. It is much more tricky sailing than at sea.

If I waste time writing letters I won't have any for writing books.

Good luck to the skipper, mate and crew of the *Mavis* and best wishes for fair winds![3]

Arthur Ransome.

Best wishes to the Blood Brother too.[4] I like your sign.

1   John and Juliet Berry, twins, were born in 1928.
2   Walton figures anonymously in *Secret Water*; Bowness is Rio in the lake stories.
3   The Berry family had sailed on the Broads in 1939, in a yacht called *Mavis* (by coincidence also the name of the original of *Amazon* and the real name of 'Titty' Altounyan).
4   John Berry had evolved a game of Blood Brothers from chapter XII of *Secret Water* ('Blood and Iodine'); it 'involved a reluctant school friend'.

To Charles and Margaret Renold

Feb. 13 1941   The Heald

Dear Margaret and Charles,

You have put off coming so long that we think now you had better wait till the fishing begins, when there will be chances of fishing along our shore, judging from the rises we have seen and the steady work of heron and dipper. Those two wouldn't be hanging about as they are unless there was something to hang about for.

We have both been ill, with this blasted flu or some similar germ. Better now, more or less.

I have made a few flies of the elementary kind, and am very pleased with a new body for the waterhen bloa, made with blue grey herl from hawk's tail feather ribbed with yellow tying silk. I think it looks better than the usual mole dubbing.

Poor Miss Lee[1] is in extremis. And I have wasted six whole weeks on her. She'll do all right some day, but not now, and I am again desperately hunting for a Swallows and Amazons plot with Wild Cat Island and perhaps the river as main background. At least seven in ten of my infant correspondents write demanding another S. and A. with the lake background. Ditto, even from America. But what on earth can they have as a motive? . . . Mining used up in *Pigeon Post*, North Pole used up in *Winter Holiday*, mere exploration etc. in *Swallowdale*. What the hell? VITAL R.S.V.P. S.O.S.[2]

Also I desperately need a new pair of breeches. Is there any tailor in Manchester who can COPY a pair of breeches if sent to him? I heard of a firm at Wigton, but the miserable wretches say they can only do trousers!

Pity about Miss Lee. She has good points, but just is not ripe. She is too fantastic to be done before she has properly rooted herself in reality.

The infernal sheep are chewing up all the young stuff in our coppice.

A tufted duck is visible from the window. Also of course the heron and dipper. AND eleven marauding muttons. They stand up on their hind legs like goats and simply murder every living sprout.

We are much looking forward to your coming.

I am told that at the beginning of the season spinning is the best way of getting the lake trout, but the old books seem to think that they can be got with Winter Browns and Spring Blacks.

DAMN IT, what CAN those young devils, Nancy and Co., devise as a main object to stretch their wills on this time?[3]

My old brain is truly bust and wore out . . . It can run headaches but not yarns.

My own suspicion about the early fly fishing is that IF as now appears to be true, the trout do go heartily for minnow at the beginning of the season, it ought to be possible to meet their tastes by fishing flies that resemble little fish. The locals do fish Butchers. Now Butchers seem to me very bad portraits of little fish. My own fry flying is better, but, I think, unnecessarily elaborate in the tying. Is it worth while to aim at (a) very tiny perch (b) salmon fry (c) minnows. There must be lots of (a) in the lake. What about teal feather dyed greenish with pale olive hackle?

Yours ever

A.R.

1   The title of this book was changed by his publisher in due course to *Missee Lee*, to Ransome's continuing regret.
2   VITAL R.S.V.P. S.O.S. inserted in large, agitated pencil letters.
3   Urgent vertical scorings in the margin emphasise this paragraph.

To Margaret Renold

Feb. 19 1941   The Heald

Dear Margaret,
    I don't think you were at Cambridge, but I have an idea that some of your little friends were . . . rude Lady Barlow[1] for example? And perhaps some of your little friends have brats at Cambridge.
    Poor Miss Lee was at Cambridge for about one ecstatic month or term before being called back to China to receive the instructions of her papa, then on his deathbed. He, I may tell you for your PRIVATE information, was a Chinese pirate and at the very top of his profession, for which reason he had done his best to give his daughter (he having no sons) a slap up western education. Now, he dying, she has to give up Cambridge and come back to take charge of his affairs, rule his fleet and territory and keep the pirate business going. It is very important to the story to get the whole Cambridge background vivid in her mind and so in the reader's, and therefore I must get sure of it myself. I won't waste time now in explaining how Captain Flint and the Ss and As get mixed up in this, but they do (I think you will like the picture of Captain Flint in a bamboo cage) and in the end

Miss Lee's (Li's) yearnings after Cambridge count for a lot in the final get-away. Don't let out all this part of things to a soul. What is wanted is simply the background for a Chinese girl student in her first term at Cambridge. She MUST, I think, be in college, and I dare say that could be arranged. She has also of course been to English schools, and been a girl guide.

Has Charles, Hans, Peter, Timothy[2] thrown away (as alas I did) his School Latin Grammar? I want the one with 'Common are to either sex Artifex and Opifex . . .'

To ease the task of putting the questions without giving owt away, I have made a questionnaire, which I enclose with this.[3]

The book is growing . . . but so far like a snowball . . . the stuff is piling up, but I am still much bothered over the intricate girder business of the skeleton which at present it lacks, except for head and tail. Lovely head . . . Elegant tail . . . but suet pudding in the middle. But that will come right . . . The scene of a pirate chief airing his singing lark while the pirates are set to catch grasshoppers for it (true to life) . . . the scene of the Dragon processions (which I watched at Hankow) . . . the dreadful burning of the *Wild Cat* . . . Miss Lee's backsliding from her duty to her father's spirit, starting back for Cambridge and an academic career, but recalled to the path of virtue and piracy by the sound of the twenty-two gongs that show her position and dignity have been usurped . . . all these things are pretty nutty. But TIME is darting on, and Cape's send a howl a week saying they must have the book early, and I am far behind schedule, and that damned Hitler . . . etc. etc., So do, please, dear Margaret, tackle firmly the girl friend who has the necessary dope and let me have it quick . . . QUICK . . . QUICK . . . *QUICK*!!

Love to both of you,
Arthur.

The weather is so damned awful that it almost *must* turn nice early in the fishing season when I hope you will get here. Now it is cold and snowing and blowing and we are just through one lot of colds and thinking about starting another.

1   Esther, Lady Barlow, was the wife of Sir T. D. Barlow; by birth a Gaselee. She had been an undergraduate at Newnham

College, Cambridge, and was one of Margaret Renold's closest friends. Miss Penelope Renold writes, 'though a kind woman, she did not suffer fools, as she saw them, particularly gladly . . . I never knew her to be rude'. Her daughter, Theodora Winter, indignantly denies that anyone could so accuse her. The Barlows and the Renolds met each other in the Manchester business world.

2   The Renold sons.

3   Questionnaire now missing.

To Margaret Renold

Feb. 24 1941   The Heald

My dear Margaret,

   Well done and thank you very much. And please transmit my politest thanks to rude Lady Barlow . . . A kestrel has perched on a tree within direct easy view . . . Excuse me while I have a squint at him through the glasses . . . The *Cambridge Student's Guide* gives no end of help (I will duly send it back). The Latin Grammars puzzle me . . . I thought old Kennedy (was it?) survived the Great War.[1] And I miss 'Artifex and Opifex' etc . . . the substitute rhymes are not so good. But they'll be useful too. All shall be duly returned. I find it hard to believe that rude Lady B. is right in saying that female undergraduates do not fall for plates etc. with the arms of Cambridge . . . though no doubt they are presently ashamed of them and hide them away. But I've no doubt R.L.B. was strongminded and ruthless and above such frivolities from the very start. My Miss Lee collects them, and, in exile, treasures them, and also a varnished oak plaque with the arms of Newnham . . . Hi! Hey! You know Hans' oars . . . Well, coxes preserve their rudders . . . Does Newnham have a college boat and could my Miss Lee cox it, and bring a rudder proudly back to China to hang on her wall, just as the Troutbeck vicar, who coxed his college boat, has his rudder hung up on the wall of his study to help inspire his sermons? This would be fine for a whole lot of different reasons . . . Would Hans know?

   Your parcel was delivered direct to my workus BUT, with an honesty beyond compare, I did not hoard your lovely chocolate mints (God bless Elizabeth Shaw!) but nobly handed over the box intact to the Boss, who is, I believe, writing to thank you for them. I thank you for them too, very much so, and have been given a share as a reward for honesty.

Poor Miss Lee is trudging along . . . page 87 . . . about 90 pages behind last year's schedule . . . I work at her morning noon and night as ordered by Mrs. Morrison[2] . . . but am still in a desperate fog over a lot of the story. Still, there's no getting away from it . . . there are pleasant bits and Miss Lee is a tough but a darling. Gosh, the moment of escape, when lights ahead in the dark show them the pirates have pulled the boom across the river closing the trap . . . And the Dragon processions in the pirate town . . . And Miss Lee's tale of her father's career . . . No, there really are points about it if only I can put the bones together so as at least to look as if the tale had an articulated skeleton.

Genia has had a fresh invasion of flu germs, but today seems to have swept them out and is now walking the hillside followed by the two cats.

Have you ever heard of an illustrator called Ardizzone?[3] Cape's offer him to illustrate a more or less grown-up book about the Lake Country of fifty years ago.[4] Not for *Miss Lee*, alas. That I have to bungle myself, and I am hard at work on dragon banners, Chinese junks and what not, and much handicapped for lack of Chinese landscape and costumes.

Well, as you say, no meandering. Back to *Miss Lee*.

Yours ever,
        and very many thanks.
                Arthur Ransome

1   At Rugby and earlier, Ransome probably used B. H. Kennedy's *Revised Latin Primer* of 1888; it was revised again in 1930. He may also, or instead, have used the *Shorter Latin Primer*, which was revised in 1931.
2   Unidentified.
3   Edward Ardizzone, who was rapidly becoming Britain's best-known and most successful illustrator.
4   Not again referred to, unless, which seems unlikely, *The River Comes First* (never finished) is meant.

To Margaret Renold
Aug. 13 1941   The Heald

My dear Margaret,

There are five spare minutes before the postman comes, so I give the machine its head and it rattles away to you.

The main news is that Genia has had a flock of teeth taken out and, though feeling bad at the moment, will, I hope, feel better for it later. She is reading P. G. Wodehouse and when I went to work the house was rocking with her chuckles in spite of toothless jaws.

Next. Gosh! What tomatoes! The very best ever seen or tasted, and they arrived absolutely pristine and unsquashed.

Next. The lake is full again, and there will be good fishing in the Crake for anybody who has time to go there. I have none. But I did get a couple of rabbits last night before dark.

Next. Your book the Big 6 seems to have taken the fancy of the Yanks . . . It is now out there and the *Times* and the *Tribune* go all out, mistakenly of course, but lucky for me.

Next. *Missee Lee* is now being printed, or rather set up while I am desperately trying to get pictures done before the proofs arrive . . . And . . . I . . . can . . . NOT . . . draw.

Next. This winter will probably be my last, because my method of keeping going by pouring down milk will be brought to an end by that damned grocer Woolton and that means the end of me. I've tried the experiment of stopping the milk three or four times and each time the result has been pretty disastrous. However anyhow, that'll mean an end to having to write book after book.

None the less, I am hunting round about [for] a new one, which both Yanks and Cape's want *quam celerrime*. Subject . . . I think the Great-Aunt of *Swallowdale*. Captain Flint takes Mrs. Blackett off for a jaunt abroad, leaving Nancy and Peggy in charge of Beckfoot . . . Damned good for them. The G.A. hearing this, writes a letter to them refraining from giving her opinion of their mother but making it very plain, and invites herself to Beckfoot to look after them[1] . . . Now then . . . WHAT? Or have you an immense idea of your own?

Next. Have you any book with a lot of Chinese pictures in it, from which I could crib?

Next. The only water supply in the district that did not wilt
during the drought was ours. We had lashings of bath water etc.
all the time.

Next. For the last fortnight a man with a devoted wife has
anchored every day after breakfast in our bay, and fished until
dark. His best catch was 8 perch and a 1lb pikelet. His twelve
worst catches were blanks. And still, from breakfast till dusk that
superhuman female sits in the boat with him, making tea on a
spirit stove, and herself desperately trying to catch bait for her
lord and master. Gosh! How do these blighters manage to put it
across? I think Charles and I ought to take lessons from him.
One of his secrets I do know. He does not allow a watch or
clock in the boat. Again and again when I have gone down to
see what they were doing, she, in a quivering voice, has asked
the time. Tell this to Charles (or don't you dare?).

The Chinese pictures are terrific. I want trees and Chinks . . .
and donkeys . . . and chopsticks . . . and opium pipes . . .
sampans . . . Water kongs . . . costumes . . . what not. I got a
catalogue of the Chinese Exhibition but the wretched cataloguer
happened to be exclusively interested in crockery.

Poor *Missee Lee*. I wish I had the old title, but they all hate it.
Love to both of you.

A.

1   The first mention of his idea for *The Picts and the Martyrs*.

To Margaret Renold
Dec. 31 1941   The Heald

My dear Margaret,
I think it quite likely that I shall not be your dear Arthur by
the time you have read a few more words. So hold tight.

I know very well that Charles is worked off his hoofs so that
it is sheer unpatriotic villainy to ask him to do anything extra.
But all the same, being anything but anybody's dear Arthur, here
is what we want him to do.

The man in Ulverston says that he thinks he can get hold of an
autocycle of some kind by March, adds that he has several

customers with their mouths open for it, and winds up by urging me to try to get hold of one through a larger firm (he's a nice chap and a friend of my solicitor). Well, you who make chains for everybody, no doubt make the chains that are used by the autocycle people. Do you think Charles could tell his secretary to order one? (This is assuming that you were a good woman and looked in the shop windows and saw there were none in Manchester.) They'd almost certainly let him have one right away.

The trouble is just this: our car is now pretty old . . . tyres very worn, etc., and we are in plumb terror lest we should any fine day find ourselves without transport of any kind. Hence urgent need of a standby.

What we want is the best autocycle made. I think that James and the Excelsior are the best known. The thing is a sort of pip-squeak of a motor bicycle, in fact a sort of bicycle with a motor (1½ or 1¾ horsepower or something like that) that will just get you there somehow. It's a thing that either of us could ride. Cost recently about £35. I am prepared to pay up to £50 if we can get one quick. The private individual ordering one gets one all right after about nine months to a year . . . and we are afraid of being immobilised by some miserable thing going wrong (that we nowadays can't get replaced) any blooming minute.

What about it?

Damn the fellow! Curse the blasted nuisance! How can he expect Charles or anybody else to be bothered in these days about his miserable scooter?

You will be able to think of much more along the same lines.

The odd thing is that the Ulverston man says he hears there are plenty to be had in Liverpool . . . but that may be just gossip . . . like the onions that are said to be all over Windermere when you go to Ulverston and all over Ulverston when you go to Windermere.

Anyway, if the thing can be done, don't worry about price. I think the thing to do is to get the best made, in the hopes that it won't go wrong so soon. If the thing can't be done at all, why then, I've sketched out for you the opening paragraph of your letter to say so.

New Year's Eve, and the new book not started, and Cape's already starting their hurrying-up methods.

Well, I hope 1942 won't be quite such a beast as 1941, though I rather think it will be. 1949 is the year I pin my hopes on.

And tonight we shall duly drink your health, with our very best wishes for you in 1942, whatever that year's character may turn out to be.

Yours ever (dear or damned), Arthur.

From G. Wren Howard [extract]

Feb. 2 1942 Thirty Bedford Square,
London W.C.1.

Dear Ransome,

We are getting a number of entries for the *Now & Then* competition from one school.[1] One of the mistresses is a friend of Miss Wedgwood,[2] and writes to say that she had hoped to get more entries but that nearly the whole school was deflected by finding some alleged errors in the semaphore page of *Missee Lee*. I enclose the findings[3] of one committee that sat to consider the question, but have not yet been able to have the illustration checked by the local experts.

Paper for a reprint of *Missee Lee* has been snowed up in Scotland for some weeks, but I hope that they may have been able to dig it out and despatch it southwards before this last lot of snow set in.

Yours ever, G. Wren Howard.

1 *Now and Then* was a literary journal published by Cape in the thirties, forties and fifties.
2 C. V. Wedgwood, the historian: published by Cape.
3 The 'Robin Patrol' decoded the original message and identified eight mistakes: e.g., GXORGE for GEORGE.

To G. Wren Howard

Feb. 4 1942 The Heald

Dear Howard,

Curse and confound Captain Flint. It isn't the first time that fellow's carelessness has got me into trouble.

What's to be done? I have corrected the original and should like a new block made at Captain Flint's expense, damn him.

Or, if there's not time for that,[1] remove the title from under the illustration (page 190) and print in very small type the following note, which, I think, should be given to Miss Wedgwood to send her friend with the school cram full of yeomen of signals.

> NOTE: This is not the original S.O.S., which is somewhere in China. Captain Flint had to make a copy of it for this book. While he was doing it Roger was playing the penny whistle and somebody else was not doing any harm just fingering Captain Flint's new accordion. He says that is why there are at least eight mistakes in the signals. Really of course his beastly carelessness. N.B.

I do hope you'll manage the block in time for the reprint. Fry, frizzle and broil that fellow, Flint. What's the good of my taking trouble, when he goes and lets me down like this?

Yours ever,

Arthur Ransome

1   There was.

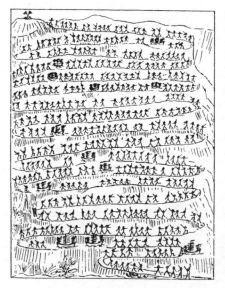 

Captain Flint's S.O.S. – the original and corrected versions

To Charles Renold

March 12 1942   The Heald

Dear Charles,

Snowing again hard!!!!!!!!

Genia has an awful cold. I have a moderate ditto. A heavy cloud of blue smoke overhead shows where the Heald is and what the inhabitants think about it.

URGENT. You said that there would be various sums to pay for delivery, packing etc. for the monster.[1] Do please let me know what I owe, so that I can settle up (though the amount I ought to pay for the miracle working that got hold of the animal is of course incalculable) (many times the value of the mere machine, of course).

I am getting the hang of the animal, and yesterday shamelessly took him for a joy-ride over High Cross down into Hawkshead and so to High Wray to play chess with Liddell Hart[2] (whose book on *The Strategy of the Indirect Approach* you probably know). I arrived there so little exhausted that I won all three games (really because Liddell Hart don't practice what he preaches, and is prone to make a direct and premature attack of the exact kind that his book deprecates). I got back without trouble, having to pedal only a bit on the worst stretches of those two snorting hills.

Riding that animal is rather like donkey-driving. Much depends on sympathetic handling. But by thunder I am grateful to you about it.

Genia saw a fish rise at the head of the lake. It must have got its nose frostbitten.

Book desperately stuck.[3] If I didn't know Margaret was so busy I'd send the rotten synopsis and beg for suggestions.

Yours ever,

A.

1 His new motorcycle.
2 Basil Liddell Hart, the most influential of all modern British military theorists.
3 *The Picts and the Martyrs.* Two weeks earlier he had told Renold, 'My mucky book has reached page 232 in the rough squish . . . But what squish. Still it's got to be done somehow for export, even if it gets too hectic here and publishers give up and leave the field to the B.B.C. and the M.O.I.'

                         To Edith R. Ransome
March 28 1942   The Heald

My dear Mother,

Just a scrap for the week end. Good. I am glad you are getting painting things, though shocked that you do not yet know the delights of caviare. Absolutely lovely stuff, for which I long ago acquired a greedy taste.

I went out one day after five o'clock and found traces of deer in one of my woods, took up a good strategic position and waited, filling in the time by working on rough sketches of illustrations. At last I heard a twig break and presently spotted the white rump of a deer, unfortunately not one of the reds but one of the little roes. I had an awful job to get within shot without betraying my sinister presence, but did it in the end and got it through the heart. It didn't move a yard, and then I was very sorry and wished I hadn't fired. However, there it was, and I had an awful time getting the beast down from close up under Bethecar to within reach of the road. We ate the kidneys the same night, the liver made yesterday's lunch, and Braithwaite came over and skinned it yesterday and cut it up. Sunday dinner for us, for the Gnossies, for Braithwaite and for the farmer who sends my milk. But they are very small animals, compared with the reds. The Forestry people are pleased, because the roe deer do a terrific amount of damage and hardly ever get shot even in the big deer drives. If I hadn't been drawing and therefore quiet and still I don't suppose I'd have had a chance at it. There are some reds about somewhere. The tracks I had seen were reds. So I have still hopes of a big one. All the same, they are such lovely-looking beasts that it seems a pity to shoot them, and I wouldn't if it wasn't for the rejoicing of the hungry.

Still awfully cold. New snow on the Old Man today.

No fishing.

Book[1] just awful morass.

Much love,

                    Your affectionate son,

                                          Arthur.

1   *The Picts and the Martyrs.*

To G. Wren Howard [abridged]
June 19 1942   The Heald

Dear Howard,

But for being held together with artificial pads and props which more or less knock out the sort of exercise I like, I am all right, thank you.[1]

Picts and Martyrs, however, are all wrong. Position today: first rough draft completed and ghastly. First 100 pages of second draft now typewritten and rather less ghastly. Total length will be as near as nothing 350 pages of my usual typewriting (specimen page from last book enclosed herewith). Usual 20 full page pictures, I suppose. That means a book slightly, though not a lot, shorter than *Missee Lee*.

I am making Dick and Dorothea the main thread, as in *Winter Holiday*, with Nancy working away as the motive force of the messes, seen mostly through their eyes, and the Great Aunt herself looming in the background seen by the D.s mostly through the eyes of Nancy, that is to say two degrees removed . . . until just before the final climax. It is a devilish job and is taking a long time to do. It's the sort of thing that simply can't be rushed at. However, there it is, dull and dutiful, plodding steadily along.

I gather from your letter that a good lot of the books are out of circulation at the moment, but I think you have done very well to keep up with them in spite of all the difficulties so far.

The road below this house is a steady stream of motor cars every week end, carrying people with picnic baskets, who hurl their waste paper into my coppice. Meanwhile we, who are 12 miles from the nearest market town, have not got the petrol to go shopping even once a week. My poor Missis is finding things pretty difficult. However, it looks as if I am going to be able to get about a dozen acres planted with mixed timber, larch, spruce, Douglas firs, beech and birch this coming winter. And I still get an occasional rabbit, though I can't get up hill.

We see practically nobody. Liddell Hart comes over sometimes to play chess, but that's about all.

1   Ransome had recently suffered two ruptures.

From Evgenia Ransome
(Written across the top of the letter in AR's hand:
'Picts & Martyrs. I stopped it for a year but in the end
let Cape have it.')

August 8 1942   The Heald

My dear darling,

I am very sorry I am going to hurt you very much – but I don't believe in Fools Paradise or in beating about the bush.

I finished reading your book[1] and I think it is hopeless. It is the best manuscript you produce – it can be sent to printers' as it stands – but the book as a whole is dead.

If the Swallows & Co. are not allowed to grow up, if they are put back in the same background with the same means of enjoying themselves as they have done holiday after holidays – they can't help repeating themselves – so that the arrival at Rio, the setting up of camp, taking possession of their own boat, are no longer new things done for the first time – fresh and exciting – but pale imitations of something that happened many times before. This feeling of imitation and rehash is continually forced upon one by references to previous adventures in the same places.

Such adventures and excitements as this book offers are entirely spurious, they are dragged in not too convincingly and they really are not adventures of S. and A. and D.s – but the troubles between grown-up natives. The characters are either new or allowed to develop a bit more fully than they did in previous books are secondary and they are preoccupied with their relations to 'great-aunt' as to each other the butcher-boy with his darts, Mary Swainson with her young man, the postman's grumbling, the cook's opinion of G.A., the doctor, Col. Jolys and his home guards[2] – they make the book too grown up and facetious for a children's book – while they would really make a grown-up book childish.

After *Peter Duck, We Did Not Mean to Go to Sea* and especially after *Missee Lee* I think that even your faithful readers who always ask for the same characters doing the same things in the same places would find it dull. Your rivals would be very happy and well justified in saying that you 'missed the bus'.

If – being certain of selling as many copies of this book as he can print – Howard persuades you to publish it – I am sure that before very long you are going to be very sorry you let him.

I really hope that by now it is a physical impossibility to have it produced in time for Xmas – because that may make it easier for Howard to be honest in his opinion of the book.

You don't know how awfully sorry I am not to be able to say: 'It is your best yet.'

I hope Howard will use such paper as he saved up for it in reprinting the others. But if not – and if as a result our income drops down with a bump – never mind. Anything is better than to have a book to your name of which you are ashamed. So cheer up!   Love

G.

1   Ransome had left the script of *The Picts and the Martyrs* for Evgenia to read while he paid a visit to London and spent two days fishing. He found her letter waiting for him at Cape's office.
2   Given the year of the letter, an understandable slip. Colonel Jolys and his men are actually volunteer fire-fighters in peacetime.
3   The book finally went to the printer in December after his mother said that she liked it.

To Margaret Renold

Aug. 15 1942   The Heald

My dear Margaret,

I have come a cropper with the new book. I had plenty of suspicions about it, but talking about it is not allowed, and there was nobody handy for reading bits aloud to (another way of testing the ice) and so, with my mind more than half set on the patriotic pursuit of American dollars, I plodded doggedly on with dreadful result. I finished the beast, as far as the second complete typescript, sent it to Howard of Cape's who (no doubt blinded by the prospect of selling 20,000 copies before Christmas) said he liked it, agreeing to let me have a few more days to telescope two chapters somewhere in the middle. I had just got to the end of five days in town on that and other business and had gone to Cape's office on the last day to say goodbye when I found the bombshell in the shape of Genia's verdict (she had read it for the first time) . . . 'Hopeless. No use thinking of revising it. I should always be ashamed of it if I allowed it to be published. All wrong in characters, details and as a whole' . . . Consternation and monkeyhouse at Cape's! Howard, after telling Cape it was all right, had gone off on holiday. Paper for 25,000 copies already at the printer's waiting for it. Etc. etc. etc. I think I was more cheerful than any of them. But it is pretty ghastly after putting in such an awful period of non-stop sweat. I haven't yet had even an evening's fishing this year.

Chiefly I kick myself for not having accepted your invitation early in the summer and come to Woodheys and given you hell with the beastly thing, when perhaps I should have found out its hopelessness a bit sooner.

There it is. I feel as if with much thought and trouble I had built a motor car, and painted and varnished it all pretty, only to find that it wouldn't move and never could.

And the maddening thing is that I can't pretend to myself that Genia's wrong. She's right.[1]

Here are two books you should get hold of:

(1) *Evenfield* by Rachel Ferguson.

(2) *Financial Times* by Ronald Fraser.

Both published by Cape's and both full of good stuff.

Fraser's story of the family of artists and the one changeling in the midst of them who sees everything in terms of money is gorgeous fun. *Evenfield*, not yet published I think, but it must be coming very soon if not, has stuff about late Victorian and Edwardian family life which will go straight to your heart.

About my having no new book this year . . . there are two ways of disappointing people, one by not giving them an expected chocolate, the other by giving it them and letting them bite into it to find it stuffed with soap. It's better, I think, not to give them the chocolate.

BLAST anyway!

Have you noticed the lovely Trollope letter sold at Sotheby's . . . and the correspondence about it in *The Times*?

Love to Charles or words to that effect.

A.

1   If Ransome had remembered his oft-repeated doctrine that good books are written by authors solely for themselves, he might have brushed Genia's criticisms aside, for her arguments were chiefly that publication would damage his market.

To Edith R. Ransome

Dec. 10 1942   The Heald

My dear Mother,

Back again. All well here. But raining hard for days and such a gale blowing with it, one can hardly stand outside the house.

Well, on your decision, the book has actually gone to the printers, and I have to work like smoke to have the illustrations ready before the proofs begin to arrive. They have got the paper for printing. And they have also (even more difficult) got the zinc for making the blocks.

PLEASE, WHATEVER YOU DO, DON3T MENTION TO ANYONE MY PROJECT OF DEDICATING THE BOOK TO AUNT HELEN. I want to surprise her with it . . . she suggested a great deal of it.[1]

I got back just in time to charge the batteries up before they had run down so far that it would have been hard to start the engine.

Cactuses all right, and I believe my rare astrophytum is going to flower in the Spring. I think I can see the first hint of a bud. The flower, if it comes, will be as big as the whole cactus.

Weather such that my hope of a grouse is gone for this year. The season ends today.

It was very jolly seeing you and Aunt Kit. You would have been amused if you had seen the relief your letter caused at the office. One of the partners rushed off to the room of the other with "We've got the Ransome manuscript!" 'God bless his Mother,' was the reply.

           Much love,

               Arthur.

We have just eaten the last of your stewing pears. MOST AWFULLY GOOD.

1   The dedication to *The Picts and the Martyrs* reads:

To

AUNT HELEN

C.F.C.A.

PLUS 100. A1.

(These letters mean Certificated First Class
Aunt. There are Aunts of all kinds, and
all the good ones should be given certificates
by their nephews and nieces to distinguish
them from Uncertificated Aunts, like Nancy's
and Peggy's G.A.)

To Pamela Whitlock

Dec. 24 1942   The Heald

Dear Pamela,

This is just to bring you good wishes for Christmas (a bit late I am afraid).

I wonder what you have decided about turning into a wren or other uniformed bird.[1] No one has any right to give advice about it. As far as helping in the war generally, of course you are doing as much where you are as you would be in uniform . . . and, I expect, working a good deal harder. So the 'moral' question hardly comes into it. Thinking of it from the point of view of your future as a writer, you might come to feel you had missed something of general experience by not having buttons to polish and sergeants to salute. On the other hand you might not.

This amounts to saying you ought to follow your own internal compass and nothing else. Which you will do in any case. Good luck to you whatever you do.

Yours sincerely

Arthur Ransome

PS. How can you expect elderly, short-sighted persons to recognise you if one day you wear spectacles and the next you don't?

1   Evidently Pamela Whitlock was hesitating as to whether she should enlist in the Women's Royal Naval Service (WRNS – hence 'wrens') or not.

To Edith R. Ransome

Dec. 29 1942   The Heald

My dear Mother,

PLEASE do not mention my wretched book in your letters. Genia was completely miserable because in the end I decided to publish it and every mention of it reopens the wound. So please don't mention the wretched thing again.[1]

As for your letter having anything to do with Cape's decision, it, of course, did not influence Cape in any way. He, his wife and Howard, all liked the book from the beginning and wanted to publish it at once. Publication was stopped by ME, because of Genia's dislike of the book. She said that no amount of revision could make it fit for publication. I did, however, revise it, and, in its revised form, showed it to you. Your letter influenced ME, not Cape, though Cape naturally rejoiced when I told him that, after trying it on you, I had made up my mind to let him send it to the printers. The fact remains that the decision has been made, and that the book is at the printer's against Genia's judgement. She knows this and is miserable about it. The book cannot and must not be mentioned again in this house, and I do hope people will not bring the subject up again by mentioning it in letters.

Nobody has ever suggested that your opinion influenced Cape in any way. His opinion was decided last August. Nothing has stood in the way of the book being published except that I, for the reasons which you know, refused to let him have the book to send to the printers.

So that is that, and, I do hope, the end of it.

I never thanked you for the lovely Chinese fisherman. If ever I do another fishing book, I think I will use that for a frontispiece. 'Winter fishing.' It's easily the most shivery picture I know.

Northerly winds at last and very cold.

much love, your affectionate son,

Arthur.

1   *The Picts and the Martyrs*, which Evgenia continued to reproach AR for publishing against her sternest warnings.

To Pamela Whitlock

Jan. 4 1943   The Heald

My dear Pamela,

Good. I am glad the compass has settled down. They are an awful nuisance when they keep on swinging about.

And, if I may say so, I think your reasons are sound ones. There is a real danger of getting high and dry on the bank and out of the general stream. That's what I meant when I wrote (or did I in the end not write?) that you might afterwards feel you'd missed something.

I'm sorry for Collins[1] though, who, as he said, will have three men's jobs to fill when you go. Can't you lend him a Great Aunt, or a Grandmother to do your work while you are throwing machinery about.

I see something very jolly . . . a long way ahead . . . when you look back on the female sergeant in action and all the rest of it. And you'll find it lovely to escape into the real world where only character counts from the fantastic pantomime of literary freaks . . . who, if it were not that now and then one in a thousand of them produces by accident a book worth reading, could all be marched into a lethal chamber to the great benefit of their at present unlucky relations.

Do let me know what happens and how you get on. (Groans

sent here will find no echo and go no further.) And, of course, if you are sent up in this direction, as you well may be (all the best hotels in Windermere are turned into schools for W.A.A.F.s and what nots) we shall hope to see something of you if the female sergeant lets you have an afternoon off. Incidentally, I shall again fail to recognise you in yet another incarnation.

Good luck to you and best wishes from both of us,

Arthur Ransome.

1   William Collins, the publisher, for whom Pamela had been working.

To Pamela Whitlock [abridged]
[April 24?] 1943[1]   The Heald

Dear Pamela (18 buttons, a buckle and a cap badge),

I am a pig for being so bad at answering letters. Particularly as I enjoyed yours very much. For one thing, it showed that you made the right choice, and, for another, it showed . . . well, never mind that. Some day you are going to be a very good writer indeed. No hurry or fuss about it. The thing lies inevitably ahead. Sooner or later you are going to find a form that lets you do just what you want, when all you will have to worry about is careful listening to your own internal tuning fork so as to know what to leave out. The training of a real writer (we're not talking about the ambitious industrious people who want to BE 'writers' and to manufacture books) is just that, learning by long practice to know the note of the internal tuning fork and to reject almost before hearing it anything that does not ring true with it. But never you mind about that. Buttons, buckle and badge. Badge, buckle and buttons. Buckle, buttons and badge. It doesn't matter. The training for your own private job is going on all the time.

Forgive this prosing. But you, I think, are going to be a novelist. Perhaps not, but I think so. And, being interested, off rattles the typewriter giving impertinent advice (from one who could not be a novelist if he lived a hundred years).

Now, Forgive me for being so slow about letters, and go on

giving me news about the three Bs and all that goes with them.
Queer to think of you at Morecambe. As a small boy I spent a
lot of time at Arnside, and I often was over there watching the
Crossfields build boats in their shed by the shore, up to about
1935. They built one of the boats I have now.[2] One of the
brothers is dead, and their business may have come to an end.
They used to build in the old way using hardly any tool except
an adze and doing grand work. Over 500 fishing boats they built.
Good luck to you

Arthur Ransome

1　The date has been half-destroyed by a tear in the paper.
2　*Coch-y-bonddhu*. See letter to the Renolds, 6 March 1934.

To Pamela Whitlock

Telephone:
CONISTON 81
May 5 1943　　　　　　　　　　　　　　　　　The Heald

Dear Pamela,
　　You are a bit of a donkey. In your letter before the last you
talked of the perfect public for which you wanted to write books.
Now, do get it into your head that to think of your public is the
way NOT TO BE ABLE TO WRITE BOOKS. Good books are not written
FOR anyone. They are OVERHEARD. If you want to make
sure of becoming just one of the many manufacturers of passable
books you will choose a public and write books for it. But, surely,
you want to do better than that. You are a person in your own
right and you are the only public you ought to consider.
　　Never mind. It's not my business to give advice, so I won't
　　This is just to tell you that if, as may well happen, you are sent
on a route lorry drive that brings you along the EAST side of
Coniston lake, you must make your lorry break down just as you
pass a one-storey stone building just above the road about half
way up the lake. You can't miss it. There are actually two
buildings, one being my workshop. We shall both be very glad
to see you.
　　When you were at Kendal you were about 15 miles from

here, but, except by road, it is an impossible place to get at. However, nearly every day long strings of lorries, two telegraph poles apart, come rumbling by, driven by Pamelas of all kinds, male and female, and it would be very jolly if one of them came up to the house with a plug in her pocket and explained that unaccountably her engine was working on only three cylinders. We would give her tea, find the plug, and send her off again working on all four. We have a telephone.

Yours sincerely

Arthur Ransome

Anyhow do go on telling me of your adventures.

To Mary E. C. Fletcher

July 29 1943   [The Heald]

Dear Madam,

My publishers have sent me a cutting of your very gallant letter to the *Spectator* in answer to what I think must have been a complaint that my books can be enjoyed only by children of the rich.[1] They did not send me the original review, but quoted a sentence from it to the effect that I write about 'children whose parents can afford to buy dinghies, rent a farm for the summer holidays, and give eight-and-sixpenny books as birthday presents'.

Authors cannot very well reply themselves to such statements, though I should rather like to point out to the reviewer that it is cheaper to take lodgings in a farmhouse than to take lodgings at Blackpool, that boats are much cheaper than, for example, motor bicycles, that books cost less than legs of mutton and last longer, and that the children in my books are the children of naval officers, boatbuilder's workmen, doctors, farmers, teachers, etc. Also, of course, one might ask if the reviewer really thinks that none but birds can read Hans Andersen's *Ugly Duckling* and that it is necessary to be of the blood royal to enjoy *Hamlet, Prince of Denmark*.

I should be very sorry indeed to think that only children of one particular background can share the fun of open air doings, and the feelings that have been common to all young human beings from the beginning of time.

But I think I recognise in the complaint that called forth your letter something that I watched with great interest in Russia in the early years of the revolution there. Young devotees quite honestly believed that after 1917 literature must concern itself exclusively with the 'proletariat', and some of them went even further and believed that it must be written only by the 'proletariat'. It was a sterile and short-lived movement and was killed by the 'proletariat' itself which preferred to read the best books it could get and was not in the least interested in books that tried to be 'proletarian'. Within a very few years that movement became a memory and a joke, and the same thing will happen here.

But here I am wasting your time instead of doing what I set out to do which was to thank you for your letter. I am grateful to the reviewer too, but for whom your letter would not have been written. It is a great pleasure to me to know that my books are liked in such a school as yours.

Yours faithfully,

Arthur Ransome.

1   What Janet Adam-Smith asked, reviewing *The Picts and the Martyrs* in the *Spectator*, 9 July 1943, was: 'I wonder whether Mr. Ransome's stories appeal to children who live entirely outside the world of nannies, cooks and private boat-houses? Or may the line between Ransome readers and non-readers be drawn between town and country-minded children . . . ? . . . perhaps the children's librarians could tell us.' Mrs Fletcher was librarian at a girls' school in Shrewsbury and wrote in to say that AR's books were popular with pupils of all types and ages. See *Life*, pp. 399–499. Her letter appeared in the *Spectator* of 23 July 1943.

To Margaret Renold

Sept. 10 1943   The Heald

Dear Margaret,

We both thank you very much for the tomatoes which just make all the difference to everything one eats with them. And such good ones.

Yesterday for once was a fine day and Genia decided she'd give herself a day's fishing. So she joined the aged doctor Morris (our neighbour's father just back from Canada) in the only obtainable rowing boat. I sailed with an extra anchor so that they could get their boat steadily moored across the wind (you will remember that this is a point on which G. admits no half measures) and enough rods to empty the lake. And we went to the best place, and fished as hard as we could, and she caught three perch and Dr. Morris caught one but it got off, and the day would have been a total failure but for Margaret's TOMATO SANDWICHES!!!!! Explanation of the coyness of the perch came in the night with a gale from the north and another downpour of rain. But there it was, the day would have been wretched but was in fact most enjoyable thanks to the tomatoes.

And also thank you for sending the books which shall be sent back at once. I very much enjoyed the Chinese one, which is amazingly true to life. I laughed like fun over the Lunghai train running its daily gauntlet. It reminded me of going up the Yangtze with a captain who had an aviary aboard. There we all were talking on deck, when the old skipper remarked, 'Now, gentlemen, we join the canaries'. You see, he had armourplated the bit of deck where he kept his bird cages, and he explained that for the next two or three miles of river the boat was always shot at; so he got up and, carefully balancing his half-full glass, moved into shelter, accompanied by his passengers, and there we sat, admiring his birds, while he rang down for full speed ahead, and the engines did their damnedest and the whole boat quivered with their efforts, and ping ping ping from the banks until the danger point was passed when the old bird went along, peeking over the side to see the damage done, accompanied by the Chinese bosun, who had already stirred up a pot of paint, and mixed some putty, and was presently covering holes and dints, so that the marksmen on shore would lose face when the condition of the steamship was reported down river.

Love from both of us,

Arthur.

To Edith R. Ransome

Sept. 14 1943   The Heald

My dear Mother,

This is to report a joyful discovery, namely that though I can no longer row a boat at all, I can catch char by sailing. The method is that of the Bay of Biscay tunny-fishers, you must have seen them, with mast-high rods, travelling under easy sail. The whole difficulty is to sail slow enough. Finally, after a lot of experiment, I have got the thing to work, and last night we had a most luxurious supper on a brace of char, each close on half a pound (big for Coniston) caught by sailing. The trouble comes when you hook your fish, sixty to eighty yards away, and have to manage sail, rudder, rod, reel and net all at the same time with only two hands and false teeth. But the thing can be done and last night's supper was the proof of it. It can only be done during the two short seasons when the char come up from the deeps, June and again in September.[1]

Torrential rain again, and a howling thunder storm, which woke us by hitting us, blowing the telephone box to bits, and scattering fragments of it all over the sitting-room, luckily not setting anything on fire, though bits of the vulcanite fuse-box had obviously been burnt and melted. Last time it happened, the station-master had his fuse box blown up and found bits of it in his piano. This time, us. We had a good shaking and the roof leaks. But otherwise no damage. Lucky it didn't hit our electric light arrangements.

The B.B.C. write to say that their foolery comes in the Schools programme at 11.40 a.m. on September 23.

Much love,

Arthur.

---

1   Ransome proposed to introduce char-fishing into *Coots in the North*, the book he apparently began to work on after abandoning *The River Comes First*. *Coots in the North* was also dropped, in favour of *Great Northern?*, when Ransome had reached the usual stage of thinking that it had 'Beginning – End – but No Middle or backbone'. (I now accept that the date I attributed to this MS in *Coots in the North* was mistaken.)

To Pamela Whitlock

Dec 20 1943   The Heald

My dear Pamela,

As always it was very pleasant to hear from you.

Stick to it, filling your notebooks. Nothing is odder than the way in which a big slice of life, vivid at the time, fades utterly away when you escape from it into something different. It's like coming back from a year abroad. But notes, no matter how scrappy, are like stones dropped into a pool of still water. They stir up the whole picture and bring to life all sorts of other things, including the things you don't happen to have written down at the time. And sooner or later, I am quite sure, you are going to bring something very good out of it all, quite different from anything that anyone else produces.

Yes. I hope your next move brings you within looking-in distance and not merely within sight of the hills.

You are quite right. It is maddening to know that all that rubbish is being printed when Cape's have not got enough paper . . . But still more maddening to think of the huge masses of paper being used in printing forms for us all to fill in (I seem to be filling forms, the same forms, again and again and again).

I got up to London a few weeks ago, but spent the whole of my time there having flu in an hotel bedroom, worse even than a Nissen hut.

Best wishes for Christmas and for a New Year that may bring the worst of this beastliness to an end.

GO ON WRITING THINGS DOWN!

Yours sincerely,

Arthur Ransome

I hope I have read your address rightly!!!

To Pamela Whitlock

May 10 1944   The Heald

My dear Pamela,

I always felt fairly confident about you but am now absolutely sure. There are lovely things in the new book, dozens and dozens of them. And it is clear now that apart from just being able to write well you are really going to have something of your own to write. You've got nothing to worry about. All you have to do is to go on listening accurately to the secret tuning fork that other people can't share with you. And, of course, DON'T be in a hurry.

Now, for a change, listen to me instead of to the tuning fork. Howard is right in not wanting to publish this book as it stands now. It would be utter waste of good Pamela. I think I see a way in which you could turn it into a good book *but* when the time comes you will find that way yourself. I do not think you ought to touch it or to use bits of it until you can come at it from far away.

One thing wrong with it is that you have never made up your mind WHOSE book it is. Plaiting view-points is a very tricky business. If it does not come off, it is like setting up ladders only to kick them down. It means too many beginnings, instead of being able to stand on one in order to reach the next.

Another thing is that you have never been quite sure WHICH book it is.

Partly, no doubt, this is due to the difficulties under which it was written. But there is a deeper reason. You are growing. You can't help it. You can't stop yourself. All you can do is to re-member an old definition of Free Will, which is: 'To want to do what you would have to do whether you wanted to do it or not.' You would only do yourself harm if you tried to stay put at any particular stage. One of the very best things in this book is that you don't try not to grow.

Have you ever watched a moth working its way out of its chrysalis? The book is like that. It is simply crammed with promise. Whether you know it or not, you are reaching out towards something better but much more difficult than anything you've had a shot at yet. You are not writing about this or that 'adventure' but about life itself. You tug at heart strings again and again with the unmistakable (forgive this beastly hand-writing) tug of real power. I think you are going to do things that it is too late for me ever to try at.

I hope I've said enough to show you what very good, and often lovely stuff you have been writing . . . much better than anything you have done before. It is just because of that that I think it would be a good thing if you let me send it back to Howard to be kept in the safe, well out of your reach for at least a year.

Meanwhile: go on writing things down. But do forget the rubbish you once wrote to me about wanting to write for one particular audience. It is precisely that mistaken notion on your part which has caused most of the trouble about WHICH and WHOSE that I mentioned earlier. The ONLY audience you have to think about is Pamela. And Pamelas, of course, are like Chinese boxes, one inside the other. You have to get at the insidest you can and for ever be suspecting that there is yet another inside that. As for the people who will eventually read your books, leave them to sort themselves. They don't concern you. All good books are *overheard*. In all the really beautiful things in this book you were listening to the internal tuning fork and to nothing else.

I know it is very upsetting to write something and not publish it, but I think your own instinct is telling you something very like this. You need not be in a hurry . . . Lucky Pamela. And not one minute of the time you put into this has been wasted.

> Yours sincerely
>
> Arthur Ransome

Well: may I send the typescript back to Howard? It's just because the stuff is so good, and because you are going to be a writer, that I think you should hold it back. If you were a mere industrious manufacturer of books I should say 'Publish and be damned!'.

To Pamela Whitlock

Oct 23 1944 The Heald

Dear Pamela,

Sorry I've been such ages in answering your last letter, particularly because there was one bit of donkeyishness in it that I ought to have answered at once.

Get into your head the melancholy fact that children are omnivorous. They will like almost anything. They cannot distinguish between originals and imitations because all alike are new *to them*. They have no standards. And anybody who is such a fool as to try in editing a children's magazine to 'give them what they want' is trying to swim in a vacuum. Give them what *you* want, and, if you are the right editor you will presently find that *they* are wanting it too (and thinking they have wanted it all the time). It is as stupid to try to 'give them what they want' as it is to try to 'write books *for* children'. Give them what *you* want. Write books for yourself. That way you may produce the best children's magazine there has ever been, or you may not. You can only try. The same with books. You can not on purpose write a book (a good book) by addressing it to a particular audience outside yourself.

Do get it into your sensible head that good books are not addressed to their readers but are overheard by them . . .

                                                        A.R.

                        To Joyce Lupton
Dec. 9 1944   The Heald

HOLD IN TONGS
& BURN. GERMS.
My dear Joyce,

Hugh's voice on the telephone carries with it an extraordinary impression of solid, unshakeable, dependable competency. I don't suppose he knew for a minute what a comfort it could be 300 miles away to know that the owner of that voice was at hand and looking after you. Mother's death must have been a pretty bad shock for you, no matter what the reasoning part of your mind may have told you.[1] It's no use talking about that. But it could hardly have happened in a better way for her. She was tremendously enjoying being at home again and troubled only at the thought that she might some day be bedridden, which she has been spared.

And remember that all your life you have been the greatest possible pleasure and comfort to her, and that your marriage gave her Hugh as well and then your nice brats in whom she took such pride.

When Hugh spoke over the telephone, he said you had written, but the post here is awful, and the letter will probably come only today by the postman who must take this with him. He said you could manage a bed for me.

Unless Genia is well enough to be left alone here I shan't be able to come, even if I get clear of my germs by Monday. I came back from London with a flu cold, which I gave to Genia. We both more or less got right and rashy boasted of it, but now are in the thick of it again, running at the nose, dribbling horrible spectacles, cut off at the moment even from our neighbours. I can't twist my head more than about an inch, and it would be no help to anybody for me to come to Kew to turn your spare room into a sick-room and germ incubator. If I get right by Monday, I would like to come. We are both worse today, which may mean that the thing is coming to its natural end. The trouble is that we can neither of us go properly to bed or avoid going out of doors to deal with chickens fires and electric light.

You won't get this till Monday. I will telephone on Sunday night.

Very much love to you my dear old Joyce, and you can perhaps let Hugh know how very grateful I am to him.

Your affectionate brother
Arthur

1 Edith Ransome died on 7 December 1944, Kew.

To Joyce Lupton

Dec. 31 1944   The Heald

My dear Joyce,

All right. I will pound out on the typewriter such news as there is, when there is any, but mostly there isn't. I used to keep up a regular supply to Mother simply because I knew she liked to get a post, even if there was nowt to put inside the envelope.

I dare say you are right about the house, though I had thought myself that if one had to live in London or its neighbourhood, one could hardly do better.[1] Anyhow I have long ago made up my mind that our next house MUST be chosen by the one who has to run it. No more misfortunes like the Heald. And it would have been quite impossible for Genia to get away just now. So we will think no more about it.

The man who is clearing our gorse spotted a fox and came to the back door in great excitement about it. Would I come? So, chilblains and immovable neck and all, I got out, and presently saw the fox, coming along at a steady trot. He gave me a goodish chance, and I put a bullet in his brain killing him instantly. I felt a brute, but much better so than to leave him to be filled full of shot by half a dozen farmers. Our neighbour lost nine out of a dozen ducks, and we have been worried for some time, knowing he was nightly prowling round the hen runs. A most magnificent skin, of course quite undamaged. The gorse man went off with it in triumph for his wife.

My aforesaid neck is no better. I suppose it's all part of the same flu-cold or whatever it was. But it is very unpleasant being unable to turn one's head without a squeak of pain. I think the actual germ is now dead. I no longer am dribbling non-stop or sneezing ditto. Genia is also better, though she had a very bad fall in the scullery and hurt her shoulder, cut her hand and badly bruised her knees.

Page 290 of the dullest ditchwater I have ever produced.[2] High time I retired and took to writing sonnets.

Best wishes to you all for the New Year.

Arthur

1   After Edith Ransome's death, AR had the idea of buying her house in Kew.
2   He was now writing *Great Northern?*

PART SIX

Retirement

1945-1964

G REAT NORTHERN?, published in 1947, was the last of the Swallows books and, essentially, marked the end of Ransome's career as an imaginative writer. He was only sixty-three, but after all the vicissitudes of his life and health it is hardly surprising that he no longer possessed the power of concentrated, single-minded application over many months which had always been necessary for completion of his bigger literary tasks. In other ways his energy and determination were still remarkable. He even found the resources to godfather the Mariners Library for the publisher Rupert Hart-Davis, and as late as 1959 brought out a collection of essays, *Mainly About Fishing*, the preface of which shows no sign of flagging powers. For the rest, he fished, he sailed, he played billiards at the Garrick Club, he kept up his correspondence and, in short, until his health began its final decline in 1958, he enjoyed the sort of old age his friends and admirers would have wished for him.

Inevitably, there were some annoyances. He and Evgenia were unable to find a dwelling which suited both, or either of them. Ransome himself seems to have been hyper-sensitive to other people's noise. He complained about a tiresome child next door when he lived at Levington. C. E. Alexander reports, in his *Ransome At Home*, that he made himself unpopular at Harkstead by complaining of the noise of the children playing at a nearby school, and his postwar letters are full of lamentation about the noise of wirelesses when he was trying to live in London. He yearned for the quiet of the countryside, which for him meant the Lake District. Evgenia, for all her dislike of the constant rain, was prepared to accommodate him, but the experiment with Lowick Hall was a failure, and by the time they settled at Hill Top, Haverthwaite, Ransome was beginning to fail physically and mentally. In 1964 he was just about able to enjoy a quiet celebration of his eightieth birthday; then the letters come to an end.

★

From Myles North
Major M. E. W. North,
c/o Civil Affairs Branch,
East Africa Command H.Q.,

June 22 1944 Nairobi, Kenya.

Dear Mr Ransome,

My mother has copied your letter to her of May 12,[1] with its very kind messages to me, which this is to thank you for. There is nothing I should like more than to come and sail with you, and on the earliest possible day, whenever that may be!

As you will have seen from my letters, I have enjoyed your books tremendously; they offer such a delightful contrast to a world at war in general, and in particular, to the rather exasperating country Somaliland in which I am working. I like the people you write about, and their quite remarkable 'aliveness' and characterisation. Given any set of circumstances, the reader knows just how Nancy or Roger or Susan would feel; they are real people, and such lively and nice ones at that. Then I like the way you write, and in particular, your descriptions of the lakes and mountains I know and love so well. There are so few people who can do this. I am a great admirer of W. G. Collingwood in this respect. I take a copy of his *Lake Counties* round with me, to read when homesick, and the other day was pleased to see 'Wild Cat Island' mentioned![2] Walpole (to my mind) canNOT describe the lakes. You do it admirably; as well as, and more simply than, Collingwood. I'd be inclined to compare your way with Buchan's and Conan Doyle's, both of whom to my mind, do it very simply and with great charm. I hope I'm not dropping bricks?

I had, as a matter of fact, read *Swallowdale* and therefore knew about the origin of Peter Duck, but this was no reason why you shouldn't have brought him to life if you wished. In fact, I suspect that you had to! And that something on the following lines may have happened:

Scene: Your study. *Enter* gang of nephews and nieces.

NNS: Look here, Captain Flint, we want a book about Peter Duck.

Yourself: There is no Peter Duck. He's an invention of Titty's.

NNS (menacingly): Who invented *Titty*?

Yourself (trapped): Well I suppose I did.

NNS (in triumph): Right. Now you can go on and invent Peter Duck.

Your parts about sailing and seamanship give me the greatest pleasure, and my goodness, it's practical! This line is your *forte* of course, but the motive of practicality runs through all your stories and is one of their great charms. Everything works.

I am no expert at sailing but enjoy it immensely, more on inland waters than on the sea, for reasons Nancy would have sympathized with after her first day on the *Wild Cat*! I began at Cambridge, when an expert friend took me in a minute 20 foot sloop down the Clyde and all round the Outer Hebrides and Skye. I've also done quite a lot on Windermere, a lake one only appreciates properly when sailing. I have never sailed on Coniston but it must be grand.

Birds are my main hobby. You clearly are a bird-man too: your descriptions and pictures of them show that. But as far as I know, you have not yet written a story which centres round a *wild* bird (which excludes parrots and pigeons).

The other day, I was jolting along in a truck over some rather unattractive country in the hinterland of Cape Guardafui, and fell to thinking what sort of bird might fit into one of your stories? The result is attached. If you took it and moulded it and breathed life into it, would it 'go'? Ornithologically, at any rate, I don't think there is anything that could be disputed.

Again, thank you for your kind letter and for all the pleasure your books have given me.

Yours sincerely,

Myles North

Suggested Great Northern Diver Story.

1. *Central Idea*. Great Northern Diver breeds in British Isles for first time. Nest found by Dick with Swallows and Amazons. Complications (a) laird owns loch where bird is breeding and keeps place strictly preserved; (b) egg collector also discovers nest and attempts to steal eggs. Aims of Dick & Co (a) to observe and photograph bird (obstacle, laird); (b) to preserve nest (obstacle, egg collector).

2. *Ornithological Background*. For this, you are referred to Witherly's *Handbook of British Birds*, 1940, vol. IV, which deals with the divers. The bird is, apparently, a winter visitor, but in the Outer Hebrides and the Shetlands it is present at most times of the year, and has been thought several times, but never proved, to have bred in the latter.

The Black-Throated Diver, a regular Scottish breeding species, nests in the Hebrides but not in the Shetlands.

The Great Northern and the Black Throated are very similar.

It would be very easy for somebody to find a breeding pair of Great Northerns in the Outer Hebrides, but not realise the importance of his discovery, thinking that they were just the ordinary Black Throated.

Any egg collector would sell his soul for the first British-taken eggs of the Great Northern Diver.[3]

3. *Plot*. *Wild Cat* with Capt. Flint and Swallows-Amazons-Scarabs, is cruising round the Outer Hebrides early in the August summer holidays. Dick is the ornithologist of the party and has taken up bird photography.

They land and see an interesting fresh-water loch but get chased off by ghillies. So next day, Swallows and Amazons create a diversion and draw off the ghillies, while Scarabs take the *Wild Cat*'s folding dinghy and find the Diver's nest on an island.

Dick thinks it's a Blackthroated, but afterwards is puzzled by his description written down on the spot, and eventually, much excited, tracks the bird down in his book as a Great Northern. He then says he's got to photograph it at the nest, from a hide, to prove his discovery. This will entail two more forays – one to put up the hide, and one to do the photography. And each time, someone must draw off the ghillies.

Now the egg collector turns up. Like a proper egg collector, he must be wearing a cap and plus fours, and have protruding teeth and an acquisitive nose. He is a nasty bit of work.

He comes by yacht from Shetland, where he has been unsuccessfully looking for Great Northern Divers.

The crew of the yacht happen to be none other than Peter Duck and Bill the red-haired boy. This is most useful, as they are allies in the enemy's camp, and can provide information.

The putting-up of the hide is done successfully, but only just, and it is clear that the laird is all out to defeat the Child Menace and may do so next time. The services of a loyal, but rather embarrassed, Capt. Flint are therefore requested, he having sensibly kept clear of the trespassing hitherto.

The photography foray goes off well, suspiciously so, in fact. But Dick does get his photographs, which should be good ones. The laird who has been foxing all the time, now pounces, and Scarabs, Swallows and Amazons, plus an even more embarrassed Capt. Flint, are captured and hauled off in triumph to the lodge.

As they go, someone looks back, and sees a sinister plus-foured figure, with field glasses, intently studying the loch.

The prisoners are locked up in the cellar, while the laird who's a decent old thing really, wonders what the devil he's going to do with them now.

Night draws in. The prisoners are disturbed by someone tapping on the bars of the cellar. It is Bill, who says the egg-collector has returned to the yacht, collected his folding dinghy and gone off towards the loch.

Clearly there is no time to lose. The laird is called and told the truth at once. He is much surprised, having, like Dick, casually assumed that his birds were Black Throateds. He is at once filled with proprietorial indignation that anyone should rob HIS birds, and in his rage quite forgets about the previous exasperating behaviour of his prisoners, who now become his devoted allies. He turns out to be a nephew of 'My dear friend Miss Huskisson',[4] which makes everyone wonder what the G.A. will say when she hears about this?

All now rush quickly, but quietly, down to the loch, which is shining in the moonlight. They are too late, as just as they arrive, they see a portable dinghy land on the islet. They have no boat handy in which to follow, so they have to wait and waylay the egg collector on his return.

The interval, for Dick especially, is an anxious one, owing to his knowing that —

(a) Egg collectors often blow, or partly blow, their eggs immediately, to make them lighter, and thus stronger, to travel.

(b) An ornithological saying runs 'What's hit's history; what's missed, mystery.' i.e. if you want to prove your bird beyond all doubt, you must *shoot it*.

However, no shot is heard, and the dinghy returns to land, where the egg-collector is duly shanghaied. Dick opens the egg box with trembling hands, and finds the two eggs unblown and still warm.

So they are rushed off to the nest and replaced there, and a few moments later, the Diver is seen, stealing back . . .

That is really the end of the story, but in this sort of story, one may, and should, have P.S.s, so here they are:

1. A month later, Dick is seen, sucking his pen, considering how to write his triumphant account to *British Birds*, concealing, of course, all reference to the exact locality. In front of him are the accompanying illustrations, two magnificent half-plate enlargements of the nesting Divers.

2. Dorothy [*sic*], who has of course been busy writing 'A Romance of the Hebrides', has discovered a most life-like villain, who has protruding teeth and an . . .

3. The laird, filled with proprietorial satisfaction, is watching at the edge of the loch, and sees his Divers sailing along, proudly escorting two fine young.

4. The G.A. writing to Mrs Blackett 'I have heard from my dear friend Miss H . . .'

5. Comment of Nancy: 'Shiver my timbers. What's coming now?' — but this is enough and more. How one does roll on!

1   Letter missing.
2   W. G. Collingwood, *The Lake Counties* (London: Dent, revised, illustrated edition 1932), p. 61, on Peel Island: 'Many readers of the recent books of Mr. Arthur Ransome . . . will no doubt recognise this place, altered a little by the usual literary camouflage, but with all its charm preserved.'

3   To judge by the emphatic vertical lines in the margin, this detail especially struck Ransome's imagination. Elsewhere he covered North's pages with many a large, emphatic *no*. Readers of *Great Northern?* will easily see which details he rejected, and guess why.

4   *The Picts and the Martyrs*, ch. XXIX.

To Joyce Lupton

March 19 1945   Coniston

My dear Joyce,

I think, knowing nothing about it, it [is] quite probable that Boham's would do us very well if we could RENT it un-furnished . . . and if its innards include a room I could use for work, and if it is a civilised house in the matter of bath, drainage, electricity and the things that matter to Genia. I am blankly terrified of *buying* another house until Genia is absolutely sure she wants it. But Blewbury does seem to meet the case, giving easy access to London.[1]

But I will say no more. Genia herself is writing.

We clear out of here on June 1. Our furniture goes into store temporarily at Manchester (100 miles on the way, making the final shift easier) and we go for six weeks to Loweswater, Scale Hill Hotel, where G. can recover a bit after the struggle of getting out. She will be seriously ill if she doesn't have a bit of a rest.

She can leave me at Scale Hill while she goes to look at things. If we can rent an unfurnished house within reasonable distance of town (which Blewbury would be) we should try to get in before the end of the summer.

I have got about as far as I can with my book[2] before going up to Stornoway to go over details on the spot. I go there about the middle of May. I think there are bright spots in the book but it's hard to tell. I've well over 200 pages of it in the rough, and am busy on tailpieces and such of the illustrations as I can do without making sketches on the spot.

Do hang on to my bits if you can.[3]

It's going to be an awful job winding up here, with a view to being cut off from library etc. just when finishing up the book, but the sooner it's over the better.

There's the text of *Racundra* to be revised too, with notes because otherwise people would be mixing up references to one war with mistaken beliefs that that war is another. Cape's are doing a new edition, having bought out Stanley Unwin.

I think myself that Boham's sounds as if it might be the thing, at any rate as a half way house, IF we could rent it for a year or two unfurnished.

But, on that subject, Genia must have the final word.

Jolly to think of you at Seend. I hope Aunt Helen was well.[4]
much love,

Arthur

1   They did not settle at Blewbury, but took a flat in Weymouth Street, Marylebone, in central London.
2   *Great Northern?*
3   Some of Ransome's belongings (including, probably, his letters) found among his mother's possessions.
4   Helen Boulton, the dedicatee of *The Picts and the Martyrs*.

To Joyce Lupton
Aug. 27 1945   [London]

My dear Joyce,

The die is cast and we turn townsfolk. The flat is in No. 9, Weymouth Street, just off Portland Place. It includes a very big room for a work room, nearly as big as the old barn at Ludderburn, in which somehow or other I shall have to turn to and produce books in order to keep up the payments of rent. Rent £600 a year!! But it includes central heating and hot water day and night, and the ground floor being occupied by 'Harley Street' specialists, for whom warm consulting rooms are essential, we shall probably be kept from freezing. The rest of the flat is not really quite large enough. No spare room of any kind . . . though 2 bathrooms! Unfurnished, of course, and we are hoping to get in some time in September. Genia will have to go to Manchester to pick over our furniture, and after that to stay somewhere in London, superintending decoration, electric engineers, etc. I shall probably clear off to Cockermouth and keep well out of the way. Seven year lease.

We heard of it by accident on the day it had been advertised for the first time. By five o'clock over SEVENTY people had been to see it. Of these TWENTY-FOUR wrote, some with deposits etc., to say they would take it. The moment it was clear that Genia really wanted it, before leaving the building, I telephoned to the agents and said I wanted it. They said, 'Put it in writing'. I did so on the spot and posted the letter, and first thing next morning went in to Lombard Street to see the agents, who showed me my letter plus the twenty-four other acceptances, and told me that their representative who had told me about it when we were looking at a house had muddled the rent which should have been £600. The acceptances were for that amount. But they also said that more important than the rent was the tenant . . . I said nowt on this, but merely gave them references and had got as far as saying that 'if they wanted to know who I was . . .' when the senior partner at the other end of the room suddenly butted in, and said, 'We know very well who you are. My children have talked of you for years as one of the family, and we are advising the owners to let you have the flat.' So there really are some points in having pumped out all those books. There followed twenty-four hours of doubts, and then came a definitive letter to say that subject to our respective solicitors approving the lease the flat was ours.

So there it is. If one MUST live in London, it is just about as good a place as one could get. The big work room, really two rooms turned into one, and very well done, first-rate floor, looks to me as if I shall be able to work in it. The address, Weymouth St., W.1., is almost snobbish. It is within a walk of the Garrick, Cape's, British Museum, and Regent's Park. There is a porter in charge below, who checks visitors and telephones up to find out if you want to see them. And, one can simply shut up the place and go away in absolute security. Automatic lift. No. 9 is what is known as the Stone House, Weymouth Street. It is just off Portland Place, turning right when walking north from Broadcasting House.

I think Genia is really pleased.

But it means that I must go on pumping out books . . .
possibly a good thing . . . if only I can.

Yesterday we went to Chislehurst, and I went sailing with
Busk and his boy,[1] putting out from Greenhithe, a real W. W.
Jacobs place, with a sailor walking about with the finest monkey
I've ever seen . . . and big ships moving up and down the river.

I hope it's all right. Anyhow, there it is.

Queer to think of you in Dover. I've had lively times getting
in and out of there. My favourite berth is in the submarine
harbour, right at the eastern end . . . but I've also spent a night
in the Granville Dock, in *Nancy* in there. I wish young Arthur[2]
had tested himself for sea-sickness. No good taking him to sea
properly until he has found out that essential point. So if he gets
a chance of going out with a fisherman from Deal or somewhere
during the holiday, he'd better take it. If he goes to Deal, he'll
find fishermen going out, and if he turns up and asks to be
allowed to come, they'll probably let him if he has a bottle of
beer in each pocket. Of course it would be a good thing if he
could *shrink* a bit, so as to fit into a fo'c'sle.

> Much love,
>
> Arthur

1   Lt. Col. E. W. Busk of West Mersea: one of the friends of the
    Pin Mill period.
2   Arthur Lupton, Joyce's son.

To Charles Renold

| | 9 Weymouth Street, |
| Nov. 19 1945 | HELL, W.1. |

My dear Charles,

I have just heard from Gordon Dickson that the disaster of the
salmon season continued unbroken to the bitter end. 'Heap a
people,' he says, 'never had a pull.' He himself had none and
many of the very best and most assiduous also ended with a
season's blank.

I saw Dunne, the Pres. of the Flyfishers, the other day and he
told me that master mariners in the Atlantic had noticed a

southgoing VERY COLD stream where there should have been a warm stream in the other direction, and this does seem to suggest some sort of explanation why the fish were deterred right through the summer from coming up our rivers. It seems to have been the same everywhere . . . no fish.

I am giving up my big ship[1] on doctor's orders and am hoping to replace her by a much smaller, easier run vessel (without having to spend money. I shall get enough for the old to pay for the new), a sort of marine bath-chair for my old age. Anyhow, even if I can't do much voyaging I shall be able to escape with her help from the incessant noise and beastliness of town, and be able to look at something better than chimney-pots.

Cocky arrived at Hampton after repainting by Borwick's with every single bit of her inside left loose in the bottom of the boat, every seat, thwart, tank, mast-step, etc. etc., pulled up for the painting and never replaced. I spent all yesterday in her with screwdriver and screws, and have made a bit of headway with the job Borwick's ought to have done. Maddening, but very pleasant to see wild duck on the water. They seem to know quite well that on the Thames they are safe from guns, and swim gaily all round Thornycroft's yard, the anchored yachts, etc., and take small notice even of racing eights.

But, even at Hampton, the Thames is mostly factories.

The one good thing about this place is my work room, which, but for what is outside it, is the best I have had since Ludderburn, and I am doing my damnedest to work in it. I propose to experiment with anti-gunfire ear protectors to deaden the din of other people's wireless.

Oh. Tell Margaret that my French publisher has come to life again and sent me four copies of *Swallowdale* in French. If among all her numerous *protégés* she has a French brat, I'll gladly be rid of one or two.

I doubt very much if I'll get any fishing next year, salmon-fishing, I mean. I shall try to catch eels when at anchor in the new boat which the designer, without consulting me, has christened *Peter Duck*. She will be P.D. among friends. A comic little boat, with two masts, so as to keep each single sail small and light to handle. She'll sleep two in comparative comfort. The designer wants to put a 12 H.P. Diesel (marine) in her, but in these grim times it seems impossible to find such a thing. So we shall have to be content with a Stuart Turner Petrol engine (8 H.P.) which there seems to be some faint chance of obtaining.

Have you any views on Diesel *versus* Petrol, or on small marine engines generally? Engines designed for use on land are NEVER any good in a boat.

A hint in one of Margaret's letters suggested that even this ghastly season has not disheartened you and that you are gaily making flies for next year. True?

Best wishes to both of you,

Arthur

1   *Selina King*. She was sold to Peter Davies, who was a publisher, and one of the originals of Peter Pan.

To Myles North

Mar. 20 1947   [Weymouth Street]

Dear North,

I have persuaded my publishers to make me a set of proofs to be hurled across continents to you (long before they would normally be ready) so that you can comment, if necessary, *without holding up the book*.

Here are the proofs, and printers, binders etc. are all straining at the leash, while I hang grimly on in case the ornithologist detects some absolutely monstrous bloomer (I do not think the possibly over-rapid change-over on the nest matters, because, though it might not happen always, Dick assures me that it actually did happen while he was watching and precisely as here described).[1] But of course there may be some other vital point.

No need to send the proofs back. But for goodness' sake, hurl off an air mail letter at the very earliest possible moment.

I fear you will hardly recognise the story as a whole, what with the scenes in harbour, and the Gael business and young Ian, etc. etc., but the essential point is there, the bird and its eggs being as you wanted, the pivoting centre of the yarn. I wonder very much what you will think of it. I think it is bound to fall flat in America, where the bird in question is no great rarity and nests regularly . . . though perhaps the human struggle may save it from complete collapse.

Anyhow, sit down to it, let the affairs of Africa go hang until you have struggled through to the last page and sent your blessings or curses hurtling through the stratosphere.

Still bothered about the dedication . . . At all costs it must do nothing to weaken the *reality* . . . nothing to suggest that it is a mere story and not the record of an actual happening, even if, for bird protection's sake, the details are somewhat disguised. I'll find a way. I dreamt of a good one the other night but could not remember it on waking.

> to Myles North
>> who said we ought to put on record what happened
>> when a series of accidents allowed us to snatch
>> a Hebridean holiday.
>>> ? ? ? ? ?
> I may find something better.[2]

AGAIN. Do let me point out that EVERY MINUTE MATTERS. HURRY UP. NEVER MIND ABOUT MEALS. LET WORK GO HANG. LOCK YOUR DOOR TILL YOU'VE DONE. HURRY. HURRY. HURRY.

> Yours ever,

> > Arthur Ransome

1   *Great Northern?* ch. VI.
2   The dedication eventually read:

TO
MYLES NORTH
who, knowing a good deal of what happened,
asked me to write the full story.

To Joyce Lupton

Lowick Hall,
Ulverston,
Lancashire.

June 8 1948   I feel a little like Sir Walter Scott.

My dear Joyce,

We start camping here from tomorrow in one small room in
the old part, with one room in the new part painted and clean,
but soon to be messed up again with the wiring for electricity,
etc., etc. Also the restoring and cleaning of the main staircase
will make the good room inaccessible. It is a terrific business, but
I do begin to see what a very nice house it will be when Genia
has worked her will on it.

The rhododendrons are perfectly gorgeous seen from this
window where I am writing, and from the garden there is the
most beautiful view of the Old Man I have ever found. We have
heard a cock pheasant, ONCE, and seen quite a sprinkling of
young rabbits. I have also seen three fingerling trout in the beck,
and am told that in the beck end when the sea-trout are up, they
can be caught just behind the house.

Who was the 'poet', cousin of old Mr. Calvert, who wrote his
poems under the big oak which that greedy fellow from whom
we bought the place had cut down before I could save it? Miss
Calvert is said to be going about making what mischief she can,
but as everybody else is extremely friendly, it won't matter very
much. By everybody else I mean farmers, millers, etc.

I don't think from the way things are going that we shall be
visible for the next two or three months. And I gather that I am
to be ejected and sent off to Cockermouth to be out of the way
for a bit.

WHEN all the plasterers and painters and plumbers and what nots are gone, the place will be really quiet, and I ought to be able to get on with some writing to pay for it all!!!

Chickens laying well!

Mice by the thousand.

We were glad to meet a hedgehog near the house. Also woodpigeons, and a few rooks.

Genia seems quite undismayed and sees the vision of the house as it is to be, gleaming before her all the time.

your affect. brother,

Arthur

To Joyce Lupton

March 1 1949   Lowick Hall

My dear Joyce,

Thank you for your kind enquiries. The infernal leprosy[1] is subsiding, but it has been pretty beastly for five solid weeks. But I got through last night and the night before without sleeping draughts. And I have several times been toddling about in the sunshine.

I hope quite soon now to get rid of my long white beard, have a bath, and make my much belated dash to London.

But golly what a disease.

The bit of news that really started the cure was that, after 23 years, I have been elected into the Leven Angling Association, so that I shall be able to fish the Leven all the way down from Newby Bridge, about the best mixed fishing in the north of England, brown trout, sea-trout and salmon. And of course within reasonable reach for a day's fishing from here, instead of having to stop a night or two as at Cockermouth.

Further, a great help to the larder. The day before the leprosy stuck its poisoned talons all over my head and face and neck, I was up on the moor by Groffa Crag and shot a snipe. Since then of course nothing, so that Genia is really almost waiting for the fishing season to start. It doesn't, alas, till the 1st of April, this year. Usually the 15th of March. But once the season does start it ought to be possible to keep up a modest supply of fish.

I hope all goes well with you and am glad you enjoy the National Book League.

Read if you get a chance *Memoirs of a Northumbrian Lady*, presently if not yet to be published by Cape. No. Not *Memoirs* . . . *Recollections* of a N.L. by Barbara Charlton.

Love,

A.

Both gardener and char deserted!!!! Just when at last gardening is possible. Very hard on Genia who has just kept the fellow on all winter in hopes of getting him to do some work now.

1	Shingles.

To Rupert Hart-Davis

June 4 1949									Lowick Hall

My dear Hart-Davis,

Are you sure your fellow Directors have not passed a vote of censure on you for gross extravagance? What chance has the firm got of ultimate success if it begins by hurling *Great Oxford English Dictionaries* quite unnecessarily at people who never expected anything of the kind?[1]

But I can't pretend not to be pleased.

IT has arrived. We are planning to move to a larger house to make room for IT. When the new part of Lowick was built in 1748, no-one foresaw that it would have to house a *Great Oxford English Dictionary*. Not one of my hats will any longer fit my head as I go prancing round, the owner of a *Great Oxford English Dictionary*. Long ago, in the time of the Zulu wars, Sir Garnet Wolseley[2] told the drill sergeant of my prep. school that the British soldier should walk 'as if one side of the street belonged to him and he expected the other shortly'. What sort of walk would he have prescribed for owners of *Great Oxford English Dictionaries*? Hang it, with that book in my room, I have got BOTH sides of the street already.

TWELVE volumes, plus the Supplement . . . (That way of counting is in itself delightful and humane . . . Oxford University, free, of course, from all superstition but taking no chances with the number that comes between twelve and fourteen.)

Nothing is missing but an inscription to put in the beginning and I strongly suspect that your fellow-directors would indignantly refuse to sign one. And I don't blame them.

IT has the most extraordinary effect upon me. Looking at IT full face, or even feeling ITS blue buckram presence arming my back, I have the oddest illusion that after all I must be some sort of a writer.

I daren't risk the loss of that illusion by trying to write.

And, anyhow, I have now a full-time job. I am an Owner of a GREAT OXFORD ENGLISH DICTIONARY. That's enough of a job for anybody. I have and shall have no time for anything else.

Yours ever,

Arthur Ransome
O.G.O.E.D.

1   Hart-Davis, whom Ransome had met before the war when he was a director at Cape's, had started his own publishing house in 1946. When Hart-Davis began to publish his Mariners Library series, Ransome 'acted as godfather and nanny . . . No title was included without his approval'. (*Autobiography*, p. 354.) AR refused all payment for the work, so Hart-Davis gave him a set of the *Oxford English Dictionary* in gratitude. In his will Ransome left the dictionary to Hart-Davis.

2   The model of the modern Major-General.

To Rupert Hart-Davis

Nov. 5 1949   Lowick Hall

My dear Hart-Davis,

Many thanks for the five *Down Channels*, and for sending one for me to Buckle.[1]

Cruise of the 'Alerte'. Nothing against it at all.

BUT

I think another book of Knight's is far more likely to find buyers, and that is

The 'Falcon' on the Baltic (NOT 'Cruise of the Falcon' which concerns a much bigger vessel).

Reasons. *Alerte* was a big vessel, crew of 13, with 4 paid hands among them, whereas the *little Falcon* was a converted P. and O. lifeboat, and her crew was Knight himself and one hand. Now lots and lots of people at this day are converting ship's boats and planning cruises in them. The whole adventure is one possible even to the young men of this day in spite of Government Restrictions. I remember what enormous pleasure I had in that book as a young man. I remember what enormous pleasure W. G. Collingwood had in it as an old one. It is a real beauty of a book, from the sailing point of view, and from the merely human. It is without one single dull paragraph, and this cannot be said of the *Alerte* book and still less of the earlier book concerned with a much bigger *Falcon*.

The *'Falcon' on the Baltic* is by far the best book *qua* book that Knight ever wrote.

If you have not read it, I can lend you a copy, but God preserve you if you lose it, for I read it at least once a year.

It is really a first-rate BOOK, whereas the other two, though good enough in their way, are without whatever the thing is that makes the difference.[2]

Yours ever,

Arthur Ransome.

1   R. T. McMullen, *Down Channel*, with a foreword by AR, was No. 7 in the Mariners Library. 'Buckle' is presumably Colonel Cuthbert Buckle, C.B., like Colonel Busk an inhabitant of West Mersea and a friend from the Pin Mill days.

2   The *'Falcon' on the Baltic*, with an introduction by AR, became No. 15 in the Mariners Library in 1951 and was followed by *The Cruise of the 'Alerte'* in 1952.

To Pamela Whitlock

March 3 1950   Lowick Hall

Dear Pamela,

Just back from London to hear of you diving kerwallop off the high springboard.[1] I don't know whether you are right or wrong, but hope you are right and in any case send best wishes.

I remember what a terrible hurry I was in, once upon a time, and how the only result of all the hurry was that I had about thirty years to wait before getting properly started.

But never mind that. You have sacked Mr. Collins and by the time you get to the end of your safe year you will probably know something about what you want to do next. I don't think you have lost anything by the time you have put in at being an editor (and what not). But I do think you will have to steel yourself to bear some very nasty moments when (inevitably) you will find that writing won't come and you feel perhaps it never will. Jobs, of course, cushion such moments whereas, when you have no other job, you have no protection at all. Almost it's worth while to have two sorts of writing going at once, so that if one goes bad on you, you just take it as a sign that you ought to be doing the other.

I am quite sure that 'For the First Time' wants writing and that you are the right one to write it. I hate giving advice (which is almost bound to be bad) but unless you have a very clear bony skeleton, don't you think it may be worth while to make sure of your last chapter first, down to T H E   E N D and to keep that last chapter in your mind while you are doing all the others? It is sometimes possible in this way for your own foreknowledge to do for you what might be done by the bone-work. But for all I know, you may have a beautifully articulated set of bones and nothing at all to worry about.

Anyhow, go ahead, and (no need to laugh) keep a strict record of how many pages each day. *For as long as you can, profit by the hangover from regular work in an office (as Masefield[2] did from his watch-keeping at sea.* He told me this after he had been years ashore.)

'All sails spread and a fair wind.'

A.R.

---

1   Apparently she had decided to leave her job at the Collins publishing firm and live as a full-time writer. Before long, however, she was lured back to edit *The Young Elizabethan*, the Collins magazine for young people.

2   Ransome got to know the poet John Masefield during his bachelor days in Bohemian London. See *Autobiography*.

To Joyce Lupton

40 Hurlingham Court,
London S.W.6.[1]

Feb. 10 1951

My dear Joyce,
The feathers you sent are all WING
feathers. The feathers are big *hackles*
from the MANTLE, cloak or tippet.
I would send you a specimen but
have used my last (hence the urgent
need). But instead I send you a black
one of similar character though rather
too small.
These HACKLES sprout all round the
neck and chest of the bird.
THESE are the feathers.   →
You'll see hundreds of them lying
round the hen run.
Those you sent are from the Right
Bird but from the wrong place on that bird.
My drawing does not show the wings.
The whole of the MANTLE from the
crown of the head down is composed of
hackles. What is wanted is big HACKLES
long ones.
Very good of you to bother with
them. When I have them I strip all
the feathery fibres off, and then
WIND the bare central flexible spine
round and round a tiny hook. The result is a minute ribbed body
like a fly's, which can be got in no other way. A wing *quill* is too
stiff.
I am glad to hear that the Blackies are already inspecting
Hugh, while Hugh is inspecting the Blackies. I should like to see
their reports set out in parallel columns.
Please give my profoundest respect to the Lupton lasses. I
envy them their Leeds. There is summat about t'owd spot as

suits me. You too, I think. I suppose it's being born there.

I wish it was Leeds and not Durham that had given me a degree. Twice the fun.[2]

Does Hugh go through Kenya? I have a friend there who is a District Commissioner or something, having a splendid time investigating the noises of birds.[3] He makes the birds teach him to match their squawks on a penny whistle, so that they can be written down on music paper. He also chases the squawks with some sort of dictaphone. He is a very happy man, as you can imagine, and is so busy listening to Blueheaded Orangetailed Jungle Warblers that he cannot hear the fantastic noises emitted by MacArthurs and similar unfeathered bipeds.[4]

Well, Goodbye for now.

Arthur

1   In October 1950 the Ransomes had moved back to London.
2   In 1948 AR had been awarded an honourary M.A. by the University of Durham, an honour which he did not much value (see *Life*, p. 419). In 1951 he was to be given an honorary doctorate by the University of Leeds, which gratified him immensely.
3   Myles North, who had suggested the plot of *Great Northern*? He also sent AR feathers of the Vulturine guinea-foul, with which Ransome made his famous salmon-fly.
4   U.S. General Douglas MacArthur, who had just sustained a fearful defeat in the Korean War and as a result was clamouring to be allowed to extend it.

*

ALTHOUGH designed to be sailed single-handed, *Selina King* was a large yacht and Ransome's doctor thought her rig too much for him to handle safely after the war. She was sold, after a spell in the West Indies, to a buyer in the USA. Between 1947 and 1949 the Ransomes sailed in *Peter Duck*, a yacht designed by Laurent Giles and built for them by Harry King, but the boat did not please either Ransome or his wife: the engine gave constant trouble, the bunks were too narrow, the cabin leaked in heavy rain and Ransome often cracked his head on a low beam. Finally disposing of it, they hired a Hillyard 5-ton sloop, *Barnacle Goose*, for a cruise in September 1951, and that winter bought a yacht from the same yard, which they named *Lottie Blossom*. The boat not quite to their liking, so Ransome commissioned David Hillyard to build on the same lines a last successor to *Racundra*, *Nancy Blackett* and *Selina King*, which they also named *Lottie Blossom*, and they cruised in her in the English Channel in 1953 and 1954, Ransome making his last crossing to France at the age of seventy.

★

To Barbara Gnosspelius

40 Hurlingham Court,

Dec. 9 1951   London S.W.6.

My dear Barbara,

Oh no. Postcards don't earn answers. Not from me anyhow, so I don't expect my postcards to bring answers from other people. As you ought to know by this time I think postcards rather rude, in the same class as digs in ribs. They please the giver's vanity but are certainly no compliment to the receiver.

I do congratulate you on your news, and wish to goodness we could do what you are going to do. But we can't because of the horror of wireless aboard ship. You won't mind that and by Dec. 29 will be already enjoying the sun on deck, and the Portuguese coast and the African. Golly, what fun. And I bet Oscar is rejoicing, and, back in his old Africa, he'll flourish like the lions, and enjoy the ancient smells and the properly penetrating warmth. And you'll pick oranges off the trees and eat them and the local wine will flow like water and you'll wonder why on earth you put off going for so long.

Meanwhile we shall freeze and enjoy our rheumatism, etc. I had nearly a month of lumbago so vile that it took half an hour to get a foot to the floor. But that's gone now, Thank God. Our fires smoke and we have no central heating but we cheer ourselves with thoughts of our new ship.[1] Yes. With incredible idiocy we have bought a new 6-tonner which is to be launched on the First of April (Yes.) Bermuda sloop. 2 cabins. 8 h.p. engine. 350 square feet of sail. 27′ 4″ o.a. × 7′ 8″ beam × 4′ 3″ draught – making bankruptcy loom before us. We chartered a 5 tonner on the East Coast in the first half of September to see if we still liked it. The bunks were sopping (hence the lumbago) but we both enjoyed it enormously and decided that we must have some sort of annexe to the flat in summer so that we can escape from the fiendish row, and why not a floating one. And so we are having *Lottie Blossom*. Named after our favourite female character in fiction . . . P. G. Wodehouse's fiction to be exact. She will be Lottie to her friends.

Is Janet going with you or is she to hold the fort with Stripes? As you say 'The House of Gnosspelius' I suppose that includes Boss, Missis and Infanta . . . if Liverpool can temporarily do without her . . . or if she's going to stir up South African architecture. It'll be a pity if she misses the chance of adding a new world to those she has already. Please give her our love. And we send our love to you and Oscar with every good wish for your tremendous adventure.

Keep a DAIRY.[1] All young adventurers should.
> Your elderly friends
> > Genia and Arthur

1   *Sic*, most decidedly.

To Pamela Whitlock

March 30 1952   40 Hurlingham Court

Dear Pamela,

Don't be disturbed by *The Times* review.[1] Even the very best of reviewers don't really like packets of seeds they have once upon a time labelled Virginia Stock to turn out something else, particularly if the 'something else' is new and not in the seedsman's catalogue at all.

I am sorry I have been so long in writing. I have been head over ears in compasses and rigging and winches and folding dinghies, and hurrying to and fro between here and Littlehampton, looking after our new boat who is now in the water and should be finished by Tuesday.

I have so far read your book twice and liked it very much and still more the visible signs of bursting chrysalis. You have again aimed at something all but impossible. But that is just what it is so well worth while to do. And although the book is not likely (it seems to me) to gather a huge crowd of readers at once you will find, as time goes on, that more and more people thank you for it, believing that it must have been written for themselves in particular, for their most secret selves. And, as always, there you go spilling fine images in all directions, like a greedy child who has gathered more flowers than she can carry. Lovely images some of them are too, and I am more than ever sure that there are miracles ahead. It is a 'tip-toe' book, like no other, and standing on tip-toe prevents movement and compels your book to be static rather than dynamic. When you say the next is 'all story', I wonder if it means that you feel just this and for a change want to be bustled along. Anyhow every book you will write will gain by your having written this one.

Some things puzzled me, chiefly the lack of reading aloud at Pound. Between Queen Victoria's first and second Jubilees, reading aloud by my Mother was the peak of each day. The other difference between your childhood and mine of forty years earlier is that in the nineteen thirties the little victims grew up with some sort of consciousness of the darkling sky, whereas the 1914 war came on us, most suddenly, out of a blue one. (The Boer war, of course, was different altogether and in this comparison does not count. It was one with the Zulus and Fuzzy-wuzzies and the good untroubled Mr. Henty.)

Let me know more about your new book (unless you think it better to keep it wrapped up and secret) and thank you very much for giving me so much pleasure with this one.

> Yours sincerely,
>
> Arthur Ransome

1   Of her first adult novel, *The Sweet Spring*.

To Barbara Smith

Oct. 9 1952   Garrick Club, W.C.2.

Dear Miss Smith,

Thank you for your altogether delightful letter which gave me a great deal of pleasure . . . and thank you also for your good wishes, which seem to be taking effect. It is true that I have been in hospital rather often this year, but, after all, old engines expect to go to the garage now and then, and I am well enough now.

You are just the reader I like my books to find – though, of course, you are not old enough for them yet.[1] They were written for a much older person (myself) and you have a number of years to catch up even now. But no hurry about that.

I was interested to hear you had been to Pin Mill. I missed going there this year, but I saw Miss Powell a year ago when I sailed up the river and anchored and went ashore to have a talk with her.[2] If it was a fine day when you were there you probably saw her too, a white haired old lady sitting on a bench at the top of the steps going up to her cottage, chattering away like anything and keeping two or three of her friends laughing at her stories. If you go there again you should walk up those steps and tell her you are a friend.

Yours sincerely,

Arthur Ransome

1   As a child, Barbara Smith discovered the Ransome books in the public library and became a passionate admirer. 'My brother, two years my senior, feigned indifference, but when he lay desperately ill with pneumonia it was *Pigeon Post* he wanted to be read aloud at his bedside.' He died, and Barbara Smith wrote a 'plaintive little letter' (she says) to AR, and got the answer printed on p. 259. She wrote again (as Barbara Ward) when a grown-up and married. Her love of Ransome's works eventually led her to settle in the Lake District. She wrote a charming article, 'I Never Met Arthur Ransome' for *The Lady*, 13 August 1981.

2   Annie Powell has a walk-on part in both *We Didn't Mean to Go to Sea* and *Secret Water*.

To Barbara Gnosspelius

March 11 1953   40 Hurlingham Court

My dear Barbara (Damn my typewriter!)

I doubt very much if we shall come north this year before the back end, unless Genia makes a dash for it to get a few things from those stored at Hawkshead . . . We left enough there to furnish a couple of rooms, but it looks as though that was but a pious hope, and we may sell the lot . . . There are some ship's stores there, ropes, etc., that we should like to have aboard *Lottie*, who is out of her shed and should go into the water almost at once.

Today I have sent off my subscription to the Leven fishing, a gross extravagance as last year I never wet a fly, but I can't bring myself to resign, though I must if I never get north.

We go down to Littlehampton once a week getting the boat ready, and we should be sailing very early in April if not before.

There is wild talk of Cherbourg.

The investiture business,[1] which I was funking, went off very well, and the Queen said very kind things about my blessed works, after which we went off to lap champagne at a friend's near by, and I rushed away to scrape the MOSS off and discard my tophat, and then joined Genia at Simpson's where we did ourselves proud with oysters and ducklings . . . then to a party at the *Spectator* office . . . and finally billiards at the Garrick in the evening with Peter Fleming[2] and two friends of his, one of them General Carton de Wiart who with only one eye and only one arm uses a little gunmetal gadget instead of a left hand, and brings off some very good shots indeed.[3]

I confess I still blush and giggle at the sight of the address on envelopes, but I suppose I shall grow quickly out of that.

Don't forget the telephone number if you come to town. RENown 5805.

Love to both Janet and yourself,

A.

1   Arthur Ransome had been awarded the C.B.E.
2   Journalist and travel-writer; husband of the actress Celia Johnson, brother of Ian Fleming; at this time on the staff of the *Spectator*. His classic travel books include *Brazilian Adventure* and *News from Tartary*
3   Lt. Gen. Sir Adrian Carton de Wiart, V.C. (1880-1963), a particularly brave and distinguished soldier. He served in the Boer War, both world wars, and three continents. In 1950 he published his autobiography, *Happy Odyssey*.

To Barbara Gnosspelius

June 16, 1953   40 Hurlingham Court

My dear Barbara,

What do you know about the Low Bank Ground boathouse? Is it of any historical or biographical interest? If you know owt about it, do please help me out. I know nowt.

We came back from the Beaulieu River today, train to Chichester after a drive through the forest, then to Itchenor where we picked up the ancient car, VERY rusty after three weeks in the open, and then drove it up to town. The ship is at Buckler's Hard. We had a 30 mile voyage from there, right through the assembled fleet to the Spithead forts and back (on Saturday) but did not go to the actual review as our allotted berth was on a bank in the middle of the Solent, all right for big boats, but not for little *Lottie*.[1] We were very glad we hadn't, for with strong wind against tide the little boats had a baddish time, dragging their anchors, etc., and we should have been unable to get home again until today. But the fleet, reviewed by us on Saturday, was magnificent, and best of all the three-masted sailing vessel (a copy of the *Victory*) with which the Italians fairly stole the show.[2] She was a gorgeous sight, and I only hope my photographs, taken under difficulty among hoards of vessels, come out.

Another small voyage was up to Southampton Dock, when we saw the big liner *Caronia*, which made no wash at all as she went out, while the harbourmaster, rushing about in a little launch to say *Caronia* was coming, produced a wash that must have upset a lot of cooking in other vessels. Another day we went to Lymington and back. But no really long voyages. I am too old.

Now do please write a word – 2 words – no, 3 words, 2 about you and Janet and *one* about Low Bank Ground boathouse. Who put it up, and *when*?

Love from both of us.   Arthur

1   The grand naval review to celebrate the coronation of Queen Elizabeth II.
2   The 3,000-ton Italian schoolship *Amerigo Vespucci*.

To E. W. Busk

Yacht 'Lottie Blossom'

July 7 1953   R.C.C.

My dear Busk,[1]

I think you will be amused to hear that purely by chance we picked up and are lying on *Overlord's* majestic but very weedy mooring, on arrival here [Southampton] yesterday, after leaving Cherbourg on Sunday evening and, thanks to finding something wrong with the engine while coming out from the inner harbour, missing the weather report and forecast which would I gather have made us sit tight.

We met John and Helen Tew coming in, not within speaking distance, and saw John Tew making some kind of signal which we think must have been due to his having heard the forecast which we missed.

Anyhow we had been long enough in Cherbourg,[2] and so, luckily for us, kept the engine ticking and old *Lottie* forging ahead through the night, with things getting more and more uncomfortable, so that when the real beastliness began yesterday morning we were already seeing the loom of St. Catherine's. Finally the engine stopped (foul jets) and after I had cleaned them, losing one in the casing of the flywheel and getting it out with a wire from the pump, we found petrol pouring from the carburettor, and so did the last fifty miles under sail only and found that when *Lottie* has a wind we think too strong, she has a wind that she thinks just right. I rolled three turns just before six, as she was getting hard to steer and inclined to bury her bows. We had intended going to Chichester, but before we had the Nab abeam it was quite clear that Chichester Bar would be not place for *Lottie*. I changed course for the forts, and thought of finding shelter under the island shore from the wind which up to then had been SW, but it changed, the spiteful brute and we had our hands [full] beating through Spithead. Decided against Portsmouth with no engine to go nosing round with looking for a place to bring up so went bucketting on, finding both shores lee shores! and finally decided to seek shelter under the Fawley side of Southampton Water. Visibility all but nil in the bad patches. But we picked up the Sturbridge buoy, and the East Bramble, and finally Calshot after a board across from the Lee on the Solent side, and here found we could just lay up Southampton Water, which we did, rejoicing in each bit of smooth water, and went right up to the docks, where, looking for Gen. Gate's boat, we spotted a vacant mooring, picked it up and having made fast looked at it, and saw the magic name of *Overlord*.[3] Then, a gent called Mr. Pickford appeared in a boat, and said that the Royal Engineers would want 10/- a week[4] from us, but presently went away seeing that we were too sleepy to produce his ten bob at that moment, and promised to tell Husband's that I wanted an expert to look at my carburettor. He did not do this. Nobody came and this morning I found the loose nut and all is well. Just 90 miles direct from Cherbourg, and *Lottie* proved herself a good little boat, though groaning and squeaking horridly during the worst of the battering. It sounded like wood working on wood, and we think must have been mast strains transmitted through tabernacle and cabin trunk. Water coming in a bit at one place, but not in any great quantity, and I suspect that the shrouds ought to have been set up harder (Hillyard always likes them rather too slack, for the good of the boat, but when being thrown about, I think the slackish shrouds are not fair to the wooden tabernacle which is fastened to the cabin trunk.)

[no signature][5]

1 Lt. Col. Busk was a friend from the Pin Mill days. His yacht, *Lapwing*, figures in *Secret Water*, which is dedicated to 'the Busk Family', who partially inspired the Eels in that work.
2 Where they had been since 27 June.
3 Of which boat Michael Busk was the mate.
4 Ten shillings, or 50 pence in today's money.
5 Since the letter ends so abruptly, and is unsigned, it may be that it was never finished or sent.

To Barbara Gnosspelius

July 12 1953   40 Hurlingham Court

My dear Barbara,
    Your letter leaves me in a thicker fog than ever about the Altounyan Appeal.

WHEN did the chatty stuff about the Altounyans appear in the *Observer?* Who can have been responsible? I have missed lots of newspapers while away in the little boat.[1]

The Cherbourg expedition[2] was a bit idiotic really. All right for lads of fifty, but not really sage in one's seventieth year, without some younger tough aboard.

The crossing was easy enough, but very tiring, sixteen hours on end, seeing nothing after a final glimpse of a bit of cliff by the Needles which soon disappeared in the fog, until next morning we got a momentary vision of a tall lighthouse in a patch of lighter mist, Cap Levi, and then the forts on the Cherbourg Breakwater.

We then had a pleasant eight days in Cherbourg *Avant-port*, ready to start back as soon as there was a touch of south in the wind. Unfortunately, when the southerly started, it tried to make up for lost time. We started just before six on Sunday evening, motoring out into the outer harbour and finding that only one cylinder was firing. So we drifted about while I put the engine right, and so missed the 5.55 forecast which would have sent us hurriedly back to the inner harbour. Instead we set forth and about three miles out met another English vessel, friends, and observed extraordinary signals from one of them, which we now know were warnings to turn back (they having heard the forecast of a southerly blow). We thought the signals were an odd form of greeting, and sailed on. The sea got up, quite slowly, but by the time we were forty miles south of St. Catherine's, we had all we wanted. It grew then rapidly worse, and the poor little ship was being badly battered, groaning and squeaking, and inclined to bury herself. I had been making for the Nab instead of for the Needles, meaning to go to Chichester or Littlehampton, but long before we sighted the Nab, it was clear that the bar at either place would be no use except for suicides, so I decided on finding shelter under the North shore of the Wight. Thereupon the wind shifted and blew more westerly, turning the Wight into a lee shore, visibility very poor indeed, and in the end I took her right up to the top of Southampton Water where I found a mooring up by the docks, eighteen hours and ninety miles out from Cherbourg – distance made good; *not* allowing for tacking after sighting the Nab and through Spithead and so to Southampton Water. The Customs came along in answer to our yellow quarantine flag, and were most kind, filling up the papers themselves, and telling us to go to sleep, which we jolly well did. We lay two uncomfortable nights at Southampton, rolled all over the place by the wash of tugs etc., and then on Wednesday took the little boat to Bursledon, up the Hamble River, where she is being given a coat of paint which she has certainly earned. I only hope it will not be found that she needs more serious repairs. Just a bit afraid that she has strained tabernacle and cabin trunk. But she is a good little boat, and exhausted as we were, it was a great pleasure to find the Nab on our bows to justify the aged navigator.

Idiotic all the same and we are still very tired.

Love to Janet and Stripes.

A.

Put on your Library list *Henry James: the Untried Years* by Leon Edel and Max Beerbohm, *Around Theatres*, a great stirrer of forgotten first nights.[3]

1   AR had heard that Ernest Altounyan was appealing for funds to revive his hospital in Aleppo, and was afraid that Altounyan was trying to exploit *Swallows and Amazons* for the purpose.
2   26 June – 6 July 1953. See *Ransome At Sea*, pp. 156-162 for the log of the voyage.
3   Both books were published by Rupert Hart-Davis.

To P. G. Wodehouse

n.d. [1953]   Hurlingham Court

Dear P. G. Wodehouse,

Ian Hay gave my your address last year and said he thought you might be amused to know that my wife and I have given our boat the name of our favourite female character in fiction, and that LOTTIE BLOSSOM appears in Lloyd's Yacht Register as a five tonner. Several earlier photographs were failures but in these[1] the name at least is legible.

There are, of course, some ignorant persons who, knowing all the rest of your books, do not know the best of all[2] and ask 'Who was Lottie Blossom?' We refer them to the book, a copy of which is always aboard (another remaining at home in the long shelf of orange Wodehouses, orange but for a few regretted exceptions)[3] and tell them merely that she is a red-headed American film star who, to please her publicity agent, travels round with a small alligator in a wicker basket and, when the Customs came aboard to go through her luggage, asks them to begin with the wicker basket, after which they go no further. This usually raised a laugh, but on one occasion it did not. I was registering the name of the boat at the Customs Office, and the Customs officer who was taking down the particulars for the Registrar asked the usual question. I, unthinking, replied with the usual story. It did not seem to amuse him at all. 'A very unpleasant young woman!' he remarked when I had done.[4]

You must be tired of being thanked for your books, but I cannot write to you without telling you what lasting pleasure those orange coloured books have given us both throughout the last thirty years.

Yours sincerely,

[Arthur Ransome]

1   Ransome enclosed photographs of *Lottie* with his letter.
2   *The Luck of the Bodkins* (London, 1935).
3   One of them being *The Luck of the Bodkins*, bound in red.
4   This incident occurred on 13 March 1953; for AR's full account in his log, see *Ransome At Sea*, pp. 128-9.
5   Wodehouse replied warmly ('I am very flattered about the name of the boat. How pleased Lottie would be if she knew!') but it is hard to resist the impression, from the manner of the letter, that he had never heard of Arthur Ransome, though he suspected that he should have.

To Barbara Gnosspelius

Jan. 23 1954   40 Hurlingham Court

My dear Barbara,

Thank you very much.

I rather enjoyed it although my seventieth. There was a very pleasant little party at the Garrick and I was given the new and magnificent edition of Sydney Smith's *Letters and* two bottles of Burgundy to take home. Very touching indeed. You'd have been amused at the menu which included 'smoked salmon à la Russe' for Genia 'filet de something Amazones', 'Swallow Maryland' and 'Soufflé à la *Racundra*.'!!!

What did Ruskin say about 'As Pretty as Seven' by Bechstein, illustrated by Richter? And when did he say it? I rather want that book republished.[1]

Genia sends her love to you both. So do I.

Arthur

1 Ludwig Bechstein, *As Pretty As Seven: popular German tales*, illustrated by Richter. In a later letter to Barbara Gnosspelius, Ransome wrote: 'As a child I liked it better than Grimm, probably because the pictures are much pleasanter than Cruickshanks's.' (Feb. 3 1954.)

To E. W. Busk

c/o The Harbourmaster,
Buckler's Hard,

June 25 1954   nr. Beaulieu, Hampshire.

My dear Busk,

We bitterly regretted that you were not aboard last night when at about three in the morning we waked more than suddenly, Genia with the firm belief that we had been struck by lightning. I shot out through the cabin door, for once not cracking my skull, to find a walloping great boat bumping into us. This was *Arion*, an ocean racer of some kind, some 15 tons I should think, that had been lying on a mooring a little ahead of us in the incoming tide. There should have been a hand aboard her but he was not. She had broken her mooring chain, just missed another boat ahead of us, and drifted (I think broadside on) across our bows, her stern then swinging in on us. I fended off, and was presently (instantly) joined by G. and prepared to pass her along, get a line on her forrard and let her hang astern of us, though I doubted much whether our mooring would stand it. No good. She went half way and stuck with her bows about level with the fore end of our cabin. With a torch I could see that her chain went right down under our stem. Nothing to be done to ease things, and wind steadily increasing, and tide rising. G. got the foghorn, and we let fly short short short long, yelling for assistance, and hoping to rouse the harbour master. But Beaulieu is a good place for sleeping. No one came, and there we were expecting any minute to bust our own mooring and be squeezed in to the steep shore as a handy fender to break the shock of the big fellow. Finally after an hour of this or more, the two boats lying fairly quiet and experiment having shown that G. could keep them separate by herself, plus all fenders we had in place, I went off in the dinghy to another boat up towards the Hard, woke a sleepy owner (yacht *Lafiya*, an interesting little centreboarder) and he nobly took his dinghy for the Harbour Master while I went back to relieve G. left alone with the two boats. After what seemed an age, we heard an engine, and the H.M. arrived in his dinghy, with *Lafiya*'s owner. He made fast alongside *Arion*, went aboard, and tested her chain. He gave one hefty jerk and the chain came loose, and away went *Arion* or would have gone if we had not hung on. The chain was the actual mooring chain, and the shackle holding it to the mooring (which runs across the river) had lost its pin. After that, all was easy, and the three of us took *Arion* and moored her to the posts by the hard. What would have happened if that end of chain, which had caught my forefoot (I think) by some rusty conglomerate of links had come off before I don't much like to think. Nothing would have stopped the big boat's going ashore on the steep bank at a place well armoured with old stumps and ship's timbers. And if our chain had gone there would be only the wreck of the *Lottie* today. The whole affair was one that called for the *sang froid* of E. W. Busk, and he would have enjoyed it tremendously. Our stem above water is a bit scratched, but the real mess must be somewhere under *Lottie*'s forefoot. Whatever it is, it is less than it would have been if we had not eased the strain almost from the second it came, but we are putting her against the posts tomorrow morning to have a look, and possibly slap some more antifouling on. She has not sprung a leak, and may be merely scratched. Later this morning the H.M. came with the absent skipper, and fished up the cross length of the mooring, with a huge rusty shackle dangling from it without a pin. The Greek shipowner who owns *Arion* or rather his under-writers ought to thank their stars that *Lottie* came in her way when she went adrift. But we both feel it a shame that E.W.B. was not aboard to give the affair 'style' as he undoubtedly would have given it. Blowing like fun again and drizzling, and we shall lose nowt by going on the hard tomorrow.

N.B. I have said nothing about costume.

P.S. It seems you can have a lot of fun in a boat without ever leaving your mooring. All the same we think with envy of you in the good little car piling up your fifteen hundred miles or so. I do hope that tremendous voyage was successfully completed and that you are now playing in *Tern*.

We both send our love to Mrs. Busk.

> Yours ever,
>
> [no signature on copy]

To Joyce Lupton
Jan. 18 1955   40 Hurlingham Court

My dear Joyce,

Thank you for your letter with its news which on the whole, I think and hope, is good. Once they know what's up these doctors do seem able to do something about it. And a week or two lying in bed and keeping the nurses amused gives one time to get one's second wind as it were. You'll come out new made like the mouse that lapped up the spilt whisky and pranced round thumping its chest and shouting, 'Bring out that damned cat!'

I hope your hospital is as civilised as King's. There, when you are in the Private Wing, they see to it vigorously that you do not hear a hint of other people's wireless and similarly see to it that you turn your own on only just loud enough to be able to hear it when it is close beside your pillow. But, of course, King's is the best of all hospitals. I have always enjoyed being there. But at Norwich too the matron was a civilised being. No wireless to be heard. And the sister in charge at night had a magnificent cat called George. He was not allowed in the patients' rooms . . . but he became very clever at nipping in. 'You're so much better today, I think I must let you see George, just for a minute . . . I'll go and fetch him.' Whereupon George shoves his head out from under the overblanket where he has been for the last two hours.

Sunshine today, thank goodness. Everything went pitch black the other day, as black as night, just for about half an hour . . . like an eclipse . . . but only a dense black dirt cloud caught in London. And at high tide, the water pours over the top of the river wall and into the garden.

Thank you for your birthday wishes. Here is a pome concocted in my bath. A nursery rhyme of second childhood:

> Seventy one:
> Seventy one!
> It isn't much fun
> To be Seventy one.
> Wool's nearly spun:
> Sand's nearly run:
> The end has begun:
> Life's nearly DONE.
> It isn't much fun
> To be seventy one.

With those blood transfusions you ought to be careful WHOSE blood you borrow. It might affect your prose. I could very well do with a pint or two from De la Mare or Masefield, but think of the horror of getting even a gill from — or — or Miss — by mistake.

Much love,   A.

To Rupert Hart-Davis

March 25 1956   40 Hurlingham Court

My dear H-D.,

We got back exhausted last night . . . to find the Tilling cheque, winding up a venture that I have thoroughly enjoyed and never regretted for a moment . . . Well worth it.[1]

Now then. We have got the cottage after incredible struggles, but we have got it.[2] And on Wednesday when all was still uncertain, I took omens by going to the river for an hour and three quarters, and caught six trout, the best one close on a pound, which is very big for our brown trout. A lovely warm bit of a lovely day. We have got the whole building in its ground, just under an acre. But the barn is not so good a building as we had thought. Anyhow, we shall camp there this summer and see. And you must come up there soon and have a look.

Yours ever,

Arthur Ransome

1 Ransome had bought a few shares in Hart-Davis's publishing company after it was set up in 1946. It was when he was over-committed at Lowick Hall or he would probably have bought more. The firm prospered in every way except financially, and in 1955-6 it was taken over by Heinemann, which itself was owned by a company called Tilling. Hart-Davis wrote to George Lyttelton (11 December 1955): 'My original share-holders, poor lambs, will lose half their money (which they've long expected to do, for the shares were written down by half some three years ago) . . .' (see *Lyttelton-Hart-Davis Letters*, i 410.)
2 Hill Top, Haverthwaite, the cottage near Newby Bridge which the Ransomes were to rent for their summers between 1956 and 1960, when they bought it: they gave up the London flat in 1963.

To Rupert Hart-Davis

Haverthwaite,

May 24 1956 near Ulverston, Lancashire.

My dear Rupert,

We are beginning to feel we have been in this house for a long time. Last year's cat met Genia at the farm down below, greeted her with enthusiasm, walked all the way up the hill uninvited and has taken up residence. I have been lucky with trout, but the sea-trout have not yet arrived, though I saw one leap at the top of the tidal water. Genia is over-working as usual in the nettle-choked wilderness that she means to turn into a garden. The gutters round the roofs have been mended, slates placed over a yawning hole in the roof of the barn, the rodent operator has got rid of a fearful plague of other rodents as operative as himself, the barn door has been so altered as to make it easy to get my chariot in, Great Spotted Woodpeckers are busy in the oak below my windows, we see buzzards daily, the worst rush of Whitsuntide trippers has ebbed, and we want to know when Rupert Hart-Davis is coming north.

We badly need rain so the weather will probably be fine. It is glorious today except for fishermen.

I forgive because it did rain last night after I had planted eighteen pansy seedlings. But that drop, though welcome, has not raised the river a quarter of an inch. We want a good deluge, to bring the salmon bouncing in.

Yours ever,

Arthur Ransome

AVOID June 1 to June 9.

To Rupert Hart-Davis

Sept 3 1956   Haverthwaite

My dear faithless Rupert,[1]

We are beginning to think of the return journey. Sunset comes so early that I have a faint chance of being fed at a convenient hour, for while sunlight lasts the Boss is digging, deeper and deeper, here and there, taming the wilderness, making rocks seem weak, and cannot stop for a moment.

Your last parcel was the best of any, with the admirable portrait of George Moore, a real beauty of a portrait, and done so delicately. I do like people who write with their fingertips and not with their fists. I shall be reading that book half a dozen times at least.[2]

And Humphry House[3] now goes with me to the river. You have to give a pool a rest sometimes while fishing for salmon. I don't say that his *Aristotle* has yet lost me a fish by keeping me reading on the bank instead of wading up to my neck, but it will lose me one if I don't look out. Those were lucky lads who had him as a tutor. He is such an alert and friendly lecturer and a critic to put beside Coleridge. I wish I'd met him in the days when Lascelles Abercrombie and I used to walk and talk. Ass!! In those days he would have been six years old and could not have kept up with us (with his feet I mean. With his head he would have been far ahead.) He is interested in just the things that used in those old days to make nothing of twenty miles for us, and he makes me want to hurry back to London to look at Bywater's translation.

MISPRINT in *George Moore*. Page 118, line 21.

Yours ever,

Arthur

1 Hart-Davis had not yet visited Haverthwaite.
2 Nancy Cunard, *GM: memories of George Moore* (London: Hart-Davis, 1956).
3 Humphry House (1909-1955), Reptonian; critic, scholar, friend of Rupert Hart-Davis, who had just published his posthumous *Aristotle's Poetics: a course of eight lectures, revised by Colin Hardie*.
4 In answer to his letter Hart-Davis wrote: 'It's uncanny the way in which you always pick out for special praise those books in which I myself am particularly interested and which I have almost always decided to publish on their merits, without much hope of profit. You've no idea how encouraging your approval can be.'

From Mary Agnes Hamilton

May 27 1959   Fulham [postmark]

My dear Arthur,

Unable to sleep, last night, I took down a quite forgotten tale of my own, called *Life Sentence*;[1] out of it fell a wonderful letter from you. I expect I thanked you for it, at the time; it has, once again, carried an unspeakable encouragement. Which is why I am writing. That letter has pulled me out of the slough of despond about writing, into which I was sunk; no human being can do a greater service to another. It's all a very long time ago; but my gratitude glows afresh, and I want you to know it.

I am still somewhat *piano*; I hope you and Genia are well. This brings much love to you both.

Ever affectionately,   Molly

1 Published by Hamish Hamilton in 1935. AR's letter untraced.

To G. Wren Howard

June 19 1961　　　　　　　　　　　　　　　Haverthwaite

Dear Howard,

I have had another very bad tumble down from the steep hill outside my house, but am extremely lucky in that my spectacles though wrecked were not driven into my eyes. A further bit of good fortune was that after I had lain for some time in a puddle of gore, I came to and heard a car coming UP the hill (if it had been coming down, nothing could have saved me from at least damaging the car. I, lying flat on my mug (I literally 'came a smeller') lifted a Red Hand of Ulster and flapped it from road level, pouring with blood, and the car pulled up instantly, and from it on the run came a young woman, full of good sense, who pulled me round so that my head was no longer downhill, and explained that she was a qualified nurse and happened to be driving slowly because she once upon a time had two aunts who lived in this house. Anyhow, lucky as I had been, I had had a bit of a shock, which is most *un*lucky just when I want to look at the Penguin cover.[1]

I shall be another two days before writing a considered report. I expect you will agree that it is important that the figures on the jacket shall not in any way contradict what is said by the figures in the illustrations. Anyway I will write in detail in two days time.

Penguins have made a very good job of their De La Mare Puffin book. If they treat me as well I shall be delighted.[2]

Yours ever,

Arthur Ransome

1　The first paperback of *Swallows and Amazons* was published in 1962 after several earlier requests to produce paperback editions of the books had been turned down by their author.

2　Although Ransome was always grateful to his original publishers at Cape, a long-running, politely acrimonious correspondence with Wren Howard over reduced royalty payments went on for years after the war. In October 1955, his patience was at an end. He wrote to Wren Howard: 'Bearing in mind that in the years *since the war* I have forgone something like £12,000 in royalties, I cannot agree that any further reduction in my percentage would be fair . . . and hope that these will be the last words necessary on "this sordid subject".'

To Rupert Hart-Davis

July 15 1961   Haverthwaite

My dear enviable Rupert,

Enviable because not engaged in pulling a house to pieces while still inside it.

I am thankful to have your Colossus[1] to look at because it lets me have an illusion of being at work while in fact I am merely running alongside in the dust doing nothing but admire and envy. I think you have struck exactly the right note and you maintain it apparently quite without effort, without visible effort that is. I am going steadily through it from start to finish. But it is a huge work and I can't send it back at once.

The builders thunder upstairs and downstairs and fill the rooms with dust and rubble, besides WHUSTLING non-stop. Small hope of going fishing. Not that I really want to. What I do want is someone with whom to chatter. My best and oldest friends up here have fallen into the bad habit of dying and I am extremely lonely.

I expect Montgomery Hyde[2] is delighted with your book. Has he now finished with the Far East? I have a faint impression that he has resigned from the Garrick. No-one should ever do that.

I live, work and sleep in a dense fog of cement-dust and see changes being made of which I don't approve. And I can't even go out into the field to see what is happening. I can't walk with longer than six-inch strides!

A shocking spectacle.

You, of course, are now all set to be a new Lord Houghton and will have to spend much of your life in shrugging off your past in order to give a chance to your present. (I hope you divine that I am referring to his being entangled with Keats.)

Since I began this letter I have become involved in Ruskin and his psychoanalyst admirers. Rupert page 380 . . . Ruskin lags . . . and the wretched Ransome sticks fast in the quagmire. I am more than ever persuaded that I ought to chuck any idea of auto-biography.[3] We'll talk of it again when I come back to town, but I don't want to have to contradict things said by other people who seem to me to have been trying to write my life for me. Further my new teypewriterxxx [sic] seems unnecessarily wilful.

I seem to be writing to you without ever saying what I do most truly believe, that you have for all time eliminated all other biographers of Oscar Wilde. You may say you haven't written a biography. You have made all others absolutely unnecessary. Incidentally you have completely justified the biographical part of my little piece of impertinence, and at the same time made my old book of fifty years ago altogether unnecessary. What cheek I had in those old days. Never mind! It was justified *then*.

I am looking forward to the Garrick, though I have become so very immobile that it will be almost impossible to get there. Nowadays I can't even get into Ulverston without misgivings. For the past six weeks (except for that one headlong idiocy)[4] I've not been outside the gate.

Later (July 23/4). Rupert into the six hundreds (pages). I hope to breast the tape tomorrow . . . but I have been reading far too fast and must have missed lots.

Yours ever, love from both of us.

Arthur

1   *The Letters of Oscar Wilde*, edited by Rupert Hart-Davis, published in 1962; Hart-Davis sent Ransome a set of proofs for correction. AR was pleased to discover that Wilde had been an angler. 'I am delighted to think of shocked littery gents learning for the first time that O.W. can be counted a writer on sport . . . I think of course that you are being a flatterer when you say that I have spotted a few things missed by the Argus-eyed Rupert' (AR to R. Hart-Davis, Aug. 14 1961.)

2   Biographer of Oscar Wilde. He was still a member of the Garrick Club when he died in 1989.

3   Gently encouraged by Hart-Davis, Ransome had been writing his *Autobiography* intermittently since 1949.

4   The fall described on p. 352.

To Morgan Philips Price

April 15 1962   Haverthwaite

Dear Price,

I am really very glad to have seen this number of the Survey and am most grateful to you for sending it to me. And I must tell you at once that you have been very handsome in your treatment of my performance on that stage. It must have been hard for all you practised political philosophers not to be worse than impatient with the intrusions of so obvious an amateur. I can well see now why Harold Williams was so cross at being contradicted by me . . . though I still think it was very regrettable that he should have been.

We had an awful journey to get here being heavily gassed *en route*.[1] And it is still far too cold for us to think of moving into our own cottage. But we do expect to move thither in this coming week. Tanya[2] will be amused and I think pleased to hear that at long last contracts have been signed for a TV production of one of my books and I look forward to a comic and exasperating summer observing the antics of actors trying to be Swallows. But, of course, we are fully expecting that at the last moment the whole thing will fall through. A celebrated film-star gave me the good advice: 'grab every bawbee you can lay your hands on . . . and then forget the whole affair.'

Yours ever,

Arthur Ransome

Oddly enough on the very day that your admirable article arrived, I had a Russian letter from a Petrograd friend of 1915, Dmitri Mitrokhin who did the pictures for my book of Russian folk stories. I had not heard from him since 1917 when he did a very good picture of the Litevsky Prison in flames,[3] meant as a cover design for a book that, alas, I never wrote. I envy you for having made so much better use of your opportunities. I was delighted to hear from Mitrokhin, because I had assumed that he was dead like so many other friends of those days. And here he was quite evidently still painting and full of energy.

This time I really do wind up.

Please convey my best wishes to Tanya when you see her.

Yours ever

A.R.

---

1 Probably through travelling in a car leaking exhaust fumes.
2 Price's daughter, Tania Rose.
3 See *Life*, pp. 119-20.

To Dora Altounyan

July 16 1962   Haverthwaite

My dear Beetle,

I have been very slow in writing to you, for reasons quite beyond my control. But I know that you know that the delay is not for want of sympathy. Ursula's death must have come as a dreadful shock to you.[1] Neither you, nor anybody else who knew her, can have expected anything of the sort. She always seemed to have the secret of perpetual youth. I go on remembering her, and always remember her doing very young things, such as swimming over to the island with a bundle of proofs tied in her hair when Robin and I were camping there. I think of her catching eels in the Medway and always, at any age, being much younger than whoever she was with. You and I were the old ones who watched the sunsets from the Lair on the bank at the bottom of the Lanehead garden. And now we linger on when all those younger ones have gone without waiting for us.

With much love, dear Beetle,

Arthur

Would not your Father have been delighted by Janet's Icelandic exploit?[2]

1 Ursula Collingwood, the youngest of the three sisters, had died on June 29, 1962.
2 While in Iceland in 1897, W. G. Collingwood painted a vast number of landscape watercolours, some of which were exhibited in Reykjavik in 1962. As a Collingwood, Janet Gnosspelius was invited to visit Iceland, where the pictures are now in the National Museum.

To John Berry

September 23 1962   Haverthwaite

Dear Mr. Berry,

Thank you for your (and your wife's) kind sympathy over the misfortunes of my book. I wholeheartedly agree with your remarks and wish to goodness you had been here all this summer so that, being immobilised myself, I could have asked you to keep a stern eye on these scoundrels.[1]

I entirely agree with your remarks, though I think they would have been more disgusted if you had seen the script.

It looks as though we should be going to London pretty soon. But I fear it is too late now for a rescue. All we can do is to lay in a stock of motor-horns with which to make a nasty noise when the thing is actually shown. Alas, with TV the scoundrels will never hear it. I hope a few people will be enraged by it and write letters complaining. The awful thing is that 'my agent' has given them an option on *Swallowdale* and *Peter Duck*.

I here hand over.

Arthur Ransome

1   The team adapting *Swallows and Amazons* for television. As he expected, Ransome disapproved of the way they went about it; he also disliked the finished product. See *Life*, p. 431.

★

Ransome had never entirely recovered from the effects of his accident in 1958, and from 1963 onwards his final decline, slow but inexorable, was under way. In that year he went into hospital again, and his condition there is well indicated by a letter from Colonel Busk of 26 May:

'It was distressing to us to see you so incapacitated, and to know that you had once more to face the ordeal of an operation. When I telephoned to you at the hospital you sounded so remarkably cheerful that I naturally expected to hear that the doctors had decided that the op. wasn't necessary – and instead I heard the very bad news that you had to wait another day for it. "As brave as a lion" I think is the only right comment.'

It was indeed an apt comment, and Ransome's enormous vitality had pulled him through many an earlier crisis, not to mention the sheer grit which he seems to have inherited from his father; but by now his resources were exhausted. After his return to Hill Top he was largely confined to a wheel-chair; his energy failed, and his mind began to fade. Tragically, he was to some extent aware of his decline. On 21 September 1963 he wrote to Dora Altounyan, 'My dear Old Beetle, I was very happy to get your letter, and if only I could I should like to write you a good gossipy scrawl that might remind you of sunsets seen

from the old Lair at the bottom of the Lanehead garden. But I
can't; and only hope that you will understand and forgive me for
being so incapable.' At times the clouds lifted, and he wrote with
something of his old vigour; but such occasions grew more and
more rare. He became alarmed and agitated if more than two or
three people were in the room with him, so his eightieth
birthday (18 January 1964) was celebrated with only the Luptons
and Genia; but a letter which he wrote to Joyce four days later
shows that he could still receive and give enjoyment:

Jan. 22 1964　　　　　　　　　　　　　　　　　Haverthwaite

Dear Joyce,

I am sorry I have been in such a feeble and wool-gathering
state that I have never thanked you properly for all your gifts. I
know how much you love the water-hen and chick so I realise
what it meant for you to part from them. I like them too and it
is a great pleasure to look at the picture. But please remember
that I consider it (like the rest of the Audubons) as a family
property and that sooner or later it will return to you or one of
your children. In the meanwhile I enjoy having it and thank you
very much.

I am not feeling too well so I have not sampled your sloe gin
yet but have to be content with admiring its pretty colour and
still more the wonderful label of Hugh's manufacture, a labour
of love indeed, thank you both for this combined offering.

It was nice to have you here.

　　　　　　　　Yours affectionately　　　　　Arthur

On the same day he wrote to Pamela Whitlock (now married to
John Bell): 'I blush to read your letter but lap up the affection
which prompts your exaggerations.' Then he went on sadly: 'I
would like to see you both before very long. But I am losing
mobility so fast I expect I shall be stuck here for the rest of my
life. Nice enough place to be stuck in but difficult for friends to
get to when we want to see them . . .'

His situation was no better sixteen months later when Evgenia
wrote to Wren Howard (24 May 1965): 'I am sorry to say that
Arthur is steadily if very slowly deteriorating and is now

completely housebound . . . Luckily our library is fairly large and he likes re-reading old favourites, but it is a great help being very well served by the country library too. Our three cats (when not too busy mousing) do their best to amuse and entertain the invalid. Our cacti do rather well, the flowering season has just begun, the first plant in flower has been moved into the invalid's room a week ago . . .'

In the autumn she had to admit defeat to Rupert Hart-Davis (1 October 1965): 'Arthur went to Cockermouth on Aug. 9th and came back on Sept. 9th. This was all rather sudden and August is the most awkward month for doing anything unless everything has been planned and booked well in advance. I only managed to get 11 days of complete rest in Newby Bridge Hotel – not nearly long enough to restore the loss of sleep and energy during the last timeless months. Almost as soon as he came back I began to feel ill again. Two days ago I had a heart attack. I had a milder one the day I took Arthur to Cockermouth and another a few weeks earlier while shopping in Ulverston.' She reluctantly accepted that for the sake of her health as well as his, Arthur would have to go into the geriatric ward of the Royal Cheadle Hospital, on 6 October. 'I wonder if you could come to see us before he goes. He was talking of wanting to see you, he even tried to write a letter to you – his efforts are quite pitiful – like a very small bird walking over the paper after its claws have been dipped in ink.'

There would be no more signalling from Mars or anywhere else. But his ending was tranquil. Rupert Hart-Davis responded to Evgenia's appeal, like the true friend he was, and perhaps his words in the epilogue to the *Autobiography* make the most suitable end to this volume too:

'. . . he lingered on for twenty months, not noticeably unhappy and only occasionally conscious of his surroundings. He died peacefully on June 3, 1967, and lies buried, surrounded by his beloved hills, river and lakes, in the lovely valley of Rusland.'

Appendix

Notes on Arthur Ransome's
principal correspondents

This list is arranged in alphabetical order of surnames, and when a surname is shared, by alphabetical order of Christian name. Women are listed under the surname they used when Arthur Ransome first wrote to them (or they to him).

Taqui Altounyan, b. 1917; eldest child of Dora and Ernest Altounyan; identified herself wholeheartedly with the Swallows as a child, but found the identification tiresome as she grew older. Some character traits of Nancy Blackett have been attributed to her. She has written two excellent volumes of memoirs, which include material on Ransome: *In Aleppo Once* and *Chimes from a Wooden Bell*.

John Berry, b. 1928. Artist. In about 1943 he managed, by bicycle and phone book, to track Ransome to the Heald, but was rebuffed by Evgenia Ransome. He befriended the Ransomes in their old age, and is now working on a book to be called *Discovering Swallows and Ransomes*.

Lt. Col. Edmund Wesley Busk, M.C. b. 1892. In the 1930s he was employed by Ransome and Rapier and lived near Pin Mill, where he met Arthur Ransome. A keen yachtsman, Busk owned a cutter, *Lapwing*, which features in *Secret Water*. The book was dedicated to 'the Busk Family', who probably inspired the Eels in the story.

K. Adlard Coles, b. 1901. Accountant, publisher, yachtsman, yachting writer, he bought *Racundra* from Arthur Ransome, sailed her back to England from Estonia through rough weather in 1925 and sold her in 1926. His book *Close Hauled* (1926) and his autobiography, *Sailing Years* (1981), contain much about *Racundra* (disguised in *Close Hauled* as '*Annette II*') and Ransome himself. He comments on Ransome's letters about the sale of *Racundra*: 'Reading them now, I am amazed at the infinite pains he took in advising me on every detail for the fitting-out of *Racundra*, together with the personal introductions to all that could help us on arrival at Riga . . . He was one of the most remarkable men I have had the privilege of meeting' (*Sailing Years*, p. 41). Unfortunately, Ransome did not return the compliment. He could not forgive Coles for having bought *Racundra*, and for writing about her, and for proposing to make money out of her. Probably the real problem was that he could not forgive himself for selling this precious fruit of his imagination.

Barbara Collingwood, 1887-1961, daughter of W. G. and E. M. Collingwood. Ransome's first love. She was a capable artist and sculptor and Ransome made some use of her work while preparing the illustrations for *Winter Holiday*. Earlier she had corrected the proofs of *The Elixir of Life* and was rewarded with the dedication of *Old Peter's Russian Tales*. She married Oscar Gnosspelius (1878-1953), the engineer whose attempt to re-open a copper mine on The Old Man of Coniston inspired *Pigeon Post*, which is dedicated to him. Her only child, Janet, was born in 1926.

Dora Collingwood ('Beetle'), 1886-1964, was also an artist and one of Ransome's early loves: he asked her to marry him several times. She was known as 'Beetle' because she wore spectacles, like the character in Kipling's *Stalky & Co.*; Ransome was known as 'Toad', from *The Wind In The Willows*. He frequently drew a toad by or as his signature when writing to Dora. Dora married Ernest Altounyan (1889-1962), in  1915; their five children, Barbara ('Taqui'), Susie, Mavis ('Titty'), Roger and Brigit were the inspiration for the Swallows.

Edith Mary Collingwood ('Dorrie'), 1857-1928, was the mother of Barbara, Dora, Ursula and Robin Collingwood, the wife of W. G. Collingwood, and Arthur Ransome's honorary aunt. She gave him the warm, unanxious affection which during his youth he badly needed and which his mother could not manage. She was a professional painter, like her husband.

William Gershom Collingwood, 1854-1932, who was an artist antiquarian, historical novelist and, in his youth, John Ruskin's indispensable assistant and first biographer. He was an authority on Saxon crosses, and designed a monument in that style for Ruskin's grave in Coniston churchyard. He was immensely kind and encouraging to Ransome, who called him 'The Skald'.

A. G. Gardiner, was the Editor of the Liberal newspaper, the *Daily News*. He first hired Arthur Ransome as his Russian correspondent in 1915 and continued to employ him until 1919, when he himself was dismissed by his proprietors, the Cadbury family, on account of his stubborn opposition to Lloyd George. Ransome then moved to the *Manchester Guardian*.

Mary Agnes Hamilton ('**Molly**'), 1882-1966, politician, journalist and author. After a brilliant undergraduate career at Newnham College, Cambridge, and a disastrous marriage, she became the first woman member-of-staff at *The Economist* in 1912, which she left (with the editor, F. W. Hirst) in 1916 over the issue of conscription. It was through Hirst that she met Arthur Ransome. She was a Labour M.P. from 1929 to 1931 and PPS to Clement Attlee. Among her books were a life of Carlyle, which Jonathan Cape published at AR's suggestion, a history of Newnham, and two volumes of memoirs. A few of her letters to Ransome survive; I hope that one day his to her will surface.

Sir Rupert Hart-Davis, born 1907, publisher and man of letters; knighted in 1967; biographer of Hugh Walpole, editor of the letters of Oscar Wilde and Max Beerbohm, of his own correspondence with George Lyttelton, and of Ransome's *Autobiography*. He is one of Ransome's literary executors and one of his most dependable friends. Ransome tried to make an angler of him but did not succeed.

George Wren Howard, 1893-1968, was Jonathan Cape's partner, fourteen years his junior, and succeeded to the chairmanship of Ransome's publishers when Cape died in 1960. Educated at Marlborough and Trinity College, Cambridge, Howard was awarded the M.C. after going missing briefly at the fighting front in the First World War. He was 27 and working as a designer at the Medici Society when he borrowed £5,000 from his father to help Cape set up their own publishing company in 1921. His son, Michael, was managing director of Cape from 1960 to 1968 and chairman from 1968 to 1970.

Lupton, see Joyce Ransome.

Morgan Philips Price, 1885-1973. His great-grandfather was one of the founders of the *Manchester Guardian*, for which he was Russian correspondent from 1914 to 1918. It was thanks to him that in November 1917 the *Guardian* published the hitherto secret treaties between Tsarist Russia and the Western powers, which the Bolsheviks had printed in *Izvestia*. He and Arthur Ransome gave one another moral support in Moscow in 1918. Later he became a Labour Member of Parliament and published his memoirs, *My Three Revolutions*, in 1969.

Edith Rachel Ransome, 1862-1944, AR's mother. *Née* Boulton, she married Cyril Ransome in 1882, and had four children: Arthur, Cecily (born 1885), Geoffrey and Joyce (*see separate entries*). She was a lovable and highly intelligent woman, who emulated her historian husband after his death by writing *A First History of England* (1903); she was also an accomplished if ladylike water-colourist. Her loyalty to her elder son never wavered, but his early life was overcast by the anxiety, shading into disapproval, with which she regarded his plunge into the life of letters. After Arthur's escape to Russia in 1913 all was at last unclouded affection between them, as is still to be seen in the hundreds of letters which he wrote and she preserved.

Evgenia Petrovna Ransome, 1884-1975, the daughter of Peter Shelepin, was secretary to Lev Trotsky when Arthur Ransome met her at the very end of 1917. She married him on 8 May 1924, shortly after his divorce from his first wife. Many found her difficult to like, both during her life and afterwards. She was hot-tempered and intractable; but she was also warm-hearted, intelligent, and deeply devoted to her husband. She was perhaps blamed unduly for her sincere but obtuse comments on his books, of which she became a passionate defender once they had been published. She carried her husband through years of ill-health heroically if not without complaint.

Geoffrey Cyril Ransome, 1887-1918, Arthur's younger brother and good friend. A printer by trade, his hobby was the bagpipes. He served bravely in the Great War until he was killed in January 1918. Photographs show a striking resemblance to Arthur.

Marjory Edith Joyce Ransome, 1892-1970, married Hugh Lupton, an engineer, in 1920, and had four children: Francis Geoffrey Hugh (born 1921); Arthur Ralph Ransome (born

1924); Cecily Margaret (born 1927); Geoffrey Charles Martineau (born 1930). Like her brother Joyce was a writer. *The Hill of the Ring* was published by Rupert Hart-Davis in 1960; *The Great Elm* and *The Seekers*, posthumously, by Kaye Ward, in 1971 and 1973. She has left a valuable memoir of her childhood.

Tabitha Ransome, 1911-1991, AR's only child, by his first wife, Ivy Walker. Her difficult relationship with her father is amply revealed in the letters in this volume. She married John Lewis in 1934 and had two children, Hazel (born in 1936) and John (born 1940). By 1944 her marriage had failed; at the very end of her life she married again. From 1934 she lived in the West Country.

Sir Charles Renold, 1883-1967, knighted in 1948, was a Manchester businessman, director (and later chairman) of the family firm, Renold Chains Ltd, from 1906 to his death. In *Who's Who* he gave his recreations as fishing and gardening: Ransome spoke of him (on what grounds cannot be determined), as 'my fishing pupil'. His first wife, **Margaret Hilda Hunter** (1883-1957) was also born into the Manchester business world: a woman of character, who refused to be shipped off to India to find a husband in the army, civil administration, or the church, as happened to her sisters, but instead took a job at the John Rylands Library. She married Charles Renold in 1909, had four children and devoted herself to charity work. She did not fish, but was happy to encourage her husband to relax by doing so. She was an ardent reader, and was glad to know that Ransome used some of her ideas in his books.

Edward Taylor Scott, ('Ted'), 1883-1932, was the youngest son of C. P. Scott, the greatest editor of the *Manchester Guardian*. He was in the same house (Whitelaw's) at Rugby at the same time as Arthur Ransome. He married J. A. Hobson's daughter Mabel (perhaps it would be more accurate to say that she married him). He worked on the *Daily News* before joining the family paper in 1913. He enlisted in 1914, was captured, and was a prisoner of war. He returned to the *Guardian* in 1919, became his father's chief assistant, and endured a long and difficult apprenticeship before being allowed to take over as Editor in 1929. Even after that his father went on breathing down his neck. Ransome was his closest friend on the paper, and befriended him nobly; but he introduced Scott to sailing and was thus – to his immense distress an indirect cause of Scott's premature death.

Richard Tizard ('Dick'), born in 1917, was educated at Rugby and Oriel College, Oxford, where he read engineering science; he became a founder fellow of Churchill College, Cambridge, in 1960. As an undergraduate he was Vice-Commodore of the Oxford University Yacht Club (Captain of the Varsity team). After the war he took to cruising in the North Sea and the Channel and on the Atlantic coast from Sweden to Spain.

John Ronald Reuel Tolkien, 1892-1973, successively Bosworth and Merton Professor of English at Oxford, is world-famous for *The Hobbit* (1937) and *The Lord of the Rings* (1954-6). His extremely interesting letter to Ransome (quoted in this volume) is preserved in the Ransome archive at the University of Leeds.

Clifford Webb (1895-1972), illustrator and engraver, was a fellow of the Royal Society of Painters-Etchers and Engravers and served in the army in the Great War. He specialised in animal drawing, and became author and illustrator of children's books, including *Swallows and Amazons* and *Swallowdale*. For his relations with AR, see *Life*, pp. 341-4.

Pamela Whitlock (1920-1982), was born in Penang but schooled in England. At St. Mary's School, Ascot, she met Katharine Hull, and together they wrote *The Far-Distant Oxus*, a novel for children heavily influenced by the Ransome books; AR secured its publication with Jonathan Cape. It had two sequels (*Escape to Persia*, 1938, *Oxus in Summer*, 1939) and there was one further collaboration with Katharine Hull – *Crowns*, 1947. Pamela Whitlock worked for Collins, the publishers, as children's books editor and as editor of the firm's children's magazine, and in 1952 published *The Sweet Spring*, her first adult novel. In 1954 she married John Bell, chairman of the Oxford University Press (and later AR's literary co-executor with Rupert Hart-Davis); they had five daughters. She died on 3 June 1982, fifteen years to the day after AR's death.

Sir Pelham Grenville Wodehouse (1881-1975), the most successful English comic novelist of his day, much enjoyed by both the Ransomes. His Mulliner stories are always set in a fishing inn, *The Angler's Rest*, but this does not seem to have been an important part of his charm for Ransome.

Select Bibliography
of works that tell the story of
Arthur Ransome's life

Alexander, C. E., *Ransome At Home* (Amazon Publications, 1996)

Altounyan, Taqui, *In Aleppo Once* (London: John Murray, 1969)

—— *Chimes From A Wooden Bell: a memoir* (London and New York: I. B. Tauris, 1990)

Brogan, Hugh, *The Life of Arthur Ransome* (London: Jonathan Cape, 1984)

Coles, K. Adlard, *Sailing Years: an autobiography* (London: Coles/Granada, 1981)

Hardyment, Christina, *Arthur Ransome and Captain Flint's Trunk* (Cape, 1984)

Hunt, Peter, *Approaching Arthur Ransome* (Cape, 1992)

Lockhart, R. H. Bruce, *Memoirs of a British Agent* (London and New York: Putnam, 1934)

Muggeridge, Malcolm, *The Green Stick* (London: Collins, 1972)

Ransome, Arthur, *The Autobiography of Arthur Ransome* (Cape, 1976)

Swift, Jeremy, *Arthur Ransome on Fishing* (Cape, 1994)

Wardale, Roger, *Nancy Blackett: Under Sail with Arthur Ransome* (Cape, 1991)

—— *In Search of Swallows and Amazons: Arthur Ransome's Lakeland* (Wilmslow, Cheshire: Sigma Press, 1996)

—— (ed.), *Ransome At Sea: notes from the chart table. A transcription of Arthur Ransome's various logbooks, 1920–1954.* (Amazon Publications, 1995).

Index

KING ALFRED'S COLLEGE
LIBRARY

KING ALFRED'S COLLEGE
LIBRARY

THE

ARTHUR **RANSOME**

SOCIETY

The Arthur Ransome Society aims to celebrate Ransome's
life and to promote his works. A variety of meetings and
activities are arranged by the six regional groups. There are
three annual publications and regional newsletters. For more
information, contact the Society: c/o Abbot Hall Gallery,
Kendal, Cumbria LA9 5AL